CONFLICTING WORLDS
New Dimensions of the American Civil War
T. Michael Parrish, Editor

A Black Patriot and a White Priest

A Black Patriot
and a White Priest

André Cailloux and Claude Paschal Maistre
in Civil War New Orleans

STEPHEN J. OCHS

Louisiana State University Press / Baton Rouge

MM

Designer: Glynnis Weston
Typeface: Galliard
Typesetter: Coghill Composition
Printer and binder: Thomson-Shore, Inc.

Library of Congress Cataloging-in-Publication Data

Ochs, Stephen J.
   A Black patriot and a white priest : André Cailloux and Claude Paschal Maistre in Civil
War New Orleans / Stephen J. Ochs.
      p.   cm.—(Conflicting worlds)
   Includes bibliographical references and index.
      ISBN 0-8071-2531-8 (alk. paper)
      1. New Orleans (La.)—History—Civil War, 1861–1865.   2. Cailloux, André, 1825–1863.
3. Maistre, Claude Paschal, 1820–1875.   4. New Orleans (La.)—Race relations.   5. New
Orleans (La.)—Church history—19th century.   6. Afro-American
soldiers—Louisiana—New Orleans—Biography.   7. Soldiers—Louisiana—New
Orleans—Biography.   8. Catholic Church—Louisiana—New Orleans—Biography.   9. United
States—History—Civil War, 1861–1865—Participation, Afro-American.   10. United
States—History—Civil War, 1861–1865—Religious aspects. I. Title. II. Series.

F379.N557 O25   2000
973.7'463—dc21   99-053403

For Meghan Elizabeth Ochs

CONTENTS

ILLUSTRATIONS

TABLES

PREFACE

All history begins "once upon a time" because it is first and last a story. By sharing the collective stories of our past, we come to a better understanding of our common humanity and of our identities, both individual and societal. In this book, I hope I have told a significant, human story about a black captain and his regiment and a white priest who, at great personal risk, supported them during the Civil War.

I have long been fascinated by the relationship between religion and race. While researching a book on black Catholic priests, I first encountered the Afro-Creoles of New Orleans, about whom I read with growing interest and fascination. Two individuals appeared frequently, if briefly, in that reading: Captain André Cailloux of the 1st Regiment, Louisiana Native Guards, the first black military hero of the Civil War, and Father Claude Paschal Maistre, the lone clerical voice of Catholic abolitionism in New Orleans. Both men played significant roles in Civil War New Orleans and in Afro-Creole history, and their lives intersected dramatically at Cailloux's funeral in 1863.[1]

Because Cailloux and Maistre so captured my imagination and fired my interest, I set out to become better acquainted with them. This proved a daunting task, since no photographs, drawings, or paintings of either man survive and only a few of Maistre's letters. Still, in my enthusiasm I convinced myself that both men somehow wanted me to find them, and that they had left more clues to their respective lives than initially met the eye. This proved to be the case. Military service and pension records, regimental papers, census returns, municipal tax ledgers and emancipation records, notarial acts,

---

1. I use the term "first black *military* hero" to distinguish Cailloux, an officer in the U.S. Army, from Robert Smalls, the first black hero of the Civil War, who, as a slave pilot on the Confederate steamer *The Planter* daringly commandeered the vessel in the dead of night, steered it past Fort Sumter and delivered it to the Union squadron blockading Charleston harbor. See Okon E. Uya, *From Slavery to Public Service: Robert Smalls, 1839–1915* (New York, 1971).

wills and successions, conveyance records, sacramental registers, ecclesiastical archives, and newspapers all yielded pieces of a puzzle that coalesced into the narrative told in these pages. The absence of letters, however, leaves lacunae and necessitates more speculation throughout the narrative than I would ordinarily prefer.

This book is intended to contribute to a growing literature on the lives of free persons of color in New Orleans, the black military experience, black Catholicism, and Afro-Creole radicalism. It attempts to build on this outstanding body of scholarship and to fill some historiographical gaps. Few studies of free people of color in Louisiana, for example, focus specifically on individuals. Those that do concentrate on elite, mulatto, slaveholding planters outside New Orleans. I have attempted to address that void by tracing the life of André Cailloux, a black Creole who was born a slave, attained freedom, carved out a niche for himself and his family as an artisan in the antebellum Afro-Creole society of New Orleans, and died a U.S. Army captain and Civil War hero whose courageous example continued to inspire civil rights activists in New Orleans down into the mid-twentieth century. Benefiting from the fine recent study of the three Native Guards regiments recruited in New Orleans in 1862, this book describes in detail the experiences of Cailloux's 1st Regiment and provides additional information about that unit, particularly after Cailloux's death at the Battle of Port Hudson. That death led to a public funeral presided over by the controversial Fr. Maistre. He surfaces in a number of books on black troops and on the Catholic church in Civil War New Orleans, but always as a shadowy, vague figure. Although many of the shadows remain, I hope that the present study sheds more light on this complex, paradoxical figure whose relationship with Afro-Creole radicals and whose battle with the archbishop of New Orleans suggest much about the admixture of war, race, religion, and political radicalism.[2]

2. See Gary B. Mills, *The Forgotten People: Cane River's Creoles of Color* (Baton Rouge, 1977) and David O. Whitten, *Andrew Durnford: A Black Sugar Planter in the Antebellum South* (New Brunswick, 1995). Cyprian Davis, O.S.B., will soon publish a biography of an urban Creole woman of color, Henriette Delille, the foundress of the Sisters of the Holy Family. See also James G. Hollandsworth, Jr., *The Louisiana Native Guards: The Black Military Experience During the Civil War* (Baton Rouge, 1995) and C. P. Weaver, ed., *Thank God My Regiment an African One: The Civil War Diary of Colonel Nathan W. Daniels* (Baton Rouge, 1998). The

*   *   *

Ignatius Loyola, the founder of the Jesuits, valued two virtues above all others: generosity and gratitude. In the course of writing this book, I have received an immense amount of the former and would now like to express the latter. Caryn Cossé Bell, James A. P. Byrne, S.J., Julie A. Collins, Thomas F. Conlan, Bonita Hanes, Peter E. Hogan, S.S.J., James G. Hollandsworth, Jr., Daniel C. Napolitano, Keith W. Olson, Joseph P. Reidy, and Benjamin D. Williams read all or parts of this manuscript and offered invaluable advice in matters historical, grammatical, and syntactical. In this regard, I am especially indebted to the late Joseph Logsdon, who graciously shared his encyclopedic knowledge of New Orleans' Afro-Creole history with me and meticulously critiqued two drafts of the manuscript. Patrick J. Foley, Charles E. Nolan, and Sally K. Reeves also provided me with valuable feedback on an earlier article that eventually grew into this book.

In addition to nourishing me intellectually through their publications, a number of historians and genealogical researchers graciously answered my questions, suggested sources, and/or provided me with materials gleaned from their own research: John B. Alberts, Jack Belsom, Peter Caron, Cyprian Davis, O.S.B., Mary Gehman, Virginia Meecham Gould, Paul F. Lachance, Diane Batts Morrow, Ann Middleton, Molly Mitchell, C. P. Weaver, and Mary White. Archivists and librarians assisted me at various depositories: Judy Bolton and Faye Phillips of Hill Memorial Library at Louisiana State University; Diane Blanton, Stuart Butler, Mike Meier, Mike Musick, Trevor Plante, and Jane "Budge" Weidman at the National Archives; Marc Cave, Chuck Patch, and Sally Stassis at the Historic New Orleans Collection; Cordelia Cappiello in the Office of the Clerk of Court of Plaquemines Parish; Sister Madelaine Dalle at the Archives of the Diocese of Orleans, France; Wayne Everard and Irene Wainright at the New Orleans Public Library; Mike Frearing at the Port Hudson State Commemorative Area Museum; Brother Hans Norbert Huber, OFMCap., at the Provincial Archives of the Austrian Province of

---

interpretations of Afro-Creole radicalism offered in Caryn Cossé Bell, *Revolution, Romanticism, and the Afro-Creole Protest Tradition in Louisiana, 1718–1868* (Baton Rouge, 1997) and Arnold R. Hirsch and Joseph Logsdon, eds., *Creole New Orleans: Race and Americanization* (Baton Rouge, 1992) have proven particularly helpful to me.

Capuchins; Sr. Eva Regina Martin, at the Archives of the Sisters of the Holy Family; Charles E. Nolan, Dorenda Dupont, and Charles Guerin at the Archives of the Archdiocese of New Orleans; Beatrice Rodriguez Owsley and Marie E. Wendell at the Special Collections Division, University of New Orleans; Sally K. Reeves at the New Orleans Notarial Archives; the late Ulysses Ricard at the Amistad Research Center, Tulane University; Rev. J. Alphonsus Sprinkart, OFMCap., of the Provincial Archives of the Bavarian Province of Capuchins; Rev. Joachim Strupp, OFMCap., of the Detroit Province of Capuchins; Lester Sullivan at the Xavier University Archives; Sharon K. Sumter at the University of Notre Dame Archives; Reverend Paul Thomas at the Archives of the Archdiocese of Baltimore; and Donald Wisnoski at the Oneida Historical Society.

I am especially blessed by wonderful, supportive colleagues at Georgetown Preparatory School, some of whom I have already noted above. My thanks go out to Thomas A. Roach, S.J., president, and Dr. James P. Power, headmaster, for their support of this project through Prep's faculty development fund, and to Patricia M. Morgan and Brian J. Hayes of the Georgetown Prep Development Office for a grant from the Georgetown Prep Student Alumni Association. Grace L. Perry, Marialuise A. Collins, and Guy M. Fraiture translated documents. Frank H. Alden and Gary L. Daum, our computer "gurus," saved me, technologically speaking, during a particularly dark twenty-four-hour period. Robert C. Barry, Vincent G. Conti, S.J., Aloysius C. Galvin, S.J., Henry J. Haske, S.J., and Garrett D. Orr, S.J., while reading not a page, provided more than they ever realized. John Raskauskas, a former student and colleague, now living in France, served as my "French connection." The gracious hospitality of my in-laws, Dodd and Jean Ouellette, and of Drs. Bruce Ouellette and Melanie Andrews, made writing this book possible. I owe them an immense debt. My students at Georgetown Prep kept me away from this manuscript for nine-month stretches and filled my life with great joy by their enthusiasm, humor, intelligence, inquisitiveness, hi-jinks, and goodness. To them I say, "Live the Fourth!"

I have enjoyed the support of the excellent editors at LSU Press. These include the unfailingly helpful and professional John Easterly and Sylvia D. Frank, and T. Michael Parrish, editor of the Conflicting Worlds series, whose mixture of encouragement and prodding led me to reshape the narrative. Sara Anderson's skillful wielding of her

blue pencil during copy editing significantly strengthened the manuscript and saved me from numerous inconsistencies. In light of all
the help and advice that I have received, any remaining shortcomings
in the book are clearly my responsibility.

In addition to Joe Logsdon, four people—three already cited
above—have been my special companions in this endeavor. For their
friendship, kindness, and significant contributions to this book, I am
deeply grateful to historians John Alberts, Caryn Bell, and Jim Hollandsworth, and to Helen Johnson, an indefatigable genealogist and
the great-great-granddaughter of André Cailloux.

My wife, Phyllis Linda Ouellette, has been for almost thirty years
a font of patience and love, support and strength. I can never suffi-
ciently thank her for all that she has meant to me. Finally, during the
writing of this book, a most remarkable, wonderful, and in some
ways, wrenching change occurred; one familiar to many fathers. My
baby girl grew up before my very eyes into a lovely young woman. It
is to her, Meghan Elizabeth Ochs, at "sweet sixteen," that I dedicate
this book.

Abbreviations

AANO   Archives of the Archdiocese of New Orleans

ADJ   Archives of the Diocese of Jackson

ANOC   Archdiocese of New Orleans Collection in Archives of the University of Notre Dame

CCPP   Clerk of Court, Plaquemines Parish

CUL   Colgate University Library

HNOC   Historic New Orleans Collection

JA   Josephite Archives

LC   Library of Congress

NA   National Archives

     RG 15   Record Group 15: Records of the Veterans Administration.

     RG 94   Record Group 94: Records of the Adjutant General's Office, 1780s–1917.

     RG 109   Record Group 109: War Department Collection of Confederate Records.

     RG 153   Record Group 153: Records of the Office of the Judge Advocate General (Army)

     RG 233   Record Group 233: Records of the United States House of Representatives

     RG 393   Record Group 393: Records of the U.S. Army Continental Commands, 1821–1920

NONA   New Orleans Notarial Archives

OR   *The War of the Rebellion: A Compilation of the Official Records of the Union and Confederate Armies*

PA   Congregation of the Propaganda Fide Archives in the University of Notre Dame Archives

PHCM   Port Hudson State Commemorative Area Museum

SHFA   Sisters of the Holy Family Archives

SLC   St. Louis Cathedral Book of Baptisms of Free Persons of Color
       and Slaves

A BLACK PATRIOT AND A WHITE PRIEST

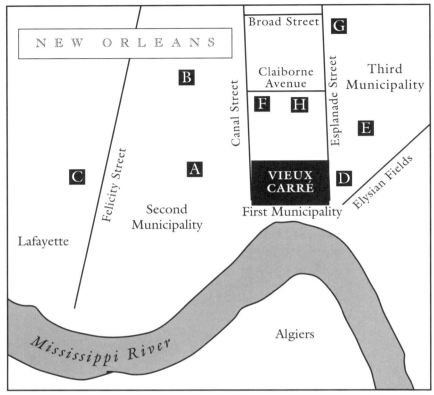

The New Orleans of André Cailloux and Claude Paschal Maistre

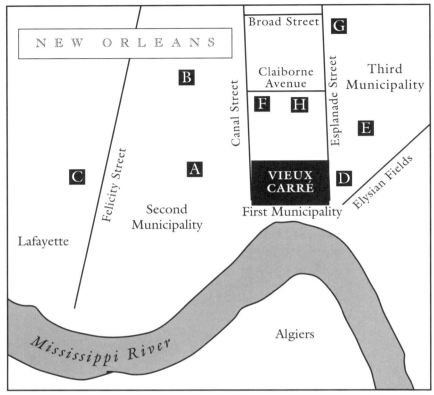 **A** The residence of Aimée and Mathieu Lartet, where André Cailloux lived as a slave.

B André Cailloux's first real estate purchase

C André Cailloux's home on Baronne Street

D André Cailloux worked in this location in 1861.

E The Hall of the Friends of Order

F Square #3 of St. Louis Cemetery #2, where Father Claude Paschal Maistre and probably André Cailloux are buried.

G St. Rose of Lima Church

H Holy Name of Jesus Church

Prologue:

A HERO'S FUNERAL

The lives and legacies of two men converged on Wednesday afternoon, July 29, 1863, a hot, humid, oppressive day typical of New Orleans in the summertime. The life of Captain André Cailloux, a thirty-eight-year-old Afro-Creole had ended two months earlier, on May 27, 1863, as he gallantly led Company E of the 1st Regiment of Louisiana Native Guards in a doomed assault on the Confederate bastion at Port Hudson, Louisiana. He would be buried that day in the Federal-occupied city, lauded as the nation's first black military hero, one of the first black men to hold an officer's commission in the United States Army, and a member of the first black regiment to be officially mustered into the Union army and to engage in a major battle.[1]

The priest who would officiate at the funeral was the French-born Claude Paschal Maistre, one of the earliest white radical voices in New Orleans and practically the sole public champion of abolitionism and racial egalitarianism among the local Catholic clergy. Maistre would perform the funeral rites of his church in defiance of New Orleans' formidable archbishop, Jean-Marie Odin, who, like Maistre,

---

1. In this book, I use the following terms interchangeably: free people of color, Afro-Creole, Creole of color, colored Creole, *libre,* and *gens de couleur libre.* During the eighteenth century, *Creole* designated any person born in the Americas. In the antebellum era, the term came to mean a white or black person who traced ancestors to the colonial era, spoke French, and was Roman Catholic. See Kimberly S. Hanger, "Patronage, Property and Persistence: The Emergence of a Free Black Elite in Spanish New Orleans," in Jane G. Landers, ed., *Against the Odds: Free Blacks in the Slave Societies of the Americas* (London, 1996), n. 1.

1

was a native of France, but who, unlike the priest and like nearly all white New Orleanians, sympathized with the Confederacy. Two months earlier, Odin had suspended Maistre and placed his parish church, St. Rose of Lima, under interdict, or censure. Odin had banned all services there in reprisal for Maistre's refusal to desist from openly advocating emancipation and encouraging black enlistment in the army, or, as Odin termed it, "inciting Negroes." The immense crowd of people of color who gathered for the service and who lined the route of the funeral procession to pay their respects did so in defiance of Odin's proscription. They were aware of the archbishop's warning that participation in public services conducted by Maistre would constitute a grave sin, the absolution of which Odin had reserved to himself.

A black patriot and a radical white priest: two relatively ordinary men transformed by their responses to the crisis of war into symbols of freedom and hope for people of color in New Orleans and of dangerous radicalism to many southern whites.

Captain Cailloux's funeral made a profound impact in New Orleans. The *Daily Picayune* reported an "unprecedentedly large" turnout of people of color for the occasion, by far the largest public event since the burial of the first Rebel Louisiana officer killed in the war. To blacks, this funeral for one of their own attested to their capacity for patriotism, courage, and martial valor. They also intended the public tribute to atone for the desecration of Cailloux's corpse, which had lain neglected and rotting on the battlefield for forty-one days until the surrender of the enemy fortress. As word of the captain's death had filtered back to New Orleans, women of color had donned crepe rosettes in mourning. Immediately after the Confederate surrender of Port Hudson, black troops recovered Cailloux's body, identifiable only by a ring on his finger. Union officials sent Cailloux's remains, accompanied by wounded members of his regiment, to New Orleans via the steamer *Old Essex*. Arriving on July 25, the body lay in state in a closed casket for four days in the Urquhart Street hall of the Friends of the Order, a mutual aid society in which Cailloux had played a leading role and whose ring he had worn at the time of his death. Flowers and lit candles, characteristic of Catholic funeral rites, framed the flag-draped coffin; Cailloux's sword, belt, uniform coat, and cap lay on the flag. A guard solemnly paced back and forth near the casket.

At the appointed time on July 29, the band of the all-white 42nd Massachusetts Regiment made its appearance, and "played the customary solemn airs." According to a witness reporting for the New York *Times,* Father Maistre read the Catholic service for the dead. The clergyman then delivered a glowing and eloquent eulogy on the virtues of the deceased. He called upon all present to offer themselves, like Cailloux, as martyrs to the cause of justice, freedom, and good government, and he characterized Cailloux's death as one that the proudest might envy.

The enormous crowd of people of color had, by this time, gathered around the building, rendering impassable the surrounding streets. After a short pause, a sudden silence fell on the throng as the band commenced playing a dirge. Eight soldiers, escorted by six black captains and six members of the Friends of Order, brought the casket on their shoulders from the hall. Two companies of the 6th Louisiana (colored) Regiment acted as an escort while representatives of more than thirty black male and female mutual aid, fraternal, and burial societies, many of which Maistre had helped organize, lined Esplanade Avenue for more than a mile, waiting for the hearse to pass. The names of many of the organizations reflected their Catholic origins; their number witnessed to the rich communal life of the Creoles of color. Besides the Friends of Order, these included the Society of Economy and Mutual Advance, the United Brethren, the Arts and Mechanics Association, the Free Friends, the Good Shepherd Conclave No. 2, the Artisans Brotherhood, the Good Shepherd Conclave No. 1, the Union Sons' Relief, the Perseverance Society, the Ladies of Bon Secours, La Fleur de Marie, Saint Rose of Lima, the Children of Mary Society, the Saint Angela Society, the Sacred Union Society, the Children of Jesus, the Saint Veronica Society, the Saint Alphonsus Society, the Saint Joachim Society, the Star of the Cross, the Saint Theresa Society, the Saint Eulalia Society, the Saint Magdalen Society, the God Protect Us Society, the United Sisterhood, the Angel Gabriel Society, the Saint Louis Roi Society, the Saint Benoit Society, the Benevolence Society, the Well-Beloved Sisters' Society, the Saint Peter Society, the Saint Michael Archangel Society, the Saint Louis de Gonzague Society, the Saint Ann Society, and the Children of Moses.

The procession to the cemetery included a large number of black officers as well as the carriage bearing Cailloux's widow, Felicie Cailloux, and their four children. Thousands of black people, free and slave, the latter emboldened enough by the events of the war to appear in the city's streets, waved miniature United States flags or wore them on their clothing.

After moving through the principal downtown streets and past Congo Square, the cortege arrived at the "Bienville Street" cemetery (St. Louis No. 2) where Cailloux was interred with military honors. Because ecclesiastical censure prevented Maistre from securing the aid of any other priests or assistants, he turned to Colonel Spencer H. Stafford, commander of the 1st Louisiana Native Guards, who had once bragged that his regiment represented so many trades and professions that he could build a town on the prairie in sixty days. Two privates immediately volunteered to help at the graveyard services. Another private also left the ranks to perform the duties of bricklayer in opening and sealing the above-ground tomb.[2]

Northern newspapers such as the New York *Times,* the New York *Herald,* and *Harper's Weekly,* which had urged the use of black combat troops in the war, gave extensive coverage to Cailloux's funeral. The *Times* correspondent eulogized the fallen captain as a soldier who "had sealed with his blood the inspiration he received from Mr. Lincoln's Emancipation Proclamation," and noted that the scene called forth a single sentiment in those who witnessed it: "the struggle must go on until there is not legally a slave under the folds of the American flag."[3] *L'Union,* a newspaper published in New Orleans by activists committed to emancipation and equality for free people of color and freedmen, observed, "In Captain Cailloux the cause of the Union and freedom has lost a valuable friend." Captain Cailloux,

2. New Orleans *Daily Picayune,* July 30, 1863; David C. Edmonds, *The Guns of Port Hudson: The Investment, Siege, and Reduction* (Lafayette, La., 1984), II, 131, 377; Deposition of Mary Lewis, June 26, 1894, in Pension Record of John Louis, RG 15, NA, Washington, D.C.; New York *Times,* August 8 and 9, 1863; *Harper's Weekly,* August 29, 1863.

3. New York *Times,* August 8, 1863. Opponents of the use of black troops also reported on Cailloux's funeral. The New York *World* mocked it in an article headlined, "A Defunct Darkey———[illegible]." See New York *Times,* August 9, 1863, which reprinted the piece from the *World* as an example of what it called "Copperhead journalism."

defending the sacred cause of liberty, "vindicated his race from the opprobrium with which it was charged." The American flag in New Orleans flew at half-mast for thirty days in Cailloux's honor, and popular poet George H. Boker memorialized Cailloux in an ode. Afro-Creole radicals and their white abolitionist allies regularly invoked the compelling image of the heroic captain as part of their campaign for emancipation, suffrage, and equal rights. Some fifty years later, Rodolphe L. Desdunes, in his history of Creoles of color written in the wake of the unsuccessful Afro-Creole challenge to segregation in the infamous *Plessy v. Ferguson* case, apotheosized Cailloux as "this American Spartacus" who had proved that "the black man is able to fight and die for his country."[4]

In life and in death, Cailloux, an Afro-Creole who took great pride in his ebony color, helped to bridge the gap between Creole free people of color and slaves on the one hand and Anglophonic, Protestant blacks on the other. His wartime experience pointed to a growing alliance between leaders of the two groups and to their shared embrace of radical politics. Cailloux's heroics represented the zenith for black combat officers during the Civil War. No other black officer figured so prominently in a major engagement, since most were forced out of the army within a year. With Cailloux's death, Union officials effectively buried the brightest hope for black combat officers in the U.S. Army.

While Northern advocates of the use of black combat troops initially made much of Cailloux's valor, they quickly shifted their attention to the supposedly more important eastern theater of the war and the Massachusetts 54th, which included two of Frederick Douglass's sons in its ranks and was commanded by Robert Gould Shaw. The scion of a prominent Massachusetts abolitionist family, the twenty-five-year-old "boy colonel" was killed leading his black regiment in its doomed assault on Fort Wagner in Charleston harbor about two months after the Battle of Port Hudson. But the Cailloux myth—the symbolic embodiment and expression of the reality of his life—

4. *L'Union* quoted in *Harper's Weekly,* August 29, 1863; Roland C. McConnell, "Louisiana's Black Military History, 1729–1865," in Robert R. Macdonald, John R. Kemp, Edward F. Haas, eds., *Louisiana's Black Heritage* (New Orleans, 1979), 60; Rodolphe Lucien Desdunes, *Our People and Our History,* ed. and trans. Sister Dorothea Olga McCants (Baton Rouge, 1973), 125. Boker's poem appears in Joseph T. Wilson, *The Black Phalanx* (1890; repr. New York, 1968), 217.

remained potent among blacks for many years. In their works on black troops in the Civil War, pioneering nineteenth-century African American historians—William Wells Brown (1867), George Washington Williams (1888), and Joseph T. Wilson (1890)—retold and sometimes embellished the tale of Cailloux's heroics at Port Hudson. Black Union veterans named lodges of the Grand Army of the Republic after him. From the 1860s to the mid-twentieth century, black activists in New Orleans especially embraced and appropriated the figure of Cailloux. These ranged from James Ingraham, a key figure at the 1864 Colored Convention in Syracuse and in the founding of the Equal Rights League, to Rodolphe Desdunes and the Comité de Citoyens, which raised the legal challenge to Jim Crow laws that culminated in the *Plessy* decision in 1896, to intellectual and civil rights figures of the early and mid-twentieth century such as Charles B. Rousseve, A. P. Tureaud, and Marcus Christian.[5]

Claude Paschal Maistre, the enigmatic and paradoxical figure who presided at Cailloux's funeral, maintained his standoff with Archbishop Odin for seven years—years that corresponded with the remainder of the Civil War and part of Reconstruction in Louisiana. The recalcitrant clerical champion of black rights became the paladin of anticlerical, Afro-Creole activists who, in the pages of *L'Union* and its successor, the *Tribune*, bitterly assailed the institutional Catholic church in New Orleans for what they regarded as its pro-Confederate sympathies and its racism. Still, most Afro-Creoles adhered to the

5. McConnell, "Louisiana's Black Military History," in Macdonald, Kemp, and Haas, *Louisiana's Black Heritage,* 60; Russell Duncan, *Blue-Eyed Child of Fortune: The Civil War Letters of Robert Gould Shaw* (Athens, Ga., 1992), 1–68; William Wells Brown, *The Negro in the American Rebellion: His Heroism and His Fidelity* (Boston, 1867), 168–70; Wilson, *The Black Phalanx,* 214–17, 527; George Washington Williams, *A History of the Negro Troops in the War of the Rebellion, 1861–1865* (1888; repr., New York, 1969), 218–19; Desdunes, *Our People and Our History,* 125; Charles B. Rousseve, *The Negro in Louisiana: Aspects of History and His Literature* (1937; rpr. New York, 1969), 4; Marcus Christian, "Captain André Cailloux: The Rock," Parts I and II, *Louisiana Weekly,* August 3, 10, 1957, typescript copies in Box 17, Marcus Christian Collection, Earl K. Long Library, University of New Orleans; Joseph Logsdon, telephone conversation with author, August 27, 1993; Rodolphe Lucien Desdunes, *Our People and Our History,* 125. Professor Logsdon had in his possession many hours of taped interviews with A. P. Tureaud, the NAACP lawyer who brought the major desegregation suits involving Louisiana schools. The definition of *myth* is from Douglas L. Wilson, *Honor's Voice: The Transformation of Abraham Lincoln* (New York, 1998), 54.

Catholicism that in part defined their identities, even as the institutional church often accommodated itself to the racial status quo and dealt severely with Maistre when he challenged it. Eventually Maistre, satisfied that he had played his part in forcing the church to attend more closely to the needs of its black communicants and believing like other white radicals that Reconstruction had effected substantive political changes in Louisiana, submitted to a new, but still conservative, archbishop. Maistre's death in 1875, however, coincided with the fraying of the nascent alliance between leaders of the Afro-Creole and Anglophonic free black communities, and with the political resurgence of white supremacist Democratic forces in the city of New Orleans.

A soldier and his regiment, a priest and his church—the story of how Cailloux and Maistre arrived at that day in July 1863, and what followed—offers a prism through which to view the complex, often paradoxical interplay of slavery, race, and religion, during American democracy's most violent upheaval.

During the antebellum era, free Afro-Catholic Creoles like Cailloux carved out lives and forged identities within the recesses of the Gulf South's volatile tripartite racial system of slaves, free people of color, and whites. They initially sought military service in the Civil War for the purpose of protecting and advancing their fragile position in society, but after the Union occupation of New Orleans, they quickly grasped the war's revolutionary import for social and political relations. The conflict radicalized both Cailloux and Maistre, just as it did many other free people of color and some whites. It forged a tacit alliance between the two men and a more explicit one between free people of color and freedmen and their white radical allies. The lives of the captain and the priest, intertwined so dramatically on that July day, provide a window into the world of Afro-Creoles, many of whom, like Cailloux, traveled a road from slavery, to freedom, to military service, and then to radical politics, establishing in the process a tradition of black Catholic protest.

Institutions, however, proved resistant to change. Conservatives in the Church, the military, politics, and society at large ultimately weathered and defeated most of the war-induced radical challenges to the racial status quo, with the exception of slavery. Nevertheless, Captain André Cailloux and the Reverend Claude Paschal Maistre, though relatively obscure figures today, played significant roles in the history of New Orleans' people of color. Their lives illustrate the era of slavery, the Civil War, and Reconstruction writ small and concretely in a unique community. Their stories capture something of the valor, trials, triumphs, and frustrations of those who helped to destroy the peculiar institution but met defeat in their efforts to forge a new era of justice and equality in race relations during and after the war. Paraphrasing the Book of Sirach from the Bible, however, their virtues were not forgotten; their heritage remained with their descendants. Cailloux and Maistre helped to sow seeds that others would harvest at a more favorable time.

1

PATHS TO FREEDOM

André Cailloux shared a common Afro-Creole, Roman Catholic ancestry and culture with most of the eleven thousand free people of color in New Orleans in 1860. Like so many of them, who were only a generation or less removed from bondage, he had entered the world a slave. But Cailloux, who was born in 1825 in Plaquemines Parish and later bragged of being "the blackest man in New Orleans," died a free man fighting against the hated institution. In the interim, he and his wife, Felicie, traveled separate paths to freedom—paths marked by guideposts of family, religion, and culture.

Cailloux's father, also named André, was born on November 30, 1793, to a twenty-year-old slave named Francisca in Spanish-controlled New Orleans, then a squalid, fetid, port city, originally founded by the French in 1718 and retrieved with the aid of slave labor from the vast cypress swamps that surrounded it. Francisca gave birth to André a year after the second of two fires (1788 and 1792) that had nearly razed the city, three years before the first great yellow fever epidemic, and approximately ten years before the Spanish retrocession of Louisiana and New Orleans to France that would lead to the subsequent sale of the territory to the United States. She probably belonged to Madame Louise Laprade, the wife of Antoine Duvernay, though the baptismal register lists a "Madame Pretel" as her owner—most likely a misspelling of "Laprade." At his baptism, on December 15, 1793, at the St. Louis Parish church, Francisca's child received the name "André," which he shared with one of Antoine Duvernay's sons.[1]

André, however, also had a nickname: "Cayou," or "Caillou." It may originally have been a corruption of an African word or name; he lived in a household that included both African and Creole (American-born) slaves and his own father may have been African. Slaves often had both "official" names given to them by their masters and African "nicknames" chosen by their parents. "Cayou" could have been his father's name. The nickname might also have had geographic significance since Caillou Bay, Bayou Grand Caillou, Caillou Lake, and Caillou Island were all located in what is now Terrebonne Parish below New Orleans. Perhaps it signified a hoped-for personal quality or occupation. In eighteenth-century French, *caillou* had a number of meanings, including "flint" or "flint stone," "pebble," "rock," "stone," and "gravel." In popular usage, it could also signify "precious stone" or "bald pate." In Haitian Creole, an increasingly common tongue among Louisiana slaves and free people of color in the first decade of the nineteenth century, "caillou" meant "wood chips." Wood chips and stone—since the elder André eventually became a carpenter and mason, perhaps this nickname indicated that he was "a chip off the old block" (his father) from whom he learned his trades.[2]

Whatever the origins of the name, André and his mother belonged to Antoine Duvernay, an octogenarian (born in 1719) sugar planter from the German Coast in St. Charles Parish, about fifteen to twenty miles upriver from New Orleans, and his wife, Louise Laprade Duvernay. Antoine Duvernay's background mirrored some of the racial, social, and political complexities of colonial Louisiana. He was of mixed ancestry: his father, François Duvernay de Riviera of Mar-

1. Gwendolyn Midlo Hall, *Africans in Colonial Louisiana: The Development of Afro-Creole Culture in the Eighteenth Century* (Baton Rouge, 1992), 120; Christina Vella, *Intimate Enemies: The Two Worlds of the Baroness de Pontalba* (Baton Rouge, 1997), 6–11, 37; Winston De Ville, *The 1795 Chimney-Tax of New Orleans: A Guide to the Census of Proprietors and Residents of the Vieux Carré* (Ville Platte, La., 1994), 10; SLC, Bk. 5, December 15, 1793, p. 132, Act 520, in ANNO.

2. Inventory of the Estate of Antoine Duvernay, June 22, 1803, in Notarial Acts of Narcisse Broutin, Spanish Louisiana Slave Records, HNOC, New Orleans, La.; Peter Caron, e-mail to author, June 23, 1997; H. Ferrar, J. A. Hutchinson, and J. D. Biard (eds.), *The Concise Oxford French Dictionary,* (2nd. ed., New York, 1980), 76; Hall, *Africans in Colonial Louisiana*, 408.

seilles, was French, while his mother, Roseta ("Natchez"), was an Indian. He himself married a woman of mixed French and Indian blood: Louise Laprade. A subject of the king of France while Louisiana remained part of the French empire, Duvernay served for a time in the 1770s as a fusilier in the service of "his most Catholic Majesty, the King of Spain," after the colony's cession to Spain in the Treaty of Paris of 1763. By 1803, shortly before his death, Duvernay had sold his St. Charles plantation and taken up residence with his wife and slaves on Camp Street in the Faubourg (suburb) St. Marie of New Orleans, just upriver from the Vieux Carré, or what became known later as the French Quarter. André, Francisca, and André's sister Maneta were three of eight slaves (one an African) owned by the Duvernays in 1803, the year the United States purchased Louisiana. Over the next few years, Francisca gave birth to several more children: Marie Louise (January 1805), Therese (March 1807), and Antonia (August 1811). Each was baptized at St. Louis Cathedral, and André stood as Therese's godfather.[3]

The Catholicism of André's family, as was the case with many slave families, probably owed a great deal to the mother, Francisca. Born about 1773, before large-scale importation of African slaves resumed in the 1780s (during the French regime, most slaves had been imported between 1719 and 1731), Francisca was most likely a native of Louisiana, part of the Creole group that Ira Berlin has called the "charter generation" of slaves. Many of them imbibed their Catholicism either directly or indirectly from Ursuline nuns. After arriving in Louisiana in 1727, the Ursulines not only instructed slaves and free people of color in the catechism at their convent school, but also between 1730 and 1744 sponsored a women's confraternity, the Children of Mary, dedicated to the evangelization of slaves and free people of color. The membership of the Children of Mary ran the gamut of New Orleans society from plantation mistresses to a few slaves, and the confraternity grew to eighty-five members by the mid-

---

3. Jacqueline Voorhies, trans. and comp., *Some Late Eighteenth Century Louisiana Census Records, 1758–1796*, (Lafayette, La., 1973); Testament of Antonio Duvernay, October 13, 1800, in Pedro Pedesclaux, vol. 37, 609–12, NONA; Jack Belsom, "Duvernay Genealogy," in the possession of Jack Belsom of New Orleans; Inventory of the Estate of Antoine Duvernay; SLC, Bk. 8, January 4, 1805, p. 27b, Act 110, Bk. 9, April 6, 1807, p. 151, Act 775, and Bk. 12, August 17, 1811, p. 82, AANO.

1740s, a ratio of approximately one evangelizer per thirty-eight enslaved blacks in New Orleans. Women of the confraternity served as godparents for many of the slaves baptized between 1730 and the mid-1740s, not en masse as the first arrivals from Africa had been, but in church ceremonies with masters participating. Women of color, both slave and free, appropriated Catholicism to their own lives and played a key role in transmitting it to their kinsfolk and to the larger community. After 1765, the great majority of godparents at slave baptisms were of African descent, rather than white. André's role at his sister's baptism reflected that reality. Indeed, as a boy, he may have received religious instruction from Ursuline sisters at their convent on Sundays and on holy days.[4]

The household in which André and his family lived, with its Catholicism and its Creole and African slaves, embodied the melding of European and African cultural and religious traditions in New Orleans. First brought to Louisiana in 1719, slaves soon outnumbered whites in the colony. In 1746, the black population—almost all slaves, with two-thirds born in Louisiana—stood at 4,730, while the white population of the colony numbered 3,200. By 1805 New Orleans' population had swelled to 8,500, with slaves constituting a majority and free blacks accounting for about one-fifth. André found himself immersed in a local culture that had, as a result of increased slave importation spurred by the growth of the plantation economy in tobacco, indigo, and then sugar, become significantly more Africanized, as seen in its cuisine, forms of entertainment, and worship. As he moved about the city, enjoying far greater freedom than plantation slaves, the aroma of African cookery such as gumbo and jambalaya no doubt wafted through the air, competing with less appealing odors emanating from the reeking slaughterhouse on the riverbank, the myriad dogs, pigs, and cows that roamed freely, and the garbage and dung that covered the streets. Like many of the

---

4. Gwendolyn Midlo Hall, "The Formation of Afro-Creole Culture," in Hirsch and Logsdon, *Creole New Orleans,* 67; Ira Berlin, *Many Thousands Gone: The First Two Centuries of Slavery in North America* (Cambridge, Massachusetts, 1998), 12, 198–99; Emily Clark, " 'By All the Conduct of Their Lives': A Laywoman's Confraternity in New Orleans, 1730–1744," *William and Mary Quarterly,* LIV (1997), 790–93, and "Evangelizing and Empowering Free Women of Color in New Orleans, 1727–1862: The Early Ursulines," paper delivered at the annual meeting of the American Historical Association, January 9, 1999), 5–7, 12.

other city slaves, André probably enjoyed and participated in the dancing ("gyrations" in the view of some Europeans) that so characterized slave life and highlighted feast days, funerals, parades, and religious processions. He likely joined the crowd at the *Place Congo* on the lake side of Rampart Street to watch or perform in traditional dances that occasioned protests from dismayed ecclesiastical authorities, and he no doubt witnessed voodoo priests accompanied by dancers and priestesses as they prepared their spirit worship at the lakeshore at Bayou St. John, a popular recreational site for slaves.[5]

Latin Catholicism and traditional African animism proved remarkably compatible in Louisiana. Catholicism aided the acculturation of Africans who brought with them traditions of pantheons, conjuring, witchcraft, sacred talismans, and cults of feminine fertility, each of which had their analogies in Catholicism. Slaves could relate to the Catholic liturgy, with its formalized adaptations on universal primitive rites, and to the Church's vestuary saints, sacramentals (scapulars, crosses, and medals that ordinary people wore as much to ward off evil as to signify their faith), intercessory prayers (which resembled African conjuring), and most especially the Spaniards' central religious motif: the Holy Virgin and the cult of feminine fertility. For all of their oft-noted religious indifference and moral laxity, slave masters, often at the urging of their more pious wives and other lay women who took the initiative in matters religious, did provide for the baptism of their slaves according to the provisions of the French and Spanish slave codes, albeit tardily at times. In 1800, slaves, who constituted approximately 37 percent of the city's population, accounted for 52 percent of the baptisms at St. Louis Cathedral.[6]

5. Berlin, *Many Thousands Gone*, 198, 333, 342; Hall, *Africans in Colonial Louisiana*, 10, 122; Alfred E. Lemmon, "Spanish Louisiana: In the Service of God and His Most Catholic Majesty," in Glenn R. Conrad, ed., *Cross, Crozier, and Crucible: A Volume Celebrating the Bicentennial of a Catholic Diocese in Louisiana* (New Orleans, 1993), 21; Thomas Marc Fiehrer, "The African Presence in Colonial Louisiana: An Essay on the Continuity of Caribbean Culture," in Macdonald, Kemp, and Haas, *Louisiana's Black Heritage*, 25–26, 30. For a graphic description of New Orleans circa 1800 see Vella, *Intimate Enemies*, 6–11.

6. Thomas Marc Fiehrer, "The African Presence in Colonial Louisiana," in Macdonald, Kemp, and Haas, *Louisiana's Black Heritage*, 27–29; Lemmon, "Spanish Louisiana," in Conrad, *Cross, Crozier, and Crucible*, 28; Emily Clark, " 'By All the Conduct of Their Lives,' " 790–93. Kimberly S. Hanger, *Bounded Lives, Bounded Places: Free Black Society in Colonial New Orleans, 1769–1803* (Durham, 1997), 22.

When Louise Laprade died in 1815, the twenty-two-year-old André was still living in the Laprade household with his four sisters, but not his mother. In 1818, the terms of Laprade's succession displaced and dislocated the family, awarding André and two of his sisters (Marie and Therese) to Laprade's daughter Felicite and her husband (and cousin) François Duvernay. Laprade also left her daughter five pieces of real estate valued at $13,000 in the Faubourg St. Marie. François and Felicite already owned a small plantation that fronted the Mississippi River at Place du Portage, about 11 leagues (26 miles) below New Orleans on the left bank, descending, of the Mississippi River in Plaquemines Parish. When they decided to employ their new slaves on that plantation, André left the urban slavery of New Orleans for the harsher rural environment of Louisiana's burgeoning sugarcane area.[7]

André apparently resided on the modest Duvernay plantation in Plaquemines for at least two, and perhaps as many as five, years. His masters regarded him as the most versatile and valuable of their eleven slaves, which included eight males and three females. André became "something of a craftsman" in carpentry and masonry, performed well as a field hand, and earned a reputation for reliability ("bon sujet") unlike his younger sister Marie, a laundress with a penchant for running away. Caillou and his fellow slaves grew rice, the dominant cash crop in the area prior to the sugar boom of the early nineteenth century, corn, and peas, and raised cows, pigs, chickens, sheep, and geese. The inventory of François Duvernay's estate following his death in an accident in 1820 placed a value of $1500 on André, "dit Caillou," whom the document described as both a versatile field hand and artisan.[8]

Felicite Duvernay's will, dated December 17, 1822, reflected

7. Heirs of Louise Duvernay, December 12, 1818, copy of a notarial act before Philippe Pedesclaux, Receipt, François Duvernay to Sieur Fromentaire, July 7, 1804, copy of a notarial act before Narcisse Broutin, both in Succession of François Duvernay, no. 201, Probate Court Records, CCPP, Pointe-à-la-Hache, La.; Inventory of the Estate of Antonio Duvernay; Succession of Louise Laprade Duvernay, 1815, in Orleans Parish, Court of Probate, Succession and Probate Records, microfilm in Louisiana Division, NOPL; Heirs of Louise Duvernay; Third Census of the United States, 1810, Plaquemines Parish, Louisiana Territory, 363.

8. Inventory, January 14, 1824, in Succession of Felicite Duvernay, no. 87, Probate Court Records, CCPP.

some solicitude for the fate of her slaves. After assigning some specifically to individual family heirs, she indicated that she would leave the fate of André to their judgment, with the proviso that neither he nor any of the other slaves should, under any pretext, pass into the possession of strangers. Mrs. Duvernay's death in December 1823 initiated a chain of events that saw André change hands three times over the next four years, although the owners remained within the Duvernay clan. Felicite left four heirs: her children Antoine Duvernay and Aimée Duvernay Bailey, both of whom lived in New Orleans, her son Joseph, the twenty-eight-year-old executor of the estate and a bachelor who lived on a modest plantation in Placquemines Parish close to his mother's property, and Edmond Duvernay of St. Charles, the illegitimate son of François Duvernay. In June and July 1824, as a result of the division of Felicite's estate, André, and six other slaves, including his sister Therese, were conveyed to Felicite's daughter, Aimée Duvernay Bailey, and her husband, William, who also purchased the plantation for $5000.[9]

During the same year, twenty-seven-year-old André became involved with a nineteen-year-old slave woman, Josephine, one of approximately seventy slaves on the large sugar plantation of Samuel Packwood, which lay across and down the river from the Bailey property and fronted the Mississippi for 50 arpents (acres) at Pointe-à-la-Hache. It also lay close to and on the same side of the river as Joseph Duvernay's farm. Josephine had already borne two mulatto sons by the twenty-eight-year-old Duvernay: four-year-old Molière (conceived when she was fourteen or barely fifteen) and two-year-old Antoine. Now, in late 1824, Josephine was pregnant again, but this time by the slave, André. The two may have known each other prior to their arrival in Plaquemines Parish, because Josephine had lived on the so-called German coast in St. Charles Parish near Antoine Duvernay's plantations there. The area had been the scene of a large-scale slave uprising in 1811, which had been bloodily suppressed. In 1816, Josephine's owner had sold her downriver to Plaquemines Parish. She and André also could have met at Joseph Duvernay's

9. Testament of Madame Widow of François Duvernay, December 17, 1822, *Note des Articles adjuges à Madame Duvernay,* July 22, 1820, Inventory, all in Succession of Felicite Duvernay; Sale of Slaves by Joseph Duvernay, exécuteur testamentaire, to William Bailey, June 23, 1824, Act 460, Sale of Land, Joseph Duvernay to William Bailey, July 9, 1824, Act 462, both in Notarial Bk. 3, CCPP.

plantation at Point-à-la-Hache if Duvernay contracted with Bailey for the use of his skilled slave. Or André may have sought female companionship away from his own plantation because only one of the four slave women on the Bailey farm other than his sister, Therese, was younger than forty.[10]

On May 3, 1825, with Josephine pregnant by André, Duvernay purchased her and his sons Moliere and Antoine from Samuel Packwood. The sale marked the fourth time Josephine had been sold since 1813, when the death of Pierre Marie Cabaret D'Etrépy of St. Charles Parish had initiated a series of transactions that eventually brought her to Pointe-à-la-Hache. There, on August 25, 1825, Josephine gave birth to a son who bore his father's first name, André.[11]

The elder André meanwhile continued to labor on William Bailey's small plantation. Inventories indicate that he and the nine other slaves on the Bailey farm lived and worked in spartan conditions. The plantation buildings consisted of a modest, two and one-half room main dwelling, a detached kitchen, a rice mill, barns for some livestock, and "Negro huts" in which André and the other nine slaves (five of them male) lived. The cultivation of rice required arduous and hazardous work involving long hours of stoop labor, knee-deep in murky waters infested with water moccasins and disease-carrying mosquitoes. André's skills as a carpenter and mason, however, may have spared him some of the difficult work associated with rice culture. Planters who employed a dozen or more slaves could turn a

10. Agreement between the heirs of Cabaret D'Etrépy, April 22, 1814, Act 207, Vol. 8, Sale of Land, Dame Delphine to Albin Michel, May 31, 1816, Act 425, Vol. 11, *Partage* (Division), January 30, 1817, Act 425, Vol. 12, Sale, Michel to John Lafarge, May 21, 1819, Act 289, Vol. 17, Sale of a Plantation, Lafarge to Samuel Packwood, March 26, 1821, Act 102, Vol. 20, all in Michel DeArmas, NONA; Acte de liberté, 1828(?) (damaged), Act 599, in Notarial Bk. 4, CCPP; acte de liberté (damaged); SLC, Bk. 20, p. 211, Act 590, AANO; Inventory of the Estate of William Bailey, October 31, 1826, in Succession of William Bailey, no. 273, Probate Court Records, CCPP. On the slave uprising, see Glenn R. Conrad, ed., *The German Coast: Abstracts of the Civil Records of St. Charles and St. John the Baptist Parishes, 1804–1812* (Lafayette, La., 1981), 100–110.

11. Sale of a Slave, May 3, 1825, Act 198, in Philippe Pedesclaux, Vol. 30, NONA; SLC, Bk. 20, p. 211, Act 590, AANO; Belsom, "Duvernay Genealogy"; Agreement between the heirs of Cabaret D'Etrépy, sale of land, Delphine to Michel, partage, sale, Michel to Lafarge, Sale of a Plantation, Lafarge to Packwood; SLC, Bk. 20, July 15, 1827, p. 197, Act 618, AANO.

profit in indigo, tobacco, and rice until about 1790, but thereafter, as a result of market conditions, such crops became less profitable and sugar began to dominate. When Bailey died in October 1826, his plantation was appraised at $13,560.50, including slaves worth $6,250.[12]

Bailey's death eventually united André, Josephine, and young André albeit on the plantation owned by the man who had already fathered two of Josephine's children. Bailey's widow, Aimée Duvernay Bailey, inherited not only the plantation in Plaquemines Parish and real estate in New Orleans (where she appears to have resided), but also $17,500 in debts. She therefore authorized the sale of her plantation and slaves in Plaquemines Parish as well as her lot in New Orleans. Since the Bailey estate still owed Joseph Duvernay $1,190 for the earlier purchase of the senior André back in 1824, Mrs. Bailey conveyed him to her brother on March 12, 1827, as part of the liquidation of the estate. Subsequently, the two Duvernay siblings evidently attempted to honor familial relationships among their slaves. Having paid off creditors, Mrs. Bailey reacquired some slaves who had belonged to her family but had been scattered as a result of the estate sale, including the elder André, Josephine, and little André, on December 27, 1827. Her acquisition of the three from Joseph Duvernay indicated at least informal recognition on the part of the owners that the slaves constituted a self-conscious family unit.[13]

* * *

12. Inventory of the Estate of William Bailey and Description of Property, October 19, 1826, both in the Succession of William Bailey, CCPP; Hall, *Africans in Colonial Louisiana*, 122; Fiehrer, "The African Presence in Colonial Louisiana," in Macdonald, Kemp, and Haas, *Louisiana's Black Heritage*, 9, 12, 13, 11; Inventory of the Estate of William Bailey.

13. Joseph Duvernay, Tuteur du mineur Ed. Duvernay, to Joseph Duvernay, Exécuteur Testamentaire, Quittance, Act 553, and William Bailey to Joseph Duvernay, Mortgage, Act 554, both on August 12, 1826, in Notarial Bk. 3, CCPP. See also document dated November 1, 1826, and Inventory of a portion of the Bailey estate located in New Orleans, November 16, 1826, Petition of Aimée Bailey, *Doit la Succession*, Wm. Bailey to Joseph Duvernay, January 4, 1827, and Adjuducation, December 23, 1826, all in the Succession of William Bailey, CCPP; Aimée Bailey, Exécutrice de la Succession, William Bailey to Joseph Duvernay, Vente d'esclave, comptant (cash), March 12, 1827, in Notarial Bk. 4, Act 584, Notarial act, January, 1828 (?) (damaged), Act 609, p. 36, in Notarial Bk. 4, and Conveyance Bk. 1, p. 35, all in CCPP.

Perhaps suffering from poor health and increasingly aware of his own mortality, Joseph Duvernay turned his attention to his children by Josephine. Catholicism (including that of the slaves) was part of Duvernay's family heritage, just as it was part of Louisiana's, stretching back to the earliest days of exploration and settlement by the French at the beginning of the eighteenth century. The names of cities, towns, civil parishes, streets, and rivers, and the celebration of such festivals as Mardi Gras reflected the Catholic heritage of the Gulf Coast. But under both the French and Spanish regimes of the eighteenth century, and then under the Americans after 1803, Louisiana's Catholics, especially the men, displayed what one historian has described as a laissez-faire attitude toward their religion. Nonchalant about doctrine and church laws and often anticlerical, many Catholic Louisianians turned to the church at key moments of their lives—birth, marriage and death—but were otherwise indifferent to the moral demands of Catholicism.[14]

Certainly the weakness of the institutional church contributed to the situation. Though supported financially (albeit sometimes grudgingly) by the colonial French and Spanish governments under the terms of the *patronato real* (royal patronage), not until the creation of the diocese of Louisiana and the Floridas and the appointment of Luis Peñalvar y Cárdenas in 1795 did Louisiana finally obtain a resident bishop to preside over the diocese's twenty-one scattered parishes and twenty-six priests. The absence of such ecclesiastical leadership for so many years meant that missionaries from already overextended religious orders such as the Capuchins (and earlier the Carmelites and Jesuits) had to maintain parishes and provide the pastoral care normally associated with diocesan clergy. A shortage of women religious also plagued the church, though the Ursuline Sisters (who had first arrived in 1727) labored heroically, establishing a school, operating a royal hospital, sponsoring a lay confraternity of women, and providing religious instruction to black and Indian girls and women, even though they also owned slaves. Rivalries and divisions within the clergy, the growth of skepticism and anticlericalism associated with the Enlightenment, the reluctance

14. Dolores Egger Labbé, " 'Helpers in the Gospel': Women and Religion in Louisiana, 1800–1830," *Mid-America*, LXXIX (Summer, 1997), 155–57.

of colonial governments to enforce the church's moral strictures, and the intellectual and political ferment associated with the French Revolution all further weakened the Church.

Numerous observers in the late eighteenth and early nineteenth centuries, focusing especially on the prevalence of concubinage, commented on the low level of morality shown by many of the city's residents, including some of the clergy. One priest stationed in New Orleans called his city "this sewer of all vice and refuge of all that is worst on earth." The transfer of Bishop Cárdenas to Guatemala in 1801, which left Louisiana without a resident bishop for another fourteen years, and the purchase of Louisiana by the United States two years later in 1803, which led to a flight of clergy, precipitated what one historian has called the darkest page in the history of the Church in Louisiana. By 1812, only twelve priests and eleven sisters remained in Louisiana. Although William Dubourg, appointed bishop of New Orleans in 1815, began to address that problem in 1816 and 1817 by recruiting priests and sisters in France to revitalize the church in Louisiana, by 1830 the number of priests in Louisiana had increased only to twenty-four. Given the scarcity of priests and nuns during this period, lay women played an especially crucial role in preserving and transmitting Catholicism to their children.

Beginning in 1805, the Church also found itself riven by a schism that pitted the city's most popular pastor, the Capuchin Friar Antonio de Sedella (known as Père Antoine), against the self-styled vicar-general of the diocese, the Reverend Patrick Walsh, and Bishop John Carroll of Baltimore, the temporary administrator of the New Orleans diocese. Sedella eventually submitted to Bishop Dubourg after the latter's appointment as bishop, but remained—rightly as it turned out under canon law—pastor of the cathedral until his death in 1828. Sedella's case became enmeshed in a larger struggle for control of St. Louis Cathedral, which lasted until 1844. This bitter conflict pitted successive bishops of New Orleans (two of whom, William Dubourg and Joseph Rosati, chose to reside in St. Louis rather than in the hostile atmosphere of their see city) against the increasingly strident and doctrinaire lay wardens (*marguilliers*) of the cathedral, who controlled its finances and refused any income to the bishop. During these years, nominally Catholic white Louisianians neglected the minimal requirement for practicing Catholics: to make their Easter duty by receiving the sacraments of penance and the Eucharist yearly. In 1820, for example, fewer than three hundred people in the city received the sacraments during the Easter season, nor did white masters ensure that their slaves did so.[15]

Such seems to have been the case with Joseph Duvernay. Like many other Catholic Louisiana slaveholders, Duvernay procrastinated in his moral obligation to see to the baptism of his slaves. When it came to the religious lives of their slaves, Catholic slaveholders frequently restricted their involvement to baptism, neglecting their obligations to see that their slaves received religious instruction, married in the church, or made their Easter duty. Writing in 1823, newly arrived Vincentian missionary Jean-Marie Odin, complained that "in southern Louisiana most of the French do not want even to hear about having instructions for their slaves, to have them get married; often they do not permit them to go to church. You can easily imagine what disorders result from that." The elapsed time between the birth of a Catholic slave and his or her baptism might sometimes stretch to years depending on a number of factors, including the distance from the church and/or the indifference of the master. Both factors may have operated in Joseph Duvernay's case, compounded perhaps by the absence of a wife, since women typically took the

15. Roger Baudier, *The Catholic Church in Louisiana* (New Orleans, 1939), 244–50, 264–74; Clark, " 'By All the Conduct of Their Lives,' " 770–71, 788–89; Labbé, " 'Helpers in the Gospel,' " 154, 156; Raymond H. Schmandt, "An Overview of Institutional Establishments in the Antebellum Southern Church," in Randall M. Miller and Jon L. Wakelyn, eds., *Catholics in the Old South: Essays on Church and Culture* (Macon, Ga., 1983), 57–58; Charles E. Nolan, "New Wine in Old Wineskins: Women Religious and the Revitalization of Louisiana Catholicism, 1803–1836," paper delivered at the annual meeting of the American Historical Association, Washington, D.C., January 9, 1999, p. 3; Lemmon, "Spanish Louisiana," in Conrad, *Cross, Crozier, and Crucible,* 16–29; Cyprian Davis, O.S.B., *The History of Black Catholics in the United States* (New York, 1990), 72; Charles Edwards O'Neill, " 'A Quarter Marked by Sundry Peculiarities': New Orleans, Lay Trustees, and Père Antoine," *Catholic Historical Review,* LXXVI (April, 1990), 235–77; Baudier, *The Catholic Church in Louisiana,* 244–50, 310–311, 313, 321–24, 335–44. Abbé Étienne Rouselon described the turmoil between Archbishop Antoine Blanc and the *marguilliers* of the Cathedral in a letter to the Lyon Society for the Propagation of the Faith, October 20, 1843, no. 2810, in Lyon Society Collection, ANNO; Labbé, " 'Helpers in the Gospel,' " 156–57.

initiative in arranging for the baptism of babies, the blessing of marriages, and the reception of Holy Communion by children.[16]

Although some slaves, like some masters, wore their Catholicism lightly, for many Catholicism mattered. Its ameliorative influence led both the French (in the *code noir*) and then the Spanish to include provisions in their slave codes requiring baptism and instruction of slaves in the Catholic faith, marriage for Catholic slaves, and burial in consecrated ground. The codes also prohibited work on Sundays and holy days, though many masters, with the tacit approval of the government, ignored these and other provisions of the codes. After the Spanish took control of Louisiana in 1769, slaves did enjoy the right to sue their masters for freedom under certain conditions and to self-purchase, or *coartacion*—rights that led to a significant increase in the number of free people of color but which disappeared after the American acquisition of Louisiana and the imposition of yet another slave code, this time by the state of Louisiana. And while Church law supposedly required instruction and marriage for slaves, most Catholic masters refused to allow their slaves to marry in church ceremonies. Priests and bishops acquiesced in this situation which, objectively speaking, required most slaves to live in a state of concubinage—a clear violation of church and moral law which made it difficult for slaves to receive Holy Communion with a clear conscience and which condemned slave children to bastardry.[17]

Catholicism, then, played a complex role in the slave system, both collaborative and ameliorative. As a result of the holdings of religious

16. Jean-Marie Odin to the seminary rector, August 2, 1823, in *Annales de la Propagation de la Foi* 2:74, Woodstock Theological Center Library, Georgetown University, Washington, D.C.; Davis, *The History of Black Catholics,* 73; Labbé, " 'Helpers in the Gospel,' " 158.

17. Kenneth J. Zanca, ed., *American Catholics and Slavery, 1789–1866: An Anthology of Primary Documents* (Lanham, Md., 1994), 23–26; Thomas N. Ingersoll, "Free Blacks in a Slave Society: New Orleans, 1718–1812," *William and Mary Quarterly,* XLVIII (1991); 187; (Lois) Virginia Meacham Gould, "In Full Enjoyment of their Liberty: The Free Women of Color of the Gulf Ports of New Orleans, Mobile, and Pensacola, 1769–1860," (Ph.D. dissertation, Emory University, 1991), 269–73. The baptismal registers of St. Louis Cathedral and St. Mary's Church (the Ursulines Convent Chapel, known for many years in the nineteenth century as Our Lady of Victory Chapel) record many slave marriages, but those numbers pale in comparison to the number of baptisms.

congregations, such as the Capuchins, Ursulines, and the recently suppressed Jesuits, the Catholic Church was the single largest slave-holder in Louisiana in 1769. In addition, it reinforced the subordinate position of slaves in society through its appeasement of planters and its acquiescence to various aspects of the slave codes which, for instance, forbade slave marriages without the master's permission and marriages between whites and blacks (slave or free), although the latter did sometimes take place as a result of Church dispensation or complicity by a priest. But the Church could also show pastoral concern in its approach to slaves. Bishops and priests, for example, wrestled with the problem of slave marriage. In 1818, Bishop Du-Bourg asked the Sacred Congregation of the Propagation of the Faith (Propaganda Fide, or simply the Propaganda), the Roman curial department that oversaw the Church in the United States, whether slaves whose masters forbade them permission to marry might do so clandestinely even though the Council of Trent had forbidden that practice. Although no record of a response to Du-Bourg exists, in 1828 the Propaganda did reply to his successor, Joseph Rosati, bishop of St. Louis and administrator of Louisiana. The Propaganda indicated Pope Leo XII's assent to valid secret marriages of slaves by priests since marriage was a natural right that superseded the laws of the state. The Propaganda instructed priests to keep written records of such secret unions. How widely Rosati disseminated and priests implemented this directive in Louisiana is not clear.

Ten years later, however, Bishop Antoine Blanc and priests in the diocese of New Orleans were still struggling with the question. In a letter to Blanc, Theodore DeTheux, a Jesuit stationed in Grand Couteau, Louisiana, suggested that priests advise slaves in confession "to mutually take each other." Priests would regard such marriages as valid and would encourage those involved in them to receive the sacraments. In order to avoid scandal, DeTheux suggested that priests announce openly from the pulpit that slaves whose masters would not allow church ceremonies could, on the advice of their confessor, marry secretly and still receive the sacraments. DeTheux and other priests, motivated by a desire to ease the consciences of pious slaves, were probably already doing what he proposed, even if they could not take the risk of making public pronouncements on the subject. André and Josephine may well have received such pastoral care, although there is no way of definitely ascertaining whether they did.[18]

The church's sacraments, rituals, sacramentals (rosaries, scapulars, etc.) and holy days provided slaves with a means of maintaining their sense of individual worth and identity. Baptism implied the intrinsic spiritual equality of slaves with all other Catholics and also established a written record of familial ties. The discovery of rosaries in excavated slave graves in New Orleans and the accounts of visitors to New Orleans describing the piety of slave women testify to the importance that religion held for them. In Catholic churches such as St. Louis Cathedral, slaves often sat intermingled with their white masters during services, and slave women constituted the majority of worshippers at weekday masses. As they had in colonial New Orleans, so too into the third decade of the nineteenth century "both free blacks and slaves constituted the city's most active churchgoers." Visitors to the city witnessed slave children receiving religious instruction and making their First Communion at the Ursuline convent. They also reported seeing slaves light candles before the cathedral's side altars of St. Francis and the Virgin Mary, make small cash donations after venerating the cross on Good Friday, and march in funeral processions behind priests and altar boys to cemeteries to bid farewell to friends and family. Catholicism helped slaves to locate themselves within the world. If Josephine shared the piety that was common among slave women, she saw herself as the person charged with fostering religion in her children and yearned for the day when they would become full members of that church through baptism.[19]

18. Hanger, *Bounded Lives,* 92; Theodore DeTheux, S.J. to Bishop Antoine Blanc, June 3, 1839, in V-4-h, ANOC, Notre Dame, Indiana; Davis, *The History of Black Catholics,* 42–43, 274; deposition of Julia Henry, November 24, 1881, in pension file of Patrick Henry, RG 15. Julia Henry, a former slave and widow of Union veteran and former slave Patrick Henry, recounted a slightly different experience that nonetheless reflected the pastoral approach of her priest. She recalled in a deposition that she and her husband "were not married by a religious ceremony, or by a priest, but her mistress talked to the priest, and then told her in the presence of a Brother and Nephew that she might live with said Patrick Henry."

19. Theresa A. Singleton, "The Archaeology of Slave Life," in Edward D.C. Campbell, Jr., with Kym S. Rice, eds., *Before Freedom Came: African American Life in the Antebellum South* (Charlottesville, 1991), 173; Hanger, *Bounded Lives,* 140; Charles E. Nolan, "New Wine in Old Wineskins," 4–5; Thomas Hamilton, *Men and Manners in America* (London, 1848), 34, 344; Liliane Crété, *Daily Life in*

In the summer of 1825, Duvernay finally fulfilled his spiritual duty. He provided for the baptism of Josephine's two-year-old son, André, at St. Louis Cathedral in July 1827. Several weeks later, he acknowledged Antoine as his natural son by Josephine when the boy was baptized at the age of five on August 8, also at the cathedral, by Fr. Antonio de Sedella, the controversial Capuchin whom the slaves revered for his pastoral attention to them. In recognition of familial ties, Aimée Duvernay Bailey, the child's aunt, stood as his god-mother. Early in 1828, according to a damaged Plaquemines Parish notarial act, Joseph Duvernay freed both of his mulatto children: six-year-old Antoine and eight-year-old Molière. The boys became legal wards of their aunt Aimée and were thus reunited with their mother and half-brother, André; their thirty-two-year-old father died in No-vember of that year. Like his contemporary Frederick Douglass, young André was about to complete an urban-rural-urban odyssey.[20]

By 1830, Aimèe Bailey had taken her slaves and two mulatto wards to New Orleans, a city that, thanks to the market revolution fueled by cotton, had exploded from a population of less than 10,000 in 1810 to 102,000 by 1840. She resided at the corner of Girod and Carondolet Streets in the Faubourg St. Marie, which as a result of the partition of the city into three self-governing municipalities in 1836 had become known as the Second Municipality. The perceived need for a division of the city had sprung from the ethnic tensions between Creoles and Americans. Although the two groups lived in all three jurisdictions along with increasing numbers of immigrants, Creoles dominated the First Municipality, which corresponded to the boundaries of the old city, or Vieux Carré, and lay between Canal and Esplanade Streets. Upriver from the First Municipality, between Canal and Felicity streets, Americans dominated the economically vibrant Second Municipality, where Aimèe Bailey and her slaves

Louisiana, 1815–1830, trans. Patrick Gregory (Baton Rouge, 1981), 144–51; Ben-jamin Henry Latrobe, *Impressions Respecting New Orleans, Diary and Sketches, 1818–1820* (New York, 1951), 33–35, 60–62, 119–23, 137–38; Labbé, " 'Helpers in the Gospel,' " 158–59, 174.

20. SLC, Bk. 20, p. 197, Act 618, and p. 211, Act 590, ANNO; Belsom, "Du-vernay Genealogy"; Acte de liberté (damaged), and Inventory, November 28, 1828, in Succession of Joseph Duvernay, no. 183, Probate Court, CCPP.

lived. Downriver from the First Municipality, Esplanade and Chef Menteur demarcated the Third Municipality, with its Creole majority but burgeoning population of Irish and German immigrants who began to arrive in great numbers in the 1840s.[21]

Aimée Bailey's household included nine slaves, a relatively large number for New Orleans, where 80 percent of the city's slaveholders in 1820 owned fewer than six. The elder André had traveled full circle back to the Crescent City, a city that offered opportunities to slaves like himself for advancement, autonomy and, in some cases, formal freedom. His return to New Orleans ran counter to the trend of the city's slaveholders to divest themselves of male slaves by selling them to rural planters. But André's carpentry and masonry skills made him more valuable to his owners in an urban context than if he had been an unskilled slave, for they could not only use him in their own household, but also hire him out for income.[22]

While holding out the possibility of greater autonomy, the world of urban slavery to which André, Josephine, and young André returned also placed enormous strains on slave family life. As the antebellum years progressed, slave owners increasingly employed their slaves in New Orleans as domestics: cooks, laundresses, house servants, and nannies. Females came to far outnumber males. The use of slaves in domestic service and the necessity of housing them led to a decline in the average size of slaveholdings in the city as owners sold unskilled male slaves to outlying plantations. Only one-third of the slaveholding households by 1850 contained slaves who were part of discernible family units and of those, 93 percent were nuclear families headed by females. Male and female slaves in the city were rarely able to cohabit. Moreover, the chances of slave children living in

21. Gerald M. Capers, *Occupied City: New Orleans Under the Federals, 1862–1865* (Lexington, 1965), 1; Testament of Joseph Duvernay, April 14, 1834, p. 376, L. T. Caire, vol. 37, NONA; Leon Cyprian Soulé, *The Know Nothing Party in New Orleans: A Reappraisal* (Baton Rouge, 1962), 14; Joseph Logsdon and Caryn Cossé Bell, "The Americanization of Black New Orleans, 1850–1900," in Hirsch and Logsdon, *Creole New Orleans,* 208.

22. Fifth Census of the United States, 1830, New Orleans, 89; Virginia Meacham Gould, " 'The House That Never Was a Home': Slave Family and Household Organization in New Orleans, 1820–1850," *Slavery and Abolition,* XVIII (1997), 93, 95.

family groups decreased with age, so that, in 1850, for example, almost half of slaves ages ten to fourteen did not live in a family group.[22]

André, Josephine, and young André thus enjoyed a unique situation, but not for long. On June 20, 1830, they experienced slavery's cruelest power when Aimée Bailey separated the thirty-one-year-old mother from her children by selling her for $300 to Celeste Fernerette, a free woman of color. The reason for the sale is unclear, but Josephine was sold without guarantee against vices and sickness, suggesting that she was either in ill health, handicapped, or incorrigible. Within six months, Fernerette, refusing to warrant against "vices and maladies," sold Josephine at a loss for $230 to Michael Jones, a white man, further suggesting that her owners found Josephine's behavior problematic. Young André still lived in the same household as his father for at least four more years, a situation that defied the normal pattern of urban slavery.[23]

The slave system sought to weaken ties of kinship by denying slaves legitimate identification with a father. In registering slave baptisms, for example, priests usually omitted the name of the father and recorded the baptism under the planter's surname. In legal documents, however, Aimée Bailey used both a first and a last name—"André Cailloux"—to identify the elder André. Surnames for slaves, though not widespread, occurred more often in commercial-urban contexts such as New Orleans where for practical reasons related to hiring skilled slaves like André needed a more distinct identity. Young André, then, had the benefit of living and identifying with his father, whose first name he bore and whose surname he later adopted when he gained his freedom. Sometime between 1834 and 1846, however, for reasons that remain unclear (sale, emancipation, escape, death), the elder André left the household.[24]

In April, 1834, Aimée Duvernay Bailey married Mathieu Lartet

22. Gould, " 'The House That Never Was a Home,' " 92–93, 95–97, 99–101.
23. Sale of a Slave, Aimée Bailey to Celeste Fernerette, May 20, 1831, act 50 in Joseph Cuvillier, vol. 1, NONA; Conveyance Office Book, 9-207, Office of Recorder of Conveyances, New Orleans, Louisiana: Gould, "The House That Never Was a Home," 97. The act of sale was executed before Greenbury Ridgely Stringer on December 24, 1831, but the notarial act was destroyed in a fire.
24. Gould, "In Full Enjoyment of their Liberty," 300–306; contract de marriage, April 30, 1834, Act 326, pp. 185–87, L. T. Caire, Vol. 37, NONA.

(sometimes spelled Larthet). Lartet was part of the large French immigrant wave that continued to enter the city through the first three decades of the nineteenth century and that served to bolster and refurbish the white Creole community in its ongoing struggle with Anglo-Americans for social and political supremacy. The forty-seven-year-old Lartet, a native of Condom in the department of Gers Royunne, France, had lived in New Orleans for eight years prior to the marriage and appeared in the 1834 city directory as a grocer. On March 10, shortly before the wedding, Lartet secured a divorce from his first wife, Marie, who lived in France. Lartet and Aimée Bailey evidently cohabited prior to their nuptials as their marriage contract listed the same address for both on Girod Street, indicated that Aimée was pregnant, and recognized as legitimate the child to be born. (Firmin Lartet, the child born to the couple in September 1834, died later that same year.) They had a combined worth of $18,000 in slaves, real estate, cash, and notes.[25]

Aimée and Mathieu saw to it that Aimée's nephews, Molière and Antoine, acquired a trade; through them, young André eventually did also. In December 1834, Lartet apprenticed fifteen-year-old Molière and thirteen-year-old Antoine, along with a nine-year-old slave, John, who was also probably related to Aimée, to J. B. Glaudin, Lartet's next-door neighbor, for four years. Glaudin, a free man of color, a slaveholder, and a tobacconist, whose father, an emigré from St. Domingue, had evidently learned cigar making while in Havana, agreed to teach the young men the trade. In addition, he promised to pay Lartet $20 per month as well as the occasional expenses associated with the youngsters attending the evening school for apprentices from April through November. Apparently, Molière, Antoine, and John informally instructed André in the trade as he grew to maturity. The Lartets then had several options. They could hire André out to a cigar-making establishment such as J. B. Glaudin's in return for a fee, or, as was commonly done, allow André to "hire his own time" in return for a fixed monthly payment to them, permitting

25. Contract de Marriage, April 30, 1834; Paul F. Lachance, "The Foreign French," and Joseph G. Tregle, Jr., "Creoles and Americans," both in Hirsch and Logsdon, *Creole New Orleans,* 101–130; New Orleans City Directory, 1834, microfiche in Louisiana Collection, NOPL; St. Louis Cemetery No. 1 Death Records, November 27, 1834, AANO.

him to keep any surplus. By his late teens, André was probably able to earn at least $10 per week from cigar making.[26]

André and John, part of the shrinking number of Lartet slaves that numbered five by 1841, may have lived in the house with Aimée and Mathieu, but more likely resided either in a small cabin enclosed by high walls behind the main house or in the two-story kitchen building in the backyard. While they lived in proximity to their master and mistress, they spent many hours away from them, especially if they did not reside in the big house. Like other urban slaves, André and John enjoyed far greater autonomy than did their counterparts on rural plantations. They left the house each morning for work and, beyond the gaze of the master amidst the bustle and relative anonymity of the city, they probably spent a part of their day roaming freely, congregating with friends, transacting business with both slave and free, black and white. They no doubt shopped in the markets and exchanged news and gossip with other slaves and free people of color, many of them female *marchandes* (peddlers) who plied their wares throughout the city.[27]

The relationship between André and his master and mistress remains speculative, though they apparently held him in high regard. Nevertheless, André most likely harbored private feelings of resentment over the sale of his mother, although he probably would have taken care to mask them. André and John may well have entered into an informal agreement with the Lartets to pay them an agreed-upon amount for their eventual emancipation, or the owners may have decided at some point to grant the two young men their freedom

26. Indenture Bk. 5, no. 376, December 2, 1834, in Records of the Office of Mayor, City Archives, NOPL; Fifth Census of the United States, 1840, New Orleans, 82; Depositions of Aguillard Belcourt, May 13, 1895, and Hippolyte Pépé, May 21, 1895, in Pension Record of Aguillard Belcourt, RG 15. For Henry Glaudin's background and family, see SLC, Bk. 19, p. 301, Act 1050, and Bk. 24, p. 130, AANO, and New Orleans City Directory, 1846, in Louisiana Collection, NOPL. According to the 1860 census, J. B. Glaudin had accumulated property assessed for tax purposes at $16,900.

27. Early Assessment Records of New Orleans, 1836–1847, Second Municipality Record Book, microfilm in City Archives, NOPL; purchase of land by Aimée Duvernay, Widow of William Bailey and spouse of Mathieu Larthet, February 28, 1835, p. 559, Octave de Armas, vol. 15, NONA; Gould, "In Full Enjoyment of their Liberty," 51; Richard Wade, *Slavery in the Cities: The South, 1820–1860* (New York, 1964), 26–27, 142–79, 326.

without any payment when they reached their majority. Whatever the details, in 1845, the Lartets petitioned the Police Jury of Orleans Parish and the Third District Court of New Orleans for permission to manumit the two twenty-one-year-old slaves. Between 1827 and 1846, Louisiana law required the approval of at least three-quarters of the parish police jury and the permission of a judge for the manumission of slaves born in Louisiana who were younger than thirty years of age. The Lartets' decision to manumit André and John reflected the increasing stagnation and subsequent decline of urban slavery in New Orleans in the fifteen years between 1845 and 1860. During that time, the number of slaves in the city dropped from 18,208 in 1840 to 17,011 in 1850, and then to 14,484 in 1860.

On October 10, 1845, and again on March 8, 1846, the Orleans Parish police jury favorably considered Aimée Lartet's petition. It ordered the posting for forty days of a printed notice in both French and English, announcing Aimée Duvernay's intention, with the consent of her husband, to emancipate the two slaves. Aimée declared in her petition to the Third District Court that "both slaves form part of a family of slaves who have always given much satisfaction by their good behavior." She assured the court that both bondsmen were fully capable of earning their livelihood as cigar makers, as did C. S. Leonard, a commissioner of the second ward of the Second Municipality, who had lived in the same square as André and John for several years. He testified to their industry, sobriety, and perseverance, and expressed confidence that they possessed the skills to support themselves and eventually prosper. After securing the approval of the judge, the Lartets executed the act of manumission before a notary, as required by law, on July 8, 1846. Since André declared that he did not know how to write his name, he made his mark on the notarial document and moved, along with John and sixty-nine other slaves that year, into the ranks of New Orleans' large population of free people of color.[28]

28. Laurence J. Kotlikoff and Anton Rupert, "The Manumission of Slaves in New Orleans, 1827–1846," *Southern Studies,* XIX (1980), 172–181; Wade, *Slavery in the Cities,* 18–19, 26–27, 326; Joseph Logsdon and Caryn Cossé Bell, "The Americanization of Black New Orleans," in Hirsch and Logsdon, *Creole New Orleans,* 206; Orleans Parish Police Jury Records, 1813–48, Petitions for the Emancipation of a Slave, Vol. 3, October 10, 1845, and March 8, 1846, microfilm in City Archives, NOPL; New Orleans City Directory, 1846, NOPL; Act of Emancipation,

* * *

André was soon joined by another recently emancipated slave: his intended wife, Louise Felicie (sometimes written in ecclesiastical and legal records as "Félicité") Coulon, who had traveled a different road to freedom. She had been born about 1818, to Feliciana, the slave-concubine of Valentin Encalada, a sugar planter who lived at Grand Isle, a barrier island in the Barrataria region of Jefferson Parish, near the mouth of the Mississippi River. Felicie's father, whom she later identified as Antoine Coulon, was probably a slave of the Coulon family, one of the first four families to have settled in Grand Isle.[29]

Valentin Encalada, born about 1773 in Bacalari in the province of Campeche (Yucatan) in Mexico, came to Grand Isle around 1800. In 1804, he inherited property (15 by 40 arpents, or acres) from his brother Manuel and, according to family tradition, became the first planter to raise sugar on the island. In addition, he gathered wax from wild myrtle bushes on his property to produce candles. As a result of the shortage of white females and the preponderance of black women in the population and of the power imbalance between master and slave, Valentin engaged in a common practice of slave-holders of the late eighteenth and early nineteenth centuries of taking one of his slaves, the Creole Feliciana, as his concubine. Evidence suggests that Valentin may have acquired her in 1810. Louisiana slaveholders frequently exploited their female slaves sexually; in Feliciana's case, it impossible to determine how willing a partner she was.

Aimée Duvernay to André, July 8, 1846, Act 233, in Achille Chiapella, Vol. 11, NONA. Beginning with William Wells Brown's *The Negro in the American War of the Rebellion: His Heroism and His Fidelity,* which was published in Boston in 1867, historians have consistently described Cailloux as "finely educated" and prominent. None have indicated his origins as a slave. See, for example, Brown, 169, Joseph T. Glatthaar, *Forged in Battle: The Civil War Alliance of Black Soldiers and White Officers* (New York, 1990), 124, and Hollandsworth, *The Louisiana Native Guards,* 27. Relying on earlier accounts, Hollandsworth states that Cailloux was educated in Paris.

29. Testament of Valentin Encalada, July 14, 1828, Act 185 in T. Seghers, Vol. 1, NONA; SLC, Bk 22, p. 107, Act 611, AANO; Extract from the Register of the Acts of Marriage of the Church of St. Mary's Assumption, June 22, 1847, in Pension Record of André Caillaux [*sic*], RG 15; Sally Kittredge Evans, Frederick Stielow, and Betsy Swanson, *Grand Isle on the Gulf: An Early History* (Metairie, La., 1979), 26; Fifth Census of the United States, 1830, Lafourche Parish, 19.

Given their vulnerability in the master-slave relationship, some slave women participated in liaisons with their masters in order to improve their living conditions and those of their children and, in some cases, to effect their freedom. The latter was the long-term result of Feliciana's cohabitation with Valentin.[30]

The twenty-year-old Feliciana, almost thirty years younger than her master, bore him a son, Sebastien (Bastien), in 1815. Father Antonio de Sedella baptized the child at St. Louis Cathedral as a free person of color, and in two subsequent wills, Encalada recognized Bastien as his son and heir and stated his intention to free both the boy and his mother. Feliciana subsequently gave birth to two girls by another man or men: Felicie (Félicité) in 1817 or 1818, and Noel in 1819, though both were baptized belatedly in 1830. That Feliciana gave birth to children by men other than Valentin suggests that the cohabitation between the two probably ended by 1817 or 1818. Regardless, the two remained connected in the person of their son, Bastien. And for Feliciana, as with a significant number of slave

30. Testament of Valentin Encalada; Sale of a Tract of Land, Valentin Encalada to Samuel B. Bermet, October 21, 1829, in L. T. Caire, Vol. 8, NONA; Evans, Stielow, and Swanson, *Grand Isle,* 26; Sally Kittredge Evans, "Some 18th and 19th Century Families of Grand Isle, La. and their Migrations," paper delivered at the 1984 Nicholls State University Symposium; Conveyance Book 1, Jefferson Parish, 259, in Jefferson Parish Conveyance Office, Gretna, La.; Paul F. Lachance, "The Formation of a Three-Caste Society," *Social Science History,* XVIII (1994), 211–13, 216–22, 225–29, 233–36; Petition of Valentin Encalada for the Emancipation of the Negresse Feliciana and her son Bastien, December 18, 1834, 23-E, Orleans Parish Police Jury Records, 1813–1848, Petitions for the Emancipation of a Slave, City Archives, NOPL; Gould, "In Full Enjoyment of Their Liberty," 339. Feliciana's parents are not known for certain, but in May 1798, a slave named Feliciana who belonged to Miguel Dragon was baptized at St. Louis Cathedral. Her mother was Sophia and her godparents were Joseph Guidi and Eugenia Matatos. See SLC, Bk. 6, Act 1825, AANO. The 1830 census for Jefferson Parish lists a Victor Coulon, age between fifty and sixty, who owned sixty-seven slaves and had four free people of color living in his household. On April 28, 1835, Coulon sold his plantation and slaves to Thomas Bibb; among the slaves was Antoine, a sixteen-year-old male and perhaps the brother of Felicie. The plantation lay on the left bank of Bayou Lafourche about one mile above Thibodaux. See Sale of a Plantation, Victor Coulon to Thomas Bibb, April 28, 1835, in the Lafourche Parish Historic Records Preservation Project Collection, Allen J. Ellender Archives, Nicholls State University, Thibodaux, La.

women during this period, the concubinal relationship led to manumission for herself and her son. Indeed, studies indicate that approximately 42 percent of adult emancipated slave women had been concubines of the masters from whom they received their freedom.[31]

Clearly, family ties motivated the fifty-five-year-old Valentin Encalada, when, perhaps sensing his mortality and desirous of protecting his kin, he made out a will in July 1828. Disregarding the familial relationships of slaves not related to him by blood or marriage, he bequeathed Feliciana's two daughters, Felicie and Noel, to his nephew Jacques. He gave freedom, however, to their mother, Feliciana, and he expressed his desire that fourteen-year-old Bastien receive his liberty as soon as the law permitted. In the meantime, Encalada entrusted Bastien to the care of his godfather, Jacques, who would instruct him in a trade that would enable him to earn a living. Since Louisiana law technically prohibited the emancipation of a slave mistress if her value exceeded 10 percent of the estate, and since it further defined slaves as immovable property and prohibited couples living in open concubinage from donating any immovable property to one another (emancipation being defined as a donation), Encalada sought to circumvent the law by stipulating that Feliciana's grant of liberty be made free of his succession. He recognized Bastien as his natural son and, again ignoring the law that restricted inheritance for a natural child to one-fourth of the estate if there were any other heirs, named Bastien as his sole heir, who would inherit all that remained of his succession after the above-mentioned deductions.[32]

For reasons that remain unclear, Valentin revoked the first will on October 28, 1830. By 1831, he had sold his plantation for $1500 and moved to New Orleans, where he resided on Pritanee Street, near Polymnie in the Faubourg Annunciation in the Second Municipality. In March 1832, he wrote a new will, in which he acknowledged that he had never married but had cohabited with Feliciana,

31. SLC, Bk. 18, p. 134, Act 582, AANO; Testament of Valentin Encalada, July 14, 1828; Revocation of Testament, October 28, 1830, Act 338, Vol. 3, T. Seghers; Testament of Valentin Encalada, March 27, 1832, Act 319, in L. T. Caire, Vol. 19; SLC, Bk. 22, p. 107, Act 611, p. 190, Act 1110, AANO; Petition for the Emancipation of the Negresse Feliciana; Gould, "In Full Enjoyment of their Liberty," 90.

32. Testament of Valentin Encalada, July 14, 1828; Judith Kelleher Schafer, *Slavery, the Civil Law, and the Supreme Court of Louisiana* (Baton Rouge, 1994), 184–85.

the mother of his natural son. He voiced his intent to emancipate not only Bastien and Feliciana, but also Feliciana's two daughters. He implored his executor to fulfill immediately after his death all of the formalities demanded by the law in order to free them and he charged Feliciana to feed, maintain, and lodge Bastien, whom he described as an "idiot," unable to support or provide independently for himself. He named executor Joseph Sauvinet as his residuary legatee and entrusted him with a sum of money on which Feliciana could draw after his death.[33]

Feliciana and Bastien did not have to wait until Encalada's death, however, to obtain their freedom. Declaring that at sixty-eight years old and approaching death he wished to recompense his loyal slave Feliciana and his twenty-year-old son, whom he had baptized as free and whom he and others described as somewhat mentally retarded but possessing a sweet disposition, Valentin petitioned the police jury in late 1834 and early 1835 for permission to emancipate Feliciana and Bastien. The jury responded affirmatively and unanimously, and on September 21, 1835, Valentin manumitted Feliciana and Bastien, making money ("quelques reserves") available to them for their support.[34]

Feliciana's family thus became one of the majority of Afro-Creole households in that it was headed by a woman. She had benefited from the wave of emancipations that occurred in New Orleans dur-

TABLE I

Free People of Color in New Orleans, 1830

Total Number of Free Colored Males	4,864
Total Number of Free Colored Females	7,042
Total Number of Free Persons of Color	13,906

SOURCE: Census Data for the Year 1860, United States Historical Census Data Browser

33. Revocation of Testament, October 28, 1830; Sale of Land, October 21, 1829; New Orleans City Directory, 1833, microfiche, Louisiana Collection, NOPL; Sale of Land, January 29, 1831, L. T. Caire, Vol. 19, NONA; Testament of Valentin Encalada, March 27, 1832. By 1830, Encalada was living on the Cheniere Caminade. See Fifth Census of the United States, 1830, Jefferson Parish, p. 177.
34. Petition for the Emancipation of the Negresse Feliciana; Emancipation of Feliciana and Bastien, September 21, 1835, Act 715 in L. T. Caire, Vol. 47, NONA.

TABLE 2

Free People of Color in New Orleans, 1840

Total Number of Free Colored Males	8,438
Total Number of Free Colored Females	10,788
Total Number of Free Persons of Color	19,226

SOURCE: Census Data for the Year 1860, United
States Historical Census Data Browser

ing the decade of the 1830s. Hers was one of 119 manumissions in
New Orleans in 1835; indeed, emancipations in the city exceeded
100 in every year between 1834 (the highest with 163) and 1839.
Felicie, however, did not share in her mother's good fortune and
remained a slave of Valentin. In 1839, she bore a son, Jean Louis.
The baptismal record of the child named Antoine Philippe, evidently
a free man, as the father.[35]

Jean Louis's grandmother, Feliciana, was determined to gain possession of her daughter and grandson, with an eye to eventually freeing them. She had access to some money, likely augmenting

TABLE 3

Number of Slaves Manumitted During the 1830s in New Orleans

1830	8
1831	75
1832	103
1833	30
1834	163
1835	119
1836	138
1837	121
1838	140
1839	129

SOURCE: Laurence J. Kotlikoff and Anton Rupert, "The Manumission of Slaves in
New Orleans, 1827–1846," *Southern Studies,* XIX (1980), 175.

35. Gould, "In Full Enjoyment of Their Liberty," 305–307, 54; Kotlikoff and
Rupert, "The Manumission of Slaves in New Orleans," 175; SLC, Bk. 27, April 13,
1839, Act 230, AANO.

Valentin's "reserves" by working in one of the occupations common to free women of color, such as a domestic or a *marchande*. The 1838 New Orleans directory lists a "Felicite" as a washerwoman at 28 History Street. By whatever means she acquired it, in 1841, six years after securing her own freedom, the illiterate Feliciana paid Valentin the considerable sum of $1200 for her daughter, her two-year-old grandson, Jean Louis, and a forty-eight-year-old slave also named Jean Louis. Why did Feliciana make such a large investment when she undoubtedly knew the terms of Encalada's will, which provided emancipation for Felicie? First, of course, the will did not provide freedom for her grandson. Then too, Valentin may have changed the terms, omitting freedom for Felicie. Or perhaps Feliciana feared that if she did not purchase her daughter and grandson, a third party might challenge the will, secure her daughter and grandson, and never agree to freedom. Whatever the reason, Feliciana had reunited her family.[36]

Approximately six months later, she made another significant expenditure, this time investing, like so many free people of color who had means to do so, in real estate. For $500 she jointly purchased with Bastien four lots (each measuring about 22' × 123') fronting Coffee Street (later Baronne) in the city of Lafayette, a suburb upriver from New Orleans that would be incorporated into the latter in 1852. Since neither Feliciana nor her son could sign their names, they had to make their marks on the notarial acts recording the sale. Two months later, perhaps because she had overextended herself in purchasing her son and grandson and four pieces of real estate all in the previous six months, Feliciana sold lots #3 and #4 to a free woman of color for $250, the price she had paid for them. In August 1844, Feliciana acquired more cash by selling her slave, John Louis (Louis), to André Cailloux's owner, Mathieu Lartet, for $300.[37] Lar-

36. Gould, "In Full Enjoyment of Their Liberty," 305–307, 54; New Orleans City Directory, 1833; Sale of Slaves, October 11, 1841, Act 187, in C.V. Foulon, Vol. 7, NONA.

37. Sally Kittredge Evans, "Free Persons of Color," in Samuel Wilson, Jr., *The Creole Faubourgs,* (Gretna, La., 1974), 25–36, Vol. IV of Mary Louise Christovich, ed., *New Orleans Architecture;* Sale of Property, James Armor to Feliciana and Bastien, February 17, 1842, pp. 331–32, in William Christy, Vol. 44; Sale of Property, Feliciana and Bastien to Manette Flerio, f.w.c., April 14, 1842, Act 53, p. 37, Bk. 4, Transcripts from Bk. 12 of the Parish of Jefferson, City of Lafayette, Orleans

tet may have known Feliciana and her family through other than business dealings since Feliciana's daughter, Felicie, had become involved with Lartet's slave, André.

In December 1846, the same year that André secured his freedom, Feliciana Encalada, as she now sometimes called herself, in a related move, secured the assent of the police jury to the emancipation of Felicie and little Jean Louis. In doing so, Feliciana reflected the significant role that people of color played in emancipating slaves, many of them family members. Indeed, of the 1159 successful petitions for emancipation presented to police juries from 1827 to 1846, 435 or 37.5 percent came from free blacks and accounted for 36.5 percent of the 1770 slaves manumitted. Roughly one out of every eight households of free people of color participated in the emancipation of one or more slaves during this period. Mothers and children emancipated together represented 30.4 percent of those manumissions. Since the expenditure required to purchase female and minor slaves, not to mention the more expensive prime males, exceeded the yearly wage of the average laborer, the outlays for emancipation represented a substantial economic burden and testified to the determination of free people of color to obtain freedom for slave members of their families. In her petition, Feliciana attested to her daughter's ability to earn her livelihood and further stated her own intention to provide for the support of her grandson Jean Louis until he could maintain himself. J. B. Glaudin, the tobacconist for whom André may have worked and who had taught the trade to André and Molière, testified to her good character, as did Lartet, who apparently maintained a close relationship with Valentin Encalada. Lartet and Feliciana were probably cooperating in these manumissions because they knew that André and Felicie wished to marry and that Felicie was pregnant with a child by André.[38] Feliciana also probably did not want the child born of the union to enter the world as a slave.

Parish Conveyance Office, New Orleans; Sale of a Slave, Feliciana to M. Lartet, August 10, 1844, COB 6-460, Orleans Parish Conveyance Office.

38. Manumission, Feliciana Encalada to Slave Felicie and Son, December 23, 1846, Act 419, p. 841, in Achille Chiapella, Vol. 11, NONA; Kotlikoff and Rupert, "The Manumission of Slaves in New Orleans," 172–81; Baptismal Register for Negroes and Mulattos of St. Mary's Assumption Church (hereafter, SMAC), June 1847, Act 183, in AANO; Vital Records: Orleans Deaths, Vol. 187, p. 254, Louisiana Collection, NOPL. Mathieu Larthet handled the arrangements for Valentin En-

* * *

On April 18, 1847, André and Felicie signed a marriage contract. In it, they expressed their intention to legitimize "their" six-year-old natural son, Jean Louis, thus ensuring to him the advantages that the law extended to legitimate children. The child's baptismal certificate from St. Louis Cathedral, dated April 3, 1839, had identified another man, Antoine Philippe, as the father. Since priests did not usually list slave fathers on baptismal certificates, it seems Antoine Philippe may have been a free man of color. The listing implies that either André begot Jean Louis at the tender age of fourteen and Felicie named a different man as the father, or, as seems more likely, André recognized another man's son as his own, in essence adopting Jean Louis and making him legitimate. By the time of his marriage, André (though not Felicie) could sign his name in a somewhat large, immature hand, and apparently had entered the ranks of the estimated 80 percent of free people of color who were literate. Perhaps his half-brothers, Antoine and Molière, who had themselves attended night school as apprentices, had imparted some of their education to him. Then too, cigar makers had a tradition of learning, with one man often reading aloud as the others rolled their cigars.

On June 22, 1847, three weeks after the birth of their son, Eugene, André and Felicie wed at St. Mary's Assumption in Lafayette, the predominantly German parish in which Feliciana resided. Their choice of St. Mary's suggests that they may have been living with Feliciana at the time. André's older half-brother, Molière, served as best man, thus continuing to aid André in his transition from slavery to freedom. William Robertson, a man apparently of at least some Anglophonic background, also stood as a witness. André and Felicie had Eugene baptized at the same church a week after their wedding.[39]

The Cailloux-Coulon marriage reflected not only the ubiquity of prenuptial pregnancy among free people of color, but also a marked change in behavior regarding marriages and births. As late as 1820,

calada's burial at St. Louis Cemetery No. 1 on January 18, 1848. Burial Records, 1843–48, St. Louis Cathedral, no. 2880, AANO.

39. Marriage Contract between André Cailloux and Louise Felicie, April 18, 1847, Act 88 in Octave de Armas, Vol. 40, NONA; SLC, Bk. 27, Act 230, April 13, 1839, AANO; Extract from the Register of Marriage of St. Mary's Assumption Church, June 22, 1847; SMAC, Bk. 1, p. 133, Act 10, June 29, 1847, AANO.

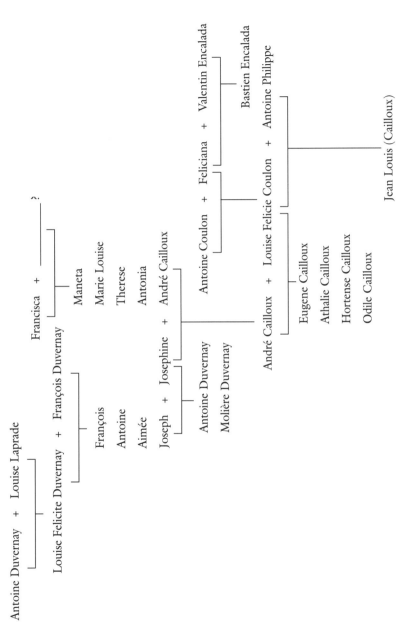

Family Connections in the Cailloux Story:
The Duvernays, Caillouxs, Encaladas, and Coulons

only 10 percent of free colored infants in the baptismal registers of St. Louis Cathedral and the Ursuline convent chapel listed parents who were legally married. The Cailloux-Coulon marriage also reflected the precipitous decline in interracial unions between free women of color and white men after 1840 and the emerging tendency of free people of color to marry within their own group. Beginning in 1815, advances in wealth and occupational standing made male free people of color more attractive partners to free women of color. At the same time, the ratio between men and women became more balanced, and a cohesive Afro-Creole society with social norms that emphasized endogamy developed and solidified. The marriage rate among free people of color, therefore, pushed upwards. By the 1850s, 65 percent of births registered by free persons of color in New Orleans were legitimate. The Caillouxs reflected these trends. They desired to enter into a legal marriage and to have legitimate children. Their marriage pattern reflected an increasingly mature society of free people of color that possessed a distinct identity and knew how to protect its interests.[40] André and Felicie began their married life in the midst of that society.

40. Lachance, "The Formation of a Three-Caste Society," 211–13, 216–22, 225–29, 233, 36; Gould, "In Full Enjoyment of Their Liberty," 329.

2

FREE PERSON OF COLOR

André Cailloux ratified his freedom by carving out an identity as a respectable, hard-working artisan, involving himself in the web of economic, religious, and social relationships that characterized the tightly knit society of free people of color, or *gens de couleur libre,* of New Orleans in the decades prior to the Civil War. In the fifteen years following his emancipation, Cailloux honed his craft, acquired property, provided for his family, saw to the baptism and education of his children, and enjoyed the esteem and companionship of his peers, who elected him an officer of one of the mutual aid societies created by Afro-Creoles in the 1850s.

The free people of color in antebellum Louisiana, whose ranks André and Felicie Cailloux joined in 1846, occupied a strangely incongruous position, both legally and socially, between whites and slaves in Louisiana's tripartite caste system. Afro-French or Afro-Spanish in culture and Catholic in religion, many had enjoyed freedom for at least a generation, and by 1860 approximately 90 percent had been born in Louisiana (83 percent in New Orleans). Though they lacked political rights, they could own property, make contracts, and testify in court against whites. They constituted the most literate and prosperous free black population in the United States. In 1850, 80 percent of their number in New Orleans could read and write, and according to the 1860 census, only 1202 free people of color twenty years of age or older in the whole state of Louisiana were illiterate. In 1836, 855 free people of color in the city paid taxes and owned property assessed at $2,462,470; they also owned 620 slaves. Their relative wealth, however, paled in comparison to that of white New Orleanians. On the eve of the Civil War, the vast majority of free people of color (77 percent) worked as "skilled laborers," or artisans, in such occupations as cigar maker, carpenter, or cabinet maker, while professionals composed only 2 percent of the population and businessmen (mostly shopkeepers) only 5–7 percent. A handful of rural elite free blacks owned substantial numbers of slaves.[1]

The free colored population had its roots in the colonial era, when first France and then Spain had ruled Louisiana. In the words of one historian referring particularly to the Spanish regime, "Demographic, economic, political, and military conditions meshed with cultural and legal traditions to favor the growth and persistence of a substantial group of free people of color." European men substantially outnumbered European women in colonial Louisiana, as did female slaves. Those demographic realities combined with laws that prohibited marriage between whites and blacks to produce concubinal interracial unions and racially mixed offspring. Manumission of many of those offspring under lenient Spanish policies, as well as natural increase, produced a population of 858 free persons of color by 1791. Immigration associated with revolutionary turmoil in St. Domingue (present-day Haiti) brought a flood of emigré free people of color to New Orleans between 1791 and 1810. By 1805, they numbered more than 1,500, 33 percent of those in the city of African descent. In 1809, the largest wave, 3,102, arrived via Cuba. The free colored population of the city stood at 4,950 in 1810, peaked at 13,076 in 1840, and still numbered close to 11,000 in 1860.[2]

1. David C. Rankin, "The Impact of the Civil War on the Free Colored Community of New Orleans," 379–86; Ira Berlin, "The Structure of the Free Negro Caste," *Journal of Social History,* IX (1976), 311–12; Eighth Census of the United States, 1860, Miscellaneous Statistics, 508; Paul Lachance, "The Limits of Privilege: Where Free Persons of Color Stood in the Hierarchy of Wealth in Antebellum New Orleans," in Jane G. Landers, ed., *Against the Odds: Free Blacks in the Slave Societies of the Americas* (London, 1996), 65–84. On rural Creoles of Color, see Carl A. Brasseaux, "Creoles of Color in Louisiana's Bayou Country, 1766–1877," in James H. Dorman, ed., *Creoles of Color of the Gulf South* (Knoxville, 1996), 67–86, and Mills, *The Forgotten People.*
2. Kimberly S. Hanger, "Origins of New Orleans's Free Creoles of Color," in Dorman, *Creoles of Color of the Gulf South,* 1–23, and Hanger, *Bounded Lives;* Brasseaux, "Creoles of Color in Louisiana's Bayou Country," in Dorman *Creoles of Color of the Gulf South,* 67–86; Lachance, "The Formation of a Three-Caste Soci-

Approximately 70 percent of free people of color in 1860 were of mixed blood (mulattos, quadroons, or octoroons), while 80 percent of the city's Negroes were slaves. Afro-Creoles ran the spectrum of phenotype. In 1860, 3,489 of 18,467 free persons of color in Louisiana were of full Negro blood. André Cailloux evidently numbered himself among these, taking great pride in his ebony hue and in fact boasting of his blackness.[3] His life reflected the complexities of the unique and anomalous society that Louisiana's free people of color fashioned amidst an environment of slavery.

At the time of Cailloux's emancipation, the free colored population in the city stood at a little under 10,000. Cailloux was one of 156 Afro-Creole cigar makers in New Orleans, the third largest group of artisans after carpenters and masons. He and many of his fellow Afro-Creoles had secured dominant positions in occupations that remained largely closed to people of color in the rest of the United States, though their hold grew increasingly tenuous during the 1850s. Indeed, most free people of color, Cailloux included, clung precariously to their place on the economic ladder, acutely aware that an illness, an economic downturn, or negative political developments could spell disaster for them and their families. Despite the uncertainties that characterized the antebellum economy, however, Cailloux sought to take advantage of the opportunities he had as a free man to earn a living and to acquire property. By 1848, two years after his emancipation, he had managed to accumulate $200 in cash. With it, he purchased from Mathieu Lartet, his former master, a small lot facing Bertrand Street, measuring 20' × 89', in a square bounded by Poydras, Perdido, Bertrand, and Prieur in the American-dominated Second Municipality.[4]

---

ety," 226–27, 234, "The Limits of Privilege," in Landers, *Against the Odds,* 69–70, and "The Foreign French," in Hirsch and Logsdon, *Creole New Orleans,* 69–70; Gould, "In Full Enjoyment of their Liberty," 95.

3. Judith Kelleher Schafer, *Slavery, the Civil Law, and the Supreme Court of Louisiana,* 21; Marcus Christian, "Genealogy: The Beginnings of the Free Colored Class," MS in Box 5, n.d., Marcus B. Christian Collection, Earl K. Long Library, University of New Orleans; Brown, *The Negro in the American Rebellion,* 169.

4. Logsdon and Bell, "The Americanization of Black New Orleans," in Hirsch and Logsdon, *Creole New Orleans,* 206; Sale, Mathieu Lartet to André Cailloux, April 3, 1848, in Achille Chiapella, Vol. 14, NONA; Evans, "Free Persons of Color," in Wilson, *The Creole Faubourgs,* 25–36. Immigrants from St. Domingue

In 1852, the year that the three autonomous municipalities of New Orleans were reconsolidated and the city of Lafayette annexed, the New Orleans city directory listed Cailloux as a cigar maker at Perdido Street between Adeline and St. Jane, three blocks toward the river from where he owned property. The cigar trade brought the personable Cailloux into contact with numerous and diverse people in New Orleans, since, in the words of tourist John H. Latrobe, "Nearly every other man had a segar in his mouth." Cigar merchants often offered their wares for purchase at tables, or *boutiques* as they called them, which they set up in various parts of the city. A man noted for his gentlemanly deportment, Cailloux likely bowed to his customers, black, white, and brown, conversed with them in French or English, and offered his own lighted cigar to the prospective customer to begin the transaction.[5]

He also evidently maintained a close relationship with the Lartets' neighbors the Glaudins. Henry Glaudin, patriarch of the clan, had fathered four natural sons by Marie Magdelaine Clemence Auger, his Afro-Creole common-law wife. Each of the four Glaudin brothers eventually opened his own tobacco shop. Cailloux may well have supplied cigars or worked for J. B. Glaudin. Cailloux gave Glaudin family names to two of his daughters and invited Glaudins to stand as godparents at their baptisms. Tax ledgers for 1852 list Cailloux as "André Duvernay," perhaps confusing him with his half-brother, Molière Duvernay, who lived in the same square, owned the same amount of taxable property and may even have worked alongside his

who sojourned in Cuba before their expulsion from that island and their arrival in New Orleans brought with them cigar-making skills learned there. See Lachance, "The Foreign French," in Hirsch and Logsdon, *Creole New Orleans,* 104–105; Reinders, Robert C. "The Free Negro in the New Orleans Economy, 1850–1860," *Louisiana History,* VI (1965), 280.

5. New Orleans City Directory, 1852, microfiche, Louisiana Collection, NOPL; Tax Ledger, 1852, pp. 300, 251, microfilm in City Archives, NOPL; *Harper's Weekly,* August 29, 1863; Samuel Wilson, Jr., *Southern Travels: Journal of John H. B. Latrobe, 1834* (New Orleans, 1986), 85; Leon Cyprian Soulé, *The Know Nothing Party in New Orleans,* 21–26, map p. 87; Joseph G. Tregle, Jr., "Creoles and Americans," in Hirsch and Logsdon, *Creole New Orleans* 156, 131–68. Under the terms of reconsolidation, the old First Municipality became the Second District; the Second Municipality became the First District, the Third Municipality remained the Third District, and the city of Lafayette, the Fourth District.

sibling. Tax ledgers for 1854 also indicate that Molière briefly owned five slaves valued at $2,000, although he no longer owned them at the next listing in 1856. In any event, Cailloux had made the transition from slavery to freedom, from bondsman to property-owning artisan, and he no doubt hoped for continuing success.[6]

The young artisan also became a slaveholder. By 1860, more than seven hundred free people of color in Louisiana owned slaves, most fewer than five. The relationships between free people of color and slaves were complex and never as simple as a somatic division between light and dark. Some free people of color owned slaves for economic reasons or as domestic servants and treated them as harshly or more harshly than any white masters. They emphasized the social distance between themselves and slaves by marrying endogamously and by jealously guarding their separate seating from slaves in church. Some of the separation between free people of color and slaves involved culture and religion. The Latin-European Catholic Creoles of color remained aloof from the predominantly Protestant, Anglophonic American slaves that flooded into Louisiana in the decades after the Louisiana Purchase. But many free persons of color, such as Cailloux and his wife, had likewise only recently emerged from slavery and they fraternized, cohabited, and intermarried with the numerous Francophone slaves in the city. Like Cailloux's mother-in-law, Feliciana, they expended considerable amounts of their limited capital to purchase and then free family members—although Feliciana apparently also sold at least one slave for cash. Free people of color formed benevolent societies such as the Perseverance and Mutual Aid Association (1783), the Société des Artisans de Bienfaisance et D'Assistance Mutuelle (1834) and Dieu Nous Protége (1844) to help blacks purchase their own or their families' freedom. One of the most devout of the religious confraternities, the all-male Christian Doctrine Society of New Orleans (1818), not only

6. SLC, Bk. 19, p. 301, Act 1050, Bk. 24, p. 130, AANO, and New Orleans City Directory, 1846, Louisiana Collection, NOPL; Rankin, "The Politics of Caste: Free Colored Leadership in New Orleans During the Civil War," in Macdonald, Kemp, and Haas, *Louisiana's Black Heritage,* 142; St. Theresa of Avila (hereafter STA), Bk. 1, October 20, 1850, Act 8, p. 101, March 19, 1854, Act 76, September 30, 1857, Act 65 AANO (recording the baptism of Odile Cailloux and attesting to the baptism of Atherlie Calliou [*sic*]); Tax Ledgers, 1852, pp. 300, 251; 1854, pp. 202, 190, and 1856, p. 254, microfilm, City Archives, NOPL.

assisted slaves in the purchase of their freedom, but also made their spiritual care its top priority.[7]

On January 22, 1849, Cailloux paid $100 cash to Charles F. Daunoy for a female slave. The forty-five-year-old woman whom he purchased from Daunoy was his mother, the oft-sold Josephine. Daunoy, who held a license for a cart, may have used her to peddle wares on the street, but the wording of the sale, which again refused to guarantee against vices or disease, suggested that she may have been ailing (or that she had remained difficult for her masters). Cailloux acquired her with the understanding that he would emancipate her "as soon as practicable." Since no record of her emancipation exists, Josephine may have died before her son could formally and legally free her. A year later, on August 20, 1850, the Cailloux couple added another member to the family, a baby daughter named Athalie Clemence. Her parents had her baptized at St. Theresa of Avila Parish church on October 20 with Meurice and Clemence Glaudin serving as godparents.[8]

Meanwhile, Feliciana continued to play an important role in the lives of her daughter and son-in-law, especially through her real-estate transactions. By 1852, her two remaining lots on Coffee Street (renamed Baronne in 1857) had appreciated in value—probably as a result of her building Creole cottages on them—so that together they were assessed at $1000 for tax purposes. In 1852, Feliciana and

7. Logsdon and Bell, "The Americanization of Black New Orleans," in Hirsch and Logsdon, *Creole New Orleans,* 204; Randall M. Miller, "Slaves and Southern Catholicism," in John B. Boles, ed., *Masters and Slaves in the House of the Lord: Race and Religion in the American South, 1740–1870* (Lexington, 1988), 146–47; Harry Joseph Walker, "Negro Benevolent Societies in New Orleans: A Study of Their Structure, Function, and Membership (master's thesis, Fisk University, 1937), 35–37; John T. Gillard, S.S.J., *The Catholic Church and the American Negro* (Baltimore, 1929), 18–19.

8. Purchase of a Slave by André Cailloux, January 2, 1849, pp. 505–507, in H. B. Cenas, Vol. 41, NONA; License 571, to Charles F. Daunoy, February 15, 1834, in Oaths and Bonds for City Licenses on Vehicles, 1834–66, Office of the Mayor, New Orleans City Archives, NOPL; Birth and Death Certificates, Louisiana State Archives, Baton Rouge, La.; STA Bk. 1, September 30, 1857, p. 13, Act 65, AANO. A free woman of color by the name of Josephine was buried on July 13, 1849, in St. Louis Cemetery No. 2. St. Louis Cemetery No. 2, Interments, September 1, 1847–January 9, 1851, p. 550, AANO.

Bastien dissolved their partnership, with Bastien taking lot #1 and Feliciana retaining #2 next door. The same day, Feliciana, evidently needing cash, sold her property to Jean Pocté for $350, one hundred dollars in cash and the balance in a note. She, however, cannily retained the usufruct, the legal right to use the fruits of Pocté's property, thus allowing her to live in the house and pay rent during her lifetime if she chose. She apparently remained responsible for the taxes.[9]

Within three years, however, the aging Feliciana apparently took up residence with her son, Bastien, and facilitated her son-in-law's purchase of the property next door. On June 30, 1855, Cailloux, with an assist from his mother-in-law, who reunited the usufruct with the property, purchased for $300 from John Pocté the lot on Coffee Street that Feliciana had sold three years earlier. Cailloux took on a mortgage, agreeing to pay Pocté $50 in cash and signing two notes for $125 apiece, the one payable at six months and the other at 12 months from the date of domicile for 6 percent interest, 8 percent for every year thereafter. The sale of his property on Bertrand (later New Orleans) for $265 ($100 of it in cash) in October helped ease the financial pinch and translated into a profit for Cailloux from his first real estate investment.[10]

Cailloux and his family then moved uptown to what before its incorporation into New Orleans in 1852 had been the city of Lafayette. They resided in a typical Creole cottage probably built by Feliciana. The white house had a shallow front porch created by the slightly fanned edge of the steep, wood-slatted roof and supported by three narrow white wooden columns. The two front casement

9. Sale of Property, James Armor to Feliciana and Bastien, February 24, 1842; Sale of Land, Feliciana and Bastien Encalada to Manette Flerio, f.w.c.; Tax Ledger, 1852, p. 692, microfilm, City Archives, NOPL; division between Feliciana and Bastien, October 14, 1852, Act 207, and Sale of the Naked Property of Land, Feliciana to Jean Pocté, October 14, 1852, Act 208, both in Joseph Cuvillier, Vol. 59; Sale of the Naked Property of Land by Jean Pocté to André Cailloux and Renunciation by Feliciana Encalada of the usufruct in favor of Jean Pocté and André Cailloux, in Paul Emile Laresche, June 30, 1855, act 197, vol. 17, all in NONA; Tax Ledgers, 1852–1854, pp. 692, 610, 704, microfilm, City Archives, NOPL.

10. Sale of Property, Bastien Enscolodo [sic] to Louis J. Frederick, November 23, 1868, COB 95-497; Sale of the Naked Property of Land by Jean Pocté, June 30, 1855; Sale of Property, André Cailloux, f.m.c., to Pane Blair, widow of John Chambers, October 4, 1855, in Paul Emile Laresche, Vol. 17, NONA.

doors, covered by green paneled shutters known as a *persiennes*, opened into two rectangular rooms of equal dimensions, each possessing a fireplace with a common interior chimney. Two *cabinets*, small rooms of unequal size separated by an open alcove, were located in the rear. A wooden fence with two green gates surrounded the house and a large oak tree graced the front yard. A detached kitchen, an outhouse, and a cistern lay behind the cottage in the backyard. The Cailloux family lived in a racially and economically diverse square bounded by Baronne (Coffee), Dryades, Philip, and Jackson Streets. The property owners in the square included seven whites (one whose real estate was assessed at $8000) and at least two other free men of color whose lots were assessed for the same amount as Cailloux's, one of whom was his next-door neighbor and brother-in-law Bastien Encalada. The free people of color living in the vicinity included a domestic, a mason, three carpenters, and a plasterer. By October 1856, Cailloux had acquired enough cash to pay off the mortgage on his property, which was then held by Thomy Lafon, an Afro-Creole businessman and real-estate speculator who acquired a fortune, served as a benefactor of the Sisters of the Holy Family, and almost forty years later, helped to bankroll the *Plessy v. Ferguson* suit. Cailloux now held clear title to his home, a not inconsiderable achievement for a man so recently removed from slavery.[11]

That home lay in a bustling urban center of 168,000, by far the largest in the South and the sixth largest in the United States in 1860. While providing opportunities, however, the environment of New Orleans also posed dangers. The city hugged a mile-wide strip between the Mississippi River and the great dismal swamp that surrounded Lake Pontchatrain to the north. Its heat, humidity, inadequate drainage, and not infrequent storms and floods made it

11. CHD13, Plan Book A, Folio B, "Plan of 1 Lot of Ground with Buildings Situated in the 4th District," New Orleans, A. Chastang, NONA; Sally K. Reeves, "The Plan Book Drawings of the New Orleans Notarial Archives: Legal Background and Artistic Development," *Proceedings of the American Antiquarian Society*, CV, pt. 1 (1995), 117; Tax Assessments, 1857, 1860, microfilm, City Archives, NOPL; Eighth Census of the United States, 1860, City of New Orleans and Orleans Parish, 839–40; Release of Mortgage by Thomy Lafon in favor of André Cailloux, October 18, 1856, Act 241, in Laresche, Vol. 18, NONA; Desdunes, *Our People and Our History*, 93–94. André Cailloux's name is listed incorrectly in the census as "Andréw Cahen."

arguably the unhealthiest city in the nation, with a soaring disease rate and frequent epidemics of yellow fever and cholera. Writing to the Lyon Society in October 1849, Fr. Étienne Rousselon, vicar-general of the diocese, lamented that, although spared "for a time" from the revolutions that had swept Europe in 1848, the city had suffered two periods of cholera during the winter. In the spring, the Mississippi had broken through levees, destroying crops, submerging one-third of the city for several months, and leaving "two or three feet of water in all our streets. . . . Yellow fever came then to add to all of the above."

In this environment the Cailloux couple raised their family. On May 6, 1857, in the Coffee Street house, Felicie gave birth to another daughter, Odile, who carried the same name as one of J. B. Glaudin's daughters. The following month, the baby girl was baptized at St. Theresa of Avila. Odile helped fill the void left by the earlier death of another daughter, Hortense, who had been born on January 28, 1854, baptized at St. Theresa's on March 18, and buried from there in the same year, perhaps the victim of one of the epidemics. The baptisms of the children manifested the Cailloux family's adherence to the Catholicism that helped to define their lives.[12]

The Cailloux family turned to the Church and specifically to St. Theresa of Avila parish particularly at key transitions in their lives—birth, marriage, and death—and at times of communal celebration or solemn observation, as the forty days of Lent. Located at Camp Street and Clio in the old Second Municipality and what had become the First District after 1852, St. Theresa's included a large number of Irish immigrants as well as some Creole families. Indeed, by the early 1850s, immigrants constituted over half of the city's white population. Political competition between white Creoles and native-born Americans and the increasing importance of the immigrant vote in that equation—only New York City received more foreign-born

12. Capers, *Occupied City,* 4–6; Vella, *Intimate Enemies,* 255–58; Étienne Rousselon to Secty. Meynis, October 20, 1849, no. 2826, Lyon Society Collection, AANO; Affidavit of Henriette Lamott, October 4, 1871, affidavit signed by Molière Duvernay, Office of Recorder of Births, Marriages, and Deaths, State of Louisiana, Parish of New Orleans, August 19, 1871, in pension file of André Caillaux [*sic*], RG 15; STA Bk. 2, p. 10, Act 162 and Bk. 1, Act 81, March 19, 1854, entries 76 and 81, AANO.

newcomers than New Orleans during the 1850s—fueled the rise of nativism and led to the emergence in 1854 of the anti-immigrant American, or Know-Nothing, Party, which became the dominant political party in the city until the Civil War. The Cailloux's had their children baptized at St. Theresa's even though, before their move to Baronne Street in 1855, they lived closer to St. Joseph's. At St. Theresa's, they may well have participated in the parish missions, or Catholic revivals, that Archbishop Antoine Blanc instructed each parish to hold during and after the tragic yellow fever epidemic of 1853. Throughout the Lenten season of 1854, the Redemptorist fathers conducted parish missions in packed churches. Priests reported that during the five parish missions in the city—including one at St. Theresa's—approximately 10,680 Catholics received Holy Communion.[13]

Parish missions encouraged popular piety and devotionalism. During missions and on Sundays or other religious occasions, free women of color like Felicie Cailloux went to church wearing brightly colored kerchiefs, known as *tignons.* If the Cailloux family participated in the widespread general observance of the forty days of Lent that followed the raucous celebration of Mardi Gras, they abstained from meat for forty days, eating instead oyster pie, jambalaya, or turtle soup. They fasted (except for bread and water) until noon, attended services during Holy Week, "kissed the cross and made the stations" on Good Friday, confessed their sins, received Holy Communion on Easter Sunday, and listened to the cannonade and watched the fireworks that marked the conclusion of the Paschal celebration. They may also have joined other Afro-Creole Catholics in singing *cantiques,* religious folk songs that bespoke their French, Catholic, and African heritage. *Cantiques* were of several types: ballads about the saints (especially Mary Magdaléne) or Christ, hymns associated with Mass, and songs and laments sung at wakes. Unlike most Louisiana folk songs, *cantiques* were sung not in the Creole patois but in French. Elements of scripture and folk traditions and

13. Roger Baudier, *St. Theresa of Avila Paris: Historic Sketch* (New Orleans, 1948), 8–15; Tregle, "Creoles and Americans," in Hirsch and Logsdon, *Creole New Orleans,* 141, 153–67; Vella, *Intimate Enemies,* 69; Marius M. Carriere, Jr., "Anti-Catholicism, Nativism, and Louisiana Politics in the 1850s," *Louisiana History,* XXXV (1994), 458; Soulé, *The Know Nothing Party,* 2–5, 27–28, 39–84; Baudier, *The Catholic Church in Louisiana,* 379–81, 376.

music from France mixed with African and Afro-Creole syncopation and repetition of the text.[14]

The French Catholic tradition informed the particular Catholicism of André and Felicie Cailloux. The historical shortage of priests in the diocese had meant that women bore the primary responsibility of handing down and interpreting the Catholic faith and practice in Louisiana, which encouraged the rise of a popular devotionalism that sometimes bordered on the superstitious. Culturally and religiously, Creoles remained part of the French world. Their Gallican Catholicism, flavored with anticlericalism and a unique popular piety, blended both liturgical and nonliturgical practices and emphasized communal devotionalism and celebration organized around holy days, patron saints, and the Lenten season, rather than a rigorous adherence to dogma or rules of conduct. This devotional piety stressed physical signs of the faith and sometimes invested sacramentals such as palms, candles, rosaries, and holy water with supernatural powers. Everyday faith was a hybrid of traditional Catholic tenets, rituals, and practices grafted with local customs, folklore, African survivals, and legends. (The most dramatic syncretism of Catholicism and traditional African religion was of course voodoo, an import from St. Domingue.)[15]

In spite of their subordinate position in the white-controlled Church, Afro-Creoles like the Cailloux family embraced Catholicism as a means of shaping individual and group identity and of giving meaning and dignity to their lives. Fr. Antonio de Sedella's zealous ministry among slaves and free people of color during the first three decades of the nineteenth century until his death in 1828 cemented their loyalty to a liberal, Latin European version of Catholicism. The

14. Mackie J. V. Blanton and Gayle K. Nolan, "Creole Lenten Devotions: Nineteenth Century Practices and their Implications," in Conrad, *Cross, Crozier, and Crucible,* 530, 536; André Prevos, "Afro-French Spirituals about Mary Magdalene," *Louisiana Folklore Miscellany,* IV (1980), 41–53.

15. Blanton and Nolan, "Creole Lenten Devotions," in Conrad, *Cross, Crozier, and Crucible,* 525–38; Ralph Gibson, *Social History of French Catholicism, 1789–1914* (New York, 1989), 161–63, 165; John W. Blassingame, *Black New Orleans, 1860–1880* (Chicago, 1973), 108. On the French connection, see LaChance, "The Foreign French," and Logsdon and Bell, "The Americanization of Black New Orleans," both in Hirsch and Logsdon, *Creole New Orleans,* 91–130 and 189–261.

church created a social sphere wherein Creoles of color mingled, at least during worship services, with other elements of the population, white and black. Indeed, black Catholics probably experienced less racial discrimination in New Orleans Catholic churches than in most places in the United States. A number of visitors to the city, including Benjamin Latrobe, Frederick Law Olmsted, and Thomas Hamilton, noted the large numbers of free people of color, especially women, who adhered to "old-fashioned devotional practices" in New Orleans Catholic churches, in contrast to the religious indifference of many white Creoles. Noting the dissimilarity to Protestant churches, which for the most part did not welcome black members, commentators such as Thomas Hamilton, a Protestant minister, marveled at scenes in St. Louis Cathedral, where he had observed white and black women of all varieties kneeling on the bare stone floors, praying in equality "before their common father," the entire floor of the extensive cathedral "crowded with worshipers of all colors and classes." Blacks received the sacraments indiscriminately with whites and sang in mixed choirs. Worshipers quickly separated on emerging from the cathedral, however, and racial mixing never extended to Catholic schools or to benevolent and religious societies associated with the Church.[16]

Distinctions of color crystallized in the decades before the Civil War as American influence replaced the older and more racially tolerant Latin Catholic tradition associated with Sedella. In 1830, the Louisiana legislature reiterated that "line of distinction" between "the several classes of this community," stipulating that violators would be charged with misdemeanors and subject to fines, jail terms (both heavier for free people of color than whites), and expulsion from the state. The Church abided by the law. Thus in 1836 Abbé Rousselon, fearing action by the state's attorney general, disbanded the Sisters of the Presentation, an early effort by two women of color, Henriette Delille and Juliette Gaudin, and a French woman, Marie Jeanne Aliquot, to form an interracial religious community. In 1842,

16. Bell, *Revolution, Romanticism, and the Afro-Creole Protest,* 70–71, 73–74; Liliane Crété, *Daily Life in Louisiana,* 144–59; Hamilton, quoted in Gould, "In Full Enjoyment of Their Liberty," 269–270. Some observers believed that a liaison existed between Sedella and his mulatto housekeeper.

concurrently with the founding of the segregated Sisters of the Holy Family, Bishop Blanc (he would not be elevated to archbishop until 1851) established a new parish in the Faubourg Tremé: St. Augustine's. While free people of color contributed to the building fund and rented about half the pews at St. Augustine's, they were required to sit separately from whites (many of them relatives), while slaves sat in galleries or on benches that lined the side of the church. Diocesan regulations required separate sacramental registers for whites, free persons of color, and slaves. Beginning with the establishment of St. Louis Cemetery No. 2 in 1823, moreover, separate sections in Catholic cemeteries marked the final resting places of free people of color and of slaves.[17]

Despite the indignities suffered at the hands of the Church, pious Afro-Creoles drew inspiration from their Catholicism to serve the less fortunate in society. In 1820, Michael Portier, a young priest at St. Louis Cathedral and a future bishop of Mobile, described a group of about a dozen young people of color serving as catechists, whom he described as "fervent, like angels." They met with him every Sunday, wore red ribbons and crosses, promised "to fight daily like valiant soldiers of Jesus Christ," taught slaves to pray, and instructed same in the catechism. Marveling at the depths of their piety, Portier insisted that they showed "as much faith as . . . seminarians" though they lived "in Babylon, in the midst of scandals." By 1829, Henriette Delille, a free woman of color, had joined with her friends Juliette Gaudin and Josephine Charles to evangelize free people of color and slaves. By 1842 they had formed a congregation of women religious: the Sisters of the Holy Family. The sisters dedicated themselves to the care, both physical and spiritual, of the poor, orphaned, sick, and elderly of their community, both slave and free. Encouraged and aided by Marie Jeanne Aliquot, Vicar-general Rousselon, and Archbishop Blanc, the sisters established the Hospice of the Holy Family

17. Bell, *Revolution, Romanticism, and the Afro-Creole Protest,* 130–31, 134, 146, 149; Sr. Audrey Marie Detiege, *Henriette Delille, Free Woman of Color: Foundress of the Sisters of the Holy Family* (New Orleans, 1976), 28–29; Baudier, *The Catholic Church in Louisiana,* 365; Randall M. Miller, "A Church in Cultural Captivity: Some Speculations on Catholic Identity in the Old South," in Miller and Wakelyn, *Catholics in the Old South,* 42; Robert C. Reinders, "The Churches and the Negro in New Orleans, 1850–1860," *Phylon,* XXII (1961), 242; Samuel Wilson, Jr. and Leonard V. Huber, *The St. Louis Cemeteries of New Orleans* (New Orleans, 1963), 22.

in 1842. After 1852, the sisters maintained a free school, St. Augustine's, as well as an orphanage for indigent children of color. They also provided religious instruction to slaves. Lay Afro-Creole Catholics rallied to their support by organizing the Society of the Holy Family, which provided invaluable assistance.[18]

Free people of color also turned their attention to schools. Finding themselves barred from the public schools that their property taxes helped to fund, those who could afford to do so sent their children to private schools, either religious or secular. In 1853 Cailloux enrolled his sons, Jean Louis and Eugene, in the most famous of these, *L'Institution Catholique des Orphelins dans l'Indigence* (Catholic Institute for Indigent Orphans, or Institute Catholique, or the Couvent School). The Institute had opened in 1848 in the Faubourg Marigny at a temporary facility on Grands Hommes and Union Streets, initiated by a bequest made ten years earlier by a native African woman, Marie Justin Camaire, a free woman of color and the widow of Bernard Couvent. The hostility of public officials to expanded educational opportunities for free people of color prevented action for ten years, but in 1847 Father Constantine Manehault of St. Louis Cathedral brought the bequest to the attention of an Afro-Creole philanthropist and slaveholder, François Lacroix. Timely passage of a law by the state legislature that year allowing six or more persons to incorporate themselves for any literary, scientific, religious, or charitable purpose opened a window of opportunity for black Creole intellectuals and businessmen. They formed the *Société Catholique pour l'Instruction des Orphelins dans l'Indigence*, obtained an act of incorporation that provided for a self-perpetuating board of directors, and solicited contributions for the school. Under the terms of the widow Couvent's will, the Institute would ostensibly

18. Michael Portier to Fr. Cholleton, September, 1820, no. 2726, Lyon Society Collection, AANO; M. Boniface Adams, "The Gift of Religious Leadership: Henriette Delille and the Foundation of the Holy Family Sisters," in Conrad, *Cross, Crozier, and Crucible*, 369–70; Baudier, *The Catholic Church in Louisiana*, 397; Detiege, *Henriette Delille*, 14–27, 31; Bell, *Revolution, Romanticism, and the Afro-Creole Protest*, 127–33; Sister Francis Jerome Woods, C.D.P., "Congregations of Religious Women in the Old South," in Miller and Wakelyn, *Catholics in the Old South*, 115–16; Virginia Meacham Gould and Charles E. Nolan, *Henriette Delille: 'Servant of Slaves'* (New Orleans, 1998), 7–18.

operate under the broad auspices of the Catholic Church and would
provide instruction in the Catholic catechism, though it would accept students of all denominations.

In 1852, the Institute moved to a permanent facility on St. Antoine Street between Bons Enfans and Morales in the Third District.
Members of the Society, defined as contributors of $2.40 or more
per year, competed for election on separate tickets to the ten-man
board of directors, publicizing their campaigns in the French-language version of *L'Orléanais,* a newspaper published in both English
and French in the Third Municipality. The Society and its school
thus provided free people of color with a venue for exercising leadership and some form of the elective franchise, both of which were
denied them in the larger society. A report by the first board at the
end of its term in 1848 indicated that in addition to $1,239.85 in
school receipts, the Society had raised $2,111.15 in contributions
and bequests (including some state funds), had spent $1,640 for
teachers' salaries, $1,239 in school expenses, $351.50 on improve-
ments and repairs to the property, and $139.70 for books, paper,
pens, and ink, leaving a balance of $1119.20. The Institute admitted
forty-three orphans in 1848.[19]

The board of directors of the Institute established policy, hired
the principal and teachers, and ruled on the admission of students.
In 1852, it chose as principal an Afro-Creole intellectual, Armand
Lanusse, one of the original incorporators of the Catholic Society for
the Instruction of Indigent Orphans and the editor and publisher in
1845 of *Les Cenelles,* an anthology of poetry by Creoles of color.

19. Bell, *Revolution, Romanticism, and the Afro-Creole Protest,* 152–54; Séance
of June 18, 1853, in Journal des Séances de la direction de l'institution catholique
pour les orphelins dans l'indigence (hereafter, Journal des Séances), AANO; Des-
dunes, *Our People and Our History,* 101–106; Baudier, "The Story of St. Louis
School of Holy Redeemer Parish, New Orleans, formerly St. Louis School for the
Colored, l'Institution Catholique Pour l'Instruction des Orphelins dans l'Indi-
gence, Widow Couvent's School," (ms., 1956, Roger Baudier Collection, AANO);
Nathan Wiley, "Education of the Colored Population of Louisiana," *Harper's
New Monthly,* XXXIII (1866), 248; Constitution De La Société Catholique Pour
L'Instruction Des Orphelins Dans L'Indigence, June 20, 1849, Charles B. Rousseve
Papers, Amistad Research Center, Tulane University, New Orleans; New Orleans
L'Orléanais, April 13, 15, 20, May 4, 1848; Donald E. DeVore and Joseph Logs-
don, *Crescent City Schools: Public Education in New Orleans, 1841–1891* (Lafayette,
La., 1991), 43.

The co-institutional school had separate floors for boys and girls and conducted classes in both English and French. The course of instruction lasted six years and included mathematics (arithmetic, algebra, and geometry), rhetoric, French and English grammar and composition, geography, history, logic, basic accounting, and personal hygiene. Each class was supposed to begin and end with a prayer. Initially, the school's faculty included three male and two female teachers. Interestingly, male and female teachers of the same rank received the same salary. The school's faculty eventually included Creole intellectuals, poets, novelists, and dramatists, whose ideas probably filtered into the Cailloux household, not only through André's personal associations with them, but also via his sons. The Institute's approximately 200 students, who sat at long tables on crude benches, included not only orphans who attended for free, but also children of Afro-Creoles who paid tuition according to their means. In 1859, 138 paid 50 cents per month; 86 paid 20 cents. The school inspired community pride and received donations from collections taken at the city's cemeteries on All Saints Day, as well as from colored Creole benevolent societies; the state legislature even appropriated funds for it.[20]

According to Afro-Creole historian and activist Rodolphe Desdunes, Felicie Cailloux, an "exceedingly intelligent, highly respected and devout woman," served as the first "institutrice," or head of the girls' branch of the Institute, though the *Prospectus* of the institution published in 1847, did not yet include her name. Between 1830 and 1838, a literate, free woman of color who signed her name, "Felicie Caill*aux*," and who may well have been the woman identified by Desdunes as "Felicie Caill*oux*," stood as a godparent for a number of free children of color and at least one slave. Her godparenting of Joseph Lavigne suggested a connection with the radical Lavigne family, whose members would later figure prominently in the Institute Catholique, the spiritualist movement, and the 1st Regiment of the

20. Wiley, "Education of the Colored Population of Louisiana," 248; Séances of June 18, October 15, 17, 1853, February 15, 1854, May 2, 17, September 1, October 5, 1859, March 9, 1860, and April 2, 1862, all in Journal des Séances, ANNO; Bell, *Revolution, Romanticism, and the Afro-Creole Protest*, 114–15, 123–27; *Prospectus de L'Institution Catholique des Orphelins Indigents* (New Orleans, 1847), copy in Howard Tilton Memorial Library, Tulane University, New Orleans.

Louisiana Native Guards. By 1851, however, following the reloca-
tion of the Institute to its permanent site and the reorganization of
the board of directors, Felicie no longer served as institutrice, though
she had clearly made a significant impression on Desdunes who regarded her as a woman of selfless and tireless devotion who had lived
Christ's injunction: "Let come to me the little children." During the
1850s, however, the Institute operated in an increasingly inhospita-
ble environment. By 1860, even though the patronage of the Church
shielded it, legislation designed to suppress free black institutions
had reduced total school enrollment of children of color in the city
from 1,008 in 1850 to 275.[21]

Wealthier free people of color often sent their sons to study in
France, a country which, after its abolition of slavery in 1848, provided a haven for black Creole artists and musicians such as Victor
Séjour and Edmond Dede, and which recruited black men into its
army and civil service. French culture heavily influenced social life
in New Orleans. Free people of color had a strong French musical
tradition, their musicians usually performing in European style and
with European instruments. They composed the band for Jackson's
forces at New Orleans in 1815, provided music for balls and parades,
formed the Société Philarmonique in the 1830s, and boasted successful expatriate composers such as Dede, Lucian Lambert, and Victor Eugene-McCarty. The French cultural link nurtured the
identification of the Afro-Creole elite of New Orleans with the intellectual and political currents associated with both the 1789 and 1848
revolutions in France. Some of the teachers at the Catholic Institute,
for example, embraced romanticism, radical republicanism, abolitionism, egalitarianism, and Freemasonry, the latter an international
secret society characterized by anticlericalism, social egalitarianism,
and religious toleration. The Church condemned the organization
for its secret oaths, anticlericalism, indifference to denominational
affiliation, and alleged near deification of reason. The ferment associated with the 1848 revolution led to the abolition of slavery and the
granting of universal suffrage to former slaves throughout the French

21. Desdunes, *Our People and Our History,* 104; copy of a letter from Rodolphe
Desdunes to René Grandjean, August 14, 1921, in Letterbook, 85-83, René Grandjean Collection, Earl K. Long Library, University of New Orleans; SLC, Bk. 24, p.
40, Act 308, Bk. 25, p. 196, Act 597 and p. 353, Act 1002, Bk. 26, p. 58, Act 189,
AANO; Bell, *Revolution, Romanticism, and the Afro-Creole Protest,* 126.

empire in 1850. Louis Napoleon continued to maintain very severe laws against slavery and the slave trade after he came to power in 1852. Some French Catholic bishops also publicly embraced emancipation. In 1853, the provincial council of Bordeaux, for example, condemned slavery. The most prominent French Catholic clerical opponent of human bondage, Bishop Félix-Antoine-Philibert Dupanloup (1802–1878), headed the diocese of Orleans.[22]

While no doubt pleased by the developments in France, Cailloux had to focus on the more immediate and mundane task of making a living as an artisan in New Orleans. In 1856 and again in 1857, the city of New Orleans attached small liens against Cailloux's property for past-due taxes. On November 7, 1857, the city secured a judgment from the Third District Court against Cailloux's property for $22.50 in back taxes, plus interest. By 1858, Cailloux worked at a shop on Union (Touro) and Casacalvo (Royal) streets, two blocks downriver from the Vieux Carré, in the Third District, the Faubourg Marigny. The 1859 tax ledgers indicate that he had $100 in capital—probably tobacco—at the Union Street address. The same ledgers list others who had similar amounts of capital at the same location, suggesting that Cailloux may have worked with other cigar makers at the site, though his specific role (partner, colleague, boss, employee) remains unclear. Contrary to later depictions of him following the Battle of Port Hudson, Cailloux did not possess significant wealth, education, or property, although by October 1856, only ten years after his emancipation, thanks apparently to careful management of his resources, he found himself free from any mortgage on his property. Owning real estate assessed for tax purposes at $500 in 1860, he nevertheless fell far short of the $2000 benchmark that signified "relatively prosperous."[23]

22. Blassingame, *Black New Orleans,* 13, 135; Charles E. Kinzer, "The Band of Music of the First Battalion of Free Men of Color and the Siege of New Orleans, 1814–1815," *American Music,* X (1992), 360–61, 368; Logsdon and Bell, "The Americanization of Black New Orleans," in Hirsch and Logsdon, *Creole New Orleans,* 195, 208–209; Benjamin J. Blied, *Catholics and the Civil War* (Milwaukee, 1945), 26–27; Davis, *The History of Black Catholics,* 63–64.

23. See attachment to Mortgage by André Cailloux to Joseph M. Zardais, October 19, 1859, Act 321 in Octave de Armas, Vol. 74, NONA; *A. Mygatt and Company, New Orleans Directory* (New Orleans, 1858 and 1859), 873:2, microfiche of

Like most of his fellow artisans, Cailloux operated on a thin margin, made even more precarious by the economic depression of 1857, which, though it hit the North hardest, had ripple effects in New Orleans. He bought tobacco on credit and did not have much access to ready cash, a situation that led to a lawsuit in 1858 over the purchase of some tobacco. This prosaic case, which eventually landed in the Louisiana State Supreme Court in 1860, illustrated not only the litigiousness of Creoles of color and the vicissitudes of small Afro-Creole artisan-entrepreneurs like Cailloux, but also the unique access to the courts enjoyed by free people of color in New Orleans even in the midst of an increasingly hostile political atmosphere, an access not enjoyed by most free blacks in states outside Louisiana.

On September 7, 1858, Cailloux, who according to testimony, had just "commenced working" at the Union Street location and "had not much money," sued François Nuba, also a free man of color and a grocer, for $420, exclusive of interest and court costs. Cailloux claimed that on August 7, 1858, after negotiating with Nuba, he had purchased for $60 two lots of leaf tobacco in boxes of 377 and 131 pounds respectively. Cailloux claimed that he had agreed to pay $20 in cash and the $40 balance in increments convenient to him. He later asserted that, in every respect, he had complied with the terms and conditions of the sale.

Nuba disagreed. On Friday, August 27, 1858, he called on Cailloux and, explaining that he had a note falling due the next day, demanded that Cailloux pay the balance owed him by the following day. Though strapped for cash, Cailloux complied with Nuba's demand, and early on the morning of the 28th tendered him the $40 in two gold pieces, silver coins, and bank notes. Nuba, however, then informed Cailloux, much to the latter's "chagrin and disappointment," that he could not accept the forty dollars because he had already disposed of the tobacco to another person, claiming that he had originally given Cailloux only eight days in which to pay him back. Cailloux claimed a breach of faith on Nuba's part that had resulted in damages and injury to him. He argued that the tobacco

---

City Directories, in Reading Room, LC, Washington, D.C.; Tax Ledger, 1859, p. 394, microfilm in City Archives, NOPL; Release of Mortgage by Thomy Lafon in favor of André Cailloux; Loren Schweninger, "Prosperous Blacks in the South, 1790–1880," *American Historical Review*, XCV (February, 1990), 33.

that he had purchased was of a quality then very scarce in the New Orleans market and that the profits that he would have realized by the manufacture of the tobacco into cigars and the loss that he suffered in consequence of his not having it amounted to and exceeded the sum of $400, which Nuba refused to pay. Cailloux therefore petitioned the Sixth District Court of New Orleans to compel Nuba to pay him $420 with interest, plus the costs of the suit.

Though Cailloux won the case, he did not receive as much in damages as he had asked. On April 19, 1859, the court ordered Nuba to pay $168, computed on the basis of testimony that the 508 pounds of tobacco, worth 45 cents per pound, would have produced $228. The court deducted the purchase price of $60, leaving $168, the amount of damages sustained by Cailloux, with 5 percent interest from September 7, plus court costs, which totaled an additional $24.45. When the court refused Nuba's appeal for a new trial, he then carried the case to the Louisiana Supreme Court. During the appeal, of course, Cailloux had neither the tobacco nor the money. On June 4, 1860, one year after the filing of the appeal, the Louisiana Supreme Court affirmed the lower court's decision.[24]

As his lawsuit suggests, Cailloux faced increased competition in the late 1850s from other Afro-Creole and foreign-born artisans and from colored businessmen such as Lucien Mansion and Georges Alcès, who operated sizable cigar factories, employing as many as two hundred men. The economic position of free people of color eroded during the 1850s as their average wealth diminished somewhat in comparison to what it had reached in 1840.[25] Indeed, the general position of free people of color in Louisiana society became increasingly tenuous after 1852 as sectional tensions grew and the consolidated city and state governments came increasingly under the control of new American leaders.

*   *   *

24. Docket no. 6358, *Cailloux. f.m.c. v. Nuba. f.m.c.* (June, 1860); 15 La. Ann. xiii. Accession *106* (unreported), Supreme Court of Louisiana Collection of Legal Archives, Archives and Manuscripts/Special Collections Department, University of New Orleans; Sixth District Court of New Orleans, docket no. 6502 in docket book C, City Archives, NOPL.

25. Desdunes, *Our People and Our History,* 90–91; Lachance, "Hierarchy of Wealth in New Orleans," in Landers, *Against the Odds,* 79; Ira Berlin, *Slaves Without Masters: The Free Negro in the Antebellum South* (New York, 1974), 231.

Many whites grew apprehensive that free people of color constituted a potentially subversive element in society that might combine with slaves to stage a rebellion. Such fears led the state legislature to restrict manumission. As a result, between 1852 and 1855 only thirty slaves in the entire state received their freedom. In 1857, the legislature simply forbade manumissions of any slaves.[26]

A growing number of whites likewise demanded the expulsion or reenslavement of the free black population, leading the state legislature and New Orleans city government to consider and enact repressive measures aimed at them. In 1855, for example, just as the Caillouxs moved to Baronne Street, the state legislature forbade the incorporation of any new religious, charitable, scientific, or literary societies composed of free people of color. Applicable to schools, the law helped to bring about the precipitous decline in the enrollment of children of color mentioned earlier, though Cailloux's own children did attend school in 1859. Other restrictions passed by the legislature made it illegal for a free Negro to keep a coffeehouse, billiard table, or retail store where liquor was sold. The city reinforced the state law on illegal entry by allowing police judges to commit all free Negroes who entered the state illegally to the workhouses, and an 1856 New Orleans ordinance supplemented the state law by preventing free colored people from obtaining liquor licenses. In addition, ordinances forbade the assembly of colored people, slave or free, and placed limitations on shooting firecrackers, playing cards and dominoes, and holding balls with slaves. Although authorities enforced many of these laws only sporadically, if at all, evidence suggests that police in the late 1850s did so in dealing with free Negro assembly, illegal passes, vagrancy, suspicion, and contact with slaves. In 1858, alarmed by free blacks, whites, and slaves worshipping together in defiance of the law, city authorities closed St. James African Methodist Episcopal Church. Certain legal rights of free people of color, however, as exemplified in Cailloux's lawsuit, remained undisturbed.

The increasingly hostile atmosphere led to stagnation in the growth of the free black population. The 1850 census recorded

26. Kotlikoff and Rupert, "The Manumission of Slaves in New Orleans," 173–74.

10,812 free people of color in the New Orleans area; ten years later, the total had risen to only 11,226, far less than natural increase would have produced. Migration probably helped to explain part of the relative decline in the numbers of free blacks, as some who could afford it migrated to Mexico, France, Liberia, or Haiti.[27]

Cailloux and his family chose not to emigrate. Rather, they remained in New Orleans and attempted to forge a better life in the face of the more difficult circumstances. Cailloux's modest economic situation was more typical of ordinary Afro-Creoles than of the stereotypical "privileged" class that some historians have painted. While Creoles of color could boast of the highest percentage of black males employed as artisans, professionals, and entrepreneurs and the lowest in lower-opportunity occupations such as laborer or domestic, and while five of the ten wealthiest blacks in the South lived in New Orleans, the vast majority of free persons of color enjoyed "privileged" status in comparison only to slaves, not to whites. Afro-Creole society featured three subclasses: a small upper class made up of professionals and proprietors, a middle class composed of artisans such as shoemakers, tailors, cabinet makers and cigar makers like Cailloux, and a lower class of unskilled laborers, mostly blacks who had only recently obtained their freedom.[28]

As the decade drew to a close, the middle strata found itself under pressure and Cailloux found it necessary to borrow money, using his property as collateral. In October 1859, he executed a mortgage to secure a loan of $325 from Joseph Martin Zardais, another free man of color. Whenever he borrowed money, Cailloux did so within the Afro-Creole community. When his note fell due in October 1860, with 8 percent interest, Cailloux, lacking the funds to retire it and seeking some extra cash, borrowed $400 from Lanoire François

27. Robert C. Reinders, "The Free Negro in the New Orleans Economy," 278; Schweninger, "Prosperous Blacks in the South," 38; Logsdon and Bell, "The Americanization of Black New Orleans," in Hirsch and Logsdon, *Creole New Orleans,* 208–209; H. E. Sterkx, *The Free Negro In Ante-bellum Louisiana* (Rutherford, N.J., 1972), 286–315; Robert C. Reinders, "The Decline of the New Orleans Free Negro in the Decade Before the Civil War," *Journal of Mississippi History,* XXIV (April, 1962), 88–91, 95; Bell, *Revolution, Romanticism, and the Afro-Creole Protest,* 82–85.
28. Lachance, "The Limits of Privilege," in Landers, *Against the Odds,* 79.

Parent against his property in order to pay the note due Zardais. Cailloux's solid reputation and demonstrated ability to meet his obligations no doubt made him a worthy credit risk.[29]

His peers also showed their high regard for Cailloux by electing him an officer of the Society of the Friends of Order and Mutual Assistance, one of the many mutual aid and burial societies that emerged among free people of color in the second half of the decade and which figured so prominently at Cailloux's funeral in 1863. Paradoxically, in light of the ban on organizations of free people of color enacted by the state legislature two years earlier, within a space of three days in February 1857, three benevolent societies, including the Friends of Order, incorporated themselves in the city. In addition to providing money for burials and sickness, these mutual aid societies provided fellowship and reflected the associational impulse that Alexis de Tocqueville described as so characteristic of antebellum Americans. The societies also created arenas within which free people of color could exercise autonomy and leadership and develop political skills, opportunities they otherwise would not have had since the traditional avenues in church and government remained closed to them. Members often placed their personal religious stamp on these benevolent societies by naming them after popular patron saints, as seen in the names of many of the societies that gathered at Cailloux's funeral.

The act of incorporation of the Friends of Order pledged the group to the diffusion of charity and to the mutual assistance of its members. It provided that every year on October 25, members of the society would elect a management board composed of a president, treasurer, secretary, assistant secretary, representative, librarian, and four commissaries, all of whom would take office on November 1 and manage and administer the society.[30] The Friends of Order

29. Mortgage by André Cailloux to Joseph M. Zardais; Mortgage by André Cailloux to L. F. Parent, October 22, 1860, Act 332, in Octave de Armas, Vol. 77, NONA; tax assessments, 1857 and 1860, City Archives, NOPL.

30. An Act to Incorporate the Society of the Friends of Order and Mutual Assistance, February 5, 1857, in Society Book 3, Folio 508, Office of Mortgages, Orleans Parish, New Orleans, La.; Séances of September 1 and October 5, 1859, April 2, 1860, and October 2, 1861, Journal des Séances, AANO; Séance des Amis de l'Ordre, October 29, 1860, Act 518, pp. 253–54, A. Ducatel, Vol. 83, NONA. The first officers were: president, Victor Lavigne; vice president, P. Manuel Fuentes;

maintained close links to other community institutions, such as the Institute Catholique. Charles Sentmanat, for example, the second president of the society, collected money at cemeteries for the Institute Catholique on All Saints Day and the Society itself made donations to the school. On May 12, 1860, Sentmanat, acting on behalf of the Society as its president, purchased a lot on Urquhart Street in the Faubourg St. Marigny, not far from Cailloux's shop, as the future site of a hall. That October, Cailloux won election as secretary of the Friends. He had obviously advanced significantly in terms of literacy from that day in 1847 when he had made his mark on his emancipation papers.

The leadership of the Friends of Order pushed for construction of a society hall. To that end, in the same month as Cailloux's election, thirty-five of the thirty-seven members in attendance authorized the treasurer to execute a mortgage on the property payable within a year in order to borrow $600 from one of their own, Charles Jolibois. The members agreed that if two months before the note's due date the society did not have sufficient funds to cover it, the members would pay from their own purses the sum necessary to retire the debt. Any who might refuse to pay his share of the contribution would forfeit his membership.[31]

The name of the Friends of Order raises an intriguing question about a possible link between its members and one of a number of Masonic lodges in the city known as *Los Amigos del Orden* (Friends of Order). Despite papal condemnation, Freemasonry had flourished in New Orleans since the late eighteenth century. In the first decades of the nineteenth century, Fr. Sedella had sympathized with the movement, allowed Freemasons to receive all of the Church's sacraments and a Catholic burial, and permitted them to display their

secretary, Crescent Theodore; assistant secretary, François Dede; treasurer, Charles Jolibois; representative, Jules Morphy; commissioners, Henry Lavigne, Jules Desale, Murville Meare, and Clement St. Cyr.

31. Sale of Land, J. B. Patrick to the Société des Amis, March 12, 1860, Act 78, pp. 375–76, Octave de Armas, Vol. 75, NONA; Séance des Amis de l'Ordre, October 29, 1860; Mortgage (and attachment confirming the decision of a meeting of the Society) by the Society of Friends of Order and Mutual Assistance in Favor of Charles Jolibois, October 20, 1860, Act 518, pp. 253–54, Ducatel, vol. 83, NONA. On December 31, the Société de La Persévérance purchased a lot for $165 in the same square as that of Les Amis de l'Ordre.

Masonic regalia in St. Louis Cathedral and on caskets. Catholic Free-masons dominated the board of church trustees (*marguilliers* or wardens) that controlled the administration of the Cathedral's finances and also exercised control over the appointment and dismissal of pastors. Between 1842 and 1844, Bishop Blanc, refusing to appoint the *marguilliers'* nominee as pastor and seeking to assert his authority under canon law to do so, and relying especially on support from English-speaking Irish and American Catholics in the city, engaged in a bitter legal struggle with the white Creole trustees. In that contest, the wardens succeeded in convincing the state senate to pass a bill that would have given effective control of church affairs to the trustees of parishes. Abbé Napoleon Perché, the fiery editor of *Le Propagateur Catholique,* the first diocesan newspaper, ably defended and explained the bishop's position and attacked his opponents. In 1844, the Louisiana State Supreme Court awarded victory to Blanc, affirming the bishop's authority in church matters and permanently breaking the power of the *marguilliers* and of other trustees in parishes throughout Louisiana, although they continued to administer the temporalities of the Cathedral parish until 1883.[32]

Many Catholics remained members of Masonic lodges nonetheless, and their numbers increased in the wake of the French revolutionary upheavals of 1848. French Freemasonry proved attractive to many free people of color who admired its professed ideals of humanism, toleration, anticlericalism, and brotherhood, and saw no incompatibility between it and their anticlerical version of Catholicism.

32. Directories, Masonic Temple Archives, New Orleans; New Orleans City Directory, 1861, michrofiche, Louisiana Collection, NOPL; James J. Pillar, "Catholicism in the Lower South," in Lucius F. Ellsworth, ed., *The Americanization of the Gulf Coast, 1803–1850* (Pensacola, 1972), 39–43. For many years, church historians interpreted the lay-trustee phenomenon as an unwarranted usurpation by the laity of legitimate ecclesiastical authority. Roger Baudier in *The Catholic Church in Louisiana* follows that line of interpretation. Recent scholars, however, have taken a more sympathetic view of lay trusteeship, which they regard as a legitimate tradition in American Catholicism. See, for example, Jay P. Dolan, *The American Catholic Experience* (New York, 1985), and Patrick Carey, *People, Priests, and Prelates: Ecclesiastical Democracy and the Tensions of Trusteeism* (Notre Dame, 1987). Caryn Cossé Bell interprets the battle between the *marguilliers* and Archbishop Blanc as a conflict between the liberal tradition of Latin Catholicism and a more conservative strain of American Catholicism distinctly influenced by southern racial norms. See Bell, *Revolution, Romanticism, and the Afro-Creole Protest,* 147.

Prior to the Civil War, some French lodges in the city evidently even admitted a number of free blacks, and anglophonic African-American Oscar Dunn secretly organized York-rite Prince Hall lodges, which even included French-speaking black Creoles such as Jordan Noble. The members of the Friends of Order, by their choice of the organization's name, may have indicated their sympathy with the ideals of Freemasonry and may have sought to create parallel organizations that might some day affiliate with the Masonic movement. The willingness of priests to celebrate masses commemorating the founding of the societies suggests either that the tolerant attitude of Sedella toward Freemasonry continued to prevail among many of the French clergy or, that the societies represented more orthodox organizations meant to fill the role played by Masonic lodges.[33]

The presence of Victor Lavigne as an officer of the Friends of Order—he served as the organization's first president—pointed not only to Freemasonry (the surname appears on postwar Freemason rolls), but also to another movement with radical egalitarian and utopian overtones that gained popularity particularly among a segment of elite free people of color in the decade prior to the Civil War: spiritualism. This religious sect insisted that human mediums could communicate with the spirit world, rejected the institutional church, and advocated a new "catholic" faith based on the Christian ideal of universal brotherhood. Lavigne became a noted spiritualist and spokesman for the movement in the city. Cailloux, however, did not follow Lavigne into the new sect and, indeed, made light of spirit communication, though subsequent events indicated that he sympathized with some of the idealistic societal aspirations of its devotees.[34]

* * *

33. Bell, *Revolution, Romanticism, and the Afro-Creole Protest*, 70, 82–84, 147–53, 182–83; Baudier, *The Catholic Church in Louisiana*, 218, 275–76, 278, 334–44; Logsdon and Bell, "The Americanization of the Black New Orleans," in Hirsch and Logsdon, *Creole New Orleans*, 211–14, 234–35; S. Toussaint to J. B. Peaucup, February 5, 1862, in Catholic Institution English Composition Copybook (hereafter, Copybook), AANO. The Persévérance Society (Société de Bienefaisance sous le titre distinctif de la Persévérance) and the True Friends Mutual Benevolent Association, chartered in 1857 and 1860 respectively, also bore names identical to Masonic lodges.
34. Bell, *Revolution, Romanticism, and the Afro-Creole Protest*, 186–87, 263, 241; An Act to Incorporate the Society of Friends; Séance, July 17, 1863, 85-30, p. 156, in Spiritualist Registers, René Grandjean Collection.

As the sectional crisis intensified and civil war loomed, the growing vulnerability and isolation of free people of color in New Orleans made them more conscious than ever before of their uneasy proximity to slavery and their need for legal and political protection of their rights—and thus more receptive to the egalitarian views of Afro-Creole radicals. Meanwhile, Cailloux clung tenaciously, if somewhat precariously, to the economic middle rung of Afro-Creole society that he had attained through his efforts in the years following his emancipation. The impending Civil War, while posing a threat to his economic well-being, would afford him the opportunity to strike a blow for a more egalitarian society in a way unique for a black man: as an officer in the military service.

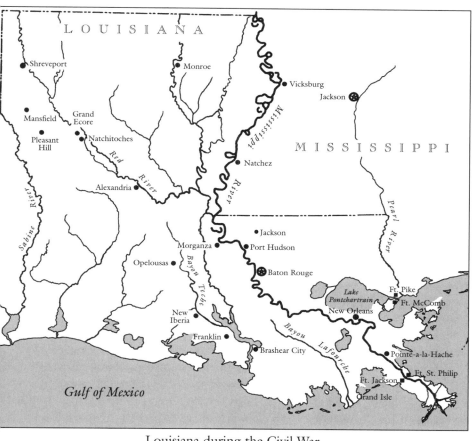

Louisiana during the Civil War

3

OFFICER OF THE NATIVE GUARDS

The outbreak of the Civil War presented André Cailloux and other free people of color with daunting challenges but also with unique opportunities. As they had done in times of war since colonial days, free people of color—including Cailloux—offered their services to the existing government in hopes of protecting and perhaps even improving their fragile and anomalous position within a slave society. The vagaries of war, however, would eventually allow Cailloux and other free people of color to move from the ranks of Confederate militia into the Union army, enabling them to fight for a society free from the curse of slavery.

Shortly after the war broke out, Cailloux, along with numerous other free men of color, responded to the governor's call to organize a militia regiment for the defense of the "Native Land" of Louisiana. In April 1861, led by Jordan Noble, the surviving drummer boy of the Battle of New Orleans, they held several meetings, the last drawing a crowd of fifteen hundred at the Institute Catholique on April 23, 1861, to show their support for their state and to offer the government their services. Governor Thomas D. Moore accepted their overture, and on May 2 authorized a regiment of free people of color and designated it the Native Guards, Louisiana Militia, Confederate States of America. The New Orleans *Daily Crescent* applauded the actions of the colored Creoles, and wishfully proclaimed, "Our free colored men . . . are certainly as much attached to the land of their birth as their white brethren" and will "fight the Black Republicans with as much determination and gallantry."[1]

Though some Creoles of color may have sympathized with the Confederacy, most, like Cailloux, probably joined the Native Guards with an eye to protecting or even improving their increasingly threatened civil and political status by demonstrating their loyalty to the state. Their forbears had done so, first under the French and Spanish during the colonial era, and then later under Andrew Jackson at the Battle of New Orleans. The French had first formed a company of free militia of color in 1735 to do battle against Indians. The Spanish had added another company and divided them into light-skinned *pardos* and dark-skinned *morenos*. Spain employed the colored militia as a counterweight to resentful French planters on the one side and restive slaves and Indians on the other.

Greater autonomy and status for the members of the free black militias, however, came at the price of greater social distance from enslaved blacks. Colored militia had played key roles in suppressing rebellious slave conspiracies such as those at Natchez in 1791 and 1795, in capturing runaways, and in dispersing *cimmaron* groups (communities of runaways) such as that of the infamous St. Malô. But the militia experience heightened color consciousness and social distance not only between *libres* and slaves but also between *pardos* and *morenos*. The colored militia, with its black officers nevertheless provided an occasion for *libres* to operate, at least theoretically, on a plane of greater equality with Europeans. The free black militia had played a crucial role in protecting New Orleans, supporting the regime, and molding the corporate identity of free people of color in the city. Even after the dissolution of the militia of color following the Louisiana Purchase in 1803, former militiamen, especially officers, enjoyed special status and exercised leadership within Afro-Creole society.

Free blacks rallied again in 1812, forming two battalions under Andrew Jackson at the Battle of New Orleans, only to be disbanded once again by the Americans. Veterans like Jordan, however, paraded

1. Mary F. Berry, "Negro Troops in Blue and Gray: The Louisiana Native Guards, 1861–1863," *Louisiana History,* VIII (1967), 167; The quotation from the New Orleans *Daily Crescent* is found in Hollandsworth, *The Louisiana Native Guards,* 1–2.

proudly every year in the commemorative celebrations of the battle, receiving the applause of the crowd and reliving, at least for a moment, the experience of greater equality. Free people of color enlisting in the militia in 1861 hoped that their service would allow them to carve out a more secure niche in society. Captain Henry Louis Rey implied as much in a toast before the officers and staff of the Native Guards during the Christmas season of 1861 when he equated the creation of the Confederacy with the earlier American Revolution and toasted the present " 'revolution' and all revolutions—for they give birth to the progress of man and lead him on the way to true fraternity."[2]

Free people of color may also have been responding, as some members later claimed, to pressure from white New Orleanians and to what they regarded as implied threats of property confiscation and bodily harm if they failed to "volunteer." Officers later told Union general Benjamin Butler that they dared not refuse to serve. A private citizen also asserted in testimony that "it is known to all under what pressure of public opinion, under what threats uttered by the promoters of secession this was done."[3]

Whatever his exact motivation for serving, Cailloux was elected first lieutenant of Order Company in the new regiment. By early 1862, approximately one thousand free people of color had enlisted in the thirteen companies that composed the Native Guards Regiment. Free men of color made up the company officer corps, but in order to ensure ultimate white control, a white man, Félix Labatut, served as colonel commanding the regiment. The men of the unit purchased their own uniforms and arms.[4]

2. Hanger, *Bounded Lives,* 15, 152, 109–35; McConnell, "Louisiana's Black Military History," in Macdonald, Kemp, and Haas, *Louisiana's Black Heritage,* 32–46; Roland C. McConnell, *Negro Troops in Antebellum Louisiana: A History of the Battalion of Free Men of Color* (Baton Rouge, 1968); Kinzer, "The Band of Music of the First Battalion," 348–56; *L'Union,* October 15, 1862.

3. Testimony of General Benjamin F. Butler in "Report of the American Freedman's Inquiry Commission, May 15, 1864," in Elon A. Woodward (comp.), *The Negro in the Military Service of the United States, 1639–1886: A Compilation,* M-858, 2552, in Records of the Adjutant General's Office, 1780s–1917, Record Group 94 (hereafter, RG 94), NA; James M. McPherson, *Ordeal by Fire: The Civil War and Reconstruction* (New York, 1982), 350.

4. Compiled Service Records, Confederate Soldiers Who Served in Units from Louisiana, First Native Guards Militia, in Records of the Louisiana State Govern-

The Afro-Creole mutual aid societies, such as Cailloux's Friends of Order, formed the basis of the individual companies and lent their names to many of them. Hence the Order, Economy, and Perseverance companies reflected the names of their parent mutual aid societies; others, however, like the Savary Company (sponsored by the True Friends Society) took different names, in this case, that of one of the black captains who had commanded troops of the Battalion d'Orléans in 1812. The officers of the mutual aid societies, having already won the trust and respect of their men, were often also elected as officers of the companies. Thus president Charles Sentmanat served as captain of Order Company, while secretary Cailloux served as his first lieutenant. The muster roll of Order Company listed three officers, five noncommissioned officers, and sixty-one other enlisted men. The company, unlike some others, soon acquired a reputation for efficiency and discipline.

Most of the men of Order Company (designated Company C) lived as neighbors in a nine-by-twelve block area bounded by Great Mans, Annette, St. John the Baptist, and Arts streets in the vicinity of the hall of the Friends of Order, just downriver from the Vieux Carré in what had become the Third District. Cailloux worked in a shop in the neighborhood, bringing him into contact with the people there, but he was the only member of the company who lived across town. That the Friends of Order elected this "outsider" to office and then agreed to serve under him in the new military company testified to the high esteem that Cailloux enjoyed among them.[5]

The companies of the thousand-man-strong Louisiana Native

---

ment, 1850–88, War Department Collection of Confederate Records, Record Group 109 (hereafter, RG 109), NA; Morning Report, 1st Regt. Native Guards La. Militia, January 10, 1862, Compiled Service Records, RG 109, NA; I. Toussaint to M. Perault, January 29, 1862, Copybook, AANO. In addition to the Order Company, the regiment included the following companies: Beauregard, Crescent City, Economy, Labatut, Louisiana, Meschacebe, Mississippi, Native Guards, Perserverance (also called Company of Native Guards), Savary, Turcos, and Young Creole.

5. See S. Toussaint to T. L. B. Peaucrup, Esq., February 15, 1862, Copybook, AANO; Muster Roll of Order Native Guards, Muster and Pay Rolls, Box 208, Records of the Louisiana State Government, 1850–88, RG 109, NA. For election results of the Economy Guards, see the insert dated June 11, 1861 in Book 30, Spiritualist Registers, Grandjean Collection, UNO.

Guards busied themselves with drills and parades and participated in two large Confederate troop reviews, one on November 23, 1861, and another on January 7, 1862. The morning report of January 10, 1862, however, indicated increased absenteeism, reflecting declining morale as the government failed to provide arms or uniforms. "The number of absentees is large," the report read, "owing to the fact that many have not their uniforms." Many also did not have muskets and those who did supplied their own antiquated models. The government clearly wanted the Native Guard as a "show" regiment to reassure the white population and to discourage any thoughts of an alliance between free blacks and slaves, not as a fighting military unit.[6]

Nevertheless, the Native Guards inspired pride in the Afro-Creole community. Students at the Institute Catholique excitedly described the regiment's activities in some of the weekly English compositions they transcribed in their copybooks. They thrilled to the "grand reviews" and tagged along on Sundays when the companies of Guards marched and drilled for most of the day on the outskirts of the city or in the various city squares such as Congo and Washington. After following the Savary Guard around the city, one boy confessed that he "was so tired on Monday morning that [he] had a fever and did not go to school."

The adults in the community also took pride in the regiment. Women, known as "godmothers," presented silk flags to the individual companies, which then had them blessed by priests. At these benedictions, money was collected for donation to the Institute Catholique. Each company marked the anniversary day of its constituent mutual aid society with a celebration featuring a military review, a march to the parish church (probably nearby St. Vincent's for Cailloux and his men) for the blessing of the company standard, a high mass, and then a party with music, singing, dancing, and a lunch of confectionery cakes and punch.[7]

6. Morning Reports, November 23, 1861, and January 10, 1862, and undated notice of return of Colonel Labatut's Regiment of Native Guards, 1st Louisiana Native Guard, in Muster and Pay Rolls, Box 208; I. Toussaint to M. Perault, January 29, 1862; Hollandsworth, *The Louisiana Native Guards,* 7.
7. H. Relf to F. Bordenave, November 20, 1861, F. Richard to H. Relf, November 27, 1861, S. Toussaint to E. Lafargue, December 18, 1861, L. L. to F. Richard, December 19, 1861, E. Perault to J. Enagerrot, January 29, 1862, S. Toussaint to

The early months of the war, though, also revealed a darker side. The economic difficulties and uncertainties spawned by the beginning of the conflict had a negative impact on Cailloux and other free people of color. An air of anxiety and uncertainty pervaded the Afro-Creole community as the economy began to suffer the effects of decreased river traffic on the Mississippi and a federal blockade of the port. In that atmosphere, on September 13, 1861, six months after the attack on Fort Sumter, Cailloux sold his property on Baronne Street at auction to James P. Freret, a noted architect and the brother of a former mayor. The promissory note Cailloux owed to Parent, which fell due the following month, probably motivated the sale; Cailloux apparently did not have the cash needed to retire it or to meet the scheduled interest payment. Freret agreed to pay Cailloux a total of $1,070, or more than three times what Cailloux had originally paid for his property. Freret gave Cailloux $200 in cash and agreed to assume his outstanding $400 promissory note. Freret also signed his own promissory note to Cailloux for the remaining balance of $470, on which he agreed to pay 6 percent the first year and 8 percent each year thereafter until final payment. Cailloux thus obtained badly needed cash immediately and counted on more to come in the near future. (Freret paid off completely on August 19, 1864.) The Cailloux family most likely moved into the four-room house next door owned by Bastien and shared with his mother, but they could also have rented from Freret or from someone else. The 1860 census already showed Feliciana and Bastien, along with Alex Gonzale, an eighty-year-old native of St. Domingue, living in a household headed by André Cailloux, though the census taker may well have erred by failing to note the two separate properties of Cailloux and Bastien Encalada, the latter of whom retained ownership of his property until 1868.[8]

M. Perault, January 29, 1862, F. Bordenave to H. Isidore, Esq., January 30, 1862, F. Richard to Janus Wells, Esq., February 5, 1862, S. Toussaint to S. S. B. Peaucrup, February 5, 1862, E. Perault to F. Drahcir, February 19, 1862, all in Copybook, AANO; Séances of January 3, February 5, and March 1, 1862, all in Journal des Séances, AANO.

8. Sale of Property, André Cailloux to James P. Freret, September 13, 1860, Act 756, in Felix Grima, Vol. 27, NONA; Tax Assessment Records, 1861, with a notation dated 1864, in City Archives, NOPL; New Orleans City Directory, 1861, microfiche in Louisiana Collection, NOPL; Eighth Census of the United States, 1860,

Despite his economic reversals, Cailloux continued to enjoy the confidence of the men of his company. State officials, however, placed little trust in the Native Guards, limiting their Confederate military service to training and ceremonial duties. This lack of confidence in the ultimate loyalty of the Guards was exhibited when Union admiral David Farragut's warships ran dramatically past Forts Jackson and St. Philip seventy-five miles below New Orleans and anchored off the city's levee on April 26, 1862. Three days later, both forts surrendered, allowing Federal troops to occupy New Orleans. The Confederate commander, Major General Mansfield Lovell, ordered his troops to withdraw from the city, leaving the militia behind. Their commander, General John L. Lewis, then ordered the Native Guards to disband rather than maintain their units in the face of the occupation. The Guards followed orders, disposing of their uniforms and hiding their old muskets in Economy Hall, Claiborne Hall, and even in the Institute Catholique, whose principal, Armand Lanusse, commanded the Mescachebe company of the regiment. Federal troops under General Benjamin F. Butler, whom southerners soon dubbed "the beast," officially occupied the city on May 1, 1862, and initiated Butler's controversial administration.

In late July, following passage of the Confiscation and Militia Acts, which authorized President Lincoln to use contraband slaves to suppress the rebellion "in such manner as he may judge best" and to enroll blacks "for any military or naval service for which they may be found competent," several parties of free colored men consulted with Brigadier General J. W. Phelps, the commander of Fort Parapet in Carrollton, upriver from the city. They suggested to the abolitionist general from Vermont the raising of one or two regiments of free persons of color for "the defense of government and good order." Phelps, in the midst of an acrimonious dispute with General Butler over the latter's refusal to allow him to raise a black combat regiment from among the contrabands who were streaming into Fort Parapet, referred them back to Butler.

A committee composed of Captains Henry Louis Rey and Edgar Davis and Lieutenants Eugene Rapp and Octave Foy met with Butler and offered their services to the Federal cause. Butler, though im-

---

New Orleans, 840; Exchange, Bastien Enscolodo [sic] to Louis J. Frederick. November 23, 1868, COB 95-497, Orleans Parish Conveyance Office.

pressed by the apparent intelligence and sincerity of the Creole officers, initially demurred and asked them to explain why they had agreed to serve in the Confederate forces. One responded "Ah! we could not help it. If we had not volunteered, they would have forced us into the ranks, and we would have been suspected. We have property and rights here, and there is every reason why we should take care of ourselves." In response to a further query about loyalty to the Confederate government, the representative insisted that "there are not five men in the regiment fighting on the side of the Confederacy." The four men withdrew and discussed their options with their friends and comrades, then returned to Butler's headquarters on August 15 to affirm their loyalty to the Union. That affirmation could not have come at a better time for Butler, who was now inclined to accept the offer because of ominous military developments. Confederate general John C. Breckinridge's attack on Baton Rouge earlier in the month seemed to presage an assault on New Orleans, convincing Butler of the need to raise additional troops to defend the city.

Unable to secure an adequate number of recruits from among white Unionists in New Orleans or additional reinforcements from the War Department, Butler requested permission from Secretary of War Edwin M. Stanton to enlist the free people of color. Receiving no reply to his repeated appeals, he decided to "call on Africa" by issuing General Order 63 on August 22, 1862. In it, he urged free men of color who had served in the Louisiana militia to enlist in three new regiments, "subject to the approval of the president." By "reactivating" those who had already seen Confederate service, Butler hoped to defuse both rebel and Democratic objections to arming Negroes against whites.[9]

According to J. B. Roudanez, one of the Afro-Creole cofounders (along with his brother Dr. Louis Charles Roudanez) of the French-language newspaper *L'Union,* within forty-eight hours of the issuance of General Order 63 more than one hundred shops and businesses of free people of color closed as men rushed to enlist. General Butler recounted that within a fortnight, two thousand men showed up to enlist, "and not a man of them who had not a white 'boiled shirt' on." They no doubt did so from a number of motives, including patriotic and antislavery sentiments, promises of land (160 acres

9. Hollandsworth, *The Louisiana Native Guards,* 9–18.

each), bounties ($100, with $38 up front and the rest at the end of the war), promises of equal pay with white soldiers ($13 per month for enlisted men), and food rations (allowances) for their families. Some may also have mistakenly thought that the regiment would perform only guard duty around the city of New Orleans.[10]

Cailloux, like other respected members of the Afro-Creole community, raised a company of a hundred men for the new regiment and served as its captain, though this 1st Regiment represented a new organization, not simply a reincarnation of the older unit. Seventy percent of the officers of the Louisiana militia regiment chose not to answer Butler's call for the three new Union regiments. Only five of the 1st Regiment's black officers—Cailloux, Edgar Davis, Octave Foy, Alcide Lewis, and Charles Sentmanat—had served as such in the old Guards. Approximately 19 percent of the "Defenders of the Native Land" militia enlisted in the 1st Regiment, and another 14 percent joined other Union regiments during the war. An additional 18 percent of the men in the original regiment had the same surnames as individuals with different first names who enlisted in the 1st Regiment of Union Native Guards, suggesting the presence of younger relatives in the new unit. Perhaps some of the original members of the Confederate regiment, for economic, psychological, familial, or similar reasons, felt a residual loyalty to the state of Louisiana and decided not to join. The presence of many of the same surnames on muster rolls of both regiments, however, suggests other explanations. It seems that older and/or more cautious men, while willing to serve in the largely ceremonial Confederate home guard in the hopes of preserving or bettering their previously declining position in Louisiana's tripartite racial society, showed less willingness than their sons or nephews or younger men in general to join combat regiments that had a greater prospect of seeing action, especially at a

10. Benjamin F. Butler, *Butler's Book: A Review of his Legal, Political and Military Career* (Boston, 1892), 493; McConnell, "Louisiana's Black Military History," in Macdonald, Kemp, and Haas, *Louisiana's Black Heritage,* 47; Howard C. Westwood, *Black Troops, White Commanders, and Freedmen During the Civil War* (Carbondale, 1992), 43–44; Supplemental Report B of the American Freedman's Inquiry Commission of James McKaye, 1863, in Letters Received by the Adjutant General's Office, Box 1054, RG 94, NA; *L'Union,* October 25, 1862; Hollandsworth, *The Louisiana Native Guards,* 29; Deposition of J. Frank Trepagnier, March 2, 1893, in Pension File of J. Frank Trepagnier, RG 15, NA.

distance from New Orleans. Acutely aware of the hostility of the conquered white population toward their Union occupiers, many of the original members of the Native Guards may not have been willing to risk their futures by incurring the wrath of white southerners who would, undoubtedly, exact harsh retribution should the war turn out badly for the Union. Still, some older officers and enlisted men did throw in their lot with the new regiment.[11]

On September 27, 1862, about five days after Lincoln issued the preliminary Emancipation Proclamation that would take effect the following January, ten companies (approximately a thousand men) were mustered into the service as the 1st Louisiana Native Guard Infantry, the first officially sanctioned regiment of black soldiers in the Union army. As the new regiment formed, at least one of the dissolved companies of the old Native Guards donated the money that it had collected from its members to the Institute Catholique. Two other regiments of Native Guards (the 2nd and 3rd, composed largely of freedmen) were also organized shortly thereafter. Cailloux, commanding E Company (nicknamed the "Halleck's Guards" in honor of Henry W. Halleck, Lincoln's general-in-chief as of July 1862), was one of the 1st Regiment's nineteen black line, or company, officers. The field grade officers, including commanding colonel Spencer H. Stafford, a lawyer before the war who had served as

11. Muster Rolls of Order Native Guards, Muster and Pay Rolls, Box 208; Regimental Muster Roll, 1st Louisiana Native Guards Regiment, September 27, 1862, in ser. 57, Returns, Muster Rolls, and Other Papers (hereafter, Regimental Papers), 73rd United States Colored Infantry (hereafter, 73rd USCInf), United States Colored Troops (hereafter, USCT), and Miscellaneous Personal Papers, RG 94, NA; Hollandsworth, *The Louisiana Native Guards,* 25. (The 1st Regiment of the Louisiana Native Guards became the 1st Regiment of the Corps d'Afrique in June, 1863; in April, 1864, the War Department redesignated it the 73rd United States Colored Infantry.) The author compared the muster rolls of the Louisiana militia regiment, found on the homepage "Louisiana Native Guards" maintained by James G. Hollandsworth, and matched them against the Civil War Soldiers and Sailors System, RG 94, NA, online at http://www.itd.nps.gov/cgi-bin/dualz.test. Arthur W. Bergeron, Jr., in "Free Men of Color in Grey," *Civil War History* XXXII (1986), 247–55, summarizes the military service of fifteen free men of color from St. Landry Parish who volunteered for and served in Confederate units, fourteen of them in Louisiana and one in Texas. The author also compared the muster rolls of the Native Guards, C.S.A., furnished by James G. Hollandsworth on his Native Guards homepage, with the Civil War Soldiers and Sailors System, RG 94, NA, online at http://www.itd.nps.gov/cgi-bin/dualz.test.

an officer in the New York State militia (the 11th New York Zouaves) and as deputy provost marshal of New Orleans, were white. Free men of color constituted the company officer corps of the 2nd Regiment, and approximately half of the 3rd. The muster roll for Cailloux's company, dated September 27, 1862, listed 82 privates, 2 musicians, 8 corporals, 5 sergeants, and 3 officers, all black, for a total of 100 men.[12]

Most of the men in Cailloux's Company E lived in the Third District of the city—the home base for the Friends of Order and the neighborhood in which Cailloux worked. Their median age fell between twenty-nine and thirty, older than the median of twenty-four to twenty-six for Union recruits during the war but about the same as that of the other two Guards regiments. A majority had not served with Cailloux in the Order Company. Of the original 67 enlisted men and 3 officers of that older organization, 15 enlisted men joined Cailloux in Company E, 11 others followed Captain Sentmanat into

12. Berry, "Negro Troops in Blue and Gray," 176; Séance, December 1, 1862, Journal des Séances, AANO; attorney's license issued to Spencer H. Stafford by the State of New York, September 1, 1840, captain's commission to Spencer H. Stafford, October 24, 1845, in the 20th Regiment, New York State Militia, and newspaper clipping, n.d., but obviously 1862, all in Spencer H. Stafford Papers, Oneida County Historical Society, Utica, New York, and Service Record of Spencer H. Stafford, RG 94, NA; Muster Roll, Company E, September 27, 1862, in Regimental Papers, 73rd USCInf, USCT, RG 94, and Special Order 411, September 26, 1862, in ser. 1767, Special Orders, Department of the Gulf, Record Group 393: Records of the United States Army Continental Commands, 1821–1920 (hereafter, RG 393), Pt. I, both in NA. "Halleck Guards" is written on the recruitment papers of men of Company E. See, for example, the papers of François Dede, Edouard Francis, Edward George, Ursin François and Jean Germain in Miscellaneous Papers, USCT, RG 94, NA. Other companies bear names such as Butler Guards, Stafford Guards, and Lincoln Guards. The origins of the names remain a mystery. Nicknames for companies were common, but it is not clear whether the names of the companies of the 1st Regiment were chosen by men, their officers, or someone as high as General Butler. It is surprising that the nickname of Cailloux's company did not reflect its Creole culture, as had the Order Guards company in the old regiment. But the selection of the 1st Regiment's company nicknames, perhaps by Butler himself, may have been aimed at garnering support for the recruitment of black troops from the politicians so honored. Butler, other officers, or the men of each company may have selected the names of Republican politicians and Union generals as nicknames to emphasize their patriotism and loyalty to the Union. Free people of color, after all, followed national events closely and would have known the major political and military figures of the day.

the newly formed Company D, and 8 others joined different companies of the 1st Regiment. Five more enlisted in the other two Native Guards regiments. Thirty-nine of the original 67, therefore, joined one or another of the Native Guards units. During the course of the war, 9 more of the original members of Order Company served in other black regiments, bringing to 66 percent the percentage of Order Guards who saw some Union service, a far higher percentage than the 33 percent average for the entire original regiment and perhaps a testament to the élan and training of the company under Sentmanat and Cailloux. The surnames of 8 of the 27 who chose to remain civilians throughout the war appear on muster rolls of Native Guards or other Union regiments, probably indicating younger relatives.[13]

Cailloux's subalterns and noncommissioned officers had all enjoyed the status of free men before the war. First Lieutenant Paul Porée at thirty-five years old and 2nd Lieutenant Hippolyte St. Louis, at thirty-six or thirty-eight (depending on the record consulted) were relative contemporaries of Cailloux's. St. Louis was a literate carpenter, while Porée, a 5′10″ free-born mulatto, made his living as a carpenter and had a wife and four children. Most of the sergeants of the company lived in the general vicinity of Cailloux's cigar shop and the hall of the Friends of Order, and may have belonged to that society. François Dede, a black-complexioned, 5′8″, twenty-nine-year-old plasterer initially served as the first sergeant. The son of a former slave, François had been born and baptized as free and had served with Cailloux in Order Company. Noel Bacchus, who eventually replaced Dede as first sergeant, was a forty-two-year-old, literate, black-complexioned carpenter and former board member of the Institute Catholique. In 1860 he owned property assessed for taxes at $1,600, including a comfortable, if crowded, house, which he shared with his common-law wife, two children, and six other people. Anselmo Planciancios, the color sergeant who bore the regimental flag, was the second of the forty-year-old NCOs of the

13. Recruitment papers in Compiled Military Service Records, series 57, and Miscellaneous Personal Papers, USCT, RG 94; Berry, "Negro Troops in Blue and Gray," 175; Muster Rolls of Order Native Guards, Box 208, RG 109, Muster Roll of Company E, September 27, 1862, in ser. 57, Regimental Papers, 73rd USCInf, USCT, RG 94, NA. The author compared the names of the muster roll of the Order Guards with the online Civil War Soldiers and Sailors System of the National Archives.

company. Born of free parents and baptized at St. Louis Cathedral in 1822, the illiterate Planciancios, described as a mulatto, also lived downriver from the Vieux Carré, supported his wife and four children as a driver, owned no real estate, and, like many struggling Creoles of color, evidently took in boarders. Victor Urquhart, a free thirty-year-old cigar maker, also hailed from the same general neighborhood. Joseph Gros, a free twenty-six-year-old, was the youngest of the NCOs.[14]

The charismatic, thirty-eight-year-old Cailloux, eight years older than the average black company officer in the regiment (the youngest, second Lieutenant John Crowder, was sixteen!) proved a resourceful recruiter and one of the regiment's most effective officers. He signed his men's enlistment papers in a strong, steady hand, using the anglicized "Andrew" Cailloux. Polished in manners, bilingual, athletic, daring, a good horseman and boxer, he was, according to contemporaries, a born leader and "a fine looking man who presented an imposing appearance" that commanded attention. His poise, carriage, manners, and ease in white company worked to his advantage. Marion Southwood, a Confederate sympathizer who resided in New Orleans during the federal occupation, recalled Cailloux as a "large, good-looking Negro, dressed to death, *a la militaire*" astride "his fine horse, caparisoned ditto, who rode up and down the streets quietly, *showing off,* making the vulgar *stare,* and enticing the Negroes to go to war. He and his horse were in danger of melting in the hot summer sun, when the perspiration would roll off both of them."

A white New York newspaper correspondent exhibited a different attitude: "Captain Cailloux was . . . fine looking and in his military dress, had an imposing appearance. I remember seeing him at General Banks' headquarters in company with at least fifteen prominent military officers: and he was a marked personage among them all." Attributes of character rather than economic or social position accounted for his prominence. Cailloux's deportment, amiable disposition, and most importantly, his capacity as a soldier and as an officer, impressed his men, who admired him and followed him loyally.[15]

14. Author's database of compiled military records, pension records, sacramental records, tax ledgers and census returns for Paul Porée, Hippolyte St. Louis, Francois Dede, Noel Bacchus, Anselmo Planciancios, Victor Urquhart, and Joseph Gros; Séance, Sept. 4, 1853, in Journal de Séances, AANO.

15. See, for example, the enlistment papers of Alexandre Chaxchon (Box 29), Jean Duran (Box 56), Francis Esquiano (Box 60), and Charles Firmin (Box 64) in

According to abolitionist and historian William Wells Brown, some soldiers boasted that each of the line officers of the 1st Regiment owned at least $25,000 worth of property, a grossly inaccurate claim. Only two of the black officers of the regiment appeared on tax rolls for 1859–61: Captain Henry Rey of H Company, a clerk with $200 in taxable property, and Cailloux with $500. The only wealthy man among the officers of the 1st Louisiana Native Guards, Captain Francis E. Dumas of Company B, had recently returned from France and had inherited a sugar plantation and a large number of slaves. Dumas left the regiment, however, to accept a major's commission in the 3rd Regiment, thus becoming the first nonwhite field officer in the United States Army. In the process, he also freed his slaves and enlisted approximately one hundred of them into his regiment. Although he was not a rich man like Dumas, Cailloux's bearing and self-confidence evidently conveyed an air of authority that people associated with wealth.[16]

Cailloux's motives for volunteering and for raising a company are matters for speculation, since none of his letters survive. His familiarity with and connection to Creole radicals through business, community activities, and institutions such as the Institute Catholique, however, suggests that he shared the egalitarian ideals they propounded. A Union colonel later recalled, "It was the magnetic thrill of his patriotic utterances that rallied a company for the services of his country." Cailloux's subsequent actions, of course, indicated

Miscellaneous Personal Papers, USCT, RG 94, NA; Joseph Glatthaar, "The Civil War Through the Eyes of a Sixteen-Year-old Black Officer: The Letters of Lieutenant John H. Crowder of the 1st Louisiana Native Guards," *Louisiana History,* XXXV (1994), 201–16; *L'Union,* January 13, 1863; Manoj K. Joshi and Joseph P. Reidy, " 'To Come Forward and Aid in Putting Down this Unholy Rebellion': The Officers of Louisiana's Free Black Native Guard During the Civil War Era," *Southern Studies,* XXI (1982), 328–29; Berry, "Negro Troops in Blue and Gray," 175; Glatthaar, *Forged in Battle,* 124; Brown, *The Negro in the American Rebellion,* 168–69; Marcus Christian, "Captain André Cailloux," Part I, Louisiana Weekly, August 3, 1957, typescript copy in Box 17, Marcus Christian Collection; Marion Southwood, *Beauty and Booty: The Watchword of New Orleans* (New York, 1867), 210–11; quote from Christian, "Captain André Cailloux," Part I.

16. Brown, *The Negro in the American Rebellion,* 168–69; Henry Rey: David C. Rankin, "The Politics of Caste," in Macdonald, Kemp, and Haas, *Louisiana's Black Heritage,* 144; André Cailloux and Noel Bacchus: tax ledgers, 4th District, 1860, p. 596, and 3rd District, p. 376, in City Archives, NOPL; Joshi and Reidy, " 'To Come Forward and Aid in Putting Down this Unholy Rebellion,' " 336; Weaver, *Thank God My Regiment an African One,* 15.

substantial devotion to the cause of the Union, and especially to the destruction of slavery. He recruited and trained his company around the time that Lincoln signaled a coming change in the war's objectives by issuing the preliminary Emancipation Proclamation. And Cailloux probably hoped, like others in the Afro-Creole community, that the Union government would reward the demonstrated loyalty of free people of color with greater political and civil rights. Cailloux no doubt also saw an opportunity to achieve greater recognition and prominence, to demonstrate his manliness and courage, to exercise his talents as a commander, and to provide a living for his family in a depressed economy with his $60 per month officer's pay.

According to Southwood, by July 1862 people in New Orleans struggled to procure a sufficient supply of food. Flour, scarce to begin with, sold at the fabulous price of thirty dollars per barrel. Construction, commerce, and trade had ground to a halt. The once-bustling levee looked "as if it had been swept by a plague, such is its bare and deserted appearance" with "embryo crops of oats . . . springing through the wharves." Cailloux at least had the consolation of knowing that his monthly salary would afford his family a better income than most and that he had left his wife and younger children with his twenty-three-year-old eldest son, Jean Louis, a carpenter by trade who he hoped could provide additional help. Others, such as twelve-year-old Joseph Bouté, had far fewer resources on which to rely. When his father enlisted, Joseph went to work in a vegetable stand in St. Mary's market and then became a boot black to help support his mother. Lieutenant John Crowder told one woman that he had joined not only to serve his country but also to earn money to support his impoverished mother.[17]

17. Union colonel quoted in Mary Ellison, "African-American Music and Muskets in Civil War New Orleans," *Louisiana History,* XXXV (1994), 313; Ira Berlin, Joseph Reidy and Leslie S. Rowland, eds., *Freedom: A Documentary History of Emancipation, 1861–1867,* Ser. II, *The Black Military Experience* (Cambridge, 1982), 382; J. B. Roudanez before the American Freedman's Inquiry Commission, 1863, in Supplemental Report B of the American Freedman's Inquiry Commission in series 360, Letters Received by the Office of the Adjutant General, RG 94, NA; Affidavit of Joseph Bouté, June 13, 1884, in Pension File of Louis B. Bouté (alias Valcour Bouté), RG 15, NA; Southwood, *Beauty and Booty,* 60–61; Deposition of Maria Wilson, October 18, 1873, in Pension File of John Crowder, RG 15, NA. The colonel's observations need to be treated with caution, for he also described Cailloux as "of pure Negro blood," but whose "features showed the result of gener-

A majority of the men in Cailloux's company had been free before the war, though many runaway slaves also joined. An analysis of 98 names on the original muster roll, based on sacramental, service, and pension records, census data, and city directories, indicates that 58 were almost certainly free at the time of enlistment and 13 others probably so. Three were definitely slaves, while 4 others likely shared that status. Insufficient data exists for 26. Military records provide descriptions for 69 men of the company and show that they spanned the range of phenotypes from black (43), to griffe or colored (25), to mulatto (7), with the latter group probably underrepresented because records omitted the skin color of a number of free men who had belonged to the Order regiment. Cailloux's company was generally darker-hued than Captain Joseph Follin's Company C, the only company whose Regimental Descriptive Book has survived. Of the 95 men enrolled in that company, between August 28 and September 8, the Descriptive Book lists 26 as "fair," "bright," "yellow," or "light"; 34 as "brown," and 35 as "black." Of the 37 designated as laborers, only 7 were described as "light," "bright," or "yellow," suggesting that lighter-skinned free people of color may have had more opportunities to learn trades than darker-skinned people. Clearly, however, the composition of both Cailloux's and Folin's companies belied General Butler's claim to Secretary of War Stanton that the darkest member "will be about the complexion of the late Mr. [Daniel] Webster," or Treasury Agent George S. Denison's declaration to Secretary of the Treasury Salmon P. Chase that "Most of them [the regiment] are very light colored." Apparently to make the enlistment of men of African descent more politically palatable, they emphasized the presence of free, nearly white men such as J. Frank Trepagnier. He was the only son of F. B. Trepagnier of St. Charles Parish, a man whom the younger Trepagnier described as "a rank rebel and secessionist." His mother, a quadroon, had been a slave of the elder Trepagnier, but had been freed by him prior to young Frank's birth. Colonel Stafford boasted, perhaps with some exaggeration, that his regiment included the sons of a former governor and a former U.S. senator as well as of numerous other white officials of the state.[18]

---

ations of freedom and culture among his ancestry." Clearly, the colonel did not possess accurate knowledge about Cailloux's family ancestry.

18. Author database; Descriptive Book, Company C, in Regimental Books, 73rd USCInf, USCT, RG 94, NA; General Benjamin Butler to Hon. Edward M.

As for the occupations of members of Cailloux's company, artisans formed the largest group. Thirty-nine plied their trades in construction (12 plasterers, 11 carpenters, 10 bricklayers, 2 masons, 2 painters, 2 slaters). Twelve worked as cigar makers, 6 as shoemakers, and 1 as a cooper. Thirty laborers, 2 cabin boys, a teamster, a basket maker, a clerk, and a dining room servant rounded out the known occupations. Those figures mirrored statistics for the regiment as a whole. Prior to the war, 20 percent had made their livings as bricklayers, 15 percent as carpenters, 12 percent as cigar makers, 6 percent as shoemakers and 45 percent as laborers.[19]

Most of the men of Company E and of the 1st Regiment shared Cailloux's Catholicism. Colonel Stafford recognized this in December 1862 when he recommended that the appointed regimental chaplain, a Methodist circuit-riding preacher from Massachusetts named Asa Barnes, be promoted to major. Stafford explained, "As most of my men are French Catholics, we have no use for a Protestant chaplain." Certainly the men saw little of Barnes. One of them recalled years later that Barnes came around only "once every other month." Later in the war, even after desertions, casualties, transfers, enlistments, and inductees had diluted the Catholicity of the regiment, Barnes's successor, Presbyterian minister Samuel S. Gardner noted that, unlike some other black regiments with which he was acquainted, "Night exhortations in the open air are not held."[20]

*   *   *

Stanton, in Woodward (comp.), *The Negro in the Military Service,* 963, RG 94, NA; G. S. Denison to Salmon P. Chase, September 9 and 24, 1862, quoted in Benjamin Franklin Butler, *Private and Official Correspondence of General Benjamin Butler During the Period of the Civil War,* ed. Jessie Ames Marshall (5 vols.; Norwood, Mass., 1917), II, 270, 328; Depositions of J. Frank Trepagnier, March 2, 1893, and William S. Fitch, September 14, 1911, both in Pension File of J. Frank Trepagnier, RG 15, NA; James Franklin Fitts, "The Negro in Blue," *Galaxy,* III (1867): 249–55; quoted in Edmonds, *The Guns of Port Hudson,* I, 49.

19. Author's database; Berry, "Negro Troops in Blue and Gray," 175.

20. Colonel Spencer H. Stafford to Major George C. Strong, December 2, 1862, in Service Record of Asa Barnes, RG 94, NA; Deposition of Joseph Fille, May 6, 1905, in Pension File of Joseph Fille, RG 15, NA; Samuel S. Gardner to General Lorenzo Thomas, November 2, 1864, in Letters Received by the Adjutant General, RG 94, NA. Pension records of the 1st Regiment contain additional evidence of the Catholicism of the men, usually in the form of extracts from parish marriage registers.

Free people of color probably constituted a majority of the regiment when Butler initially authorized it. Major H. R. Perkins, who was with the regiment from its inception, estimated in 1863 that two-thirds of the original enlistees of the regiment had been "free colored men." Many slaves, however, both natives of New Orleans and refugees who had flocked to the city by the thousands after its capture by the Federals, enlisted as a means of escaping bondage. Sometimes using aliases to mask their true identities from masters who continued to search for them, on induction they swore to their status as legally free men. Hillaire Zenon of E Company, for example, recalled that he "was a slave before the war and until I enlisted. Many men in our regiment were slaves but all were put down as free men."[21]

Reports and complaints from white slave owners about slave enlistments led General Butler to issue a warning through his aide de camp to Colonel Stafford, insisting "that no man must be enlisted who has failed to obtain his freedom from some recognized legal channel." Recognized channels were manumission by the master and the application of the two Confiscation Acts passed by Congress providing freedom for captured or runaway slaves who had been used for military purposes or whose legal owners supported the rebellion. The order, however, had little effect, as seen in the recollections of Emile Chatard, a private in Company H, who later recalled that several times the officers had called the men of his company into formation to inquire about their status, and the fugitives always responded in the affirmative when asked if they had been free when they enlisted. Chatard could not remember a single man being discharged because he had not been free on enlistment. In September 1862, Denison accurately reported the situation to Secretary Chase, an avowed abolitionist. He noted that "nobody inquires whether the recruit is (or has been) a slave. As a consequence, the boldest and finest fugitives have enlisted, while the whole organization is known as the 'Free Colored Brigade.' " In a subsequent report, he acknowl-

21. Notation on Annual Return of the 1st Regiment for 1863, in ser. 57, Regimental Papers, 73rd USCInf, USCT, RG 94; Deposition B of Hillaire Zénon, June 9, 1911, in Pension File of Basil Ulgere, RG 15, NA. A. J. B. Merrill submitted to General Banks a descriptive list of twelve of his slaves who he claimed had enlisted in the 1st and 2nd Regiments. See A. J. B. Merrill to General Nathaniel Banks, May 29, 1863, ser. 1920, Letters Received, Bureau of Civil Affairs, Department of the Gulf, RG 393, Pt. 1, NA.

edged Butler's order, but, Denison wryly observed, that included those who had received freedom from their masters, contrabands freed by military courts and by General Butler's decree freeing all slaves belonging to French and British foreign nationals whose countries had outlawed slavery, and *all* [his emphasis] those slaves who came in from enemy lines. "You see," he noted, "this includes almost all colored people." Runaway slaves, ten thousand of whom lived in the city and its environs by late 1862, may have comprised a majority of Companies F, H, J, and K. Their muster rolls, in contrast to the Francophonic character of those of Companies A through E, contain many Anglophonic names, indicating African Americans who were more likely to have been slaves. George Case, First Lieutenant of F Company, noted that his men" are mostly contrabands."[22]

Cailloux apparently cooperated in the subterfuge of allowing slaves to enlist. He personally enrolled the members of his company and counted many as friends and acquaintances drawn from the tightly-knit Afro-Creole community. Louis Borée, for example, a thirty-year-old private and former cigar maker, had testified on Cailloux's behalf in the 1858 suit against Nuba. Therefore, Cailloux almost certainly recognized any who were not legally free, but did not balk at ignoring regulations by recruiting them, including some very young boys. For instance, he allowed fifteen-year-old Steven Myers, born a slave in Lathorn, Louisiana, to accompany the unit as a drummer boy even though he had not formally enlisted. Since the boy could not legally draw pay or rations, Cailloux permitted the young-

22. William H. Weigel, 1st Lt. and ADC to Colonel Stafford, in Woodward, comp., *The Negro in the Military Service*, 969, RG 94; Deposition of Julius S. Duvernay, August 18, 1911, in Pension File of Julius Sylvester Duvernay (alias Julius Sylvester), Veteran's Administration, Suitland, Maryland; Deposition of Basil Ulgere, June 3, 1911, and Deposition of Emile Chatard, February 21, 1906, in Pension File of Wallée Ralney (alias Valsin Lemaître), RG 15, NA; G. S. Denison to Salmon P. Chase, September 9 and 24, 1862, in Butler, *Private and Official Correspondence*, II, 270, 328; John D. Winters, *The Civil War in Louisiana* (Baton Rouge, 1963), 129; Muster Rolls for Companies F, H, J, K, September, 1862, in ser. 57, Regimental Papers, 73rd USCInf, USCT, RG 94, NA; Depositions of Laura Enols, January 8 and July 6, 1909 in Pension File of Noble Enols, RG 15, NA; Glenn R. Conrad and Ray F. Lucas, *White Gold: A Brief History of the Louisiana Sugar Industry, 1795–1995* (Lafayette, La., 1995), 33; Berlin, Reidy, and Rowland, *Freedom*, Series II, 529.

ster to collect food from the soldiers and from surplus left over after meals.[23]

In his person, Cailloux appears to have reconciled both slave and free, black and mulatto. His experience indicates that the boundary between slaves and free people of color was far more permeable than some historians have suggested and that the cauldron of war further reduced barriers between slave and free and American and Creole blacks.[24] So long as equality with whites did not exist as an option, many free people of color found it in their interest to maintain social distance between themselves and slaves in an attempt to protect their unique, if tenuous position in the tripartite racial caste system and to avoid sinking to the level of slaves in the eyes of whites. The radical, universalist vision of antebellum Afro-Creole activists, combined with the Union occupation of New Orleans, the issuance of the pre-liminary Emancipation Proclamation, and the continuing abrasion of war, however, raised for blacks in general the possibility of greater equality with whites and thus encouraged increased cooperation among them in pursuit of a common goal. In December 1862, Afro-Creoles created a Comité Central des Natifs, or Freedmen's Aid As-sociation, that eventually offered premiums for the best crops and set up an employment bureau that guaranteed "fair wages" and "work among friends" to contrabands. The absence of ethnic or color con-flict within the 1st Regiment contrasted with the divisions between

23. Berry, "Negro Troops in Blue and Gray," 175; Depositions of Hillaire Zénon, June 9, 1911, and Basil Ulgere, June 3, 1911, and extract from SLC Bk. 4, March 13, 1841, all in Pension File of Basil Ulgere, RG 15, NA, Affidavit of Steven Myers, June 5, 1900, in Pension File of Steven Meyers, and Deposition of Stephen Meyers, February 29, 1908, in Pension File of Frederick Clayman, both in RG 15, NA.

24. For examples of historians who emphasize the racial, social, and class distinc-tions that separated free people of color from slaves, see Donald C. Everett, "De-mands of the New Orleans Free Colored Population for Political Equality, 1862–1865," *Louisiana Historical Quarterly*, XXXVIII (1955), 43–64; Mills, *The Forgotten People;* Rankin, "The Politics of Caste," in Macdonald, Kemp, and Haas, *Louisiana's Black Heritage,* "The Impact of the Civil War on the Free Colored Community of New Orleans," and the introduction to Jean-Charles Houzeau, *My Passage at the "New Orleans Tribune": A Memoir of the Civil War Era,* ed. David C. Rankin, trans. Gerard F. Denault (Baton Rouge, 1984), 1–67; Reinders, "The Decline of the New Orleans Free Negro" and "The Free Negro in the New Orleans Economy"; Sterkx, *The Free Negro in Antebellum Louisiana,* 247–48; and Whitten, *Andrew Durnford.*

light and dark-skinned imposed by the Spanish on the earlier colonial militia. In a letter published in *L'Union* in October and aimed at whites who had predicted friction between them, Captain Henry L. Rey had celebrated the solidarity by bragging, "In parade you will see a thousand white bayonets gleaming in the sun held by black, yellow or white hands. Be informed that we have no prejudice; that we receive everyone in the camp; but that the sight of human salesmen of flesh makes us sick."[25] A common agenda of liberation grew among the ranks and held out the promise of even greater cooperation on the political level between free people of color and freedmen in the struggle for equality.

A teenage student at the Institute Catholique expressed the growing hopes for equality in a letter penned in his copybook in November 1862. Implicitly recognizing the revolutionary changes promised by the war, L. Lamanière wrote that he was

> very glad since the Federals are here, they are telling that General Butler is going to make the colored men of this city who were born free vote, if he do that the colored men will be very glad to see equality reign here and if he is ever to be elected President of the United States, I am sure that he will be President because the colored man will vote for him, and I must tell you another thing. The creoles of this city will die when they see the Negroes vote as well as them, those Negroes whom they were always whipping in the plantations take their tickets and put it in the [ballot] box.[26]

Young Lamanière had come to interpret the war, at least unconsciously, as a struggle for emancipation and equality. Afro-Creole

25. *L'Union*, October 18, 1862; Geraldine M. McTigue, "Forms of Racial Interaction in Louisiana, 1860–1880," (Ph.D. dissertation, Yale University, 1975), 23; *L'Union* (English version), April 9, 1864; quoted in Logsdon and Bell, "The Americanization of Black New Orleans," in Hirsch and Logsdon, *Creole New Orleans*, 220–21.

26. L. Lamaniere to E. Brunet, Esq., November 26, 1862, in Copybook, AANO. Lamaniere's reference to Creoles fleeing to Havana where they "are dieing like flies" and "the negroes of that country are cursing them" indicates that the term "Creoles" in this context meant white Creoles. For corroboration, see a letter from Rev. Étienne Rousselon to Archbishop Jean-Marie Odin, October 15, 1862, in VI-2-f, ANOC. Rousselon describes the flight of white Creoles to Havana.

intellectual-activists associated with *L'Union,* such as the Roudanez brothers (Louis Roudanez was the paper's chief financial backer) and Paul Trévigne, its editor in chief and a language instructor at the Institute Catholique, had founded the paper in the same month that the 1st Regiment entered Federal service. Steeped in French intellectual and political radicalism, they viewed black participation in the war as a vehicle both for abolishing slavery and for obtaining equal civil and political rights. They were joined in their efforts by other supporters of the paper, including Blanc F. Joubert, John Racquet Clay, Joseph Tinchant, and Francis Dumas. One of the editorials neatly captured their thinking when it declared, "From the day that bayonets were placed in the hands of the blacks . . . the Negro became a citizen of the United States." In September 1862, free black leaders began to hold "Union meetings," which further enraged already embittered white conservatives.[27]

The 1st Regiment excited the interest, loyalty, and support of free people of color of the city, who viewed it as uniquely their own. They flocked to Camp Strong Station on Gentilly Road, to the site of the racetrack about four miles from the center of the city, to view daily drill and dress parades. While there, they heard the men sing the popular military song, "En Avant Grenadiers," which Creole troops had sung at the Battle of New Orleans, and also lighter marches such as "Free Market" and "New Orleans Song of the Times." Major Chauncey J. Bassett, a former captain in the 6th Michigan Infantry and a dedicated abolitionist, directed the regiment in these endeavors because Butler had given Stafford overall command of all the Native Guards while they trained. Although the maneuvers made the army seem glamorous, a student at the Institute Catholique noted the dark side of camp life: the rampant fevers, the monotonous food, and the military discipline that circumscribed personal freedom and that punished deserters. In October 1862, he wrote that a soldier's life was "not as good as I thought." He now believed it to be "a very bad thing and I would not like to be a soldier." Buoyed by community support and fired by a worthy cause, though, most

27. *L'Union,* January 13, 1863; Bell, *Revolution, Romanticism, and the Afro-Creole Protest,* 223–37, 240–48, 246; Houzeau, *My Passage at the New Orleans Tribune,* 5–11, 18–19.

young Afro-Creole men did not agree with him. They constituted a substantial percentage of the 3,000 men under arms in the Native Guards at a time when, according to the 1860 census, the number of free men of color in Orleans Parish between the ages of 15 and 59 stood at 2,578. In other words, an overwhelming number of eligible male Creoles of color enlisted, at far higher rates than in most white communities.[28]

While colored troops inspired excitement among Afro-Creoles, their presence triggered a far different reaction among white New Orleanians. Even before Butler formally authorized the formation of the Native Guards regiments, the New Orleans *Daily Picayune* had predicted failure, because of the Negro's unfitness for military service arising from his "innate inferiority, natural dullness and cowardice, indolence, awe of the white man and lack of motivation. The vast majority of Negroes," the paper declared, "are contented with their

TABLE 4

Free Colored Males in Orleans Parish by Age Cohort, 1860

15–19	480
20–29	752
30–39	581
40–49	525
50–59	240
Total	2,578

SOURCE: Census Data for the Year 1860, United States Historical Census Data Browser

28. Ellison, "African-American Music and Muskets," 309–10; Lucien Lamaniere to J. H. Sauvage, Esq., October 24, 1862, E. Perault to H. Relf, Esq., October 22, 1862, both in Copybook, AANO; Chauncey J. Bassett to Brigadier General G. S. Andrews, July 31, 1863, and official documentation of service, both in Service Record of Chauncey J. Bassett, RG 94, NA; Hollandsworth, *The Louisiana Native Guards,* 25; Berry, "Negro Troops in Blue and Gray," 167. During the course of the war, Louisiana furnished the single largest number of black soldiers to the Union Army of any state: approximately 24,052, or 31 percent of the black males between eighteen and forty-five years-old. See Berlin, Reidy, and Rowland, *Freedom,* Series II, 12–14; Census Data for the Year 1860, United States Historical Census Data Browser made available by the Interuniversity Consortium for Political and Social Research (IPSCR) at http://icg.fas.harvard.edu/~census/.

TABLE 5

Free People of Color in New Orleans, 1860

Free Males of Color	4,583
Free Females of Color	6,356
Total of Free Persons of Color	10,939

SOURCE: Census Data for the Year 1860, United States Historical Census Data Browser

situation." An English visitor to the city recalled the scowling line of white faces that lined Canal Street on a Saturday afternoon and watched as the 1st Regiment, led by Colonel Stafford and a band playing "Yankee Doodle," marched the length of the avenue. Cailloux's rank, striking martial appearance, and effectiveness as a recruiter represented a threat to the southern racial hierarchy. Alarmed and irritated, Southwood characterized him as a kind of vulgar Svengali, leering at women and enticing blacks to join the army. The very sight of black Union troops enraged many New Orleanians and they flooded Union headquarters with complaints. According to one lieutenant in the regiment, "When we enlisted we were hooted at in the streets of New Orleans as rabble." In her diary, Julia Legrand, a white resident of New Orleans, accused black soldiers of the 1st Regiment of "impudence to white people" and of depredations in the countryside such as stealing chickens, horses, and cattle, breaking into houses, and arson. She referred contemptuously to Colonel Stafford as "this creature" who commanded "Negroes armed and equipped, wearing the leather belt which other soldiers wear, having the letters U.S. in brass upon it." She lamented the once-honored "Stars and Stripes . . . borne by such hands" but, expressing a widely held belief, declared that she had "no fear of them, at least as soldiers. They will fly at the first fire."[29]

According to Stafford, whites went out of their way to insult and provoke his men. Police in the city arrested soldiers without cause

29. New Orleans *Daily Picayune*, July 30, 1862; W. C. Corsan, *Two Months in the Confederate States: An Englishman's Travels through the South*, ed. Benjamin H. Trask (Baton Rouge, 1996), 21; Southwood, *Beauty and Booty*, 210–11; *National Antislavery Standard*, November 29, 1862; Kate Mason Rowland and Mrs. Morris L. Croxall, eds., *The Journal of Julia LeGrand* (Richmond, 1911), 167–68.

on the slightest pretense, thereby provoking breaches of the peace. Segregated streetcars also proved particular flash points between black troops and citizens. Cars were marked by large black stars designating those reserved for blacks. Shortly after the Federal occupation of the city, General Butler, at the request of a delegation of free people of color, ordered the desegregation of the omnibus lines. The car companies, however, succeeded in having a local court set aside the order. Soldiers bridled at having to wait for "star cars" when other half-filled cars passed by them. Colonel Stafford attempted unsuccessfully to convince the railroad companies to add more star cars. In September and October, members of the Native Guards, displaying a new militancy born of their blue uniforms, defied the ordinances and boarded street cars designated for whites only. In one case, several troops punched the driver when he ordered them off. In another, a soldier pulled a pistol and threatened to shoot the driver. A compromise agreement finally provided that black officers could ride on all streetcars, but black enlisted men would still have to ride the star cars. Afro-Creole activists would revisit the issue again in 1864, but meanwhile concentrated their fire against slavery. White New Orleanians saw no compromise in the streetcar decision—only growing black "insolence" and danger from black soldiers.[30]

In this racially tense situation, the families of black soldiers proved particularly vulnerable. Rations, which the government had promised to distribute to their families through relief committees, proved substandard and sporadic. Since the government failed to deliver on Butler's pledge of a $100 bonus and a monthly wage of $13, and since it had, up to that point, not paid the men anything at all, families faced harassment and eviction by white landlords. Slave owners also denied soldiers access to their slave wives and children.[31]

The case of Auguste Perrauld, a private in Company B, illustrates the straits in which families found themselves. Perrauld's mother,

30. Roger A. Fischer, *The Segregation Struggle in Louisiana, 1862–1877* (Champagne, 1974), 13, 30–31; Hollandsworth, *The Louisiana Native Guards,* 31–32; New Orleans *Tribune,* January 13, 1865.
31. Spencer H. Stafford to Captain Wickham Hoffman, Asst. Adj. General, February 23, 1863, Stafford to General Benjamin Butler, October 14, 1862, Stafford to Major George L. Strong, A. A. General, October 23, 1862, all in ser. 1756, Letters Received, Department of the Gulf, RG 393, Pt. 1, NA.

who was married to a free man of color in New Orleans, was owned by Oscar Perrauld, living in the adjacent parish of St. Bernard, down-river from the city. For many years her owner had permitted her to hire her time and live in the city with her husband. Once her son entered the service, however, Oscar Perrauld showed his indignation by having the woman arrested and put in the police jail. Private Auguste Perrauld took his case to Colonel Stafford who, on October 14, 1862, requested an order for her release from General Butler. The General referred the matter to the provost marshall, who was to conduct an inquiry and discharge the woman if the inquiry showed her innocent of wrongdoing.[32]

A little more than a week later, in a letter to Major George L. Strong, the assistant adjutant general of the Department of the Gulf, Stafford officially complained about the harassment suffered by the families of his men. Failure of the government to pay the troops, he claimed, increased the vulnerability of their families. He therefore requested publication of an order forbidding landlords to meddle with those families at least until after the men had received their first pay. Stafford also respectfully called attention to his previous communication about the mistreatment of the slave wives of soldiers. Stafford's importuning produced some results. Butler issued a sharply worded letter declaring that "my colored soldiers . . . are to be protected from the insults of all persons" and promising to mete out punishment via a military commission "to the party found . . . to be in the wrong." On November 6, 1862, Butler ordered suspension of all court processes involving the eviction of families of Union soldiers because of past-due rent. Butler's edict quoted a similar non-eviction order for the families of Confederate troops issued in New Orleans in March 1862 and, with obvious relish and irony, simply applied the measure to the families of Union servicemen. On November 1, 1862, he also issued General Order 88, which forbade policemen or other persons to arrest or hold in confinement for safe-keeping any Negro unless the arresting person knew that such a person belonged to a loyal citizen of the United States. The War Department, however, turned a deaf ear to Stafford's pleas for the promised bounty and advance pay. The paymaster, who held the reg-

32. Stafford to Butler, October 14, 1862 (with endorsement).

ular pay due to the men, added insult to injury by refusing to release it.[33]

Cailloux and the men of the regiment also had to endure the blatant hostility of many Union troops, especially white officers and regulars, who opposed the very concept of black troops and especially of black officers. Groups of white soldiers frequently accosted black troops on Canal Street in the city. Staff officers who opposed the use of black troops threw impediments in the way of procuring supplies and equipment. When the regiment marched from the Touro Building to Camp Strong after its initial muster, the men wore belts and knapsacks that other re-equipped units had discarded. In Stafford's words, "altogether it was the most indifferently supplied regiment that ever went into service." Once in the field, supply officers ignored requisitions for wagons, mules, ammunition, and wooden flooring for tents, claiming that they had none while furnishing other units with those same things. And always, the lack of pay and the vulnerability of their families back home weighed on the minds of Cailloux and his men.[34]

The vulnerability of their families extended even to church, where in some cases priests, who shared the general antipathy of the white population toward the enlistment of black troops, explicitly manifested their opposition to relatives of black troops. A notable exception, however, was Claude Paschal Maistre, an enigmatic French priest who attended to the spiritual needs of the men of the Native Guards regiments and of their families. At considerable personal risk, Maistre daringly identified himself with the black troops, emancipation, and equal rights.

33. Stafford to Strong, October 23, 1862; General Order 88, November 1, 1862, in ser. 1763, General Orders, Stafford to Lt. Col. R. B. Irwin, January 4, 1863, in ser. 1756, Letters Received, Department of the Gulf, RG 393, Pt. 1, NA.
34. Butler, *Butler's Book*, 94; Stafford to Hoffman, February 23, 1863.

4

ABOLITIONIST PRIEST

As André Cailloux and the rest of the Louisiana Native Guards moved into the field, the Reverend Claude Paschal Maistre, a maverick visionary with a somewhat checkered past, waged his own lonely and personally risky battle on their behalf in New Orleans. Maistre, who ministered to the men of the newly formed Native Guards Regiments while they trained at Camp Strong, became the only Catholic cleric in New Orleans to publicly advocate abolition and equal rights for blacks. In doing so, he incurred the wrath of white clergy and laity and eventually aroused the ire of Archbishop Jean-Marie Odin. At the same time, he won the admiration and support of many freedmen and free people of color and allied himself not only with black troops, but also with the Afro-Creole activists associated with *L'Union*.

Maistre had been born on January 7, 1820, one of several sons of Claude Maistre and Anne Simonnot, who owned a farm in Laubressel in the Department of Aubé, France. Ordained on September 21, 1844, by Bishop John Mary Matthew Débélay of the Diocese of Troyes, he took up his first assignment ten days later in Thil, where he served during the revolutionary upheaval of 1848. At the end of that year, the bishop transferred him to Thuisy. There, he ran afoul of the law in a case involving money (the specifics are unclear) and resigned his post on June 1, 1849. He traveled first to England, where he secured both Belgian and French passports, and then to Belgium, where he spent five months with the Redemptorist community at St. Trond, whose superior praised his "piety and exemplary conduct." In April 1850 he departed for the United States, carrying an exeat, or letter, from his bishop, Pierre Louis-Coeur of Troyes, certifying him as a priest in good standing and asking rectors of parishes and other superiors to receive him favorably and to give him permission to exercise his priestly functions. Maistre's passports describe him as standing 5'5" with chestnut hair and beard, gray eyes, a round chin, and a strong, thick, "average French nose."[1]

Once in the United States, Maistre moved from place to place, often trailing the scent of scandal. He became an assistant at St. Anne's Parish in Detroit, but the bishop dismissed him because of accusations involving sexual immorality—accusations that at least one other bishop later characterized as "doubtful." Upon leaving Detroit, he visited Cincinnati, staying with Father Edward Purcell—who would later, as editor of the diocesan newspaper, become an advocate of emancipation during the Civil War. Purcell seemed genuinely impressed by Maistre, who hoped to obtain a mission in a French-speaking congregation. He regretted that no such vacancy existed in the Cincinnati diocese, but he enthusiastically recommended Maistre to Archbishop Antoine Blanc of New Orleans. Bishop James Oliver Van de Velde, meanwhile, accepted Maistre into the Chicago diocese in 1851 and appointed him pastor of Holy Family Parish in French Village near Cahokia, in southwestern Illinois. There, in 1852, the parents of a young girl accused Maistre of sexual improprieties. Van de Velde conducted a juridical examination and found "nothing positive," but on September 17, 1853, he transferred Maistre to Bourbannais Grove in Kankakee County, south of Chicago, to be pastor of Maternity of the Blessed Virgin Mary Church, where he remained until November 3, 1854.[2]

1. Copy of Will by Claude Paschal Maistre, January 10, 1855, originally executed in 1850 and amended February 6, 1854, V-l-i, ANOC; Information from the Archives Départmentales, Department de l'Aubé, France, furnished by Xavier de la Selle in a letter to the author, October 28, 1994; Bishop John Mary Matthew Débélay, September 21, 1844, Certificate of Ordination for Claude Paschal Maistre and Grant of Faculties to Maistre, October 1, 1844, V-5-b, Bishop Pierre-Louis Coeur, Exeat to Maistre, June 1, 1849, V-5-k, Father P. Reyners, C.C.C.R., December 6, 1849, V-5-l, French passport issued by N. Boisselier, French Consul, to Father Claude Pascal Maître-Simonnot, London, June 26, 1849, Belgian passport issued to Father Claude Pascal Maître-Simonnot, June 29, 1849, V-5-K, ANOC. A search of French archives failed to uncover the specific charges against Maistre.

2. *Metropolitan Catholic Almanac and Laity Directory,* 1851 (Baltimore, 1851), 85; Bishop James Oliver Van de Velde to Archbishop Antoine Blanc, November 6, 1855, V-l-i, Edward Purcell to Antoine Blanc, August 25, 1851, V-l-b, ANOC.

Maistre's perceived "excessive love of money" and other irregularities associated with his ministry led to problems with Bishop Anthony O'Regan, who succeeded Van de Velde in 1853. O'Regan sent Maistre to St. Louis Parish, a French Canadian congregation in Chicago. There, in 1855, allegations of financial chicanery (misappropriating parish funds for his personal benefit), indifferentism (baptizing and blessing the marriages of all who presented themselves regardless of denomination), and simony (blessing the burials of suicides and of Protestants for a fee and charging for the sacrament of Extreme Unction) surfaced. Maistre's supposed willingness to bless marriages and burials irrespective of religious affiliation may have reflected greed on his part. After all, many nineteenth-century priests in the United States operated as solitary figures, at odds with authority, lonely, overworked, and insecure about their financial situations. But the alleged actions may also have suggested Maistre's embrace of a more tolerant strain of Catholicism somewhat reminiscent of that of Antonio de Sedella, but shaped by such contemporary liberal Catholic thinkers as Félicité Robert de Lamennais, Charles Montalambert, Jean Baptiste Henri Lacordaire, and Félix-Antoine-Philibert Dupanloup. Those thinkers, who emphasized the compatibility between Catholicism and political liberty and democracy, applauded the separation of church and state, and embraced, at least initially, the egalitarian spirit of the Revolution of 1848, influenced many young French priests and seminarians during Maistre's formative years. Whatever Maistre's actual behavior and motivation, O'Regan, perhaps also reflecting some of the Irish-French tension within the American church, denounced the priest, deprived him of his canonical authorization, and cast him loose to find a bishop who would accept him into a diocese. In his distress at finding himself once more adrift, Maistre at least did not lack financial resources. By the time he left Chicago, he had acquired enough money to loan John Flageole of Bourbannais Grove $4,150 at 10 percent interest for six months. He had also loaned $300 to Toussaint Menard of Chicago on the same conditions, and he owned a small house in Bourbannais worth between $300 and $400.[3]

3. *Metropolitan Catholic Almanac and Laity Directory,* 1852 (Baltimore, 1852), 137; *Ibid.,* 1853, 109; *Ibid.,* 1854, 152–53; *Ibid.,* 1855, 167; *Diamond Jubilee of the Archdiocese of Chicago; Antecedents and Developments* (Chicago, 1920), 255, copy in the Archives of the Archdiocese of Chicago; Alec R. Vidler, *The Church in an Age of Revolution: 1789 to the Present Day* (Harmondsworth, England, 1971),

Maistre traveled to Indiana, but his past dogged him. He impressed Father Edward Sorin, C.S.C., the founder of the University of Notre Dame and the superior of the Congregation of the Holy Cross, who evidently recommended that he stay with Fr. Julian Benoit in Fort Wayne, Indiana, for a trial period. Maistre spent two months with Benoit and the latter secured canonical faculties for him. Then, Maurice de St. Palais, the bishop of Vincennes, made a personal visit. Having recently spoken with O'Regan about Maistre, St. Palais decided against extending Maistre's faculties in his diocese. Fearful of becoming a clerical pariah, Maistre turned to his old patron, Van de Velde, who had become the bishop of Natchez, Mississippi.

Van de Velde initially responded positively to Maistre's entreaties. After all, Maistre still possessed a valid exeat from O'Regan. Besides, Van de Velde, who needed priests for his diocese, knew Maistre and believed that he had shown repentance after his banishment by O'Regan. Van de Velde, therefore, decided to gamble on Maistre and assigned him to Pascagoula, on the Mississippi Gulf Coast, in return for Maistre's promise to make a spiritual retreat of prayer and meditation for several months with the Trappist monks at Gethsemane Monastery in Kentucky. A baggage mix-up, however, supposedly delayed Maistre's departure for Gethsemane. Maistre claimed that on boarding the steamer for Louisville, he realized that boat hands had mistakenly put his baggage aboard a vessel bound for New Orleans. He thereupon decided to follow his baggage to Natchez to retrieve it, and appeared on Van de Velde's doorstep. Van de Velde accepted Maistre's somewhat implausible story on its face and made new arrangements with the monks in Kentucky. Maistre agreed to start out again. But once more he had to delay his departure for several days, this time because of a change in the boat's schedule.

Maistre's appearance in Natchez and his apparent reluctance to go to Kentucky for retreat made Van de Velde suspicious about the

68–78. Vol. V of Owen Chadwick, *The Pelican History of the Church*, 6 vols.; Peter N. Steans, *Priest and Revolutionary: Lamennais and the Dilemma of French Catholicism* (New York, 1967), 82–83, 94, 104–105; Adrien Dansette, *Religious History of Modern France: From the Revolution to the Third Republic* (2 vols.; Edinburgh-London), I, 218–58; Bishop Anthony O'Regan to Blanc, June 6, 1855, Bishop James Oliver Van de Velde to Blanc, October 23, 1855, Will of Father Claude Paschal Maistre, January 10, 1855, VI-l-i in ANOC.

depth of his contrition and gave the bishop second thoughts about using him. Van de Velde seems to have suggested that Maistre travel to see Archbishop Blanc about the possibilities of working in the archdiocese of New Orleans. The French-born Blanc needed clergy and was in the process of strengthening the institutional framework of his archdiocese through the recruitment of women religious and priests (until 1869 the New Orleans Catholic clergy included only one American-born member) and through the establishment of parishes and educational and charitable institutions. In a letter, Van de Velde asked Blanc if he would be willing to employ Maistre. If he were, Van de Velde suggested that the archbishop "test" Maistre by requiring him to make a retreat of several weeks with the Redemptorist fathers or another group. Van de Velde described Maistre as possessing a good disposition but suffering from the same "sickness" as one of Blanc's acquaintances: "the mania to make money." Van de Velde reiterated his own willingness to accept Maistre and send him to Pascagoula as long as he would agree to spend two months in spiritual exercises with the Redemptorist priests and give them satisfaction as to his spiritual state. Maistre, though, apparently continued to show little enthusiasm for such a retreat.[4]

The whole episode evidently made Blanc uneasy and led him to solicit more background information on Maistre. In a letter dated November 6, 1855, Van de Velde responded by reviewing Maistre's troubled past. He repeated his opinion that the most serious charge was Maistre's inordinate love of "amassing money." Van de Velde acknowledged that Maistre's coming down to Natchez instead of going to Kentucky had raised some doubts, but he expressed confidence that Blanc himself could best judge whether he could use the priest. Father Benoit also weighed in with a letter to Blanc, observing that while Maistre had "behaved well" while staying with him in Fort Wayne, Benoit had noticed "an excessive love of money and a negligence of the functions of the ministry which made one suspect his faith." He courteously advised Blanc to "observe" Maistre and speculated, "Perhaps his past falls will serve as a lesson." In his need of clergy, Blanc took their advice and assigned Maistre a trial period,

4. Baudier, *The Catholic Church in Louisiana,* 402; Logsdon and Bell, "The Americanization of Black New Orleans, in Hirsch and Logsdon, *Creole New Orleans,* 233; Van de Velde to Blanc, October 23, 30, 1855.

sending him in late 1855 to assist Fr. Ennemond Dupuy at St. Gabriel Church in rural Iberville Parish, Louisiana, about fifty-five miles upriver from New Orleans.[5]

Very soon after Maistre's arrival, however, Dupuy, who served a number of outlying rural chapels from his headquarters at St. Gabriel, informed Blanc that he had little regard or use for Maistre. He claimed that Maistre, immediately upon his arrival and before meeting Dupuy, had looked over Dupuy's house, inquired of others about the revenue of St. Gabriel, and decided to seek room and board near St. Raphael Chapel because it had better income. In a letter to Blanc in early January, Dupuy called Maistre a "false person" and accused him of fomenting strife between two boys who lived in his household. More seriously, the slaveholding Dupuy characterized Maistre as "an abolitionist in his ideas and language," indicating, perhaps, the influence on Maistre of action taken by the French Second Republic in 1848 in emancipating all slaves in the empire and forbidding French citizens, at home or abroad, from possessing, buying, or selling them, a decree enforced strictly even after Louis Napoleon replaced the Republic with the Second Empire. Then too, the condemnation of slavery in 1853 by French bishops gathered at the provincial council of Bordeaux may also have helped to mold Maistre's views.[6]

Open advocacy of abolition in the South, of course, would have proven both unpopular and dangerous. In July 1840, for example, Étienne Rousselon, Blanc's vicar general, implored the Society for the Propagation of the Faith in Lyon, France, which regularly sent money to support the church in Louisiana, to refrain from touching on the question of slavery in its publication, *Annals*. "With this question . . . we do not judge exactly as one may do in France," Rousselon explained, and warned, "This is for the Catholic religion in our area a matter of life and death. From the moment when one suspected the clergy to be abolitionists, one would have to expect in our slave states certain deplorable excesses." Most Catholics, North and South, also abhorred abolitionists, whom they associated with a host

5. Van de Velde to Blanc, November 6, 1855, Julian Benoit to Blanc, November 26, 1855, V-l-i, and Rev. Ennemond Dupuy to Blanc, January 3, 1856, VI-l-j, ANOC.

6. Dupuy to Blanc, January 3, 1856; Bell, *Revolution, Romanticism, and the Afro-Creole Protest*, 159–60; Blied, *Catholics and the Civil War*, 26–27.

of evils, including militant evangelical Protestant nativism, temperance, European radicalism, transcendentalism, free love, and women's rights. Blanc, though, apparently did not take this particular charge against Maistre very seriously.[7]

For his part, unaware of Dupuy's private, stinging characterizations of him, Maistre complained to Blanc of too little to do and asked the archbishop to make use of him elsewhere, either at another Louisiana location or along the Mississippi coast. He assured Blanc that the archbishop need not worry too much about his "means of subsistence," as "Providence will provide it" (aided, no doubt, by his financial reserves). Maistre urged Blanc to ignore the warnings he had probably received from others and to permit him to exercise his ministry under the archbishop's jurisdiction. If Blanc had no permanent position open for him, Maistre expressed a willingness to wait and to work temporarily at Covington, Louisiana, or Pascagoula. While he acknowledged that he pronounced English badly, he noted that he had preached a little and had heard many confessions in that language and had seemed to make himself understood. Maistre implored Blanc not to send him away from the archdiocese, as he had already suffered too much—suffering, he asserted, that had purged him of imprudence and frivolity and matured him. He also plaintively appealed to vicar-general Rousselon to find "a corner" for him in the two large areas of Louisiana and Mississippi.[8]

The priest-starved Blanc again proved amenable, sending Maistre in March 1856, to a chapel at Bayou Boeuf, southwest of New Orleans in Lafourche Parish, where Maistre promised that he would do everything he could to ensure that Blanc would never regret having taken a chance on him. At Bayou Boeuf, in an echo of the larger battle that Blanc had waged and won earlier in New Orleans, Maistre encountered recalcitrant church trustees who insisted on complete control over the church and its finances. Maistre refused their claims,

7. Dupuy to Blanc, January 3, 1856, in VI-l-j, ANOC; Bell, *Revolution, Romanticism, and the Afro-Creole Protest,* 159–60; Blied, *Catholics and the Civil War,* 26–27; Etienne Rousselon to the editor, publication of the Propagation of the Faith, Lyon, July 16, 1840, no. 2799 in Lyon Society Collection, AANO; Madeleine Hooke Rice, *American Catholic Opinion in the Slavery Controversy* (Gloucester, 1964), 86–109.

8. Claude Paschal Maistre to Archbishop Antoine Blanc, January 14, 1856, and Maistre to Étienne J. Rousselon, February 11, 1856, both in VI-l-j, ANOC.

confronted them in a power struggle, and probably earned Blanc's admiration for upholding clerical authority. He insisted that the pastor should manage finances and control the affairs of the church and that trustees should play only the role of advisers. In a letter to Blanc, Maistre disparaged four of the five trustees as men who had failed to make their Easter duty and to attend Mass regularly. To resolve the issue, Maistre—in an act fraught with irony in the light of later developments—suggested the archbishop as the arbitrator and, showing little doubt about his superior's ultimate decision in the matter, asserted, that: "The people would depose the trustees rather than not have a priest." The trustees accepted the archbishop's arbitration. Meanwhile, through adroit management of Easter Sunday pew rents, Maistre demonstrated his financial acumen to trustees, parishioners, and the archbishop alike by raising enough money to pay off the debt on the church. By November 1856, however, Maistre described his position at Bayou Boeuf as untenable and looked forward to a new assignment promised him by Fr. Guillaume Le Mercier Duquesney. That assignment, part of the vast expansion of church institutions that occurred during Archbishop Blanc's tenure, brought him to New Orleans.[9]

On May 1, 1857, Maistre took over as the first pastor of a new parish for back-of-town residents. It extended from the Old Basin to Touro Street and from Tonti Street back to the lake. As a result of a donation, the energetic pastor had a modest-sized lot at Maurepas and Mystery Streets, and a shanty, to start the parish in what was more countryside than residential area. His parishioners consisted of scattered families of French Creole elite, French and German dairymen and truck farmers, and free people of color. Maistre converted the shanty into a chapel, which he named "Chapel of the Nativity of the Blessed Virgin Mary." After seven months, he decided to relocate to a busier and more promising section at the junction of Bayou Road with its branches: the Metairie Shell Road and Gentilly Road.

A parishioner, Madeleine Gueno, responded to Maistre's request for a piece of property by donating to the archbishop in July 1857 one lot and a portion of another, both fronting Bayou Road, as the

9. Maistre to Blanc, February 25, April 9, November 6, 1856, VI-l-j, ANOC.

site for the new church. Maistre purchased the remainder of the second lot under his own name and proceeded with construction. Paid for by Maistre, completed by the middle of November, and blessed by the archbishop under the invocation of St. Rose of Lima, the white frame structure contained forty pews, a sanctuary, and an altar. Pastor and people referred to it as a "chapel." Maistre had no presbytery (residence) to speak of, only a room added to the back of the chapel. He proved an effective pastor, though, delivering sermons, teaching catechism, and providing instruction in French to his racially mixed congregation. In 1858, he recorded fifty baptisms of white children and eighteen of colored and blessed the marriages of nine white and two free colored couples. The next year, the total number of white baptisms declined slightly to forty-nine while colored increased to twenty-four. Marriages stood at nine white and four colored.

Maistre conducted an active ministry among free people of color in the back-town area and encouraged the formation among them of the burial and mutual aid societies so much in evidence at Cailloux's funeral, whose numbers had surged following the yellow fever epidemic of 1853. In return for small monthly or weekly dues, these societies provided social and religious fellowship as well as assistance with medical and funeral expenses. Some of the organizations in the parish included St. Benedict, St. Louis the King, St. Aloysius Gonzagu, Holy Angels, Dieu Nous Protége, St. Bernard, St. Veronique, St. John the Baptist, and Fleurs de Marie. They sponsored special high masses at St. Rose that always included a collection for the benefit of the parish or for a charitable cause. From as early as 1858, Maistre was assisted in his pastoral work by Mademoiselle Felicie Caillau, an unmarried, literate, free person of color—quite possibly the same woman who had served as *institutrice* of the Institute Catholique. (Spelling of French names was fluid in New Orleans with "a" and "o" sometimes interchanged and "x" often dropped at the end.) Felicie kept Maistre's house, witnessed weddings, stood as a sponsor at baptisms, and, given her literacy, may have provided some religious and secular instruction to the children of the parish.[10]

10. Roger Baudier, *St. Rose of Lima Parish: New Orleans: Centennial, 1857–1957* (New Orleans, 1957), 13–21; "Enterrements," in Registre des Marriages et Baptêmes depuis 17 Décembre 1857 jusqu'à 22 Avril 1871, Book III, Schismatic Parish of Holy Name of Jesus in St. Rose of Lima Registers (hereafter, Holy Name

In May 1861, shortly after the firing on Fort Sumter, Maistre learned that he had a new archbishop. Jean-Marie Odin, a native of Hauteville, France, and an indefatigable Vincentian missionary who had rebuilt the Church in Texas and served as the first bishop of Galveston, succeeded his old friend, Antoine Blanc, as the second archbishop of New Orleans. Odin inherited a healthier and significantly strengthened institutional church, thanks to the efforts of his predecessor. During his twenty five year episcopacy, Blanc had increased the number of priests from 27 to 92 and the number of churches from 26 to 73, including the establishment of 47 new parishes. He recruited not only priests but also seven communities of religious sisters and brothers, who conducted schools, orphanages, and other institutions—and, of course, he approved the foundation of the Sisters of the Holy Family. Blanc also oversaw the founding of a seminary, a Catholic newspaper (*Le Propagateur Catholique*), two colleges, nine academies and schools, four orphanages, one hospital, and one home for girls. Catholic life showed greater vitality as revivals packed churches in the 1850s and the number of those attending church and receiving Communions soared.

In addition, the courteous and generous but also determined and resourceful Blanc had shown himself politically adept. He defeated the trustees of St. Louis Cathedral in a decisive legal battle in 1844. Then, the foreign-born leader of an overwhelmingly foreign-born clergy prudently and tactfully guided the church through the political storms and violence associated with the rise of the Know-Nothing Party in the mid-1850s. (White Roman Catholic Creoles who joined the American Party often embraced the anticlerical Gallicanism of the *marguilliers* and resented the ultramontane loyalties of immigrant Catholics.) Despite suffering blistering public denunciations from the *marguilliers* of St. Louis Cathedral in the 1840s and later from Know-Nothings in the mid-1850s, he cultivated cordial, cooperative relations with the political establishments of the state and the city, officiating on patriotic occasions at the Cathedral with public officials

Register), AANO; Walker, "Negro Benevolent Societies in New Orleans," 24, 27; *L'Union,* December 6, 1862; Eighth Census of the United States, 1870, New Orleans, 251. For some examples of Caillau's activities, see entries for August 11, 1858, October 4, 1862, April 7, 1863, October 12, 1865, July 23, 1866, March 17, 1867, March 3, 1868, March 19, 1870, all in Baptisms, Marriages and Funerals, St. Rose of Lima, 1857–64, and Holy Name of Jesus, 1864–1871, AANO.

in attendance. As a result of both his personal qualities and his role as the spiritual leader of a politically significant Catholic population, Blanc enjoyed wide respect throughout Louisiana. He even saw his political nemesis, the Know Nothing Party (which dominated city government in New Orleans) break with its parent organization and renounce its earlier anti-Catholic, anti-immigrant stance. Archbishop Odin no doubt appreciated the magnitude of Blanc's achievements, but he also inherited considerable debt connected with his predecessor's ambitious construction projects. Dealing with it in the midst of the worsening political and military crisis would require greater discipline in the archdiocese, which Odin intended to impose and maintain.[11]

A dedicated, courageous, iron-willed man, Odin possessed great piety and resolve. He had expended himself unstintingly on behalf of Texas Catholics, traveling thousands of miles around his diocese, enduring all manner of discomfort, privation, and danger to minister to his far-flung flock. He also had demanded strict adherence to Church law. In San Antonio, for example, he discontinued the custom of ringing the church bells to announce cockfights, races, and burials of non-Catholics. Odin stipulated that, in conformity with canon law, church bells would be rung only for church services and for the interment of Catholics. He stuck to his ruling even in the face of demands from prominent people to make an exception for a Protestant hero of the Texas Revolution who passed away two days after his pronouncement. Devoted to his Texas diocese, where he had spent more than twenty years and with whose people he identified, Odin considered declining the appointment to the archbishopric. But Bishop Martin John Spalding of Louisville warned him that to do so would display disobedience and effrontery to the Vicar of Christ. Accepting what he regarded as God's will, Odin consented to the appointment and sadly left his beloved Texas for the challenges posed by New Orleans.

11. Baudier, *The Catholic Church in Louisiana*, 381, 402, 394–401, 379–81, 412; Soulé, *The Know Nothing Party in New Orleans*, 57, 66–67, 83, 118; J. Edgar Bruns, "Antoine Blanc: Louisiana's Joshua in the Land of Promise He Opened," in Conrad, Cross, Crozier, and Crucible, 126–33; Carriere, "Anti-Catholicism, Nativism, and Louisiana Politics," 462, 470, 473; Rousselon to la Propagation de la fois: Lyon, October 20, 1843, no. 2810, Jean-Marie Odin to Monsieur le President et Messieurs les Membres de Conseil de la Propagation de la fois: Lyon, January 26, 1866, Lyon Society Collection, AANO.

Sixty-one years old and, in his own words, beginning to feel "the infirmities of age," Odin took the reins of the historically unruly archdiocese intent on protecting the authority of his office and enforcing greater discipline and regularity than had previously been practiced in religious and financial matters. He demanded a clear demarcation of parish boundaries and enforcement of church regulations confining the ministrations of priests to their own parishioners. He also banned grandiose evening weddings, promulgated strict regulations for the handling of parish finances, and ordered every parish to conform to standard Church practice by providing a percentage of its funds for the support of the archbishop and the archdiocese.[12]

The stern episcopal disciplinarian and the maverick priest seemed destined to clash, and clash they did, initially over money and property. Seeking to avoid any recurrence of the trustee battles that had earlier plagued his predecessors, Odin insisted that Maistre, like all other pastors of the archdiocese, legally transfer parish property to him. Maistre disregarded the advice of his friend, Abbé Napoleon Perché, who urged him to donate to the archbishop the portion of the lot and the church building that he owned. Instead, Maistre drove a hard bargain, forcing Odin to purchase title to the lot and the church edifice for $3,287.25. Odin paid part of the purchase price in cash and gave three notes for the balance with interest at 6 percent per annum. Hard feelings remained between the two men thereafter, in part because Odin suspected that Maistre had used parishioners' money to make the initial purchases and then later had fraudulently claimed to the archbishop that he had used his own. This not only offended Odin's sense of honesty, but also violated his

12. Baudier, *The Catholic Church in Louisiana,* 411; Patrick Foley, "Jean-Marie Odin, C.M., Missionary Bishop Extraordinaire of Texas," *Journal of Texas Catholic History and Culture* (March, 1990), 42–60; Diary of Jean-Marie Odin, February, 1843, copy in Vincentian Collection, Archives of the University of Notre Dame; Carlos E. Castaneda, *Our Catholic Heritage in Texas, 1519–1936, (Supplement 1936–1950)* (Austin, 1936–58), 49, 72, Vol. VII of Castaneda, *The Church in Texas Since Independence, 1836–1850,* 7 vols.; Baudier, *The Catholic Church in Louisiana,* 412; Jean-Marie Odin to Messieurs, July 1, 1861, copy in Lyon Society Collection, AANO; Hubert Joseph Bru, "Archbishop Odin: Reformer and Disciplinarian," (master's thesis, Notre Dame Seminary, New Orleans, 1938), 53–54; Baudier, *St. Rose of Lima Parish: Centennial: 1857–1957* (New Orleans, 1957), 19–20; Jean-Marie Odin to Messieurs, February 28, 1862, copy in Lyon Society Collection, AANO.

sense of the nobility of the priesthood—an ideal that he had imbibed as a young man from his Sulpician seminary professors in France. Odin did not include St. Rose of Lima Church in his Confirmation tours in 1861 and 1862. Shortly thereafter, he left for Europe to recruit priests and did not return until after the city had fallen to the Yankees.[13]

News of the surrender of the city saddened Odin who, though desirous of peace and certainly no southern "fire-eater before secession," blamed Lincoln for the war and publicly supported the Confederate cause. In an 1862 pastoral letter, Odin had declared that justice lay on the side of the South. He held the North responsible for the war because of its unwillingness to accede to the South's legitimate claim to independence. The Confederacy enjoyed widespread support among Catholic clergy and laity in New Orleans. A number of Catholic parishes in New Orleans, in response to an appeal by General Pierre Beauregard, donated their church bells for use in making cannons. Priests blessed regimental flags, and prior to his departure for Europe, Odin appealed for chaplains for Louisiana forces. At least ten priests answered his call. During Odin's absence, Abbé Perché was so outspokenly pro-Confederate in the pages of *Le Propagateur Catholique* that General Butler suspended it and placed him under house arrest for five weeks.[14]

13. Baudier, *St. Rose of Lima Parish*, 20; Christopher J. Kauffman, *Tradition and Transformation in Catholic Culture: The Priests of Saint Sulpice in the United States from 1791 to the Present* (New York, 1988), 33–38; Foley, "Jean-Marie Odin," 45–46; *Le Propagateur Catholique*, October 25, 1862.

14. James Talmadge Moore, *Through Fire and Flood: The Catholic Church in Frontier Texas, 1836–1900* (College Station, Tex., 1992), 121–23; pastoral letter of Jean-Marie Odin, February 26, 1862, in Pastoral Letters of the Archbishops of New Orleans, Vol. 1 (1844–1877), AANO; Baudier, *The Catholic Church in Louisiana*, 426–27; *Le Propagateur Catholique*, September 7, 1861; Baudier, *St. Rose of Lima Parish*, 20; Archbishop Jean-Marie Odin to James McMaster, January 21, 1863, I-l-m, ANOC. James McMaster edited the New York *Freeman's Journal* which was read widely by priests throughout the country and by Irish Americans. An opponent of the war and of abolition, he defended the principle of secession and warned his readers that they would have to seek new homes in the West after "Massa Linkum" loosed freed slaves on them through emancipation. Officials arrested him and suppressed the paper. See James Hennesey, S.J., *American Catholics: A History of the Roman Catholic Community in the United States* (New York, 1981), 147, and Frank L. Klement, "Catholics As Copperheads During The Civil War," *Catholic Historical Review*, LXXX (January, 1994), 37.

* * *

As for the peculiar institution, Odin as a young missionary in Louisiana in the 1820s had found slavery most distressing, writing to his sister that "they are treated as one would treat a beast of burden in France. In the fields they are almost always naked. I have found some who do not even know there is a God. One should not be amazed if they are corrupted; they live, alas, rather like beasts than men." But over the years, Odin, like so many other Catholic clergy, despite his abhorrence of its cruelty, came to terms with slavery as a de facto part of the society in which he lived. Odin's own congregation, the Vincentians, possessed, bought, and sold slaves, most of whom served as domestics and maintenance workers. Assigned to Cape Girardeau, Missouri, in April 1836, Odin had taken possession of the church accompanied by a slave family: Harry, Minty, and their slave daughter. As bishop of Galveston, Odin had had slave servants at least through 1850. By the 1840s, though, a majority of the congregation, probably including Odin, wished to end its connection with the institution, and under the leadership of Odin's friend John Timon gradually began to divest itself of slaves.[15]

Catholic moral teaching on slavery relied heavily on St. Thomas Aquinas and the tradition of Roman law, especially as interpreted by Francis Patrick Kenrick, the archbishop of Baltimore and author of the most widely used manual of moral theology in American seminaries. This composite outlook did not view slavery as arising from the natural order of things, but neither did it see the institution as intrinsically evil and thus contrary to natural law. It accepted the fundamental legitimacy of slavery (though not of the slave trade) but surrounded it with a number of caveats—often ignored in actual practice—based on the principle that while a master had the right to a slave's services, the slave still possessed both natural and supernatural rights that the master was morally obliged to respect. These included the right to the knowledge and practice of religion, specifically Catholicism; the right to a lawful and valid marriage; the right

15. Jean-Marie Odin to Benoite (his sister), quoted in Patrick Foley, "Odin of Texas: First Bishop of Galveston," manuscript of a forthcoming book, 47; Moore, *Through Fire and Flood*, 122–23; Stafford Poole, C.M. and Douglas J. Slawson, C.M., *Church and Slave in Perry County, Missouri, 1818–1865* (Lewiston/Queenstown, Mo., 1986), 163, 165–67, 175, 178–81, 185; 7th United States Census, Schedule 2, Slave Owners, 1850, Galveston, Texas, 917.

to unbroken family life; the right to adequate food and clothing; and the right to humane treatment. As the leading historian of the black Catholic experience points out, "Kenrick's priorities were the tranquillity of civil society first, then the good of the slaveholders who were Catholics, and finally the well being of the slaves." Many Louisiana clergy justified slavery for the moral good it might do the slaves while lamenting the spiritual neglect shown by many Catholic masters.[16]

Odin's views probably closely paralleled those of another French transplant southerner, Bishop Augustin Verot, apostolic administrator of Florida and soon to become the bishop of Savannah. On January 4, 1861, Verot delivered a widely publicized sermon titled "Slavery and Abolition." He first took issue with the abolitionists, whose association with anti-Catholic nativism made them doubly suspect in his eyes. Echoing Kenrick, he denounced their moral condemnations of slavery as "unjust, iniquitous, unscriptural, and unreasonable," and insisted that the institution of slavery in the abstract, apart from the abuses often associated with it in practice, violated neither natural nor divine law. He described slavery as a social rather than moral evil, to be tolerated and ameliorated as a concrete reality until gradually replaced at some future, unspecified time. Immediate emancipation would produce greater evil than slavery itself in the form of social chaos and worse conditions for blacks. Verot reserved his strongest words for southern slaveholders who, by abusing their slaves and thus violating their natural rights, not only did wrong, but also provided ammunition for abolitionists. He laid down conditions that he insisted had to accompany the legal and moral possession of slaves, including repudiation of the Atlantic slave trade (condemned in 1839 by Pope Gregory XVI in his apostolic letter *In Supremo Apsostolatus Fastigo*), protection of free blacks against enslavement, preservation of the chastity of slave women from the carnal depredations of masters, promotion of marriage and protection of families from separation by sale, and provision of adequate food, clothing, shelter, and the opportunity and means to know and practice reli-

16. Poole and Slawson, *Church and Slave in Perry County*, 53–58; quoted in Davis, *The History of Black Catholics*, 48–49; Elizabeth Shawn Mills and Gary B. Mills, "Missionaries Compromised: Early Evangelization of Slaves and Free People of Color in North Louisiana," in Conrad, *Cross, Crozier, and Crucible*, 46–47.

gion. Verot called for passage of a slave code that would guarantee these protections and warned that continued abuse of slaves would bring down God's wrath on the South. Verot had his sermon published as a tract, and on November 9, he wrote to Odin, expressing gratification at its reception in New Orleans and giving Odin permission to reprint it. The presses of *Le Propagateur Catholique* did so on December 8 and 9, turning out two editions, one in English and the other in French. Perché enthusiastically recommended the tract, praising it for effectively countering the "criminal" arguments of the abolitionists and explaining clearly both the rights and duties of masters.[17]

One of the bishops in Odin's episcopal province, Augustine Martin of Natchitoches, advanced a different line of argument—one that embodied the South's "positive good" thesis concerning slavery. He issued a pastoral letter on the war in August 1861, which Perché also reprinted in *Le Propagateur Catholique*. In it, Martin asserted that slavery constituted part of God's plan for the redemption of blacks but that slaveholders had abused it by exploiting the slaves' weakness and turning a "good" (slavery) into an instrument for evil. He also repeated the old canard that blacks were descended from the cursed son of Noah. Martin's letter came to the attention of Roman authorities in the Sacred Congregation of the Index, the curial congregation charged with monitoring books and writings. It directed the Sacred Congregation of the Propaganda, which exercised authority over the American church, to ask Martin to correct "errors" and "inexactitudes," specifically that God would have willed the immoral taking of slaves as captives and that a curse lay on blacks. Martin, however, did not hear from the Propaganda until after the war and by then the issue had become moot.[18]

* * *

17. Michael V. Gannon, *Rebel Bishop: The Life and Era of Augustin Verot* (Milwaukee, 1964), 31–55; Bishop Augustin Verot to Jean-Marie Odin, November 9, 1861, AANO; *Le Propagateur Catholique*, December 21, 1861, and January 4, 1862.

18. *Le Propagateur Catholique*, September 7, 1861; Zanca, *American Catholics and Slavery*, 219–25; Maria Genoino Caravaglios, "A Roman Critique of the Pro-Slavery Views of Bishop Martin of Natchitoches, Louisiana," *Records of the American Catholic Historical Society of Philadelphia*, LXXXIII (June, 1972), 67–81; Mills and Mills, "Missionaries Compromised," Conrad, *Cross, Crozier and Crucible*, 46–

A rarity among the Catholic clergy of New Orleans and Louisiana, Maistre—unlike Odin, Verot, and Martin—sympathized with the Union and the cause of immediate emancipation. As early as 1856, DuPuy had complained of his abolitionism, but another priest of the archdiocese may also have sympathized, at least quietly, with his views: Abbé Adrien-Emmanuel Rouquette (1813–1887), the first native Louisiana priestly vocation, a famed poet, and a legendary missionary among the Choctaws, who called him *Chata-Ima* (one of us). In the late 1850s, Rouquette, a charitable and humane priest who ministered at St. Louis Cathedral for fourteen years, reportedly criticized slavery in several sermons, which upset his listeners. Shortly thereafter, having experienced what he described as a mystical call from God to minister to the Indians, he left the city in 1859 for the other side of Lake Ponchartrain and life among the Choctaw. During the war he supported the Union and took the loyalty oath.[19]

Maistre undoubtedly also read the widely publicized antislavery sermon delivered by French Bishop Félix-Antoine-Philibert Dupanloup of Orleans in April 1862. Dupanloup led the liberal Catholic movement in France, had served in the National Assembly, and was the first bishop to be received into the *Academie Française* since the 1789 Revolution. Although recommending compensation for slaveholders, Dupanloup condemned the institution of slavery, declaring that it violated "the unity of the human family, the principle of dignity, of equality, of freedom, [and] of humanity among mankind." The bishop asked rhetorically, "Is it not yet time, after eighteen centuries of Christianity, for us all to begin to practice the everenduring law, 'Do not to another that which you would not he should do to you; and that which ye would your brothers should do for you, do ye for them' "? He identified the principle of emancipa-

---

47. Unfortunately, the author could find no correspondence between Odin and Martin on the subject. An archepiscopal province consists of an archdiocese and other dioceses. The archbishop takes precedence, but the bishops of the dioceses exercise ordinary powers within their sees, or jurisdictions.

19. Dupuy to Blanc, January 3, 1856, VI-l-j, ANOC; Dagmar Renshaw Le Breton, *Chahta-Ima; The Life of Adrien-Emmanuel Rouquette*, (Baton Rouge, 1947); Edward Larocque Tinker, *Les Écrits de Langue Française en Louisiana Au XIXe Siècle* (Paris, 1932; Kraus Reprint, 1970), 406–407; Baudier, *The Catholic Church in Louisiana*, 392; Baudier, "Memorandum for Rev. Robert Guste on White and Negro Relationships After War between the States," (Ms., August 22, 1956, in Roger Baudier Collection, AANO).

tion with Jesus Christ, the Apostles, and Saint Paul. In a letter to Odin in France, vicar general Rousselon, who was also chaplain to the Holy Family Sisters, bemoaned the excerpts of the speech that he saw in the French newspapers, declaring it "a pity to hear them [French clergy] speak on the slavery question. They are blind men . . . even Bishop Dupanloup." He urged Odin to use the opportunity of his visit to "open their eyes."[20]

The sight of Afro-Creoles sporting Federal uniforms in late summer of 1862 further alarmed Rousselon and some of his fellow clergy. When the Native Guards had borne arms for the Confederacy, priests had blessed their regimental and company flags and the archbishop had urged them to fight valiantly. All that changed when they donned Federal blue. In letters reporting to Odin on developments in New Orleans between August and September 1862, Rousselon expressed the fear of "A new San Domingo," a reference to the bloody slave uprising associated with the creation of the black nation of Haiti. Lamenting the announcement of the Emancipation Proclamation which would take effect on January 1, 1863, Rousselon observed to Odin, "It is the last card thrown on the table but it is also the total destruction of the South and the signal for a cataclysm." He repeated his apprehension of a "new San Domingo." He reassured the archbishop, however, that almost all of the clergy had avoided either taking the oath of allegiance or registering as enemies of the United States as prescribed by General Butler, by securing certificates as foreign nationals from their consuls.[21]

According to *L'Union,* whose anticlerical editor and publishers harbored deep suspicions concerning the church anyway, Catholic clergy showed much the same animosity toward the Native Guards

20. Bell, *Revolution, Romanticism, and the Afro-Creole Protest,* 159–60; Blied, *Catholics and the Civil War,* 26–27; Davis, *The History of Black Catholics,* 63; Félix-Antoine-Philibert Dupanloup, *Lettre de Monseigneur L'Évéque d'Orléans Au Clergé de Son Diocèse, Sur L'Esclavage* (Orleans, 1862); Étienne Rousselon to Odin, August 2, 1862, VI-2-f, ANOC. A copy of Bishop Dupanloup's pastoral is also included in *Speech of Hon. T. [Thaddeus] Stevens In Reply to the Attack of General Hunter's Letter,* (Washington, D.C., 1862), pamphlet in Library of Congress (hereafter LC), Washington, D.C.

21. Rousselon to Odin, August 23, September 18, October 15, 1862, VI-2-f, AANO.

as did the majority of white New Orleanians. Some priests threatened to withhold the sacraments from men if they enlisted, and a priest at St. Augustine's according to the paper, had carried through on that threat. Some clergy allegedly voiced their opposition to racial equality in front of Afro-Creole children during catechism classes. Supposedly, Monsignor Chalons, the archbishop's secretary and pastor of St. Mary's, traced "demarcation lines unsuitable and totally rare and unworthy of the Christian" and offered "some indecent and shameful" prejudicial words to a first communion class, instructing white children to sit in the first row, mulattos in the second, and slaves in the third row, adding that nothing would keep that "from always" being their place. Churchgoers, the paper charged, spat on black soldiers, and church doors were closed to them. Several families claimed that they had encountered difficulty in securing church burials for relatives who had died at Camp Strong during training and that only threat of scandal had led to a satisfactory resolution. One soldier who had gone to confession the previous day charged that a priest had refused him communion at Mass because he wore a Federal uniform. The Richmond *Enquirer* unintentionally gave credence to the charges of the Afro-Creole radicals when it reprinted an article from the New Orleans *Era* that identified the priest at St. Augustine's (probably Pierre-Marie Jouan, though the paper incorrectly spelled it "Joubert") who refused communion to men of the Native Guards. "It would appear," the *Enquirer* went on to quote approvingly, "that for a Negro to enlist in the United States service constitutes an offense in the eyes of the priest which should cut him off from the consolations and hopes of religion."[22]

Maistre responded to the Native Guards quite differently. He had first seen them as recruits as they marched to Camp Strong, which lay out Gentilly Road beyond St. Rose church but still within the boundaries of his parish. Detachments of marching troops continually passed by the little white church and Maistre regularly visited the Native Guards, ministering especially to the sick. (Camp fever remained a great menace throughout the war). Much to the chagrin

22. McTigue, "Forms of Interracial Interraction in Louisiana," 40, 42; Houzeau, *My Passage at the "New Orleans Tribune,"* 5; *L'Union,* December 6, 1862, April 28, May 5, 1863; Richmond *Enquirer,* May 29, 1863.

of white parishioners, moreover, he made his church a haven for contraband slaves who had fled into Union lines, and for people of color who suffered indignities at the hands of other priests in the city. Women of the Société des Fleurs de Marie, one of the benevolent societies encouraged by Maistre, asked a parish priest to sing Mass for the protection of their loved ones in the Native Guards. He retorted that he would gladly do so, if it were a funeral service. Stunned by his vituperative reply, they turned in their distress to Maistre. He willingly celebrated the mass, preaching a consoling sermon on the love of God and neighbor and on the benefits of unity and peace. At the end of the service, in keeping with the tradition of the benevolent societies, the women held a special collection that garnered $24.85 for the benefit of the Institute Catholique.[23]

Maistre also became bolder and more radical in his support of emancipation and equal rights. He assisted desperate black refugees, some of them still legally slaves, by providing food and shelter. He also provided them the succor of the sacraments, later charging that some local clergy refused them absolution and last rites unless they consented to return to their former masters. Ignoring diocesan regulations that required separate sacramental registers for whites, people of color, and slaves, Maistre marked January 1, 1863, the day that the Emancipation Proclamation took effect, by writing in the parish register: "N.B. From the date of January 1, 1863, acts [baptisms and marriages] for persons of color will be inscribed in the principal register without discrimination, together with the whites." People of color, slave and free, increasingly regarded him as their champion; many whites considered him a traitorous pariah.[24]

Maistre further enraged whites on April 9, 1863, by celebrating a high mass at St. Rose before an overflow crowd that numbered in the hundreds and spilled outside the packed church. He offered thanksgiving for the Emancipation Proclamation (which applied only

23. Baudier, *St. Rose of Lima,* 22; F. Richard to Janus, February 5, 1862, Copybook, AANO; *L'Union,* December 25, 1862; *L'Union,* December 6, 1862, April 28, May 5, 1863; Séance de December 1, 1862, in Journal des Séances, in AANO.

24. Baudier, *St. Rose of Lima,* 22; St. Rose of Lima Baptisms, Marriages, and Funerals of People of Color (hereafter, SRL), vol. 1, p. 37; AANO; Claude Paschal Maistre to Cardinal Alessandro Barnabò, May 15, 1865, Vol. 20, fols. 1461–1462rv, *Scritture Riferite nei Congressi: American Centrale,* Congregation of Propaganda Fide Archives (hereafter, PA), AUND.

to areas of Louisiana not yet occupied by Union forces) and prayed for the complete abolition of slavery in the state and nation and its replacement by free labor. In his sermon, which drew plaudits from the Afro-Creole activists at *L'Union*, Maistre marveled at the changes wrought over the course of the previous year by the war, and referred to the Proclamation as the difficult "first step" on the road to equality. He stressed the nobility and the necessity of free labor, and described slaves as "men like us," in need of guidance. He acknowledged some fears for the future but, in a peroration that brought tears to the eyes of many in the audience, he reassured them that "[God] watches and His justice finally prevails. Men might perish in the work, but a principle—a faith set loose—spreads and bears fruit."

A few weeks later, Maistre, whom *L'Union* praised as "a sincere and devoted friend of the Union," mounted the pulpit and, unlike most of the other priests in the city who ignored it, read President Lincoln's proclamation calling for a day of fasting and prayer. Those few other Catholic churches where priests, for fear of Federal authorities, also read the proclamation witnessed disorder as men and women walked out and created commotion by stomping their feet on the floor. By April 1863, most white parishioners of St. Rose, repulsed by Maistre's abolitionism and his alleged incitement of Negroes, had abandoned the church. Lynching the priest was hinted at by some whites, including one fellow priest, who declared that a cord would be too good for Maistre—that his [priestly] stole would suffice.[25] This was the situation in New Orleans that Maistre faced on the eve of Archbishop Odin's return to the city from France.

Captain Cailloux and the men of the 1st Regiment appreciated the risks that Maistre had taken in championing their cause and befriending their families. Having marched off to war unaccompanied by a Catholic chaplain, they perhaps drew a measure of consolation from knowing that this besieged clergyman stood by them. But just as Maistre felt increasingly isolated and besieged by hostile opponents, so too did Cailloux and the 1st Regiment as they attempted to demonstrate their manliness and worthiness as Union soldiers.

25. *L'Union*, April 14, April 28, 1863, December 6, 1862.

5

CHALLENGES IN THE FIELD

Once in the field, Cailloux and his men saw little combat but experienced a great deal of racism, which manifested itself in numerous ways. The troubles they endured tested their mettle and heightened their desire to prove themselves in battle and thus lay greater claim to equality of rights and treatment.

On October 25, 1862, after only a month of training, the 1st Regiment left Camp Strong. Sometimes when marching the men sang that they would "bring back the four limbs of old Jeff Davis." No doubt glad to remove the regiment from the racially charged atmosphere of New Orleans, General Butler ordered a column under the overall command of Colonel Stephen Thomas and consisting of the 1st Louisiana Native Guards and the 8th Vermont volunteers to push West from Algiers (located across the river from New Orleans) into the Bayou Lafourche along the Opelousas Railroad that ran through Thibodaux and Brashear City. Butler intended for the units to open the railway so supplies could be forwarded to General Godfrey Weitzel whose expedition at Brashear City aimed to occupy the rich sugar-producing area and prevent supplies originating in Texas from reaching enemy forces in Louisiana. Butler hoped also that the presence of Union troops would afford loyal planters an opportunity to forward their sugar and cotton to New Orleans. The prospect of having the 1st Regiment of Native Guards under his command, however, elicited vehement objections from the young, West Point–trained Weitzel. He lacked confidence in black troops and feared that their presence would incite slave rebellions. He therefore asked Butler to accept his resignation. Butler refused, insisting that Weitzel obey orders.[1]

During the early days of the operation, Butler praised the energy of Colonel Thomas and the efforts of the men of the 8th Vermont and the 1st Regiment. In the span of six days, they opened 52 miles of railroad, built 9 culverts, rebuilt a 435-foot-long bridge burned by the enemy, and pulled up by hand (they had no scythes) the rank grass that had grown between the rails to where it impeded the passage of locomotives. Colonel Stafford established the 1st Regiment's headquarters at Bayou Lafourche. Much to his chagrin, he found it necessary to scatter companies A, B, C, D, F, and J along the railroad for twenty-eight miles, a situation that prevented the regimental drill and discipline essential to prepare new troops for combat. Cailloux and Company E remained at Bayou Lafourche. Residents of the area complained bitterly about the supposed depredations of members of the 1st Regiment, including burning, stealing, rape, and lesser crimes. An officer of a New Hampshire regiment speculated that General Nathaniel P. Banks (who soon replaced Butler) would have to either disband the regiment or put it under iron rule and garrison it "at some fort far away from civilization." Slaves in the area also became restive, and many flocked into the regiment's lines. Planters pleaded with authorities to remove the black troops.[2]

Military authorities, however, kept the regiment in the area to make use of its brawn. Cailloux and his comrades spent most of their

1. Baudier, *St. Rose of Lima Parish,* 22; Report of General Benjamin F. Butler, October 24, 1862, *OR,* Vol. XV, 159; Butler, *Butler's Book,* 495–96; G. Weitzel to Maj. George C. Strong, Asst. Adj. Gen., November 5, 1862, *OR,* Vol. 15, 171–72; Butler to Brig. Genl Weitzel, November 6, 1862, in Butler, *Private and Official Correspondence,* II, 455–58; Butler, *Butler's Book,* 499–501.

2. Gen'l. Benjamin Butler to Major General H. W. Halleck, November 2, 1862, *OR,* vol. 15, p. 161; Remarks by Colonel Spencer H. Stafford in the Annual Returns of the Alterations and Casualties incident to the 1st Regiment, Louisiana Native Guards Regiment, 1862, in ser. 57, Regimental Papers, 73rd USCInf, USCT, RG 94, NA; George N. Carpenter, *A History of the Eighth Vermont Volunteers, 1861–1865* (Boston, 1886), 69; Hollandsworth, *The Louisiana Native Guards,* 33; Weitzel to Major George C. Strong, November 5, 1862, Butler to Halleck, November 6, 1862, Woodward, *The Negro in the Military Service,* 992–94, RG 94, NA; Depositions of J. Bucard and G. Chabaud, December 22, 1862, in Berlin, Reidy, and Rowland, *Freedom,* II, 233–34; Hollandsworth, *The Louisiana Native Guards,* 37–38.

time on tiring guard duty and in backbreaking fatigue duty, which consisted of hard physical labor. Captain Edgar Davis recalled that while guarding the Opelousas Railroad in late 1862 and early 1863, the men experienced the coldest, wettest weather of the season. Strong winds downed tents, and the men found themselves in water to their knees. Their camps resembled the "low wet holes inhabited by crocodiles, frogs, mosquitoes and rats" described by other Union troops. According to one of the regiment's officers: "This was the worst time and the first time we had been exposed to such fatigue." In those conditions, one of the officers of the regiment, First Lieutenant Emile Detiége of Company C, proved overzealous in trying to maintain discipline. He shot and killed an enlisted man who had shoved him during a drill after being shaken for failing to respond quickly enough to an order to join ranks. A jury indicted the captain for murder but he escaped conviction. Stafford noted in his inspection report, on the other hand, that "Considering the youth of the regiment and the duty in which it is engaged, its drill and discipline is good." But he added that for such duty "none but old and highly disciplined regiments should be selected. Such alone can withstand the demoralizing tendencies of segregation." He concluded by observing that the intelligence and earnest desire of his men to prove the capacities of their race had preserved them thus far from the worst effects of the continuous manual labor.[3]

The assignment of black troops to fatigue duty placed a stigma of inferiority on them and both reflected and reinforced skepticism among many white northerners and southerners alike about their martial capacity. On July 5, 1862, Charles Anderson Wickliffe of Kentucky declared on the floor of the U.S. House of Representatives, "A Negro is afraid by nature and by instinct of a gun." Wickliffe's Kentucky colleague, Robert Mallory, added, "one shot of a cannon would disperse thirty thousand of them." Mockingly describing how blacks would react under fire, the Richmond *Enquirer* pictured "a simultaneous effusion of mellifluous perspiration from . . . tarry

---

3. Deposition of Edgar Davis, May 28, 1884, in Pension File of Louis B. Bouté (alias Valcour Bouté), RG 15, NA; Galutia York to Brother Henry, March 12, 1863 and to Father and Mother, February 25, March 5, 1863, Civil War Letters of Galutia York, Special Collections, Colgate University Library (hereafter, CUL); Hollandsworth, *The Louisiana Native Guards,* 37; Remarks by Colonel Spencer H. Stafford, Annual Returns.

hides—there is an universal squall, as if all Africa had been kicked upon its shins, and at the selfsame moment a scattering, as if all the blackbirds, crows, and buzzards in creation had taken wings at once." A correspondent for *Frank Leslie's Illustrated Weekly,* apparently ignorant of the urban background of a majority of the men of the 1st Regiment, and reflecting stereotypical northern views of blacks, described the regiment as eminently qualified for swamp duty. He wrote that "In this swamp in the wilderness the 'nigger soldiers' are eminently useful. The melancholy solitude, with the spectral cypress trees, which seem to stand in silent despair, like nature's sentinels waving in the air wreaths of gray funeral moss, to warn all human beings of the latest pestilence around, though unendurable to our soldiers of the North, seem as eylisium to the sable soldiers, for the swampy forests have no horror to them. Impervious to miasmas, they see only the home of the coon, the possum and the copperhead, so that with 'de gun dat Massa Sam gib 'em, they have around them all the essential elements of colored happiness, except ladies' society." The New York *Tribune* of May 1, 1863, observed that loyal Northerners "have generally become willing that [blacks] should fight but the great majority have no faith that they will really do so. Many hope that they will prove cowards and sneaks—others greatly fear it."[4]

On January 3, 1863, two days after the Emancipation Proclamation became official, Stafford again took pen in hand to express his dissatisfaction to General Butler about the employment of his troops. He repeated his earlier complaint about the dispersal of his companies along the rail lines and its negative impact on drill and discipline. He urged the general to employ seasoned units in the work on the railroad, while insisting that recent engagements in Maryland and Virginia had demonstrated the combat capability of new troops in the field. His tone became more urgent as he reminded Butler, "The raising of this class of troops is an experiment important in its character and its effects and upon the success of the early organizations will depend the action of the government in that regard. . . . This

4. Congressmen and the Richmond *Enquirer* quoted in the New York *Weekly Anglo-African,* June 27, 1863; *Frank Leslie's Illustrated Weekly,* March 7, 1863; quoted in McPherson, *Ordeal by Fire,* 353–54. Joseph Logsdon graciously furnished the author with a microfilm copy of the *Weekly Anglo-African.*

experiment cannot be fairly tried in the present service in which they are engaged, and while scattered in detached companies." Stafford went on to request that Butler relieve the regiment of its present duty, brigade it with other black units, and put it into active field service, "that, by the exercise and discipline consequent thereon, their mobility and effectiveness may be sooner secured." Stafford also addressed the doubts that many whites entertained about black combat proficiency. He asserted that his experience with the mental, moral, and physical characteristics of the men made him confident that "when tried, they shall not be found wanting," and he urged the general to give his men the opportunity to demonstrate their valor and to put to rest the calumnies that circulated about them.[5]

The following day, Stafford sent another appeal for justice to the adjutant, Lt. Col. Richard B. Irwin. He emphasized that his men had not received their promised bounty and advance pay, or even their first regular pay through October 31st, which still remained in the hands of the paymaster, who refused to disburse it. He recited the hardships that lack of pay caused his troops' families and urged an investigation of the relief committee charged with distribution of food, "as the quantities distributed . . . are far below standard and . . . some . . . are wholly withheld." He argued, "The government expects the full performance of his contract on the part of the soldier, and it ought not fail in the conditions on its part to be performed." Stafford's appeals, however, proved fruitless; the regiment received no bounty, pay, or relief from hard labor, families back home continued to suffer, and fatigue duty increased.

Stafford's cause had probably not been helped by a charge he had recently faced for riding down Captain Richard Barrett of Co. B, 1st Louisiana Cavalry, while purportedly intoxicated. Although the incident may have sprung from alcohol-induced personal differences between the two men, it illustrated the continuing tension between the black 1st Regiment and the white native-Louisianian Unionists of the 1st Cavalry who objected to black troops.[6]

5. Spencer H. Stafford to Benjamin Butler, January 3, 1863, in ser. 57, Regimental Papers; 73rd USCInf.

6. Spencer H. Stafford to Lt. Col. R. B. Irwin, January 4, 1863, in ser. 1756, Letters Received, Department of the Gulf, RG 393, Pt. 1, NA; Charges and Specifications against Col. S. H. Stafford of the 1st Regiment of Louisiana Native Guards, n.d., and J. B. Gutbard, AA General, by command of Brig. Gen. Weitzel, December 29, 1862, both in Service Record of Spencer H. Stafford, RG 15.

Deciding against a court-martial of either Stafford or Barrett, General Weitzel in January 1863 scattered the companies of the regiment among three forts for construction duty. Cailloux and his company, along with companies B, F, and G, proceeded to Fort Jackson, on the right bank descending of the Mississippi below New Orleans in Plaquemines Parish, to make repairs and alterations on the structure. Companies C, G, H, and K went to Fort St. Philip on the opposite side of the river. Weitzel ordered that their labor on the forts "take precedence [over] all other work." Companies A and D, meanwhile, traveled to Fort McComb, which guarded the eastern approaches of Lake Pontchatrain at Chef Menteur Pass. When he thus returned to the parish of his birth (Plaquemines), Cailloux did not enjoy a cordial reception, as he and his company endured insults from the men at the post. Thomas Sears, first lieutenant and adjutant of Company E, observed that despite the discomforts and affronts, the men displayed admirable discipline and devotion to the cause.[7]

Though held in low esteem by many white soldiers, the men of the regiment impressed some northern observers. When the 114th New York Infantry replaced the 1st Regiment at Bayou Lafourche on January 11, 1863, Captain James Fitts of the 114th witnessed a dress parade staged by several companies of Stafford's regiment, most likely including Cailloux's E Company. He recalled looking down the "long dusky line" and seeing the soldierly bearing, proficiency in the manual of arms, and the zeal that each unit displayed, and in that moment "the barriers of prejudice . . . in my mind began to fall before the force of accomplished facts before me." One correspondent, who accompanied units from Bayou Lafourche to their assignments at the various forts, wrote that he not only observed the men but took the opportunity to converse with several of the black officers in order to come to some just conclusion as to their mental caliber, manners, etc. "Truth and honesty compel me to state," he wrote, "that as far as the privates were concerned, a more decent, orderly, obedient and soldierly set of men I never saw; while, as regards the officers, had I come in contact with the same number of

7. Special Orders 3, 7, 8, 9, 27, 1863, ser. 1767, Special Orders, Department of the Gulf, RG 393, Pt. 1, NA; Notes on Annual Return of the 1st Regiment of Louisiana Native Guards, for January 1863 (dated February 10, 1863) in ser. 57, Regimental Papers, 73rd USCInf.

white men taken at random, I could not have expected to find more general intelligence, education, and refinement."[8]

The onerous fatigue duty, however, had begun to take its toll. On one day in February, seventy enlisted men of the regiment reported sick. After an inspection that month, Stafford noted discipline in Cailloux's company as "imperfect," a departure from the previous rating of "good." The badly worn and tattered clothing of the men reflected the daily impact of heavy labor on both uniforms and morale. Ironically, Stafford's earlier boast to reporters that "my men can work. . . . Put me down in a forest with those fellows and I'll build you a city; for I have every useful trade represented among them," had come back to haunt him. The regiment also had to contend with continued complaints that it was pillaging the countryside. Stafford sarcastically dismissed the charges, insisting in one instance that his men "are not and have not been in the habit of pulling up the cane from the fields of the 'Belle Chase' plantation of James E. Zumpt. I have not seen any cane upon his place in the vicinity of my command at which they could conveniently get."[9]

Further complicating matters was the implacable opposition to black officers maintained by General Banks, who replaced Butler in December 1862 as commander of the Department of the Gulf. As governor of Massachusetts, Banks had vetoed an 1859 measure opening the state militia to blacks, and furthermore, one of his primary objectives in Louisiana was to encourage Unionist sentiment through more conciliatory policies toward the populace of New Orleans. When he assumed command of the Department of the Gulf, he had already decided that the experiment in black officers had failed. The commissioning of men like Cailloux not only implied racial equality, but also conferred upon them the prerogatives of "an officer and

8. Fitts, "The Negro in Blue," 251; *Harper's Weekly,* February 28, 1863, p. 143.
9. Inspection Reports of the 1st Regiment of Louisiana Native Guards, Colonel Stafford, December 31, 1862, February 28, 1863, ser. 57, Regimental Papers, 73rd USCInf; Stafford to Capt. W. Hoffman, AA General, February 20, 1863, ser. 1756, Letters Received, Department of the Gulf, RG 393, Pt. 2, NA; *Harper's Weekly,* February 28, 1863, p. 143; William Hoffman to Col. Rust, January 28, 1863, Stafford to Lt. Col. R. B. Irwin, AAG, March 3, 1863, ser. 57, Regimental Papers, 73rd USCInf.

a gentleman" and allowed them broad authority which, in a given situation, might extend to controlling white officers and troops. Cailloux's reception at Fort Jackson reflected the resentment of white troops about this arrangement. White officers regarded official conversation with black officers as insulting and often responded abruptly and rudely to legitimate queries. Enlisted men refused to salute or to obey orders given them by black officers. At Baton Rouge, ill-will between the black officers of the 3rd Regiment of Native Guards and the white officers and men of other units led, on several occasions, to violence.[10]

In February 1863, Banks signaled his intention to remove the black officers from the regiments, "being entirely satisfied that the appointment of colored officers is detrimental to the service" because it constituted a constant source of embarrassment, annoyance, and demoralization of both black and white troops. He blamed the black officers for lax discipline in their units and for stirring up unnecessary and injurious controversy between themselves and white troops. He then pressured the black officers to resign their commissions. Moving first against the officers of the 3rd and 2nd Regiments, respectively, Banks summoned the officers of the 3rd to his headquarters and, in effect, advised them to resign. Nearly all did so. For the officers of the 2nd, he devised an especially disingenuous plan. He ordered a board of examination which included some white officers of inferior rank, to pass judgment on the qualifications of the blacks. Most resigned rather than submit to such an indignity.

As part of his campaign, Banks also proposed a new army corps, the *Corps d'Afrique,* that would mean the end of the detached status of the 1st Regiment of Native Guards. In order to meet the perceived instructional and disciplinary needs of black troops and to maximize the influence of white officers over them, Banks envisioned small regiments of five hundred men. He wanted white officers because he attributed the defects of black regiments to the "incorrect ideas" of the black commanders, who he thought focused too much on dog-

10. Edmonds, *The Guns of Port Hudson,* I, 10–14; Berlin, Reidy and Rowland, *Freedom,* II, 304–305, 317; General Order 40, May 1, 1863, in ser. 1763, General Orders, Department of the Gulf, RG 393, Pt. 1, NA; Endorsement by General Richard B. B. Irwin, AA General, November 25, 1863, on letter of Ex-2d Lieut. Joseph G. Parker to Honorable E. M. Stanton, May 30, 1863, in Berlin, Reidy, and Rowland, *Freedom,* II, 317–21.

mas of equality. He believed this to be the reason some regiments suffered from poor discipline and had engaged in discreditable and unsatisfactory conduct. Banks hoped that his proposed new organization would eliminate what he regarded as the unnecessary and injurious controversy that had arisen between black and white troops by further segregating blacks in their own corps.[11]

Cailloux and the other officers of the 1st Regiment escaped Banks's frontal assault, perhaps in part because their commanding officers, Colonel Stafford and Lieutenant Colonel Bassett, sympathized more with black officers than did other white commanders of Guards regiments. Lieutenant John Crowder of Company K declared in a letter in April to his mother that he did not intend to resign, "nor will I resign unless I am the only black officer in the service. As long as there is a button to hold to I will hold to it." He could count on Cailloux—whose name, after all, translated as "rock"—to stand firm and provide the "button" for him to hold. Still, the 1st Regiment lost one black lieutenant in March, discharged as a result of inflamed testicles from venereal disease.[12]

Banks's actions, if not his words, undermined the authority of Cailloux and the rest of the black officers and encouraged disrespect and defiance by white soldiers toward them. Early the next year (1864), following Cailloux's death and the resignation of Stafford, officers of the 1st Regiment also began to resign. Captain Joseph Follin of Company C attributed his resignation to "daily events [that] demonstrate that prejudices are so strong against Colored Officers, that no matter what would be their patriotism and their anxiety to fight for the flag of their native Land, they cannot do it with honor to themselves."[13]

11. Genl. N. P. Banks to Brig. Genl. L. Thomas, Adjutant General, February 12, 1863, in Woodward, *The Negro in the Military*, 1054, RG 94, NA; General Order 40, May 1, 1863.

12. John Crowder to "Dear Mother," April 23, 1863, in Glatthaar, "The Civil War Through the Eyes of a Sixteen Year-Old Black Officer," 212; Octave Foy to Stafford, March 6, 1863, J. T. Paine, Surgeon, to Stafford, March 10, 1863, ser. 1859, Letters Received, 1st Division, Department of the Gulf (T. Sherman), RG 393, Pt. 1, NA; Lt. Col. Frank S. Hesseltine to Captain Hickham Hoffman, March 19, 1863, ser. 1756, Letters Received, Department of the Gulf, RG 393, Pt. 1.

13. Endorsement by Irwin on Parker to Stanton, May 30, 1863, in Berlin, Reidy, and Rowland, *Freedom*, II, 317–21; Captain Joseph Follin to Asst. Adjt. Genl. George B. Drake, February 18, 1864, in Service Record of Joseph Follin, Compiled Military Service Records, RG 94, NA.

Lieutenant Colonel Irwin, on the other hand, blamed the situation on the arrogance and intolerant self-assertion of the black officers, some of whom dared take their complaints to General Banks. He concluded that the experiment in these cases "proved a distressing failure . . . due to the incompetency [and] . . . bad character" of the men and "their nervous and uncontrollable anxiety to discount the future of their race." Within eighteen months, Banks had almost completed his purge.[14] In the late spring of 1863, however, even amidst growing pressures, Cailloux remained in command of Company E. He and his men yearned for combat in order to prove their valor and disprove the aspersions heaped on black soldiers and officers.

At the beginning of Banks's campaign to remove black officers, Stafford took the occasion of an inspection by Brigadier General Thomas J. Sherman to once again register his grievances about the obstacles facing his regiment. Sherman invited him to put his concerns in writing which Stafford did. In four and one-half pages, he reviewed the harassment of soldiers and their families by whites in New Orleans, the difficulties in securing adequate equipment, uniforms, transport, supplies, and building materials, and the failure of the government to make good on its promises of rations for families, bounties, advance pay, and regular pay. He pointed out that he had earlier addressed the commanding general on this subject and had urged the publication of orders to remedy the injustices, but to no avail. Stafford then offered an explanation. He charged that "some people have, without reflection, formed an opinion that blacks, being inferior, cannot be made soldiers and for fear that they may ultimately be convinced of their error, are determined to throw every impediment in the way of such conviction." Stafford admitted his own initially negative reaction to the idea of commanding black troops—a notion that conflicted with "all my former opinions, prejudices, and political association." He had followed orders, though, and his subsequent experiences had changed his views. In light of these considerations, Stafford again appealed for an order to rectify the situation so as to give a fair and untrammeled opportunity for the trial of "the experiment inaugurated in the formation of these regiments." He apologized for the tone of his letter and disclaimed

14. Berlin, Reidy, and Rowland, *Freedom*, II, 319–320, 305–307, 19.

any intentional bitterness or disrespect. Rather, he attributed his frustration to the difficulties already mentioned and "the fact that I am goaded daily with new acts of insults to my officers and men and oppression to their families." Sherman noted in his endorsement on the back of Stafford's letter that he had forwarded all requisitions from Stafford for supplies to the proper depot officers, over whom he had no control. He directed Stafford in the future to send his supply requisitions directly to him and promised that he would do his "utmost" to get them filled. As for Stafford's other complaints, he tended to attribute them to "the peculiar state of affairs at the present time—the state of transition through which the Negro seems to be passing—the want of some decided policy of the government relative to the Negro." He added in a postscript however, that he hoped that Stafford's claims for sufficient supplies would be met.[15]

Shortly thereafter, the 1st Regiment moved upriver to Fort St. Leon at English Turn, about fifteen miles south of New Orleans, to work on fortifications. On March 19, Cailloux and his men moved upriver again, this time to the vicinity of Baton Rouge as part of a two-month campaign to establish Union control of the rich sugar- and cotton-growing regions along the Bayou Teche. Their movement into the area attracted runaway slaves as recruits, such as twenty-five-year-old François Remy, who fled into Union lines on the soldiers' approach. Remy met three soldiers and an orderly sergeant and asked them if they needed recruits. They replied affirmatively and sent him into camp where he waited a week. After a doctor examined him twice, Remy received his uniform and was sworn in. He, along with others, carried his clothes into a camp "alley" and buried them. He then joined his assigned company, where he lived in a large tent with a number of French-speaking men.[16]

The arrival of black troops in the Baton Rouge area initially elicited favorable comments from troops of the 49th Massachusetts, who admired both their physiques—hardened by manual labor—and their proficient, "elastic, vigorous steps" on the drill field. Observa-

15. Spencer H. Stafford to Hoffman, February 23, 1863, and endorsement on back of same by Brig. General W. T. Sherman, ser. 1756, Letters Received, Department of the Gulf, RG. 393, Pt. 1, NA.

16. Special Order 27, January 27, 1863, ser. 1767, Special Orders, RG 393, Pt. 1, NA; Deposition of François Remy, August 29, 1903, in Pension File of François Remy, RG 15, NA.

tions about their military bearing notwithstanding, Cailloux and his men found themselves working around the clock on the old familiar: fatigue duty. They dug ditches and latrines, loaded and unloaded supplies, and prepared defensive perimeters, in addition to standing guard duty. An aide to General Banks observed "The white soldiers won't do anything now except make the Negroes work for them."[17]

When they had some spare time, Cailloux's men entertained themselves by climbing greased poles and shooting alligators. The officers of Company K, however, fell to quarreling, as Crowder became the object of a smear campaign waged by Captain Alcide Lewis and Lieutenant Erhud Moss. The two, apparently jealous of the efficiency, skill, and energy of the "boy wonder" and angered at his insistence on disciplining an enlisted man for lewd behavior toward a female visitor to the camp, sought his removal. Crowder dug in his heels, and in a letter to his mother referred to the two as "the most pusillanimous dirty low-life men I have ever seen."[18]

At Baton Rouge, Cailloux and the rest of the regiment also finally received their first pay. The enlisted men received only $10 from which $3 was deducted for uniform, compared to the $13 pay exclusive of uniform that went to white soldiers. Inequitable pay fell particularly hard on black noncommissioned officers, who—unlike their white counterparts—received no additional pay for their duties and responsibilities. Cailloux and his fellow black officers fared better, receiving $60 per month, the same pay as white officers. Cailloux thus could at last send money home to his family—a preoccupation of many of the men during the months that they had waited for that elusive first payday.[19]

The well-being of their families, of course, remained an overriding concern for men in the regiment, and they strove to stay in contact

17. Deposition of Basil Ulgère, June 24, 1895, in Pension File of Jacques Augustine, RG 15, NA; Henry T. Johns, *Life with the Forty-Ninth Massachusetts Volunteers* (Pittsfield, Mass., 1864), 150; David C. Edmonds, *The Guns of Port Hudson*, I, 25.

18. Deposition of Basil Ulgere, June 24, 1895; Crowder to "Dear Mother," April 27, 1863, in Glatthaar, "The Civil War Through the Eyes of a Sixteen-Year-Old Officer," 212.

19. Crowder to "Dear Mother," May 4, 1863, in Glatthaar, "The Civil War Through the Eyes of a Sixteen-Year-Old Officer," 214; Berlin, Reidy, and Rowland, *Freedom*, II, 362–64, 382.

with those they had left behind. A fragment of a letter in Cailloux's pension file, written in English, mentioning "Jean," and including the words "my love," suggests that he communicated with his loved ones back home. Officers, chaplains, and literate comrades wrote and read letters for those who were illiterate. The men filled their letters with terms of endearment, inquiries about family members, admonitions to write more frequently, requests for needed articles such as underwear, mosquito nets (one Yankee soldier described mosquitoes in Louisiana as "thicker than hair on a dog and as large as bumblebees"), and tobacco, promises to send money when paid, and expressions of concern for their relatives' welfare. Private Charles Pourcelle, anxious to know if his wife in New Orleans had received tickets for food rations promised by Union authorities, told her that if she had not, she should write a letter in English emphasizing the importance of his presence at the upcoming baptism of one of their children, thereby (he hoped) providing him with an excuse to obtain home leave so that he could take care of the ration problem. Writing what would be his last letter to his Afro-Creole wife in New Orleans, fifty-three-year-old Patrick Henry, a private in Cailloux's Company E and a runaway slave from New Orleans, closed tenderly with the words, "My dear love, I finish this letter by embracing you with all of my heart. Your old spouse for life."[20]

On May 20, under Cailloux's command, Henry and his company marched out from Baton Rouge with the rest of the 1st Regiment, their destination Port Hudson. They did so, however, without Colonel Stafford, who had been placed under arrest four days earlier for his reaction to yet another incident of racism directed against his

20. Letter fragment found in the Pension File of André Caillaux [sic] RG 15, NA; Frederick H. Dyer, *A Compendium of the War of the Rebellion* (Dayton, 1908), 1214; Glatthaar, "The Civil War Through the Eyes of a Sixteen-Year-Old Officer," 201–16; quote about mosquitoes in Galutia York to Brother Henry, February 19, 1863, in Civil War Letters of Galutia York, CUL; Charles Pourcelle to "My Dear Eloise," April 18, 1863, Pourcelle to Eloise attached to letter of Joseph Daunoy to "My Dear Wife," April 19, 1863, Pension File of Charles Pourcelle, RG 15, NA; Depositions of Julia Henry, November 24 and 28, 1881, and letter of Patrick Henry to "Ma Chère Femme," July 18, 1863, Pension File of Patrick Henry, RG 15, NA; Enlistment paper of Patrick Henry, August 24, 1862, Box 68, Miscellaneous Papers, USCT, RG 94, NA. Patrick Henry died of dysentery, an ever-present plague of camp life, within a month of his letter of July 18, 1863.

men. This time, the frustrated colonel, having reached the limits of his endurance, had exploded in wrath. Stafford had secured a multiple day pass from General Christopher C. Augur, who commanded the District of Baton Rouge, for a work detail to gather wood for fuel. Stafford dispatched the detail, which included wagon teams. The lieutenant in command showed the pass as he and his party traveled out through the lines. Later, the wagon teams returned to camp loaded with wood, while the lieutenant with the pass and his party remained at their work. When the teams attempted to exit the lines in order to collect another load, sentries refused passage, required the detail to send to Stafford for another pass, and compelled the party to return to camp—fatiguing the teams unnecessarily from Stafford's point of view. One of the teamsters reported being called a "damned black son of a bitch" by the sentries. Stafford called on General Augur for another pass, all the while growing increasingly indignant over the mistreatment of his men, for sentries had harassed previous teams.

Stafford led his wagons back to the picket line and then, without showing the pass, defiantly forced the guard, moving through the line and hurling abusive and insulting language at the sergeant, calling him a "God damn son-of-a-bitch." Captain J. P. Garland of the 31st Maine Regiment, the officer who commanded the picket line and who had initially refused passage to the wagoners, returned to his post, and when more wagons from the 1st Regiment attempted to pass out, he sent them back. Stafford soon rode up and verbally accosted Garland. "What in hell did you stop my teams for?" Stafford demanded without showing the pass. "You are a god-damned stinking white-livered Yankee," he yelled, at the same time thrusting his fist into the captain's face. He accused some of the officer's men of stealing wood and labeled the brigade "a set of god-damn thieves." Declaring, "It is enough to make a minister swear and even Jesus Christ," Stafford warned Garland that if he stopped one of Stafford's men again, with or without a pass, Stafford would arrest the captain and put him "into the guard house with my niggers, God damn you." Stafford also reportedly spoke disrespectfully of President Lincoln. Garland wrote down Stafford's words and had witnesses to the incident.

Stafford did not deny that he had acted intemperately, and claimed to have regretted his remarks as soon as he had cooled down and had had time to reflect about them. By cursing a subordinate,

however, he had transgressed military courtesy, something that soldiers of the day took very seriously. Stafford pleaded extenuating
circumstances to his superiors, citing previous occasions of harassment about which he had complained to the commanding general
and which, in his words, had "worked upon a sensitiveness in regard
to my regiment which I had perhaps foolishly fostered instead of
repressing." He explained that he had been "mad with indignation
at what I then supposed to be especially designed as an insult to
my organization." He expressed the hope "That this, though not a
justification, may be deemed an extenuation of my offense and that
in the future I may be able to repair from such swiftness to anger."
Stafford was charged with "disrespectful or contemptuous words
against the President of the United States; conduct to the prejudice
of good order and military discipline; and conduct unbecoming an
officer and a gentleman." Restricted to hospital service in Baton
Rouge pending a decision in the case, he would care for the
wounded after the battle of Port Hudson but would not lead his
regiment. Though ordered back to duty in July, Stafford was dismissed from the service on September 8, 1863. (Bassett continued
to command the Regiment.) In 1871, Stafford's dismissal was
changed to an honorable discharge.[21]

As Cailloux led his men toward Port Hudson, serious issues, in addition to his own life or death, undoubtedly weighed on him. He had
lost a staunch defender of black officers in Stafford and he knew that
the coming engagement at Port Hudson would finally answer in the
minds of many the widely asked question whether blacks possessed
sufficient manliness to fight. He knew also that the honor of black
officers hung in the balance and that this battle could afford them

21. Captain J. P. Garland to Col. E. P. Chapin, May 14, 1863, Stafford to Major
G. B. Halstead, May 19, 1863, Charges and Specifications against Colonel Spencer
H. Stafford, 1st Louisiana Native Guards, forwarded by E. P. Chapin, May 15,
1863, Spencer H. Stafford to Maj. General N. P. Banks, June 4 and 23, 1863,
General George L. Andrews, Brig. General Volunteers Commanding Corps
d'Afrique, to Lt. Col. R. B. Irwin, Asst. Adj. General, August 12, 1863, Special
Order 224, September 8, 1863, Department of the Gulf, and Special Order 1, War
Department, Adjutant General's Office, January 3, 1871, all in Service Record of
Spencer H. Stafford, RG 15, NA. For a discussion of military courtesy, see Gerald
F. Linderman, *Embattled Courage: The Experience of Combat in the American Civil
War* (New York, 1987), 51–53.

their first and possibly last chance to show their mettle in large-scale combat. He knew his men would look to him to model that core virtue so prized among nineteenth-century soldiers: courage. And he knew that many whites expected him to fall short. Perhaps he, like so many other soldiers approaching battle, drew solace from his belief in the protecting hand and providential plan of God.[22] As Cailloux prepared for the coming clash on the bluffs overlooking the Mississippi, he could count on the prayers of at least one representative of the Almighty: Claude Paschal Maistre, who was facing his own impending battle—this one with the formidable Archbishop Odin.

22. Linderman, *Embattled Courage*, 45–47, 9–10; James M. McPherson, *For Cause and Comrades: Why Men Fought in the Civil War* (New York, 1997), 64–71.

6

TWO BATTLES

In late spring 1863, both Maistre and Cailloux faced battles that would confirm their devotion to emancipation and equality. The priest would choose schism rather than submission; the captain would suffer a heroic and tragic death. The priest would bury the captain, but the efforts of both would help to energize Afro-Creole activists in the cause of greater political and racial democracy.

On Good Friday in April 1863, Archbishop Jean-Marie Odin, accompanied by a score of priests whom he had recruited in France, returned to New Orleans. According to his later report to the Propaganda, Odin quickly learned of Maistre's behavior that had offended white Catholics at St. Rose and had attracted to the church a large number of slaves and persons of color to whom, in Odin's words, "he preached the love of liberty and independence and excited . . . to insurrection against their masters." Odin viewed his own position as delicate. He hesitated to reprimand Maistre for his seditionary discourse for fear of exposing himself to reprisals from the federal military authorities, whom he contemptuously described as "partisans of abolitionism," working unremittingly to turn slaves against their masters. He no doubt had in mind the widespread Union recruitment of slaves into the military, which thereby gave them legal freedom. Odin believed that most slaves wished to remain on the plantations where they belonged, and he attributed their mass exodus to the devastation caused by the Yankees and to agitation by radicals such as Maistre. Yet he worried that Federal officials would interpret any direct steps against the priest as persecution on the basis of political opinions.[1]

Nevertheless, on May 7, Odin seized on a pretext to dismiss the troublesome cleric. (In a later report [August 7] to Allesandro Barnabó, cardinal prefect of the Propaganda, Odin explained that Providence had furnished him "with a favorable occasion to discharge Maistre.") At the monthly gathering of clergy at the archiepiscopal residence, one priest stood and declared that he could not continue to sit in a gathering that included another priest convicted of a crime. Maistre immediately arose and left the assembly. After the conference, Odin asked for an explanation from the man, who claimed that he felt bound by conscience to reveal Maistre's earlier turpitude in France, which had involved greed, violated both civil and canon law, set French police on his trail, and forced him to flee the country. Odin did not explain to Barnabó why the unidentified priest chose to risk public scandal by airing his concern about the fifteen-year-old incident in an open meeting rather than in private conference with Odin. The priest-accuser probably had access to the correspondence between Van de Velde and Blanc that detailed Maistre's early difficulties. The whole scene appeared rehearsed and choreographed—a setup that would allow Odin to move against Maistre and rid himself of the troublesome abolitionist. Odin claimed that in short order the scandalous accusation echoed throughout the city, but he indicated no disapproval of the man who had initially aired those charges publicly.[2]

Odin summoned Maistre, who had never been formally incardinated into the diocesan clergy. According to the archbishop's account, Maistre admitted that he had committed the crime in France and that he could not return there. Odin declared that given such a public stain on his reputation (thanks to the priest who had blurted out the charges), Maistre could no longer exercise his ministry without causing scandal. The archbishop strongly exhorted him to retire to a monastery to do penance. Odin judged at first that Maistre

1. Jean-Marie Odin to Cardinal Alessandro Barnabó, August 14, 1863, in Vol. 20, fols. 358rv–361rv, March 1, 1864, Vol. 20, fols. 703rv–704rv, November 8, 1865, Vol. 20, fols. 1658rv–1659rv, *Scritture Riferite nei Congressi: American Centrale*, PA; Odin to the Lyon Society for the Propagation of the Faith, July 20, 1863, F02855, in Lyon Society Collection, AANO.

2. Odin to Barnabó, August 14, 1863, March 1, 1864, November 5, 1865.

seemed disposed to follow his advice and intended to leave the arch-diocese.[3]

Maistre, however, refused to go quietly. He had become friends with a man whom Odin described as the senior Protestant chaplain of the Union forces, who used his influence to secure a directive from Captain C. W. Killborn of the Provost Marshal General's Office ordering Maistre to continue his ministry to French-speaking free people of color at St. Rose. Killborn then commanded Odin to appear before him so he could ascertain whether the archbishop had attempted to dismiss Maistre because of the latter's political views. Odin's fears that partisans of abolitionism would denounce him to the provost marshal seemed confirmed. At their meeting, Odin explained to Killborn what he called the "true" reason for his proceeding against Maistre, viz., the latter's crime. On his departure, he encountered Maistre at the entrance to the office. Once more he demanded that the priest retire as soon as possible to a monastery, and also forbade him verbally from celebrating Mass. Maistre responded with a note, dated May 16, informing Odin that the military authorities had located him after he had left St. Rose and had ordered him back to continue his ministry—an "order" with which Maistre eagerly complied.[4]

3. Odin to Barnabó, August 14, 1863, March 14, 1864, November 5, 1865. Incardination is the canonical act whereby a man is attached to a diocese and made subject to its bishop, who also assumes ultimate responsibility for him. See Albert J. Nevins, M. M., ed., *The Maryknoll Catholic Dictionary* (New York, 1965), 289.

4. Odin to Barnabó, August 14, 1863, March 1, 1864, November 8, 1865; General James Bowen, Provost Marshall, to Monsignor Jean-Marie Odin, May 25, 1863, ser. 1839, Press Copies of Letters Sent, nos. 296–99 DG, Provost Marshall General Records, Department of the Gulf, RG 393, Pt. 1, NA; Captain W. Killborn to Odin, July 30, 1863, VI-2-g, ANOC; Odin to Killborn, August 1, 1863, ser. 1845, Letters Received, Provost Marshall General Records, Department of the Gulf, RG 393, Pt. 1, NA; Buadier, *St. Rose of Lima*, 23.

The "senior Protestant chaplain" with whom Maistre collaborated may have been Thomas W. Conway. In a letter, Conway described himself as "the chaplain of the 79th U.S.C. Infantry . . . I am the senior chaplain of the Colored Troops in this department or any other, having been mustered into the 2nd U.S. Vols. Gen Ullman's Brigade, in New York, Feb. 16, 1863 . . . and furthermore, that, to the best of my knowledge, I am the senior chaplain in the volunteer service of the United States, having first entered the service April 23, 1861 as chaplain of the 9th N.Y. Vols., which regiment was held into the U.S. Service for two years except sooner discharged." Thomas W. Conway to Col. George B. Banks, Supt. Negro Labor,

Odin, who jealously guarded his episcopal prerogatives and who had all-too-painful memories of the chaos associated with the earlier clerical and lay defiance of his predecessors, would brook no further insubordination from Maistre, a man whom he regarded as personally dishonest. After gathering with his consultors, the archbishop moved quickly. On May 16, he deprived Maistre of his canonical faculties and placed him under interdict (suspension), thereby forbidding him to perform any of the sacraments. Maistre ignored the order and celebrated mass at St. Rose—a sacrilege according to canon law. In a pastoral letter dated May 19, 1863, Odin publicly announced the suspension of the priest and placed St. Rose under interdict, meaning that no Catholic rites could be performed and no Catholic could worship there. The archbishop pointed out that Maistre had the right, while submitting to the archbishop, to appeal the censure to Rome. Odin warned Catholics that any who attended a mass celebrated by Maistre would partake in his schism (defined as defiance by a congregation of legitimately appointed episcopal or pastoral authority) and his sacrilege and that whoever confessed to Maistre—except a dying person unable to find another priest—would, far from receiving forgiveness, only aggravate his offenses. Any contact with Maistre in spiritual matters would consititute participation in his crime. Any who, after reading the letter, took part in any public exercise of worship in the church of St. Rose of Lima, or who attended any public act of worship conducted by Maistre, or who had recourse to his ministry in spiritual matters, would commit a grave sin, the absolution of which Odin reserved to himself. He forbade any priest to grant a Catholic burial to those who, having committed any of the acts proscribed above, had not given signs of repentance. He further called for services of atonement in all of the churches of the city for the profanation that had occurred at St. Rose."[5]

Maistre still refused to back down. He likely considered Odin's censure invalid because it threatened pastoral care for blacks in New Orleans. In Maistre's view, obedience to the archbishop would not only imperil him personally, but also (and more importantly) endanger the salvation of blacks who depended upon his ministry. In this

Dept of Gulf, July 14, 1864, in Service Record of Thomas W. Conway, Compiled Military Service Records, RG 94, NA.
5. Jean Marie-Odin, May 19, 1863, *Pastorals*, vol. 1. (1844–1887), AANO.

instance, therefore, Divine Law had to take precedence over ecclesiastical law. In this "holy war," Maistre attempted to manipulate the military authorities to his advantage, giving Odin the impression, at least initially, that Provost Marshal General James Bowen backed him. When, in a letter of May 25, 1863, Odin requested the keys of St. Rose from the provost marshall, Bowen denied that he had ever had them in his possession. In the first inkling that Maistre might have overestimated the amount of support that he could count on from military authorities, Bowen declared that Maistre had "entirely misapprehended" his views regarding the controversy. Bowen insisted that he had told Maistre what he had told Odin at a meeting between the two: "that the question at issue was simply one of discipline of his church, in which I could take no part."[6]

Despite Bowen's assertion that Maistre had misunderstood his support, the priest still held the keys to St. Rose. And absent any military moves to oust him, he continued to exercise his ministry there, "to the great scandal," Odin wrote in his report to Cardinal Barnabó, "of the faithful" and "the spiritual detriment of a great number of irreligious and ignorant Negroes who consider him as a virtuous persecuted victim for the love that he carried for their race." In a statement that reflected the real reason for his move against Maistre, Odin bemoaned the anarchy of war, which made it more difficult for him to arrest the schism, "the more so because the military authorities work unceasingly to arm and enlist the blacks in the army, thus enabling them to liberate themselves from their masters." The baptismal register of St. Rose's, which recorded 175 baptisms (mostly black) in 1863, testified to the popularity and esteem that Maistre enjoyed among people of color, freedmen, and contrabands. The priest with the questionable past, for whatever reasons— idealism, religion, opportunism, miscalculation—had chosen to cast his lot with the outcasts.[7]

---

6. Bowen to His Grace, The Archbishop of New Orleans, May 25, 1863, ser. 1839, Press Copies of Letters Sent, nos. 296–99 DG, Provost Marshall General Records; Killborn to Odin, July 30, 1863, VI-2-g, ANOC. Odin's letter to Bowen is registerd in Register of Letters Received by the Provost Marshall, ser. 1843, vol. 1, RG 393, P. 1, NA. The letter itself, however, is missing from the Letters Received File. In the matter of Maistre's motivation, the author would like to acknowledge the insights provided in a letter by Cyprian Davis, O.S.B., October 16, 1998.

7. Odin to Barnabó, August 14, 1863; Book of Baptisms, St. Rose of Lima Parish, and Registre des Marriages et Baptêmes, Holy Name of Jesus, AANO.

Perhaps Maistre found hope in the earlier example of Antonio de Sedella, who had ministered to blacks, led a schism, and suffered ecclesiastical censure only to win exoneration in the end. True, Sedella had enjoyed the overwhelming support of white New Orleanians in an environment in which slavery was not unraveling, and neither had he faced as formidable a figure as Odin. Still, Maistre had aligned himself with what he regarded as the powerful forces and progressive policies of the Union. He also enjoyed the support of the free people of color of his parish, the Creole elite at *L'Union*, and many black New Orleanians free and slave, throughout the city. Moreover, he could appeal his case to Rome. He gambled, perhaps, that his power base might enable him to force the seemingly implacable archbishop into accepting some kind of compromise that would preclude his exile from New Orleans. Time would tell.

Meanwhile, as the standoff continued between the priest and the prelate, news began to filter into the city of things both terrible and glorious upriver at Port Hudson. There, on May 27, 1863, Cailloux and the rest of the Native Guards had finally had their chance to strike a blow for their own liberation, knowing that they might perish but, in the spirit of Maistre's emancipation sermon, hoping that the "faith set loose" would spread and bear fruit.

Cailloux and his men had advanced from Baton Rouge on May 20 as part of General Banks's operation against Port Hudson, one of two remaining Confederate strongholds on the Mississippi. (The other was Vicksburg.) Banks, a handsome and engaging politician who viewed military command as a stepping stone to higher office (perhaps including the presidency), had suffered defeat in every major military campaign he had led, though he had managed to subdue the Teche country, to the west and south of Port Hudson. This former speaker of the U.S. House of Representatives and governor of Massachusetts owed his appointment as commander of the Department of the Gulf to his political clout and to his predecessor's knack for inflaming the white population of New Orleans. His superiors in Washington wanted two things from him: conciliatory policies that would encourage Unionist sentiment among white Louisianians, especially in New Orleans, and control of the Mississippi River. Politically ambitious, painfully aware that his defeats at the hands of Stonewall Jackson in Virginia had earned him the deri-

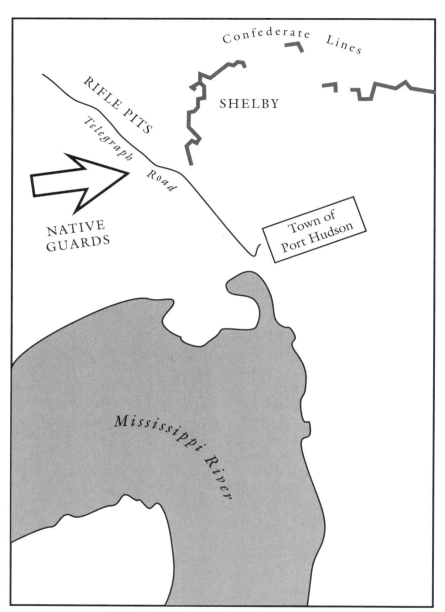

The Assault on Port Hudson

sive sobriquet "Old Commissary General," jealous of Ulysses S. Grant's growing reputation, and resentful of the latter's failure to reinforce his troops as promised, the often indecisive Banks was determined to take Port Hudson by force.[8]

In that, he and his approximately thirty thousand troops faced a formidable task. The town sat on a towering and precipitous eighty-foot-high bluff that commanded one of the sharpest and most difficult bends in the river. In addition, the land approaches to Port Hudson formed what Banks termed "a perfect labyrinth" of creeks, marshes, canebreaks, ravines, and woods. Under the vigorous and charismatic major general Franklin Kitchell Gardner, the six-thousand-man garrison aimed big guns toward the river and built a four-and-one-half mile semicircle of land defenses, composed of breastworks and batteries, that connected the upper and lower river defenses. They built abatis (arrangements of felled trees with branches facing outward) along ravines, dug rifle pits, and constructed lunettes, or three-sided field forts, to cover approaches by road.[9]

Banks ordered his commanders to launch an attack on May 27 against the fortifications commencing with an artillery barrage at six A.M., to be followed by an infantry onslaught. The general envisioned the land assault in conjunction with a naval bombardment from Admiral David Farragut's fleet in the Mississippi. Unfortunately, he failed to ensure simultaneous attacks by the elements under his command. Nor did he adequately take into account the inability of the units of his force to communicate with or even to see one another. And finally, he implied—erroneously, as it turned out—that further reconnaissance would occur during the bombardment and before the attack. Banks placed six companies of the 1st Regiment, including Cailloux's, and nine companies of the Native Guards 3rd Regiment, under the provisional command of General William Dwight on the extreme right of the Union lines. He had instructed Dwight to assist General Godfrey Weitzel's assault against the left side of the Confederate fortifications which were commanded

8. Edmonds, *The Guns of Port Hudson*, I, 10–13, For the most recent biography on Banks, see James G. Hollandsworth, Jr., *Pretense of Glory: The Life of General Nathaniel P. Banks* (Baton Rouge, 1998).

9. *Ibid.*, 44, 50.

by Colonel W. B. Shelby. Banks left Dwight the option of assisting Weitzel "as the opportunity presented itself," either by creating a diversion or by directly assaulting the works.[10]

In the approaching battle, Cailloux and his men found themselves commanded by devoted abolitionist Lieutenant Colonel Chauncey Bassett, who had taken over as a result of Stafford's arrest. Bassett had volunteered for the Native Guards out of conviction and had adhered to his belief in the "true policy" of recruiting black soldiers despite the scorn, ridicule, and abuse that he and the other officers had suffered. He fancied that he had, by virtue of his ten months' association with black troops in the regiment, become acquainted with "their peculiarities of character and disposition and . . . learned . . . their peculiar wants and . . . the peculiar tact essential to their discipline and development as soldiers." Unfortunately, Cailloux and the men of the 1st and 3rd Regiments also found themselves part of General Dwight's brigade. Dwight, a petty, vindictive, mean-spirited martinet given to drink, had little confidence in or regard for black troops and resented having to command them.[11]

As it moved into position the day before the battle, the 1st Regiment exhibited fine spirit amidst the vine-covered, flowering magnolia forest. White troops whom they passed reported high morale in the two black regiments, the soldiers bragging that "they would make no guard by taking prisoners." As the color company, Cailloux's Company E would man the right center of the regimental line, with the color bearers posted on the left. Company E would lead the charge, a tribute to Cailloux's demonstrated leadership and to the discipline and pride he had instilled in his troops. One officer, Col. William Logan Rodman of the 38th Massachusetts, noted in his diary that Col. John Nelson of the 3rd Regiment had bragged that "his niggers" would make the assault and take their colors into the town first. The black troops made such a fine impression on Rodman's men that few mocked them or showed contempt, "even . . . the Irishmen." He added, "if they will fight, and Port Hudson falls, the great problem of 'Will the blacks fight?' will be solved forever. It is a question of vast interest."[12]

10. *Ibid.*, II, 34–35, 51–52.
11. Chauncey J. Bassett to Brigadier General G. S. Andrews, July 31, 1863; Edward Bacon, *Among the Cotton Thieves* (Detroit, 1867), 159–61.
12. L. Carroll Root, "The Experiences of a Federal Soldier in Louisiana, 1863," *Louisiana Historical Quarterly*, XIX (1936), 658; Edmonds, *The Guns of Port Hud-*

The Sunday of the attack dawned clear, bright, and beautiful. By seven A.M. Weitzel, positioned to the left of Dwight, had launched a doomed attack on Confederate positions. Dwight, already drunk, met with Nelson and Lieutenant Colonel Bassett. Designating Nelson as the overall battlefield commander, Dwight indicated that he (Dwight) would monitor the situation from the rear. Six companies of the 1st Regiment would lead the attack, followed by nine companies of the 3rd. Dwight, however, misled Nelson and Bassett. He told them that the terrain that the two regiments would traverse during the attack was "easy," even though neither he nor anyone else had reconnoitered it. He also promised artillery support from two batteries and reinforcement from two regiments should the troops become pinned down.[13]

At roll call, color sergeant Anselmo Planciancios accepted the regimental standards (probably the national colors with the regimental name emblazoned on it and another banner unique to the unit) for Company E from Lieutenant Colonel Bassett. Color-bearers had the most dangerous jobs in the infantry. They attracted heavy enemy fire because of the key role they played. The rank and file aligned on the colors in battle and looked for the banners as a rallying point if they became disorganized amidst the smoke and confusion of combat. Planciancios, like other color sergeants, held his post as a result of his demonstrated "gallantry and military bearing." A color guard of five corporals, also distinguished for their military conduct, accompanied him; much depended on their courage and daring, for wherever they carried the colors, the troops would follow. Bassett ordered Planciancios to "protect, defend, die for, but . . . not surrender these flags." The men cheered his response: "Colonel, I will bring these colors in honor or report to God the reason why." His reputed words reflected the importance of both honor and religion (a belief in an afterlife) in helping Civil War soldiers overcome their fear of death and steel themselves to fight. Planciancios, who had been baptized forty-one years earlier at St. Louis Cathedral and whose wife

son, II, 37; Department of War, *U.S. Infantry Tactics for the Instruction, Exercise, and Maneuvers of the United States Infantry* (Philadelphia, 1862), 7–8; William Logan Rodman Diary in Thomas W. Higginson, *Harvard Memorial Biographies*, (2 vols; Cambridge, Massachusetts, 1866), I, 73. The author originally found this diary on the Louisiana Native Guards homepage maintained by James G. Hollandsworth.

13. Wilson, *The Black Phalanx*, 527; Bacon, *Among the Cotton Thieves*, 159; Edmonds, *The Guns of Port Hudson*, II, 52.

was pregnant with their third child, would, later that day, make his report to God.[14]

The military objective of the black troops was to overcome the force on the extreme left of the Confederate line. It occupied a nearly level crest of a steep bluff that bent back toward the Mississippi and dominated the low ground by a sugarhouse, where Telegraph Road crossed Foster's Creek. Before the battle, Cailloux displayed great confidence and self-possession, walking down the ranks of his men exchanging pleasantries. As the regiment advanced, he ordered the men into skirmish formation and moved among them shouting encouragement in both English and French as they made their way through the dense and tangled woods on both sides of Telegraph Road.

What they saw as they came to the edge of the woods must have startled them, for they did not gaze on the "smooth" approach to Port Hudson that Dwight had promised them. Instead, several hundred yards in front of them, running parallel to a road they had to cross, stood a rugged bluff about four hundred yards in length, occupied by six companies of the 39th Mississippi under Colonel W. B. Shelby. To the front, and at a lower elevation, stood a second bluff that projected boldly from the main height with a sharp return to the right to form a natural outcrop that would allow flanking fire from the rifle pits that covered it, especially in the direction of any force emerging from the road and attempting to cross the pontoon bridge over Foster's Creek. Sixty men under Lieutenant T. C. Rhodes occupied this stronghold. A Confederate-engineered backwater from the Mississippi further protected the bluffs by forming a moat about two hundred yards in front of them. Cailloux and his men could not flank these obstacles because to the right along the road lay an impassable

14. August V. Kautz, *Customs of Service for the Non-Commissioned Officers and Soldiers* (Philadelphia, 1864), 130–31; Arms and Equipment of the Union (Morristown, N. J., 1991), 244; Linderman, *Embattled Courage*, 157; McPherson, *For Cause and Comrades*, 64, 77; SLC, Book 17, p. 132, Act 1014, AANO; Pension Record of Anselmos Plaçiençios RG 15, NA. The spelling of Planciancios's name varies depending on the source. It appears as "Anselma Placencio" in the St. Louis Cathedral book of baptisms and as "Plaçiençio" in his wife's depositions in his pension file. See SLC, Book 17, p. 132b, Act 1014, in AANO, and Pension File of "Anselmos Plaçiençios." I have used the spelling found in the first muster roll of E Company, dated September, 1862. See Muster Roll of Company E, September 1862, in Regimental Papers, ser. 57, 73rd USCInf, USCT, RG 94, NA.

swamp of cottonwoods, willows, and cypress trees that ran down to the river, and to the left lay a tangled abatis of felled trees, under-brush, and gullies. To even reach the backwater, Cailloux would have to lead his men across several hundred yards of nearly impassible terrain along a shallow gorge exposed to enemy gunfire and artillery. Moreover, the troops would not enjoy the artillery support promised to them; Confederate gunners had already routed the two Union batteries, with one of the latter getting off only a solitary round in return.[15]

At 10 A.M., the 1st Regiment, followed closely by the 3rd, emerged from the willow forest in good order, each regiment form-ing a long line two ranks deep. The men advanced first at quick and then double-quick time toward the bluff about six hundred yards away. A party of skirmishers, concealed in a little copse on the attack-ers' left flank, fired on them, while to their front they faced a volley from the rifle pits and the simultaneous discharge of artillery. The barrage threw the leading elements into confusion, and they broke and ran to cover among the willows. Cailloux and other officers ral-lied their men using swords, threats, curses, and words of encourage-ment. Accounts differ as to how many times the men reformed, charged, broke, and reformed again. Some say once, some three, some as many as six times. Cailloux led a charge of screaming and shouting men that reached the backwater, about two hundred yards from the bluffs. At that point, they fired their first and apparently only volley. In response, Confederate artillery opened up on them with solid shot, grapeshot, and canister and the infantry rained down lead. Only the availability of trees, stumps, and other obstacles pre-vented a complete slaughter. As one member of the regiment re-called, "Quite a number of men were hurt in that fight by the limbs of trees falling on them." One of these was Frank Trepagnier, who remembered, "A shell from a rebel battery cut the limb of a tree and it fell on me injuring my back. It struck me across the small of the back, knocked me down and I was carried off the field." One Con-federate veteran of the battle who was positioned directly opposite

15. Richard B. Irwin, *History of the XIXth Army Corps* (1892; repr. Baton Rouge, 1985), 172–73; M. J. Smith and James Freret, "Fortification and Siege of Port Hudson," *Southern Historical Papers*, XIV (1886), 320–22; Edmonds, *The Guns of Port Hudson*, II, 53–54; Winters, *The Civil War in Louisiana*, 251–252.

the charge of the black troops recalled, "They were fighting in the timber and suffered severe bombardment and sustained several desperate charges. We ran them back on the white troops that were supporting them several times." John A. Kennedy of the 1st Arkansas Regiment watched the black soldiers move toward the moat but, refusing to attribute bravery to them, less generously explained their willingness to make the charge to Yankee troops positioned behind them, allegedly forcing them to fight.[16]

Even in the midst of the pandemonium that had broken loose, Cailloux remained true to the code of "sublime courage" that dictated that officers "lead the charge" and boldly place themselves in danger to demonstrate their valor and to embolden and rally their men. His face ashen from the sulfurous smoke, his left arm dangling by his side—broken by a ball above the elbow—while his right hand held his unsheathed sword, Cailloux hoarsely exhorted his soldiers: "En avant, mes enfants!" (Once more, my children), and "Follow me!" His color company presented an especially good target for Rebel sharpshooters. As Cailloux moved in advance of his troops urging them to follow him across the flooded ditch, he was killed by a shell that struck him in the head. Sergeant Planciancios, boldly and conspicuously flourishing the flag, was also felled by a missile that cut the banner in two and carried away part of his skull. Two men nearby struggled to raise the brain-splattered standard; one of them, the recently promoted eighteen-year-old corporal Louis Leveiller, fell mortally wounded. The other, Athanase Ulgere, a former slave, took a bullet in his left hand as he retrieved the colors.[17]

16. Depositions of Arthur Victor, March 7, 1893, and Frank Trepagnier, March 2, 1893, Pension File of Joseph F. B. [Frank] Trepagnier, RG 15, NA; Deposition of George M. Flick, March 6, 1893, Pension File of Frank B. Trepagnier, RG 15, NA; Diary of John A. Kennedy, Co. H, 1st. Arkansas Regt., April 25 to June 9, 1863, in ser. 1756, Letters Received, Department of the Gulf, RG 393, Pt. I, NA.

17. Linderman, *Embattled Courage*, 21, 44–48, 157; J. T. Paine, Surgeon, Report in Pension Record of "Anselmos Plaçiençios" in RG 15, NA; Edmonds, *The Guns of Port Hudson*, II, 49–58; McConnell, "Louisiana's Black Military History," in Macdonald, Kemp, and Haas, *Louisiana's Black Heritage*, 51–53; Diary of John A. Kennedy; Benjamin Quarles, *The Negro in the Civil War* (1953; repr. New York, 1968), 217; Wilson, *The Black Phalanx*, 214, 525–28; P. F. DeGournay, "The Siege of Port Hudson," from the *New Orleans Times Weekly*, reprinted in *Annals of War: Chapters of Unwritten History*, copy at the Port Hudson State Commemorative Area Museum (hereafter, PHCM), Zachary, Louisiana; Smith and Freret, "For-

With Cailloux and Planciancios dead, and in the midst of the fierce Confederate barrage, the 1st Regiment broke in disorder and fell back on the 3rd as it forded the creek, causing even more confusion. According to some accounts, thirty or forty volunteers from the 3rd held their ground nonetheless and even attempted to swim across the backwater to the base of the bluff, but were mowed down. Only six were reported to have survived the return trip. Meanwhile, the majority of the attackers plunged across the creek and fled pall mall into the willow forest surrounding the sugarhouse. Some men were trampled in the melee. Noel Bacchus, Cailloux's 1st sergeant and a man of sterling character, did not succumb to panic. Rather, he kept his head and managed to save the life of Lieutenant Louis Larrieu of Company A by leading him to safety. While some officers attempted again to rally their troops, others ran into the swamps for cover and were later dismissed for cowardice: Captain Alcide Lewis of Co. G, Second Lieutenant Louis H. Thibaut of Company H., and Second Lieutenant Hippolyte St. Louis of Co. E. (St. Louis later claimed that the charges of cowardice against him stemmed from his refusal to go back out onto the field to retrieve Cailloux's body.) The growing heat of the day seemed to exacerbate the intensity of Confederate fire. Artillery had the range of the willow swamp and shelled it for several hours, tearing the slender trees into splinters and causing many casualties. A Confederate soldier recalled, "Our shots tore the fragile willows into fragments and the splinters were probably as dangerous as our fire." John J. Cage, first sergeant of I Company, suf-

tification and Siege of Port Hudson," 320–22; Edmonds, *The Guns of Port Hudson*, II, 53–57; Winters, *The Civil War in Louisiana*, 253; Williams, *A History of the Negro Troops*, 218–19; Lawrence Lee Hewitt, *Port Hudson: Confederate Bastion on the Mississippi* (Baton Rouge, 1987), 147–50; Brown, *The Negro in the American Rebellion*, 168–70; Deposition of John Taylor, alias Aleck James, May 3, 1911, in Pension File of John Taylor, RG 15, NA; Charles P. Bosson, *A History of the 42nd Regiment Infantry, Massachusetts* (Boston, 1886), 365; Christian, "Captain André Cailloux," Part II; Marcus Christian, "Color Sergeant: Anselmas Planciancois—"Iron Man," typescript, Box 17, Marcus Christian Collection, Earl K. Long Library, UNO; Surgeon's Certificate, July 28, 1868, Pension File of Andre Caillaux [*sic*], RG 15, NA; Affidavit of Rose Ulgère, October 26, 1904, Deposition of Louis Snaër, August 25, 1894, Pension File of Athanase Ulgère, RG 15; Deposition of Clement St. Cyr, July 3, 1895, Pension File of Jacques Augustin, RG 15; Muster Roll of Company E, 1st. Regiment, Corps d'Afrique, June 1–August 1, 1863, Regimental Papers, ser. 57, 73rd USCInf, USCT, RG 94, NA.

fered wounds to the right knee and foot from an exploding shell. At the same time, the barrel of a gun, having been severed from its stock by a shell, struck Cage across the abdomen, bending and adhering to him until removed by a friend. Remarkably, he recovered and returned later to the regiment to become the sergeant major.[18]

Colonel Nelson notified Dwight of the failed assault and received a new order from the inebriated general to "Charge again." Faced with outright refusal by Lieutenant Colonel Henry Finnegass of the 3rd Regiment and recognizing the futility of another assault, Nelson ordered his men to remain in the willow forest and to fire at the Confederates, even though they lay beyond the effective range of his men's muskets, so that Dwight would believe that his orders were being carried out. The Native Guards retired at nightfall, having endured a day-long artillery barrage after an assault on an impregnable defensive position over almost impassable terrain without benefit of artillery support. One Confederate recounted, "During that day and the next we could hear the groans of the wounded that had fallen among the willows, and the dead lay festering in the hot sun, creating a sickening stench."[19]

The 1st Regiment, an inexperienced unit in its first test of fire under desperate ciurcumstances and with less training than most white units, had performed honorably. Every group of Banks's attacking force, white and black, had failed to breach the Confederate defenses, but the 1st Regiment had confronted what one military man called "by far the stronger part of the rebel works." As a result, they suffered 105 casualties (approximately 17 percent) including

18. Winters, *The Civil War in Louisiana*, 253; P. F. DeGournay, "The Siege of Port Hudson"; Deposition of J. T. Paine, late surgeon of the 73rd USCInf., March 3, 1880, Pension File of Douglas Brown, RG 15, NA; Depositions of Noel Bacchus, January 3, 1890, and Louis D. Larrieu, January 6, 1890, Pension File of Noel J. Bacchus, RG 15, NA; Service Records of Alcide Lewis, Hippolyte St. Louis, and L. H. Thibaut, Compiled Military Service Records, RG 94; Deposition of Hippolyte St. Louis, February 17, 1890, Pension File of Joseph T. Martin, RG 15, NA; Edmonds, *The Guns of Port Hudson*, II, 55, 59; Lt. Howard C. Wright, *Port Hudson: Its History from an Interior Point of View* (1863; repr. Baton Rouge, 1961), 36; Original Invalid Claim, November 6, 1885, Surgeon's Certificate, October 13, 1906, Pension File of John J. Cage, RG 15; Military Service Record of John J. Cage, Compiled Military Service Records, RG 94.
19. Winters, *The Civil War in Louisiana*, 253; Hollandsworth, *The Louisiana Native Guards*, 55–57; P. F. DeGournay, "The Siege of Port Hudson."

two officers (Cailloux and Crowder) and 24 enlisted men killed. Cailloux's company had five men killed in action and two who later died of wounds suffered that day. On the other hand, the Confederates under Shelby sustained no casualties in the lopsided contest.[20]

The Native Guards had suffered from both the military and the personal shortcomings of their commanding generals, Banks and the drunken Dwight, and with the less-than-inspired leadership of Bassett and Finnegan. (The latter was eventually court-martialed.) These problems manifested themselves most significantly in the faulty intelligence regarding the terrain and the promised artillery and infantry support that never arrived. And as a New York *Times* correspondent noted, "In the midst of the carnage, when men in every form of horrible mutilation were being sent to the rear . . . —after fighting as few white men could have fought—not a single ambulance or stretcher was there to gather their torn and incapacitated bodies." Nor, parenthetically, was a priest present to tend to their spiritual needs. Banks's assault on Port Hudson had completely failed in all sectors. The Union had suffered a total of 1,995 casualties, and Banks had lost the respect and confidence of his men; the Confederates had a total of 235 killed, missing, and wounded.[21]

That night, some of the Confederate troops left their lines to search the dead and dying who lay in front of them. They first encountered the body of Cailloux, which lay in advance of the others near the ditch. Some native New Orleanians recognized him. In his pocket, they found his officer's commission and eight dollars in greenbacks. During a four-hour truce the day after the assault, Union details retrieved and buried the remains of all the white soldiers. Cailloux and the other Louisiana Native Guards, however, were left to lie where they had fallen. Walter Stephens Turner of the 39th Mississippi Infantry wrote in his diary on the 28th, "The enemy

20. C. Thomas to Honorable H. Wilson (*Congressional Globe*), May 30, 1864, in Woodward, *The Negro in the Military*, 5997, RG 94, NA; *The Official Army Register of the Volunteer Force of the United States Army, 1861, '62, '63, '64, '65,* (8 vols., 1865, Washington, D. C.; repr. Gaithersburg, MD., 1987), VIII, 246–47, 250–51.

21. New York *Times*, June 13, 1863; Winters, *The Civil War in Louisiana*, 260; Field and Staff Muster Roll of Company E, 1st. Regiment, Corps d'Afrique, June 1–August 1, 1863; *The Official Army Register*, VIII, 246–47, 250–51; J. F. Moors, *History of the 52nd Regiment, Massachusetts Volunteer Militia* (Boston, 1893), 160.

have buried all their white men and left the Negroes to melt in the sun. That shows how much they care for the poor ignorant creatures. After they are killed fighting their battles, having done all they can for the Federals then for them to let the bodies of the poor creatures lie and melt in their own blood and to be made the prey of both birds and beasts." The *Times* reporter observed that although "by a flag of truce our forces in other directions were permitted to reclaim their dead, the benefit, through some neglect was not extended to the black regiments." Some northern journalists attributed the situation to rebel snipers who would not permit Union soldiers to collect the bodies of the black troops. The observations of the Confederate diarist, however, were probably more accurate in ascribing responsibility to Banks. Indeed, the stench of death became so unbearable that Colonel Shelby approached General Gardner with a request to ask for a truce for burial. Some of the Confederates even volunteered for the loathsome task, but nothing came of it. Banks rebuffed the proposal, reportedly replying "that he had not dead there." Banks's actions may have arisen from a combination of indifference and calculation—indifference toward his black soldiers and calculation that the stench of their decomposing bodies would make life more miserable and unhealthy for the defenders. So Cailloux's bloated body and those of his comrades lay amidst corruption and exposed to broiling sun, rain, vultures, flies, and rodents until after the surrender of Port Hudson forty days later.[22]

Meanwhile, officers sympathetic to the cause of black troops but not present during the attack anxiously sought word about the Guards' battlefield performance. Captain Elias D. Strunke, serving with one of General Daniel Ullman's black regiments, removed and ministered to the wounded on the evening of May 27, "gathering . . . as much information as possible concerning the battle and the conduct of our troops." He candidly wrote to Ullman of his eagerness to find out all he could concerning the black troops "for their

22. Walter Stephens Turner Diary, May 27, 28, 1863, original in possession of William T. Rogers, Brandon, Mississippi; P. DeGournay, "The Siege of Port Hudson"; Edmonds, *The Guns of Port Hudson*, II, 49–58, 377; McConnell, "Louisiana's Black Military History," in Macdonald, Kemp, Haas, *Louisiana's Black Heritage*, 51–53; Quarles, *The Negro in the Civil War*, 217; Wilson, *The Black Phalanx*, 214; Williams, *A History of the Negro Troops*, 218–19; Hewitt, *Port Hudson: Confederate Bastion*, 147–50; New York *Times*, June 13, 1863.

good conduct and bravery would . . . make more popular the movement." The account he heard from First Lieutenant Morris W. Morris of the 1st Regiment did not disappoint him, as he rejoiced to hear of their "gallantry," "coolness," and "bravery." Others heard more exaggerated reports. On May 30, three days after the battle, J. F. Moors, a member of the 52nd Massachusetts at Port Hudson, listened to accounts of sick and wounded soldiers brought to a hospital. They told Moors that the black troops had "fought like very devils" and that, through almost superhuman exertion, they had crossed the wide ditch, scaled the abatis and, once inside the fortifications, had proceeded to bayonet the Confederate gunners. Supposedly overcome by martial frenzy, they had thrown away their guns, "seized their hated foes with their hands and tore their quivering flesh from their faces," before being overwhelmed by superior numbers and compelled to retreat. That version and other embellishments found their way into some of the accounts of the battle that soon filled newspapers.[23]

Journalists sympathetic to the cause of black troops seized on the battle of Port Hudson as evidence of the valor of African Americans and the benefits that their service in the armed forces would bring the race. The *Weekly Anglo-African*, published in New York City, reprinted dispatches from other papers declaring, "The deeds of heroism performed by these colored men were such as the proudest white men might emulate. Their colors are torn to pieces by shot, and literally bespotted by blood and brains." For the editors of that paper and other abolitionists, black and white, the battle had answered definitively and affirmatively the question of how black men would fight: "Nobly . . . have they acquitted themselves, and proudly may every colored man hereafter hold up his head." William Lloyd Garrison's *Liberator* assured its readers that the black troops at Port Hudson had not died in vain, that their blood would "wash out the prejudices so long existing against their oppressed race" and would vindicate the right of all blacks to "life, liberty, and the pursuit of happiness." Washington's *National Intelligencer* printed an extract

23. Captain Elias D. Stranke to Brigadier General D. Ullman, May 29, 1863, ser. 159, Daniel Ullman Papers, Generals' Papers and Books, RG 94, NA; Moors, *History of the 52nd Regiment*, 160; New York *Herald*, June 6, 1863, New York *Times*, June 13, 1863; *The Liberator*, June 26, 1863.

from the letter of an officer of engineers at Port Hudson that appeared to confirm the *Liberator's* hopes for changed attitudes toward black soldiers in the wake of Port Hudson. The officer wrote, "You have no idea how my prejudices with regard to Negro troops have been dispelled by the battle of the other day. The brigade of Negroes behaved magnificently and fought splendidly . . . they are far superior in discipline to the white troops and, just as brave. I hope the government will raise more of them."[24]

The performance of the 1st and 3rd Regiments also drew enthusiastic praise from their commanders. Not surprisingly, Bassett applauded his men, calling his command of them on May 27 at Port Hudson an "honor." He asserted later in a letter to Brigadier General George L. Andrews, who had become the commander of the Corps d'Afrique, that at Port Hudson, "they in a measure solved the general problem that the Negro would fight even under disadvantageous conditions." General Ullman, commander of his own brigade composed entirely of former slaves who had not seen action in the battle, nevertheless later recounted that "the conduct of these Regiments on this occasion wrought a marvelous change in the opinion of many former sneerers." In his report three days after the battle to Major General Halleck, General Banks, the consummate politician who knew that official Washington favored the use of black combat troops, described the conduct of the Native Guards as "in many respects . . . heroic." He lauded their determination and daring and claimed, "Whatever doubt may have existed heretofore . . . the Government will find in this class of troops effective supporters and defenders." Beating the drum for his proposal to create the Corps d'Afrique and backhandedly denigrating black officers, he expressed confidence in the ultimate success of black troops, provided they had "good officers, commands of limited numbers, and careful discipline to make them excellent soldiers." Halleck agreed that organization of colored troops should proceed forward as rapidly as possible, especially in order to garrison posts, though with Port Hudson in mind, he added that "some of the older units will do well in the field." Ullman seized on the battle as a way of encouraging black enlistment. He issued a general order aimed at blacks in which he declared,

24. *Weekly Anglo-African*, June 20, 1863; *The Liberator*, June 26, 1863; *National Intelligencer*, quoted in Brown, *The Negro in the American Rebellion*, 175;

"Your brethren at Port Hudson have shown to the world that they can and will fight, and have displayed as dauntless courage as ever illuminated a battle field. Emulate their noble example, and fight under the glorious banner of the Republic."[25]

That banner did not yet fly over Port Hudson, for the surrender would not come until July 8, after a month-long siege. On June 14, Banks tried again to take the fortifications by storm with another futile and bloody assault, in which the 1st Regiment did not participate. By that date, as if the initial attack on May 27 had marked the end of its original, unique identity, the 1st Louisiana Native Guards, in accordance with Banks's order of June 6, had acquired a new designation: 1st Regiment of the Corps d'Afrique. On June 15, Banks called for volunteers for a storming column of a thousand men "to vindicate the flag of the Union." According to Bassett, all of the men of the regiment "expressed their willingness to go." He selected fifty-four noncommissioned officers and privates from Companies C, G, H, I, and K, but Banks chose not to accept the blacks for the storming party. Nor did he ultimately carry through with the operation, owing to high numbers of casualties in the previous two attacks and dwindling numbers of available troops because of sickness and plummeting morale. He focused instead on siege tactics, with the intent of pounding the Confederates with artillery, picking them off with sharpshooters, and starving them out. During the siege, the men of the 1st and 3rd Regiments played an important but thankless role. The two regiments were divided into two parties of seven hundred each and worked night and day building an immense battery, four hundred feet of breastworks, and a series of rifle pits. To protect against snipers, they worked behind cotton bales and fascines and

25. Chauncey J. Bassett to G. S. Andrews, July 31, 1863; *OR*, Vol. 26, p. 45; Major General Daniel Ullman to General Richard C. Drum, April 16, 1887, ser. 160, Generals' Reports of Service, RG 94, NA; Berlin, Reidy, and Rowland, *Freedom*, II, 530; Confederate Walter Stephens Turner, who had helped repulse the Native Guards, noted Banks's praise and mocked it with the observation that the general couldn't get them to charge again because "if they are Negroes they have more sense than that." Turner Diary, June 28, 1863, original in possession of William T. Rogers; H. W. Halleck to Banks, July 24, 1863, Box 27, Nathaniel P. Banks Papers, Library of Congress; General Order 7, in Berlin, Reidy, and Rowland, *Freedom*, II, 414.

hogsheads filled with cotton as shields between them and the rebels. In his diary, Colonel Willoughby M. Babcock reported that the southerners fired on blacks as much as they could and often shouted to the white soldiers guarding a work party, "Hello, Yank! Get down there. I want to shoot that damned nigger!" Blistering heat, lack of clean water, vermin, fevers, and the stench of death also plagued the troops as they labored. Flies and mosquitoes "set sleep at defiance." Fortunately, four days after the fall of Vicksburg the Confederate garrison at Port Hudson finally surrendered and the Mississippi could once again "flow unvexed" to the Gulf. Union burial parties then recovered Cailloux's body, which they identified only by the ring of the Friends of Order on his finger.[26]

While the siege of Port Hudson was taking place upriver, Federal authorities in New Orleans, seeking to deprive the rebels of any useful information, had clamped a news blackout on the city, forbidding newspapers to publish information about the battle and refusing to dispense any official word. Although large numbers of wounded had begun arriving at city hospitals, people could not obtain their names or information about their condition, nor could visitors gain admittance. Authorities worried not only about compromising the Port Hudson operation but also about inadvertently providing information to Confederate general Richard Taylor whose forces had entered the Lafourche country and presented a threat to New Orleans.[27]

Word of Cailloux's death, however, filtered into the city, devastating the Afro-Creole community. *L'Union* seized upon the circumstances to transform Cailloux into something of a martyr for the cause of black military service, emancipation, and equality. On June 16, 1863, the paper published resolutions adopted by members of the Conclave du Bon Pasteur, No. 2. The Conclave invoked the justice of God, the civil rights of men, and religious liberty (a possible refer-

26. McConnell, "Louisiana's Black Military History," in Macdonald, Kemp, and Haas, *Louisiana's Black Heritage*, 55–58; Roland C. McConnell, "The Surrender of Port Hudson," in Glenn R. Conrad, ed., *Readings in Louisiana History* (New Orleans, 1978), 194; Moors, *History of the 52nd Regiment*, 160; *OR*, Vol. X, pp. 716–17, and Vol. XXVI, pt. 1, p. 539; Dyer, *A Compendium of the War of the Rebellion*, 1214; Edmonds, *The Guns of Port Hudson*, II, 131.

27. New York *Herald*, June 9, 1863; *L'Union*, June 16, 1863; Irwin, *History of the XIXth Army Corps*, 214.

ence to Maistre) in mourning the death "of the brave and glorious martyrs who succumbed in combat against an enemy of the United States and usurper of the liberty of men of our race for 250 years." Calling Cailloux "a noble son of Louisiana," it declared that "his memory will always be dear to us," especially because he led black troops against the rebel fortifications, thereby "rehabilitating the race" in the eyes of the Army. Evidencing the hyperbole that would characterize descriptions of the engagement in later news accounts, but also communicating the reality of Cailloux's demonstrated heroism, *L'Union* described him standing for two hours, the national colors floating betwen his hands, seemingly protected amidst the hail of fire by divine Providence until he led the fatal charge. The resolutions of the Conclave promised "glorious immortality" to him and his companions, who had "showed the world that the men of color possess all the great qualities that appear in man: honor, bravery, patriotism, magnanimity, and chivalry." Members of the Bon Pasteur society resolved to wear crepe for thirty days in memory of Cailloux, Crowder, and the other fallen members of the Native Guards, and presented copies of their resolution to Cailloux's family.[28]

The Cailloux mythos continued to build. Afro-Creole radicals used the figure of the fallen captain as part of their campaign to radicalize and energize people of color, strengthening their determination to end slavery and attain equality. On Independence Day, 1863, *L'Union* published a poem by "E. H." titled, "Captain André Cailloux and His Companions in Arms." Emphasizing the slain officer's racial pride, courage, and manliness, the poem put forth the claim that his noble death would help ensure the triumph of liberty and the Union by inspiring massive black enlistments:

Captain André Cailloux and His Companions in Arms

> What! You weep for the brave captain,
> Whose valor astonished Port Hudson!
> Why, in falling in the open field,
> He struck down vile conjecture.
> We console ourselves, we, men of his race,

28. *L'Union*, June 16, 1863.

That before God alone he bent his knee.
Let both Whites and Blacks follow the noble path
    Of the brave André Cailloux.

Yes, it was among the cannon-balls, the grapeshot
That this hero of the black brow so proud
Directed his steps, leading in battle
His black brothers, brave as steel!
It was in the midst of enemy bullets,
Hissing of death, and bearing it everywhere,
That these soldiers, possessed of a thousand lives,
    Followed André Cailloux!

God, what ardor! What sublime courage!
Without any help in this bloody battle,
They made the enemy tremble in his rage;
Banks recognized the saviors of the state!
Six times that day they attempted victory:
A thousand cannons crushed them everywhere.
Those noble dead in the abode of glory!
    Always follow Cailloux!

Oh Liberty! Our mother, contemplate
What your children will henceforth be able to do?
Doubt has fled; open your temple to them,
And let the Union bide its time.
Conquered soon the unworthy rebels,
Bloodthirsty men, of your grandeur jealous,
Will disappear, and there will be faithful to you
    Over a hundred thousand Cailloux!!![29]

In a séance conducted on July 17, Captain Henry Rey of C Company of the 1st Regiment, an Afro-Creole radical and a leading spiritualist medium who contributed occasional pieces to *L'Union*, claimed to have contacted Cailloux. He avowed that Cailloux's spirit had promised to remain among his black comrades to inspire them with "manly courage and an indomitable spirit." According to Rey, Cailloux urged them to fight, pledged to welcome and guide them into the spirit world should they fall, declared that "God demands

29. *Ibid.*, July 4, 1863.

liberty," and guaranteed that "our brothers will have it [liberty], equality will follow."[30]

In death as in life, Cailloux helped to unite people of color, Creole and Anglophone. They gathered in great numbers and with great solemnity to pay their respects on July 29, the day of his funeral. Prominent among them, of course, was Cailloux's widow, Felicie, who, in addition to her grievous personal loss, also faced dire economic consequences as a result of her husband's death. Felicie's defiance of Archbishop Odin in choosing Maistre to officiate at the funeral represented a religious and political statement on her part as well as reflecting the extent to which the priest had become identified in the public mind with the Native Guards and the cause of black liberation. Among the family members at the funeral was Cailloux's twenty-four-year-old adopted son, Jean Louis, a private in the 7th Louisiana Regiment (colored), one of two that had been formed on July 4 for sixty days to defend the city against a possible attack by General Taylor.[31]

Afro-Creole radicals, working with Maistre and cooperative military authorities, no doubt orchestrated the public services for Cailloux. The activists clearly hoped to use the event to expiate the shame visited on Cailloux's body at Port Hudson, to highlight the capabilities of black soldiers, and to rally support for their campaign to abolish slavery in the state. Maistre, given his outspoken opposition to slavery, his ministry to the Native Guards and their families, his harboring of slave contrabands, and the reality that he probably was the only priest in the city willing to participate in the public ceremony, was the obvious choice to officiate, a selection that reflected his deepening collaboration with the black radicals. His public partnership with Afro-Creole leaders, which predated that of other white radicals in the city, such as Thomas J. Durant and Anthony Fernandez, may well have served as a catalyst for change—a bridge between black and white radicals that resulted in greater cooperation between them and culminated in an open alliance by the end of the year. Maistre probably also hoped to use the funeral to convince the archbishop that

30. Séance, July 17, 1863, 85-30, p. 156, Spiritualist Registers, René Grandjean Collection, UNO. The author is grateful to Caryn Cossé Bell for a translation of this register.
31. Service Record of Jean Louis Cailloux, Compiled Military Service Records, RG 94; Dyer, *A Compendium of the War of the Rebellion*, 1214.

he wielded considerable influence both among the black masses and among U.S. military authorities, and was thus not a person to be trifled with. More puzzling was why General Banks allowed the event to occur. A public extravanganza for a black officer seems inconsistent with both his purge of black army officers and his aim of winning the support of more white New Orleanians in the wake of Butler's tumultuous tenure. Perhaps Banks not only grudgingly admired the heroism shown by Cailloux but also hoped to defuse the bitterness felt by Afro-Creoles over the purge of black officers at a time when he needed people of color in the 6th and 7th Louisiana Regiments to defend the city. Or, perhaps, given his preoccupation with all of the matters clamoring for his attention after the Port Hudson campaign, Banks simply left the matter to more sympathetic subordinates without pondering the implications. On these points, the historical sources remain mute. The funeral itself, however, drew national attention.[32]

As with the battle of Port Hudson itself, the abolitionist press reported on Cailloux's funeral in considerable, though not always accurate, detail, making Cailloux the first nationally publicized black warrior-hero of the Civil War. The *National Anti-Slavery Standard* reprinted the long account of the funeral that had first appeared in the New York *Times*, as did the *Anglo-African*. *Harper's Weekly* began its piece, "Captain Cailloux was one of the bravest soldiers in our country's service, though a colored man." It accompanied its article, taken from the New Orleans *Era*, with an impressive illustratoin of the funeral procession drawn by one of the Native Guards. The piece claimed mistakenly that Cailloux had fallen "within a few feet of the enemy's parapet." The *Times*, prehaps attempting to make Cailloux more attractive to its readers, or perhaps simply equating all New Orleans free people of color with a particular phenotype, inaccurately identified Cailloux as "a fine looking mulatto." It accu-

32. McTigue, "Forms of Racial Interaction," 51–52. McTigue states that Durant's first verifiable political contact with free people of color took place in November 1863. Brigadier General W. H. Emory, writing from New Orleans, warned Banks of an imminent Confederate threat and noted that when white "so called Union people" of the city had failed to heed his call for sixty-day volunteers, "the free colored population raised two full regiments and placed them at the disposal of the government." Emory to Banks, July 4 and 11, 1863, Box 27, Banks Papers, Library of Congress.

rately characterized him, however, as one who enjoyed the respect and love of those who knew him. The description of Cailloux as a "mulatto" surfaced in several other accounts written by both northerners and southerners. It may have revealed not just faulty sources but also a reluctance on the part of some, either consciously or unconsciously, to ascribe such heroism to one fully black.[33]

On the other hand, George H. Boker, a popular abolitionist poet of the war, showed no such reluctance, drawing upon biblical imagery in apotheosizing Cailloux and his death in a poem entitled "The Black Captain":

The Black Captain

He just lay where he fell,
Soddening in a fervid summer's sun,
Guarded by an enemy's hissing shell,
Rotting beneath the sound of rebels' guns
Forty consecutive days,
In sight of his own tent,
And the remnant of his regiment.

He just lay where he fell,
Nearest the rebel's redoubt and trench,
Under the very fire of hell.
A volunteer in his country's defense,
Forty consecutive nights and days,
And not a murmur of discontent,
Went from the loyal black regiment.

A Flag of truce couldn't save,
No, nor humanity could not give
This sable warrior a hallowed grave,
Nor army of the Gulf retrieve.
Forty consecutive days,
His lifeless body pierced and rent,
Leading in assault the black regiment.

33. New York *Times*, August 8, 1863; *National Anti-Slavery Standard*, August 15, 1863; *Weekly Anglo-African*, August 15, 1863; *Harper's Weekly*, August 29, 1863. For other examples of national press coverage, see P. F. DeGournay, "The Siege of Port Hudson," and Bosson, *A History of the 42nd Regiment*, 364–65.

But there came days at length,
When Hudson felt their blast,
though less a thousand in strength,
For "our leader" vowed the last;
Forty consecutive days
They stormed, they charged, God sent
Victory to the loyal black regiment.

He just lay where he fell,
And now the ground was theirs,
Around his mellowed corpse, heavens tell,
How his comrades for freedom swear.
Forty consecutive nights
The advance pass-word went,
Captain Cailloux of the black regiment.

"He just lay where he fell," Boker intoned, soddening and rotting in the summer's sun beneath the rebel guns for forty days and nights—the same number of days that Jesus fasted in the desert before beginning his public ministry; the same number of days as the season of Lent that culminates in the celebration of the Resurrection; the same number of years that the Israelites wandered in the desert before crossing into the Promised Land. The message was clear: though Cailloux's body had suffered unspeakable dishonor, his immortal spirit and example would live on, continuing to inspire black troops. And on the fortieth day "God sent Victory to the loyal black regiment," as he would ultimately to the Union, thereby redeeming Cailloux's sacrifice and that of the other black troops at Port Hudson. Cailloux had become a redemptive figure of mythic proportions in the popular imagination of friends of the Union.[34]

The emergence of Cailloux as a heroic figure, which flew in the face of commonly held stereotypes about blacks, proved threatening to Confederates and Copperheads (northern sympathizers) alike, and they responded viscerally. In a letter to her son, Polyxene Reynes, the matriarch of a prominent New Orleans Creole family, expressed the shock, outrage, and hatred felt by many white New Orleanians. She described Cailloux's public military funeral and burial as a parody

---

34. *The Black Captain*, quoted in Wilson, *The Black Phalanx*, 217.

of that given to Colonel Charles Dreux, the first Louisiana Confederate officer killed in the Civil War, and complained bitterly that the Yankees had staged it in order to humiliate southerners. The episode had so angered, offended, and shaken her indignant husband, Joseph, that he had taken to bed with a fever after encountering "the burlesque cortege" on Canal Street, complete with its armed Negroes and military band, all led "by the Devil and his train . . . the miserable priest, Lemaitre." Well might Joseph Reynes have taken to his bed, for he, his wife, and many others correctly perceived the imminent danger to the existing social order posed by the events surrounding the interment of Cailloux. After all, as Governor Joseph E. Brown of Georgia had argued, "Whenever we establish the fact that they are a military race, we destroy our whole theory that they are unfit to be free." In an attempt to maintain the threatened stereotype, the Copperhead New York *World* ran a mocking article titled "Defunct Darkey [illegible]." It identified Cailloux as "a well-known 'ball-nigger' of New Orleans," claimed that the Native Guards had charged Port Hudson only because Union bayonets at their rear gave them no choice, and, inadvertently acknowledging the growing power of the Cailloux myth among people of color, observed acidly that "for weeks past, scarcely a wench in the city has appeared without a crepe rosette in memory of 'Saint Cailloux.'" White New Orleanians, alarmed and shocked at the determination, solidarity, and radicalism that Cailloux's death and funeral had inspired among blacks, desperately attempted to debunk the mystique and drive a wedge between blacks and white radicals and federal authorities. A mocking song, written in Creole dialect and entitled "Capitaine Caillou," took aim not ony at Cailloux but also at Maistre, whose sermons, it claimed, had misled the stupid, naive black troops into thinking that they could defeat the Confederates. Here is a translation:

Capitaine Caillou

Can I, Cailloux, escape from Africa
To go and look for freedom?
They told me in America
That Negroes could never enjoy equality.

When I got to the country of America
I heard the roar of the cannon.
The smell of the powder gave me a chill
The Confederates gave me a stomach ache.

At Port Hudson, the Yankees made me run
The black race planted the Union flag.
But the Confederates were not afraid of death
They were there to massacre us—to peel off our skin like onions.

Captain Cailloux was hit by gunshots,
In the valley they let him rot.
For the Yankees it's no big thing
Because a dead negro meant nothing to them.

When they came to look for him in all of the carnage,
They could not find him amidst the dead bodies
and the corruption.
They could only find 1,000 bones mixed
with the frogs in the marsh
In the midst of the corruption and slime of the ditch.

Fr. Lemaitre [Maistre] told us in church
That the Confederates would dance Calinda
The Negroes are stupid and believe anything
Ignore him, they are taking you for dummies.

When you guys go see our friend Fernandez
[Anthony Fernandez, the white radical]
Tell him you have to pray for the soul of Cailloux
Tell him to be aware of Judge Bermudez [another radical]
Who gave lectures in the Bayou.

Many white New Orleanians clearly linked Cailloux and Maistre together as part of the web of emerging radicalism that they abhorred.[35]

35. Polyxene Reynes to Joseph Reynes, August 7, 1863, in Reynes (Joseph and Family) Papers, Louisiana and Lower Mississippi Valley Collections, Hill Memorial Library, Louisiana State University, Baton Rouge, Louisiana; Governor Joseph E. Brown, quoted in Joseph T. Glatthaar, "Black Glory: The African American Role in Union Victory," in Gabor S. Boritt, ed., *Why the Confederacy Lost* (New York,

On July 29, 1863, the day of Cailloux's funeral, Henry Perry published another bitter piece, a broadside titled "Dirge of Andre Squash Cailloux: Killed Before Port Hudson, May 27, 1863, while in the act of Slaughtering Southerons":

Good folks who love a pensive theme,
Come listen unto me;
T'was in the month of bright July
Of eighteen sixty-three.
I heard a sound my bosom deemed
More sad than any other—
I heard a white-washed Ethiope Knight,
Bewailing his lost brother!

Henry Perry was the mourner's name,
He had no kinky hair;
But still the noble nigger traits
Shone bravely in his air.
A garb he wore of sable hue,
His tears did freely flow—
And to his sad coat-tail behind
Was pinned a mourning bow.

"Oh God!" he cried, in accents wild,
And clapped his hands together,
"How doth our wounded bosoms bleed
For thee our slaughtered brother!
Long, long, in anguish and in tears,
This crapey badge for you,
Shall float from my coat-tail behind,
Dear Andre Squash Cailloux!

Chorus:—Dear Andre Squash Cailloux!

No more thy stalwart form shall send
With vengeful, bloody hand,
The deathly leaden hail amid
The cursed rebel band!

1992), 139–40; Alcée Fortier, *Louisiana Folklore* (Baltimore, 1888), 67–68. The New York *World* article was quoted in New York *Times*, August 9, 1863.

No more thou'lt make young orphans weep,
Or Southern widows rue,
Nor sheathe thy blade in proud white hearts,
Our bloody, brave Cailloux!
Chorus:—Our bloody, brave Cailloux!

No more thy buxom blooming belle,
The kitchen's peerless Rose,
To the banjoe's dulcet twang shall sing
Thy valor and thy woes!
Yet, rest thee! mourn not for her fate!
We'll comfort her for you;
Abe Lincoln won't forbid the bans,
Dear Andre Squash Cailloux!

Go rest and soothe thy spirit's cares
With this assurance civil,
Thou was the blackest nigger next
To Ullman and the devil!
For Terry, Dostie, Durant, I,
By fate beyond control
Were born with these white skins of shame,
Though niggers true in soul!

And long thy martial name of pride,
Through southern homes shall ring,
As the bloodiest-minded sable ape
Who served the Jackass King!
Long, long in glory and in pride,
This mourning badge for you
Shall deck my long-tail coat behind,
Dear Andre Squash Cailloux!
Chorus:—Dear Andrew Squash Cailloux!

Repeating the canards contained in other pieces, Perry's verse also unwittingly reflects both the fear and the grudging respect that white southerners felt for "bloody, brave, Cailloux!" (and by extension, other black troops) by gratefully noting that "the stalwart form with vengeful, bloody hand," would no longer create white southern orphans or widows by his gun, nor strike at white hearts with his saber.

162

Reflecting southern dread of strong black men as sexual predators, the poem accuses President Lincoln of fostering miscegenation through his use of black troops and refers to Cailloux in bestial terms as "the bloodiest minded sable ape/Who served this Jackass King!" Perry further attempted to debase Cailloux's death by employing the word "squash"—a term associated with killing insects.[36]

The efforts of opponents to demean and ridicule the figure of Cailloux, however, proved futile and only exposed the deep anxiety that many whites felt when confronted with evidence of black valor and solidarity. In death, Cailloux had become the first national black military hero of the Civil War. He had entered the world a slave and had left it free and courageously in the ravines of Port Hudson. His body lay on ground littered with corpses ranging in hue from nearly white to deepest ebony, stark testimony to the growing unity among blacks that Cailloux had helped to foster. His life had been relatively short, but during it, he traced a trajectory from slavery to freedom then to military command and the verge of citizenship. In the process, he helped to vindicate black manhood in the eyes of many, legitimate the use of black troops in combat, and unite free people of color and freedmen in a common cause of liberation and equality. In giving his life to that cause, he became an inspiring icon to his community, encouraging its pride and steeling the resolve of black activists in New Orleans, both Creole and Anglophone, to achieve emancipation and the rights of citizenship, including suffrage.

Yet Maistre's obsequies over Cailloux's casket also marked, for all practical purposes, the demise of black combat officers in the Civil War. Evidence of Cailloux's bravery could neither stem Banks's campaign against black officers nor overcome white reluctance to see men of color wield authority. Indeed, about three months after the battle of Port Hudson, in a letter to President Lincoln, Banks blamed the conflicts that had arisen between white and black troops prior to that battle on the character of the black officers in command, "who were unsuited for this duty." While utterly ignoring the roles played by Callioux and Crowder, Banks charged that the black officers had

36. Henry Perry, "Dirge of André Squash Cailloux: Killed before Port Hudson, May 27th, 1863, while in the act of Slaughtering Southerons," July 29, 1863, Broadsides Collection, John Hay Library, Brown University, Providence, Rhode Island.

"been most of the time, and some still are, in arrest upon charges of a discreditable character." Adding further insult to injury, officials quietly omitted the 1st Regiment from the list of those units entitled to inscribe "Port Hudson" on their regimental flags.[37]

Most of the men of E Company and of the 1st Regiment had acquitted themselves bravely and honorably at Port Hudson. But faced with disrespect, ingratitude, and bad faith on the part of Banks and other officers and government officials, many of them protested with their feet. Just as André Cailloux's body had seemed to "melt" as it lay unburied under the blazing sun at Port Hudson, so too, the 1st Regiment began to melt away through desertions. But the symbolism of André Cailloux did not melt away. Black leaders and their white allies, including Maistre, appropriated the Cailloux icon and made it a key part of their drive for equal rights on the home front.

37. Nathaniel Banks to President Abraham Lincoln, August 16, 1863, *OR*, Vol. XXVI, 688–89; Berlin, Reidy, and Rowland, *Freedom*, II, 310–11; S. M. Quincy to Dear Mother, March 12, 1864, Quincy, Wendell, Holmes, Upham Family Papers (microfilm), LC; Special Order 42, November 11, 1864, War Department, in Woodward, *The Negro in the Military*, 2833, RG 94. A member of the regiment wrote to the *Weekly Anglo-African* in September of 1864: "The only inscription on the banner of the glorious 73rd (the regiment's designation had been changed) is the blood stain of the noble sergeant who bore it in this fierce assault and the rents made in the struggle of the corporals to obtain the dear rag from the dying man who had rolled himself up in its folds. Regiments which were ridiculed as cowards and vagabonds have 'Port Hudson' on their flags. Let us be cautious how we praise the 1st Native Guards; they have it not on their flag. Thank God there were thousands of honest privates in the ranks of the white regiments who tell their story of the 1st Native Guards!" Quoted in Noah Andre Trudeau, *Like Men of War: Black Troops in the Civil War* (New York, 1998), 397.

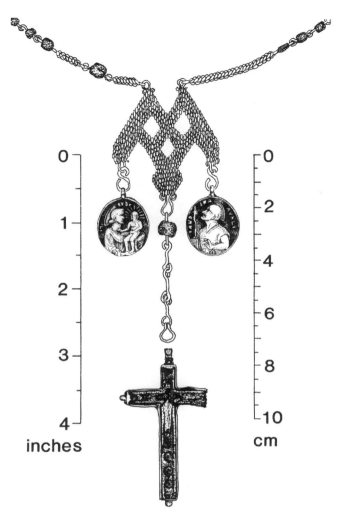

0
1
2
3
4
inches

0
2
4
6
8
10
cm

This rosary, recovered during an archaeological excavation from the grave of a slave buried in the St. Peter/Toulouse Street Cemetery, offers mute testimony to the Catholicism of Afro-Creoles in New Orleans. By the early nineteenth century, slaves and free people of color, especially women, constituted a majority of worshipers at the racially mixed St. Louis Cathedral and comprised at least half of the Catholic population of the city. *Courtesy Louisiana State Division of Archaeology*

The baptismal record of the slave André (Cailloux), dated July 15, 1827, as it appears in the baptismal register for free persons of color and slaves of St. Louis Cathedral. Reception of the sacrament of baptism signified membership in the Catholic church and signified spiritual equality for blacks. Baptismal records documented birth dates and family and religious ties, thereby contributing to the slaves' sense of heritage, dignity, and identity. Note, however, that only the first names of slaves were used and that, though the name of the master appears, that of the slave father does not. *Courtesy Archives of the Archdiocese of New Orleans*

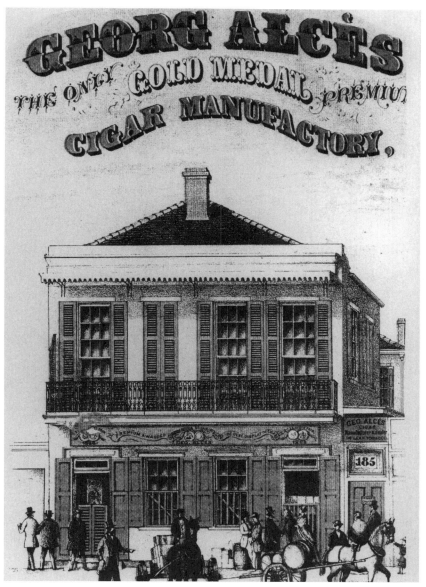

Georges Alcès' Cigar Manufactuary. Unlike Alcès, who became a prominent businessman in the city, André Cailloux remained a small cigar maker who had learned his trade while still a slave and then carved out a life for himself and his family as an artisan amidst the vibrant society created by free people of color in antebellum New Orleans. *Courtesy Louisiana Division of the New Orleans Public Library*

A slave maid, ca. 1840, wearing a red kerchief, or *tignon*. Feliciana Encalada, André Cailloux's remarkable mother-in-law, probably wore something
similar, since a New Orleans city ordinance required all women of African
descent, both slave and free, to cover their heads. Women of color, however, often transformed these intended symbols of subservience into stylish
accoutrements. *Courtesy Louisiana State Museum*

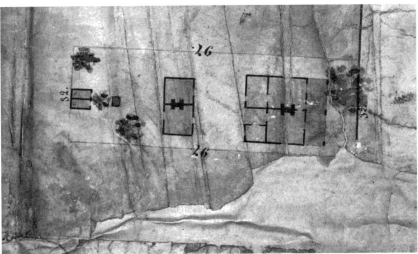

The Creole cottage, originally built by Feliciana Encalada, that André Cailloux and his wife, Felicie Louise Coulon, purchased on Bacchus Street in Lafayette in 1855, complete with floor plan as depicted in a poster advertising it for auction in 1861. *Courtesy New Orleans Notarial Archives*

The charred and gutted remains of the original structure of St. Rose of Lima Church, built by Father Claude Paschal Maistre in 1857. Maistre ministered to a racially mixed congregation and encouraged the formation of burial and mutual aid societies among free people of color. *Courtesy Archives of the Archdiocese of New Orleans*

Officers of the 1st Louisiana Native Guards (Union), February 1863, including Charles Sentmanat, who is on the extreme left. André Cailloux
served as a 1st Lieutenant in Sentmanat's Order Company in the original
Louisiana Native Guards regiment that was formed as part of the Louisiana
state militia after the Civil War began. Following the Federal occupation of
New Orleans, three new Native Guards regiments, ostensibly composed
only of free men of color but in reality including many slaves, were officially
mustered into Union service in September, 1862. Captain André Cailloux
recruited Company E of the 1st Regiment. Harper's Weekly, *February 28,
1863. Courtesy Louisiana and Lower Mississippi Valley Collections, Louisiana
State University Libraries*

Francis E. Dumas, originally captain of Company B of the 1st Regiment, was promoted to major in the 2nd Louisiana Native Guards, thus becoming the highest-ranking black combat officer during the Civil War. As fair-skinned as Cailloux was black, Dumas inherited a plantation but proceeded to enlist his slaves for service in the Union army. *Courtesy C. P. Weaver*

Company D of the 2nd Louisiana Native Guards, stationed at Ship Island, Mississippi, in 1863. Like Cailloux and his men, the members of the 2nd Regiment faced hostility from white troops and civilians. The 2nd Regiment did not participate in the assault on Port Hudson, unlike the 1st and the 3rd. *Courtesy C. P. Weaver*

Pickets of the 1st Louisiana Native Guards stationed along the Opelousas Railroad in early 1863. Colonel Spencer H. Stafford, the commander of the regiment, complained that scattering the companies of his regiment across twenty-eight miles in the Bayou Lafourche and assigning them to either picket duty or manual labor (fatigue duty) allowed little time for the regimental drill necessary to prepare inexperienced troops for combat. *Frank Leslie's Illustrated Newspaper, March 1863. Courtesy Louisiana and Lower Mississippi Valley Collections, Louisiana State University Libraries*

According to contemporary accounts, Cailloux cut a dashing figure astride his horse and was admired for his athleticism, bearing, and courage. Though the officer of the Native Guards pictured in this photo is not Cailloux, one can imagine that Cailloux looked much like this in the mist of morning. These men are from Battery S, 2nd Louisiana Native Guards, Ship Island, Mississippi, Spring 1863. *Courtesy C. P. Weaver*

Contraband slaves arrested in New Orleans on January 20, 1863. The Emancipation Proclamation did not legally apply to slaves in areas already occupied by Union forces, and the slave laws of Louisiana remained technically in effect. Father Maistre ministered to the Native Guards when they trained just outside the city, comforted their families after the regiments went into the field, called publicly for emancipation, and provided a haven at St. Rose of Lima Parish for runaway slaves like those pictured above. Frank Leslie's Illustrated Newspaper, *March 1863. Courtesy Louisiana and Lower Mississippi Valley Collections, Louisiana State University Libraries*

Lieutenant Colonel Chauncey J. Bassett, a dedicated abolitionist from Michigan, assumed command of the 1st Regiment after Colonel Spencer H. Stafford's arrest and led it during the battle of Port Hudson. *Courtesy Roger D. Hunt Collection at the United States Army Military History Institute*

The view from Confederate lines at Port Hudson on May 27, 1863. The 1st and 3rd Native Guard Regiments, with Captain André Cailloux in the lead, charged across Telegraph Road (visible in the background) toward the almost impregnable Confederate positions. *Courtesy of the Illinois Historical Society*

Captain André Cailloux (with raised sword) leading the charge of the 1st
Louisiana Native Guards at Port Hudson on May 27, 1863, during which
he was killed. Inaccurate though the illustration is in its depiction of Cailloux's complexion and of the details of the battle (Cailloux fell well in front
of his men, and the regiment got no closer than two hundred yards from
the Confederate lines), it nevertheless captures his heroism, which helped
to validate the use of black troops in combat. The flag bearer behind Cailloux is Anselmo Planciancios, though, as with Cailloux, this is not an accurate physical representation of him. *Detail from an illustration that
appeared in* Frank Leslie's Illustrated Weekly, *June 27, 1863. Reproduced
courtesy of The Pennsylvania State University Libraries, Rare Books and
Manuscripts.*

Archbishop Jean-Marie Odin of New Orleans suspended Maistre in 1863 for "inciting Negroes." Odin later placed the priest and his parish under interdict when Maistre insisted on continuing his ministry at St. Rose. Maistre eventually formed the schismatic parish of Holy Name of Jesus and did not submit to church authorities until after Odin had died. *Courtesy Texas Catholic Archives*

The funeral of André Cailloux, July 29, 1863. Much to the chagrin of white
New Orleanians, people of color, both free and slave, embraced Cailloux as
their hero and turned out in huge numbers for his military funeral, which
was conducted by Father Maistre in defiance of the archbishop. The event
reflected Cailloux's growing mystique as he was transformed into a powerful symbol of liberation and manhood by Afro-Creoles. Harper's Weekly,
August 29, 1863. Courtesy Louisiana and Lower Mississippi Valley Collec-
tions, Louisiana State University Libraries

Louis Charles Roudanez, publisher of *L'Union* and a leading Afro-Creole activist. His newspaper led campaigns to abolish slavery in Louisiana and then to obtain suffrage and equal rights for blacks. *L'Union* praised Maistre and excoriated the archbishop and Catholic clergy of the city for their alleged Confederate sympathies. *Reproduced from Rodolphe Lucien Desdunes, Nos Hommes et Notre Histoire (Montreal, 1911). Courtesy Howard-Tilton Memorial Library, Tulane University*

Sergeant Alfred Noldier of F Company, 73rd Regiment, Unites States Colored Infantry (originally the 1st Regiment, Louisiana Native Guards). Noldier, a former slave, was captured by Confederate forces at Jackson, Louisiana, in July 1863, and then escaped. Noldier's regiment endured unremitting fatigue duty and blatant racial discrimination. Believing the government to have broken trust with them, many deserted only to return to duty after President Lincoln's amnesty proclamation of 1864. In April 1865, the 73rd was the first Union regiment to breach the Confederate defenses at Fort Blakely outside Mobile. *Courtesy of the National Archives*

7

TWO FRONTS

Even as morale in the 1st Regiment plummeted in the aftermath of the battle at Port Hudson, Afro-Creole activists, energized by their groups' service in the military and united in common cause with Anglophonic blacks and white allies such as Father Maistre, continued to fight on the home front against the injustice that lay at the heart of the difficulties plaguing the soldiers. They effectively and dramatically drew upon the memory of Cailloux as a rallying symbol to bolster their campaign for equal citizenship that extended beyond Louisiana to the rest of the nation.

Afro-Creole radicals viewed service in the army as an integral part of their campaign to abolish slavery and gain equal civil and political rights, including suffrage, for both free people of color and freedmen. *L'Union* declared in its pages that military service gave blacks a claim to citizenship. The crucible of war fueled the Afro-Creole drive for equal rights and emboldened its leaders to move beyond abolition and demand suffrage for both free blacks and freedmen.

Afro-Creole political insurgency had commenced almost as soon as the Native Guards entered Federal service, with Creole leaders holding Union meetings in September 1862. White Unionists, constituting less than 10 percent of the white population and led by Anthony Fernandez, a French-speaking, native New Orleans businessman and Freemason, founded the Union Association on June 4, 1862. By the spring of 1863, the more radical socialist Thomas Durant, a prominent white lawyer and former member of the Louisiana legislature, had replaced Fernandez as the leader of both the Union

Association and the Unionist movement. Durant pressed for a new state constitution that would abolish slavery throughout the state, an effort in which he received encouragement from the Lincoln administration. Afro-Creole leaders cooperated closely with Durant and Fernandez, publishing the minutes of the Association in the pages of *L'Union*, which was its official organ. In November 1863, with an eye to the proposed election of delegates to a state constitutional convention, *L'Union* and its allies pressed for enfranchisement of blacks and sponsored an interracial rally. The gathering adopted a resolution calling on General George F. Shepley, the military governor, to order the registration of free black voters; freedmen, however, were not included at that point.

Free people of color could pitch their demand for suffrage on distinct grounds from recently emancipated slaves: treaty rights. For years, Afro-Creoles had particularly resented their exclusion from all political rights and many civil rights because of what they considered the national government's failure to honor its solemn treaty commitments under Article III of the Louisiana Purchase Treaty, which guaranteed "all the rights, advantages and immunities" of citizenship to the *ancienne population* of the territory. Appearing before the American Freedman's Inquiry Commission in 1863, *L'Union* founder J. B. Roudanez advanced that argument in urging the vote for free people of color. He also stressed their demonstrated intelligence, industriousness, respectability, and, most important, their loyalty to the government as seen in their military service. Durant's Union Association swung behind the demands of free people of color for suffrage. Afro-Creole leaders omitted freedmen from this initial thrust for the ballot, not out of indifference or hostility to them, but as a result of tactical considerations suggested by white Unionists, who argued that Afro-Creoles had a better chance of success if they limited their petition for the vote to those who had enjoyed freedom prior to the war. Once the radicals were convinced that suffrage for free people of color would operate as an opening wedge that would eventually include freedmen, they acceded to that argument.

Indeed, from the time that *L'Union* began publishing, the Afro-Creole radicals who made it their mouthpiece showed considerable concern, albeit sometimes tinged with paternalism, for slaves and contrabands. They campaigned vociferously for abolition, and in December 1862, in anticipation of the Emancipation Proclamation, had created a *Comité Central des Natifs*, or Freedmen's Aid Association. The publication of an English language version of *L'Union* in July 1863, further reflected the desire of the Afro-Creole leadership to make common cause with English-speaking black radicals. The *Tribune*, which succeeded *L'Union* in 1864, bitterly condemned the contract labor system which the military had imposed on the freedmen in 1863 to ensure a stable work force and agricultural production for the Union. The *Tribune* likened the system, which bound freedmen to yearly contracts and restricted their travel, assembly, ownership of firearms, and use of alcohol, to the antebellum Louisiana slave code.[1]

Still, distinctions between free people of color and freedmen did not entirely disappear. On September 1, 1863, for example, in response to requests by a large number of contrabands for admission to the Institute Catholique, the principal put the question to the board of directors. Perhaps concerned about the hazy legal status of contrabands at that point in Louisiana, they ordered him to refuse admission until he received explicit orders from the board to do otherwise. The directors' minutes revealed no subsequent directive, suggesting perhaps, that the question became moot after Louisiana's new constitution, ratified in 1864, abolished slavery in the state. The Sisters of the Holy Family, however, did not admit former slaves as candidates until March 17, 1869, when Chloe Preval, a cook at the archbishopric, entered the small community of half a dozen. She eventually became a professed member in 1871, taking the name Sister Mary Joachim.[2]

1. *L'Union*, January 13, 21, 28, 1863; *Tribune*, February 18, March 3, 1865.
2. Bell, *Revolution, Romanticism, and the Afro-Creole Protest*, 246–49; Ted Tunnell, *Crucible of Reconstruction: War, Radicalism, and Race in Louisiana, 1866–1877* (Baton Rouge, 1984), 84–85; Testimony of J. B. Roudanez before the American Freedman's Inquiry Commission, 1863, Supplemental Report B of the American Freedman's Inquiry Commission, ser. 360, Letters Received by the Office of the Adjutant General, RG 94, NA; *Tribune*, December 8, 1864, March 14, 18, 1865. Journal des Séances, September 1, 1863, AANO; Sister Mary Francis Borgia Hart, S.S.F., *Violets in the King's Garden: A History of the Sisters of the Holy Family of New Orleans* (New Orleans, 1976), 19. For an interpretation differing from the *Tribune* account and arguing that the leadership of free people of color lacked interest in the political rights of freedmen and maintained social distance from them, see Donald E. Everett, "Demands of the New Orleans Free Colored Population for Political Equality, 1862–1865," *Louisiana Historical Quarterly*, XXXVIII (1955),

Deteriorating relations with the military authorities and organizational difficulties within the Union Association delayed the convention movement and led to its collapse. On December 8, 1863, President Lincoln, impatient with the delays involved in forming a free state government, turned to Banks as the "master" of the state's political reorganization and issued his Proclamation of Amnesty and Reconstruction, the "Ten Percent Plan." It offered a pardon to those antebellum voters—excluding high Confederate officials—who would take a loyalty oath and accept the abolition of slavery. When 10 percent of those who had voted in 1860 took the oath, the organziaiton of a new state government could proceed. These new governments were required to provide for the education of young blacks. Lincoln did not seek to challenge southern white control, but only to replace disloyal white southerners with loyal ones. In Louisiana, this arrangement meant official disregard of a campaign to include any free black voters to help shape the new state constitution.[3]

Stymied by these developments at home, Afro-Creoles decided to take the issue of suffrage directly to the president. In December

---

43–64. According to Cyprian Davis, O.S.B., the biographer of Henriette Delille, one must use the early records of the Sisters of the Holy Family with caution because of certain inaccuracies. Gould's "In Full Enjoyment of Their Liberty" suggests that color consciousness may have been more prevalent among free women of color than men, espcially early in the antebellum period, perhaps out of concern for opportunities for their children. Gould's research in the Sisters of the Holy Family archives also suggests that Preval's admission, which came at the insistence of Abbé Napoleon Perché, proved controversial among the sisters themselves and led to a split within the community that took ten years to heal.

3. Bell, *Revolution, Romanticism, and the Afro-Creole Protest*, 250; McTigue, "Forms of Racial Interaction in Louisiana," 23; William C. Harris, *With Charity for All: Lincoln and the Restoration of the Union* (Lexington, 1997), 8–10; *L'Union* (English), April 9, 1864. The issue of Lincoln and black rights has sparked historical controversy and an extensive literature. In *Lincoln and Black Freedom: A Study in Presidential Leadership* (Columbia, S.C., 1981), LaWanda Cox sets forth the case for Lincoln as a "consistent, determined friend of black freedom," though she argues that his political style, informed by his understanding of the Constitution and concern for white backlash, obscured the extent of his commitment. See expecially pages 46–139 on the suffrage question in Louisiana. For historians offering differing interpretations, see Cox, *Lincoln and Black Freedom*, notes 1–4, pp. 185–86, and notes 42, 43, 44 in LaWanda Cox, "From Emancipation to Segregation," in John B. Boles and Evelyn Thomas Nolen, eds., *Interpreting Southern History: Historiographical Essays in Honor of Sanford W. Higginbotham* (Baton Rouge, 1987), 199–253.

1863, they launched a petition drive urging both Lincoln and Congress to extend the right to vote to freeborn men of color in Louisiana. The petition eventually bore the signatures of more than a thousand property-holding free men of color, twenty-seven of them veterans of the Battle of New Orleans, and twenty two white radicals, including Durant and Fernandez. Two of the signers, J. B. Roudanez and Albert Bertonneau, the latter a former officer in the 2nd Louisiana Native Guards, carried it to Washington. As mentioned above, freedmen were initially to be included in the petition but were excluded for tactical reasons. Once in Washington, however, Roudanez and Bertonneau, at the urging of congressional Radical Republicans like Charles Sumner, added a final paragraph to include all those of African descent, "especially those who have vindicated their right to vote by bearing arms." They presented the document to President Lincoln on March 12 and also submitted copies to the House and to the Senate. Although Roudanez had renounced the institutional Catholic church and embraced rationalism and anticlerical Freemasonry, he nonetheless echoed his universalist Catholic background and the prophetic outlook of that great majority of Afro-Creoles who remained within the Church when speaking at a dinner in Boston on April 12, 1864, about the suffrage petition. Eloquently, he declared, "As slavery is abolished, with it must vanish every vestige of oppression. The right to vote must be secured; the doors of our public schools must be opened, that our children, side by side may study from the same books and imbibe the same principles and precepts from the Book of Books—learn the great truth that God 'created of one blood all nations of men to dwell on all the face of the earth.' "[4]

The petition and its bearers clearly impressed Lincoln. The day after receiving them, he penned a private note to Governor Michael Hahn, then in the midst of preparing for the Louisiana constitutional convention scheduled to convene in April. "I barely suggest for your private consideration" Lincoln wrote, "whether some of the colored people many not be let in [to the suffrage]—as, for instance, the

---

4. Bell, *Revolution, Romanticism, and the Afro-Creole Protest*, 250–52; "Memorial of a large number of citizens of Louisiana asking that citizens of African descent residing in this state who were free at the breaking out of the rebellion may be registered as voters," in folder 3, HR. 38A-G25.6, no. 1418, Records of the United States House of Representatives, Records Group 233, NA; *Tribune*, June 21, 28, 1864.

very intelligent, and especially those who have fought gallantly in our ranks." Lincoln, nevertheless, would not violate his notion of republican self-government by dictating a suffrage requirement for the state. Showing Lincoln's letter to leading delegates, Governor Hahn urged them to accede to the president's wishes. The consititution that emerged from the convention, however, although officially abolishing slavery in Louisiana and ordaining a system of segregated public schools for all children, explicitly failed to grant even the limited suffrage to black men that Lincoln had proposed. Responding to pressure from Hahn and General Banks, the convention did, albeit reluctantly, authorize the legislature to enfranchise blacks on the basis of military service, payment of taxes, or intellectual fitness if it chose to do so in the future.[5]

Although disappointed with the results of the convention and alarmed at the conservative resurgence in Louisiana made possible by Lincoln's 10-percent reconstruction plan, Afro-Creole radicals nevertheless redoubled their efforts to obtain citizenship and the ballot. They trumpeted Fr. Maistre as the true spokesman and representative of genuine Catholicism in the city. The priest's protracted defiance of Archbishop Odin and his outspoken advocacy of abolition and black rights dovetailed both with the Afro-Creoles' political agenda and with their bitter criticism of the Catholic Church. From the end of May 1863 when Archbishop Odin suspended him and placed St. Rose of Lima under interdict, until January 1864, Maistre held the keys to St. Rose. He refused to vacate the church and continued to hold services there, often involving the mutual aid societies he continued to encourage. *L'Union* rallied to his side, and he returned the favor. On June 30, 1863, for example, a notice on the front page of the paper announced a solemn mass at St. Rose for the Fourth of July. It invited all "true friends of liberty . . . without distinction of race or color . . . to pray for the triumph of the rights of man for all," and emphatically closed with the words: "Liberty, equality, independence." On July 8, 1863, the eighth anniversary of the Society of the Ladies of Perseverance, Maistre celebrated a high mass and took up a collection for the infirm.[6]

5. Harris, *With Charity for All*, 182–84.
6. *L'Union*, May 7, June 2, June 30, 1863.

Odin, meanwhile, disseminated his version of the dispute. He sent copies of his pastoral letter censuring Maistre to the bishops of the ecclesiastical province of New Orleans and others. Martin John Spalding, the bishop of Louisville who would soon become archbishop of Baltimore, commiserated with Odin, expressing the hope that the scandal which "afflicted" him would soon end. More importantly, Odin kept Rome informed of the dispute and cultivated General Banks and the military authorities, who were anxiously trying to both conciliate white southerners and to counteract a major abolitionist attack on their policies regarding freedmen. On August 8, Odin sent a report giving his version of the situation to Cardinal Barnabó of the Propaganda. Barnabó's response no doubt buoyed him. The cardinal expressed grief to learn that a priest under ecclesiastical censure had dared to continue to exercise his ministry sacrilegiously, and added approvingly, "I see that you have left nothing undone beforehand to prevent evil, nor afterward to remove it, when committed." He indicated his desire to learn from Odin whether Maistre persisted "in his course of perdition" or whether he had returned to his duty, or at least, had ceased to lead others to ruin.[7]

Barnabó's sympathetic response may have sprung not only from his desire to uphold episcopal authority, but also from his desire to secure Odin's cooperation in a diplomatic initiative of the Holy Father. In the autumn of 1862, Odin and Archbishop John Hughes of New York received letters from Pope Pius IX exhorting them to exert themselves in the Pontiff's name to bring about a peaceful resolution of the destructive war. Such a position squared with Odin's sincere desire for peace and with his pro-Confederate sympathies. After all, the papal stance, whatever its motivation, called for a negotiated peace, which coincided with the aims of northern peace advocates and the Confederate government. In effect, it would have meant Confederate independence, a point not lost on Jefferson Davis, who, after hearing from Odin on the subject, wrote a letter to the Pope thanking him for his solicitude. Odin issued a pastoral letter

7. Martin John Spalding to Jean-Marie Odin, October 22, 1863, VI-2-h, ANOC; Barnabó quoted in Pastoral Letter of the Most Rev. Archbishop of New Orleans, January 24, 1864, *Pastorals*, Vol. 1 (1844–1887), AANO. See also the entry for August 20, 1863, in R. O. Gerow, ed., *Civil War Diary (1862–1865) of Bishop William Henry Elder, Bishop of Natchez* (private printing, n.d.), copy in Archives of the Diocese of Jackson, Jackson, Mississippi.

calling for three successive Forty Hours devotions for peace (periods of forty hours during which the Sacred Host was solemnly exposed in churches before which the faithful could pray) which Spalding characterized as "wholly free from political allusion." Archbishop Hughes, fearful of sparking an anti-Catholic reaction in the North, simply published the papal letter in his diocesan newspaper without comment.[8]

Odin maintained a correct and civil relationship with the occupation authorities under General Banks, who, mindful of the number of Catholics both among residents of New Orleans and in the Union forces, sought to avoid confrontation. They accommodated the archbishop and treated him respectfully. Odin was therefore able to mediate on behalf of those of his clergy who had run afoul of Union troops; he also observed in a letter to James McMaster, the Copperhead publisher of the New York *Freeman's Journal*, that Catholics fared better under Banks than other denominations in securing passes, food, and other privileges. Banks allowed *Le Propagateur* to resume publishing, and authorities acquiesced when the archbishop deftly deflected their efforts to have priests read Lincoln's thanksgiving proclamation of July 1863 from church pulpits, accepting Odin's strained explanation that such "is contrary to the custom of the [Catholic] church." They also looked the other way when Catholic churches held Forty Hours devotions for peace on the very day pro-

8. A. Dudley Mann to His Excellency Jefferson Davis, May 9, 1864, with enclosure of a letter from Pope Pius IX, December 3, 1863, OR, Series IV, Vol. 3, p. 401; David J. Alvarez, "The Papacy in the Diplomacy of the American Civil War," *Catholic Historical Review*, LXIX (1983), 246–47; Hennesey, *American Catholics*, 155–56; Baudier, *The Catholic Church in Louisiana*, 427; Archbishop John Hughes to Odin, September 10, 1863, Martin John Spalding to Archbishop John B. Purcell, December 19, 1863, copies in Martin J. Spalding Collection, Josephite Archives (hereafter, JA), Baltimore, Maryland. Historian James Hennesey suggests that the embattled Pius IX, who faced the resurgent forces of Italian unification from his shrunken Papal States with Napoleon III as his last protector, and who resented the United States' recognition of the Kingdom of Italy, viewed the Union cause unfavorably as a "liberal" attack on a conservative, traditionalist South. As a priest, Martin Spalding had concerned himself with the pastoral needs of slaves. He opposed immediate emancipation, and in 1863 sent to Cardinal Barnabó of the Propaganda an analysis of the American Civil War entitled "Dissertation on the American Civil War," which was sympathetic to the Confederacy. See David Spalding, "Martin J. Spalding's 'Dissertation on the American Civil War,' " *Catholic Historical Review*, LII (1966), 66–85.

claimed by Jefferson Davis for such prayers. Julia LeGrand, a resident of the city, observed that only the Catholics could get away with such things; Union authorities closed recalcitrant Protestant churches. The military, though, kept Odin under surveillance throughout the war, as well they might, since as late as March 1865, a Confederate Secret service agent claimed to have learned from him—how, the agent did not specify—about Union troop movements towards Texas.[9]

In December 1863, another disgruntled priest in New Orleans, Benedict M. Poyet, made common cause with Maistre and attempted to warn Banks about what he perceived as the dangerous "secessionist" influence wielded by Odin and most of his clergy over the Catholic laity. Betwen 1852 and 1858, Poyet had served as an assistant at the cathedral and then as rector of St. Joseph's Church until the Vincentians took control. In 1859, with Blanc's permission, he had left New Orleans for France, but by July of that same year he had obtained from the Propaganda in Rome a commission as a missionary. Returning to New Orleans, he continued to list St. Joseph's as his residence, indicating that he may have assisted there. He failed, however, to secure a permanent assignment from either Blanc or Odin for reasons not entirely clear, though Poyet later claimed that they stemmed from his Unionist sentiments. In a scathing report, entitled "Catholic Clergy of New Orleans," Poyet assailed Odin and numerous other clergy by name and condemned their actions as "calculated to create enthusiasm in favor of rebellion." Describing Odin as "the very fountain of clerical secessionism in Louisiana," he accused him of intimidating clergy by making it clear

9. Baudier, *The Catholic Church in Louisiana*, 411, 425–27; Baudier, *St. Rose of Lima*, 20; Odin to James McMaster, January 21, 1863, I-1-m, ANOC; General James Bowen to Odin, June 4, 1863, November 28, 1863 (?), ser. 1839, Press Copies of Letters Sent, Vol. 1, Provost Marshall General Records, Department of the Gulf, RG 393, Pt. 1, NA; Odin to Colonel H. Robinson, Provost Marshall General, New Orleans, January 16, February 1, February 5, 1865, ser. 1845, Letters Received, Provost Marshall General Records; Captain W. Killborn, Provost Marshall, to Jean-Marie Odin, July 30, 1863, VI-2-g, AANO; Odin to Killborn, August 1, 1863, ser. 1845, Letters Received, Provost Marshall General Records; Rowland and Croxall, *The Journal of Julia LeGrand*, 269–71; James Bowen, Provost Marshall General, to Major H. M. Porter, May 24, 1864, Porter to Captain B. W. Frost, May 26, 1864, ser. 1497, Letters Received, Provost Marshall General, Parish of Orleans, RG 393, Pt. 4, NA; General E. Kirby Smith to Major General J. G. Walker, March 7, 1865, in *OR*, Vol. 48, pt. 1, 412.

that "no Catholic priest would be allowed to profess sentiments of loyalty to the Union without jeopardizing his position and being promptly dismissed under some pretence." Urging Banks to destroy the political influence of the "secessionist administration," Poyet suggested that the general force it to take compromising steps, such as the reading of public prayers for the President in Catholic churches and the conducting of funeral Masses for those killed in battle fighting to restore the Union. More radically, he also advocated closing the "nests of rebels": all of the Catholic schools in the city. Alluding to himself and to Maistre, he further recommended that Banks compel "this infamous administration" to reinstate those clergymen friendly to the Federal cause who had been "most arbitrarily dismissed and most atrociously injured," and to require Odin to pay them damages. Banks, however, rather than embracing Poyet's approach, adopted a more accommodating one towrads the archbishop.[10]

Father Maistre sensed the changing political climate in the city. Recognizing that Banks's policy of conciliating white citizens of New Orleans, including the archbishop, in an attempt to build Unionist sentiment meant that his days of occupying St. Rose were probably limited, Maistre began making plans to construct his own church. He had financial resources, despite losing his $1,200 annual salary from the archdiocese, which gave him independence in dealing with Odin and enabled him to proceed with his building plans. On September 30, 1863, he purchased for $6,500 from Anthony Fernandez a site consisting of three lots located on the river side of Claiborne Avenue at the corner of Ursulines in the Faubourg Tremé, an area that also housed St. Augustine's Church and the Association of the Holy Family. Maistre put down $2,500 in cash and agreed to pay the rest in four yearly installments of $1,000 each at 6 percent interest for the first three and 8 percent for the last. He intended to live in a house on one of the lots and build a church on another. He retained the famous architect J. N. B. De Pouilly, who had remod-

10. New Orleans City Directory, 1859, NOPL; *Metropolitan Catholic Directory*, 1859, 1860, 1861, AAB; Attestation issued by Archbishop Antoine Blanc to Rev. Benedict M. Poyet, May 19, 1859, Vol. 132, fol. 1112rv, and Benedict M. Poyet to the Propaganda, 1859, Vol. 132, fols. 1110rv, 1111v, both *Udienze di N. S.*, PA; B. M. Poyet to General Banks, December 2, 1863, ser. 1920, Letters Received, 1863, Bureau of Civil Affairs, Department of the Gulf, RG 393, Pt. 1, NA.

eled St. Louis Cathedral, to design the new edifice that he named Holy Name of Jesus. On October 12, 1863, Maistre established a building committee responsible for securing construction materials.[11]

The committee's composition reflected Maistre's close ties to Afro-Creole and white radicals. Anthony Fernandez, for example, who lived on Claiborne only four houses away from the new church, served on a subcommittee charged with gathering lime. The other members of the building committee consisted of men of color, including Charles W. Honoré, a prominent leader of the Equal Rights League and a future officer of the Central Executive Committee of the Friends of Universal Suffrage; Armand Gonzalez, a twenty-six-year-old former Second Sergeant in the 6th Louisiana Regiment (colored); Étienne Dolliole, whose family name would appear on a Masonic lodge membership roll and who made his living as a stonemason; Joseph Souder, a carpenter; G. Lachant (Lachaut, Lachaud, or Lacheaux), a grocer; Edmond Joseph, a carpenter; Joseph Fleury, a saddler-tobacconist-commissary; G. Lubin, a printer; Hercule Le Jean; Pierre Raymond; and C. Jeannetti. Doliolle, Honoré, and Gonzalez had responsibility for securing the bricks to build the church. Soudé, Lachaut, and Joseph took care of wood, and LeJean and Fleury joined with Fernandez to obtain lime. Jeanetti, Lubin, and Raymond handled the slab, or foundation.[12]

Maistre's defiance of the archbishop apparently inspired unrest in other parts of the archdiocese. Father Gilbert Raymond in Opelousas, fearing a schism à la Maistre, reported that Rev. Clement Rigol-

11. Baudier, *St. Rose of Lima Parish*, 23; Baudier, *The Catholic Church in Louisiana*, 412; Roulhac Toledano and Mary Louise Christovich, "The Role of Free People of Color in Tremé," in Christovich and Toledano, eds., *Faubourg Tremé and the Bayou Road*, (Gretna, LA., 1980), 85–107, Vol. VI of Mary Louise Christovich and Roulhac Toledano, eds., *New Orleans Architecture*, 6 vols.: Sale of Property, Anthony Fernandez to Claude P. Maistre, September 30, 1863, no. 109 in Mortgage Book 79, Office of Mortgages, New Orleans, La.; SRL, Vol. 1, p. 38, AANO.

12. Bell, *Revolution, Romanticism, and the Afro-Creole Protest*, 246–48; New Orleans City Directories, 1860, 1861, 1866, 1870, microfiche in Louisiana Collection, NOPL; Ninth Census of the United States, New Orleans, 862; *Tribune*, September 18, 1865; SLC, Book 22, p. 160, Act 950, AANO; a list of members of the building committee and their responsibilities under the heading "l'Année Octobre 1863, Membres de la comité chargé de. . . . " Holy Name Register, AANO; Baudier, *The Catholic Church in Louisiana*, 413.

let, in an apparent dispute over salary, had installed himself "at a negro's in the country," made himself pastor of Bois Mallet, and taken the chalice and vestments from Villeplatte for himself. A schoolmaster who was also a judge at Villeplatte had drawn up a petition to Odin asking him to appoint Rigolette as the pastor. Raymond reported, "The people have made themselves masters of the church and vestments and have disposed of them" and accused Rigolette of "walking in the footsteps of Fr. LeMaître [Maistre]."[13]

In a further sign of the interplay of religious and political ferment among black Catholics—even those who would not follow Maistre into schism—Odin also received a petition on November 17, 1863, signed by Edmond Debars on behalf of the Congregation Unioniste de Bienfaisance, a federation of benevolent societies, whose charter extended back to 1813 and which, over the years, had taken upon itself the religious instruction of slaves. It had recently adopted the new name of *Congregation Unioniste de Bienfaisance de la Ville de la Nouvelle Orléans, sous le protection de Saint Abraham* (Union of Benevolent Organizations of New Orleans under the Protection of St. Abraham). The members no doubt recognized that the use of the politically charged "St. Abraham" would not please Odin and represented something of a slap at him. Emboldened by wartime developments, including Maistre's defiance, however, their more orthodox protest apparently sought to steer a middle course between the status quo and the schism, perhaps in hopes of using Odin's concerns about blacks joining Maistre's new parish as leverage to wring some concessions from the archbishop.

The Congregation sought Odin's approval to acquire a piece of property on which "to build a Catholic Church, especially destined for the use of our population and remaining forever our property during our lives, reversible at our deaths to our children and their descendants." Manifesting a growing political and religious activism on the part of orthodox black Catholics and a spirit of solidarity between free people of color, slaves, and freedmen, Debars wrote that the Congregation intended to place the proposed church under the auspices "of the great St. Abraham, patron of the illustrious President of the United States." In reverential language, he praised Lin-

13. Father Gilbert Raymond to Odin, November 4, 6, 1863, VI-2-g, ANOC.

coln as a man "who could no longer support the excessive cruelty against a part of our population" and who, "by an energetic act of his will" had broken the chains that had "restrained our brothers in a long and painful slavery, and had proclaimed universal liberty to all groups in the United States." The group invoked God's blessing on its endeavor "so that our posterity, thankful for the benefits of liberty, may ever praise and adore God and by its Christian conduct be worthy of one day being reunited together in the 'celestial homeland.'" Perhaps the Congregation envisioned a reinstated Fr. Maistre as the future pastor of such a church. Odin, however, would have found distasteful not only the Unionist rhetoric of the Congregation's petition, but also the notion of a semiautonomous, self-perpetuating black parish, which smacked of trusteeism and flew in the face of his established policy of archiepiscopal ownership of all Church property. No record survives of Odin's response, but he did not authorize the church.[14]

He did, however, maneuver effectively to reclaim St. Rose of Lima from the dissident priest. On January 14, 1864, responding to a note from Odin, General Bowen signaled that he would restore the church of St. Rose to the prelate. He denied that he had ever ordered Maistre to continue his ministry there and stated that "no permission or authority, verbal or written, has been issued by this office to any person to occupy the Church of St. Rose of Lima in this city." In an implied rebuke of Captain Killborn, he added, "if any permission has been granted for such purpose by a subordinate officer, of which, however, I have no knowledge, it is hereby revoked." Banks sent a file of soldiers to compel Maistre to vacate the church, but Odin literally had to pay for the move. He still owed $1,120 on the promissory note that he had given to Maistre back in 1862 when he had had to purchase the church and a small parcel of land from the priest. The archbishop paid off the note to Maistre on January 27, 1863, and the priest left the premises. The archdiocese reclaimed the church of St. Rose of Lima and reopened it on February 14, 1864, with an expiatory ceremony performed by Abbé Perché. In his pasto-

<hr>

14. *Preambule, Congregation Unioniste de Bienfaisance de la Ville de la Nouvelle Orléans, sous le protection de Saint Abraham*, AANO, translation and copy graciously provided by John B. Alberts; Congregation Unioniste de Bienfaisance to Charlotte Mouat, October 23, 1896, Act 72, in J. A. Eustis, Vol. 11, NONA.

ral letter announcing restoration of the church, Odin sought to emphasize the curial support that he enjoyed by quoting from Cardinal Barnabó's earlier letter to him. Attendance at the newly reopened St. Rose of Lima Parish, though, remained sparse, as most of its black parishioners left to follow Maistre.[15]

After his eviction from St. Rose, Maistre rented a public room in which he officiated every Sunday until completion of construction on Holy Name of Jesus Church. Always adroit in financial matters, and eleven hundred dollars richer from the recent payment that he had received from Odin, Maistre retired his mortgage to Fernandez on February 27, 1864. Several days later, on March 1, he sold a lot that abutted Holy Name for $3,280 to the Congregation Unioniste de Bienfaisance, the society that had petitioned Odin for a separate black parish and which now intended to build a hall on the site. The Congregation paid $800 in cash and signed four notes of $500 at 6 percent interest, one coming due each of the succeeding four years. Maistre thus had an investment that would provide him steady income for several years, though still less than the salary he would have received as a priest of the archdiocese.

The proximity of the hall to Holy Name suggested at least tacit cooperation if not an outright relationship. That would not have been surprising. Maistre, after all, had midwived the birth of many black Catholic burial and mutual aid societies and remained involved with and supportive of many, including some that comprised the *Congreagation Unioniste*. He also sympathized with the politics of two of the leaders of the Congregation: thirty-nine year-old J. B. Alexis, a cooper, and Pierre Boyer, a tailor, both Unionist political activists who would play significant roles during Reconstruction. For his part, Maistre may have hoped to ingratiate himself with orthodox Catholics in the hopes that they would eventually come to view Holy Name Church standing next to the Congregation's hall as the black parish for which that group longed. For their part, the members of

15. Odin to Barnabó, November 8, 1865, Vol. 356, fols. 448v, 449r, *Lettere Di S. Congregazione*, PA; General James Bowen to Odin, January 14, 1864, ser. 1839, Press Copies of Letters Sent by the Provost Marshall, RG 393, Pt. 1, NA; Account with Rev. Maistre of St. Rose, entries for August 3, 1863, January 27, 1864, Diocesan Account Book, AANO; Pastoral Letter of the Most Reverend Archbishop of New Orleans, January 24, 1864, *Pastorals*, Vol. 1 (1844–1887), AANO; Baudier, *St. Rose of Lima Parish*, 24.

the Congregation, rebuffed by Odin in their efforts to gain his approval for a black parish, perhaps viewed proximity to Holy Name of Jesus as a way to continue to exert pressure on the archbishop or as the next best thing to their own parish. It is not clear if members of the Congregation Unioniste attended Holy Name of Jesus, but the decision of that society to deal with Maistre and to locate so closely to his schismatic church suggested widespread sympathy among the city's black Catholics for the renegade priest, even if they did not formally join his breakaway fold.[16]

In a report to the Propaganda, Odin claimed that most of Maistre's adherents had abandoned him—a claim belied by figures from the marriage and baptismal registers which showed over a hundred more baptisms and ten more marriages than the previous year. Odin characterized most of Maistre's adherents as Negroes "whose passions he rouses or panders to." He described Maistre as a willing accomplice of evil northern men who controlled New Orleans, sought to destroy Louisiana, and exploited the slaves whom they helped to escape from their masters. (Louisiana had not yet legally abolished slavery throughout the state.) Barnbó approvingly acknowledged Odin's news that he had managed to eject Maistre from St. Rose of Lima and expressed his hope that further evil could be avoided. Meanwhile, Maistre continued to ally himself openly with Afro-Creoles who spearheaded the drive for equal rights and attacked the archbishop and the Catholic clergy for their Confederate sympathies and hostility to emancipation. With their faith that reason and scientific progress would result in social progress, and their sympathy for the egalitarian and universalistic implications of spiritualism, Afro-Creole leaders had little use for what they regarded as the benighted, authoritarian, priest-ridden, dogmatic, reactionary Church. *L'Union* referred contemptuously to "the rebel clergy" and condemned "their offensive distinctions" and "insults" aimed at

16. COB 86-637, Orleans Parish Conveyance Office; Sale, Maistre to Congregation Unioniste, March 1, 1864, Act 106, in Antoine Mondeverri, Vol. 2, NONA; Incorporation of the Congregation Unioniste de Bienfaisance, November 2, 1867, Act 257, in Octave DeArmas, Vol. 85, NONA; Congregation Unioniste to Charlotte Mouat, October 23, 1896. Maistre also officiated at the weddings of two men, William J. Rudolph (1864) and Emile L. Vinet (1867), who would later hold key positions in the *Congregation Unioniste* in 1896. Rankin, "The Politics of Caste," in Macdonald, Kemp, and Haas, *Louisiana's Black Heritage*, 109, 139.

people of color. It accused the Catholic Church of operating as an "accomplice of secession" and denounced Perché in particular, calling him "the champion of treason and rebellion." Reacting to a condemnation of the Emancipation Proclamation that appeared in the English-language Catholic newspaper, the *Southern Pilot, L'Union* asserted, "Satan has hung some relics and some rosaries at his side, he has donned a three-cornered hat [a reference to the biretta worn by priests] . . . in order to disguise his evil and to mislead the people more easily."[17]

L'Union highlighted Maistre as different from the rest of the corrupt, uncharitable, unchristian clergy. Activists valued his support, which helped to increase their credibility among many ordinary Afro-Creole Catholics, who, despite their dissatisfaction with Church policy, still clung to their Catholicism. Perhaps they viewed Maistre's "protest Catholicism" as a palatable alternative to leaving the Church completely—as a stalking horse for their own interests, with Maistre testing the limits of autonomy and ideally, pushing the church to a reconsideration and redefinition of its stance. By emphasizing his influential role among blacks, *L'Union* and its successor, the *Tribune*, hoped to strengthen Maistre's hand in his future dealings with the archbishop. In Maistre's benediction delivered at the state constitutional convention of April 6, 1864, which *L'Union* reprinted, he emphasized the theme that God could bring good out of the evil of war. He referred to Lincoln as "this noble pioneer of liberty, this other Christ," who, guided by God, had with a stroke of the pen in his "immortal proclamation" redeemed a large number of slaves and made it possible for them to live as men. Maistre went on to ask God's blessing on the president and on all who had worked for freedom. Recognizing political realities, he even included General Banks in the list. He concluded by praying that God would enlighten the consciences of the delegates so that all slaves would attain freedom. On May 11, the convention voted to abolish slavery in the

17. Notation dated February 27, 1864, No. 109, Mortgage Bk. 79, Office of Mortgages, New Orleans; Register des Marriages et Baptêmes, Holy Name of Jesus, AANO; Odin to Barnabó, March 1, 1864, Barnabó to Odin, May 31, 1864, VI-2-h, ANOC; *L'Union*, November 15, 1862, January 29, 1863, May 31, 1864; *Tribune*, January 13, 14, April 25, 1865; McTigue, "Forms of Racial Interaction in Louisiana," 40, 42; Bell, *Revolution, Romanticism, and the Afro-Creole Protest*, 244–46; Houzeau, *My Passage at the New Orleans Tribune*, 5–6.

state. The following day, *L'Union* announced that Maistre would chant a *Te Deum* four days hence at Holy Name in thanksgiving for abolition.[18]

The men in the dwindling ranks of Cailloux's old regiment undoubtedly welcomed the good news from the constitutional convention. It represented a ray of hope in an otherwise dismal situation, for precious little had gone right for them in the months following the battle of Port Hudson. During that time, morale had declined precipitously and desertions had grown alarmingly. At Port Hudson in the immediate aftermath of battle, the men endured terrible conditions. The grounds, works, and ordinance stores lay in a state of confusion and filth. The stench of death and swarms of insects filled the air, while the searing sun and soaking thunderstorms added to the misery of the troops, many of whom became sick. Black troops also bore the burden of extra fatigue duty.[19]

Noting the growing demoralization of the 1st Regiment and expressing his willingness to "abnegate" and "humble" himself in order to arrest it, on June 23, 1863, Colonel Stafford requested that General Banks allow him to resume his command. Instead, on August 12, General George Andrews, who had assumed command of the Corps d'Afrique on July 10, recommended to Banks, still the commander of the Department of the Gulf, that he dismiss Stafford. Banks did so officially on September 8. Lt. Col. Chauncey Bassett continued to lead the 1st regiment.[20]

Both the loss of black officers and the continued hostility of white troops contributed significantly to the erosion of morale. In early

18. *L'Union*, April 16, May 12, 1864.
19. McConnell, "Louisiana's Black Military History," in MacDonald, Kemp, and Haas, *Louisiana's Black Heritage*, 55–58; General George Andrews to Major G. Horman Liber, AAG, ser. 2100, Letters Sent, U.S. Forces, Port Hudson, Department of the Gulf, RG 393, Pt. 2, NA.
20. S. H. Stafford to General Banks, June 23, 1863, General George L. Andrews to Lt. Col. R. B. Irwin, Asst. Adjutant General, August 12, 1863, Service Record of Spencer H. Stafford, Compiled Military Service Records, RG 94, NA.; Winters, *The Civil War in Louisiana*, 209; Special Order 224, September 8, 1863; On January 3, 1871, the War Department revoked Stafford's dismissal and substituted an honorable discharge, effective September 15, 1865. Special Order 1, January 3, 1871; Chauncey J. Bassett to Andrews, July 31, 1863, Service Record of Chauncey H. Bassett, in Compiled Military Service Records, RG 94.

August, Bassett pressed charges against Capt. Alcide Lewis of Co. G, 2nd Lt. Louis. A. Thibault of Co. H, and 2nd Lt. Hippolyte St. Louis of Co. E for cowardice, breach of arrest, and absence without leave. Bassett, who hitherto had sympathized with the cause of black officers, insisted that unimpeachable evidence of witnesses substantiated the charges against the officers and he requested trial by court-martial or dismissal from the service. Banks chose the latter option and also continued the purge of other black officers. As for the matter of racial hostility, it came to a head when Captain Joseph Follin complained to his superiors that a solider from the 3rd Massachusetts Calvary had beaten one of his privates and authorities responded by judging it impossible to find the culprit since witnesses claimed they did not know him. The situation became so intolerable that General Andrews issued General Order 12 on July 30, 1863, to address the problem. An 1851 graduate of West Point, Andrews had left the army for a six-year stint as a civil engineer before rejoining it in 1861 as lieutenant colonel of the 2nd Massachusetts Infantry. He had seen action at Cedar Mountain and Antietam before joining Banks's staff. Intelligent, upright, conscientious, and devoid of much of the racism that infected other officers and soldiers, Andrews was determined to make the Corps d'Afrique one of the best in the army and to promote the good of his black troops.[21]

In his order, Andrews wrote that he had become aware of "the abuse of colored soldiers, and disregard of their authority as sentinels on the part of some troops and some civilians"; he condemned such conduct and ordered it to cease at once. He noted that since the government had decided to employ black troops, "it is the imperative duty of the officers and soldiers to acquiesce fully and promptly." He maintained that a black soldier engaged in the performance of his duty deserved consideration, respect, "and the protection and support of his military superiors," which he promised to provide. Andrews warned that any abuse or disobedience of black troops employed in an official capacity would represent disobedience and contempt for the authority of the commanding general, which he would

21. Chauncy J. Bassett to Capt. G. B. Halstead, A. A. Genl., August 5, 1863, ser. 57, Regimental Papers, 73rd USCInf, USCT, RG 94, NA; Letter of Captain Joseph Follin, ser. 2106, Register of Letters Received, 1863–1866, U.S. Forces, Port Hudson, Department of the Gulf, RG 393, Pt. 2, NA; Hollandsworth, *The Louisiana Native Guards*, 84–85.

not tolerate and would punish with "unrelenting severity," not only for the protection deserved by the black soldier but also "because such conduct is grossly insubordinate to lawful authority." He finished by "strictly prohibiting all discussions of the subject of employing black soldiers, all remarks disparaging them and any course of conduct tending to create ill feeling between colored troops and other troops."[22]

Despite the racial tensions, Andrews sought to recruit more black troops. He acknowledged the difficulty of securing them, listing among the factors the "covert hostility of some of our army officers," and the "bitter hostility of the rebels and planters to the employment of Negro soldiers." Since, according to Andrews, the rebels "hunt down and drive off every able-bodied Negro man that attempts to reach us," he authorized raiding parties of considerable size "to afford them the necessary faculties for reaching us." On August 3, 1863, one such recruiting mission at Jackson, Louisiana, went awry, costing the regiment approximately twenty of its men, including another of its black officers, 1st Lt. Oscar Orillion, the twenty-three-year-old leader of B Company. Orillion headed a detail of 100 men from the 1st Regiment, part of a larger force of 250 infantry drawn from the 1st, 3rd, and 6th regiments of the Corps d'Afrique, 50 cavalry of the 3rd Massachusetts, and two pieces of artillery of the 2d Vermont Battery. The detachment traveled to Jackson, Louisiana, and collected fifty recruits for the 12th Infantry of the Corps d'Afrique. About 5 P.M., a Confederate force of approximately 500 under the command of Colonel John L. Logan of the 11th Arkansas Infantry surprised the Union troops. In the ensuing engagement, the Confederates forced the Federals to retreat and captured approximately 100 men, about half of them black, including Orillion and 21 enlisted men from the 1st Regiment.[23]

The following day, Logan requested advice from Lt. Gen. William J. Hardee, the local commander who also commanded the Army of the West, about what to do with blacks captured in arms. His ques-

22. General Order 12, July 30, 1863, ser. 2110, General Orders, U.S. Forces, Port Hudson, Department of the Gulf, RG 393, Pt. 2, NA.
23. General George Andrews to Capt. James Dwight, October 28, 1863, Special Order 23, August 1, 1863, Ser. 2100, Letters Sent, U.S. Forces, Port Hudson, Department of the Gulf, RG 393, Pt. 2, NA; *OR*, Vol. XXVI, Pt. 1, 238–40.

tion reflected ongoing confusion about the matter. Between December 1862 and May 1863, both President Jefferson Davis and the Confederate Congress had announced that prisoner-of-war status would not apply to captured black troops. Confederate forces would treat officers of black regiments as criminals and would remand former slaves to state officials who would deal with them according to their respective statutes, which prescribed death to black insurrectionists. President Lincoln responded in July by promising to retaliate in kind for every Union soldier murdered or enslaved by either executing or placing at hard labor one Confederate soldier. But both Confederate and Union authorities found it difficult to implement official policy. In one set of instructions to the commander of the Department of Mississippi, Tennessee, and Louisiana, for example, Confederate Secretary of War James A. Seddon tempered the draconian official policy, informing Lt. Gen. John C. Pemberton that he could put back prisoners-of-war to work in any of the workshops of the government or on fortifications or in "any manner" that he deemed appropriate. In practice, Confederate field commanders established widely varying standards of treatment ranging from reenslavement and hard labor to summary execution. Confederate officials left unclear the status of free black soldiers, although initially state officials, with the acquiescence of Richmond, treated free and slave alike. Indeed, the refusal of Confederate officials to include free blacks in prisoner exchanges led Secretary of War Stanton in 1863 to refuse any exchanges lest he betray free black troops held in captivity. But though the Confederates continued to deny formal prisoner-of-war status to black freedmen, by 1864 they seemed to have treated them much as white captured soldiers.[24]

On the morning he sent his query to General Hardee, Logan decided to have guards of the 17th Arkansas Mounted Infantry move the prisoners toward Confederate lines. A Union surgeon who was released shortly after the action said that the Confederate troops showed great contempt "toward officers of colored troops" and that they forced Orillion to march at the head of his "niggers." Andrews

24. *OR*, XXVI, Pt. 1, 240; Berlin, Reidy, and Rowland, *Freedom*, II, 567–70, 572–73; Trudeau, *Like Men of War*, 61–62. During the war, Confederate forces executed six white officers of black units. See, "The Execution of White Officers from Black Units by Confederate Forces During the Civil War," *Louisiana History*, XXXV (1994), 475–489.

later said that he had reports that "in one or two instances black troops were struck several times by their captors." As Orillion and his men proceeded on their march, four of the black soldiers, doubtless aware of the official Confederate policy regarding black prisoners, attempted to escape. Col. Frank Powers, the commander of the guard, ordered his men to shoot them. The other black troops tried to take advantage of the ensuing confusion to make their own getaway. Powers ordered everyone shot "and with my six shooter assisted in the execution of the order." Lt. James W. Shattuck later boasted of having killed thirteen prisoners himself. Nevertheless, some of the black troops, including Alfred Noldier of Company F, a sandy-haired, 5' 11" mulatto and former slave from St. Charles Parish, evaded their captors and made their way back to Union lines. The intrepid Noldier went on to become a sergeant by war's end. Others suffered a different fate. Céline Fremaux Garcia, a resident of the area, unexpectedly came upon two black soldiers hanging from a tree limb, their feet just clear of the ground. And whether by bullet, bayonet, or rope, Orillion evidently perished. Recurrent reports of summary executions of black troops involved in the operation led Andrews to make inquiries of his Confederate counterparts, who denied the charges. Although he threatened reprisals if the reports proved true, he could not substantiate them and took no further action.[25]

Meanwhile, Andrews continued to wrestle with the second-class treatment that sapped the spirit of his troops. He admonished a surgeon for requesting burial of a white trooper apart from black soldiers, noting acidly that Robert Gould Shaw, the white "boy colonel" who had died heroically while leading the doomed charge of the Massachusetts 54th against the walls of Fort Wagner, had shared a mass grave with his black troops. In so many words, Andrews caustically observed that if an officer like Shaw, who shone as

25. Andrews to Major G. N. Leiber, A. A. General, September 14, 1863, ser. 2100, Letters Sent, U.S. Forces, Port Hudson, Department of the Gulf, RG 393, Pt. 2, NA; *OR*, Ser. 2, Vol. VI, 244, 258–59, 289, 960–61, 477; Depositions of Valsin Lamit, January 27, 1905, Henry Bradley, September 5, 1881, Mélite Noldier, January 7, 13, 1905, pension file of Alfred Noldier, RG 15, NA; Céline Fremaux Garcia, *Céline: Remembering Louisiana, 1850–1871* (Athens, Ga., 1987), 131–32; George L. Andrews to Lt. Col. R. B. Irwin, August 4, 1863, ser. 2100, Letters Sent, U.S. Forces, Port Hudson, Department of the Gulf, RG 393, Pt. 2, NA.

a man and as a soldier, could be buried with his men, so should any white man of any regiment in the Department of the Gulf. On August 21, 1863, after realizing that most of his troops would receive smooth bore muskets, Andrews wrote to Col. Richard B. Irwin, General Banks's adjutant, asking for a larger proportion of rifled muskets for his men. The old muskets would "give rise to dissatisfaction," Andrews warned. "Anything that has the appearance of treating the colored troops as unfit to receive any but inferior articles of clothing or equipment is promptly felt by officers and men alike." Keenly aware of the threat to morale, he urged that "as far as practicable, distinctions in arming the two classes of troops should be avoided, for the present at least."[26]

A letter from twenty-four-year-old private Isidore Kinney of Company G to his mother on September 1, 1863 provides a personal glimpse of the concerns of the men at Port Hudson. Kinney, an illiterate mulatto and former slave from New Orleans, had enlisted in April 1863, and had suffered a wound in the waist during the Battle of Port Hudson. He dictated his letter in French to a private from E Company. Informing his mother that "thanks be to God" he was recovering and in good health, he admonished her for not having found a way to write him since his enlistment, especially since she had received word of his being wounded. More gently, he added, "Try to write me a letter a little more often." Kinney asked her to convey his greetings to his godmother (a key figure in Creole families), his sister, and his brothers, and to send him news about them. He also requested her to pass a message through his uncle to "Constant," (apparently a friend or a cousin) "to come here and give up his foolish ways." Isidore informed his mother that he had planned to secure leave and to visit home the following week but the growing number of desertions had led authorities to cancel all furloughs—although he still hoped to make it to New Orleans after the next payday in order to give her money. He only hoped that he would receive the whole of it at once. He noted that the regiment found itself encamped in a field of flowers, that many men suffered from

26. Brig. Genl. Cmdg, written on letter from D. H. Leavitt, October 7, 1863, ser. 2106, Letters Received, U.S. Forces, Port Hudson, Department of the Gulf, RG 393, Pt. 2, NA; Andrews to Irwin, August 21, 1863, ser. 2100, Letters Sent, U.S. Forces, Port Hudson, Department of the Gulf, RG 393, Pt. 2, NA.

fevers, and that all of the black officers talked about resigning. The earnest young man assured his mother, however, that he would endeavor to do his duty and earn the respect and esteem of his superiors.[27]

The steady drumbeat of officers' resignations and dismissals to which Isidore referred created instability and disillusionment within the regiment. First Lieutenant Paul Porée of Company E received a medical discharge on August 11 for rheumatism, a common ailment exacerbated by the many nights spent in wet and damp environs. Capt. Alcide Lewis, 2nd Lt. Hippolyte St. Louis, and 1st Lt. Louis G. Thibault were also finally dismissed on August 26. First Lt. James H. Ingraham took command of Cailloux's Company E, but also found himself under pressure to resign. General Andrews reflected the bleak propects for black officers when he wrote: "I cannot at present under any circumstances approve the application of a colored person for a commission in the Corps d'Afrique. The time for this may come, but it is not now."[28]

The lone bright spot in the midst of the purge came ironically, as a result of the officer shortage created. Bassett recommended Lieutenants Ingraham and Alfred Bourgeau for the rank of captain and the recommendation was accepted. Both men also received pay equal to white officers, thanks to the insistence of General Banks, for whom, in matters of pay, an officer was an officer. The imminent convening of examining boards in February, however, and the unabated hostility of white officers and enlisted men meant that their days, like those of the other black officers, were numbered. By mid-1864, only Captain Louis A. Snaer of Company B, who served to the end of the war, remained. During the war, approximately one hundred blacks served as commissioned officers, two-thirds of those in the three Native Guards regiments. Another quarter served as

27. Isadore John Kinney to "Ma chère mère," September 1, 1863, Depositions of Gabriel Paholie and Celina Kinney, March 5, 1885, Pension Record of Isadore J. Kinney, RG 15, NA.

28. Field and Staff Muster Roll of the 1st Regiment of the Corps d'Afrique for the Month of August 1863, in ser. 57, Regimental Papers, 73rd USCInf, USCT, RG 94, NA.; George L. Andrews to Col. C. C. Dwight, President of the Examining Board, November 4, 1863, ser. 2100, Letters Sent, U.S. Forces, Port Hudson, Department of the Gulf, RG 393, Pt. 2, NA; Berlin, Reidy, and Rowland, *Freedom*, II, 328.

chaplains and surgeons. Six Massachusetts officers received commissions in 1865, all but Stephen A. Swails being so recognized only after the war's end. Three other black officers served with an independent artillery battery at Fort Leavenworth, Kansas.[29]

As in the rest of the Native Guards, the decimation of the leadership cadre of the 1st Regiment continued. By September 1, 1863, the regiment had lost its commanding colonel and a total of eleven company officers, three in battle (Cailloux, Crowder, and Orillion) and the rest by dismissal and resignation. To secure good officers, Andrews established examining boards, which he expected to apply high standards to white as well as black officers. He also established a school for white officers to upgrade their skills. On October 20, 1863, he appointed thirty-year-old, Lt. Col. Samuel M. Quincy, scion of a distinguished Massachusetts family and a veteran of the battle of Chancellorsville, acting assistant inspector of the Corps d'Afrique. Andrews wrote that with good officers, proper instruction, and strict discipline, he believed that "the colored troops will prove themselves superior to the white troops." Still, the shortage of officers continued to plague the regiment and the loss of the black officers deeply distressed the men.[30]

Cailloux's former company—the color company of the regiment that had led the assault on Port Hudson—reflected the decay. It had lost its original complement of officers—Cailloux, Porée, and St. Louis—along with its color sergeant. It also suffered the highest desertion rate in the regiment, eventually losing fifty-six of its original one hundred members by that route, a high rate even by Civil War standards. Thirty-two had deserted by October 1863—nineteen between August 19 and October 4. In the regiment as a whole, between late May and December seventy-seven men deserted from Port Hudson and fifteen from Baton Rouge, where the wounded

---

29. Berlin, Reidy, and Rowland, *Freedom*, II, 306, 310–11; Hollandsworth, *The Louisiana Native Guards*, 78.

30. General George Andrews to S. M. Quincy, October 20, 1863, ser. 2100, Letters Sent, U.S. Forces, Port Hudson, Department of the Gulf, RG 393, Pt. 2, NA; list of the officers of the 1st Regiment of Corps d'Afrique, September 1, 1863, ser. 57, Regimental Papers, 73rd USCInf, RG 94, NA; Samuel S. Quincy to Dear Mary [Apthorp Quincy Gould], May 14, 1863, Quincy, *et. al.* Family Papers, LC; Service Record of Samuel M. Quincy, in Compiled Military Service Records, RG 15, NA; Hollandsworth, *The Louisiana Native Guards*, 85.

and seriously ill were sent for hospital care. In August 1863, in apparent response to the manpower hemorrhage, the regiment received an infusion of ninety-seven new men mustered in at Port Hudson, most of them former agricultural slaves who bore Anglophonic names and whose places of birth included Woodville, Mississippi, Pickens, North Carolina, and the Maryland Eastern Shore. These new recruits diluted the strongly Creole character of the regiment.[31]

Despite the personnel problems, the regiment managed to give a good account of itself before the inspector general of the Department in September 1863. Clearly impressed, that official noted proficiency in battalion movements, some of which "would cause envy from white regiments which have been the same length of time in service." His observations regarding black officers contrasted markedly with the "prevailing wisdom" among Banks and his coterie. "The regiment is partially officered by colored men," he wrote, "some of whom exhibited as much promptness and intelligence and knowledge of their duties as a majority of the white officers of other regiments." He praised the appearance in both arms and equipment of the color guard and predicted, "This regiment fully officered will be in condition to do good service."[32]

The only service that commanders appeared to have in mind for the regiment, however, involved fatigue and guard duty. Lieutenant Colonel Bassett requested cancellation of the order requiring the regiment to furnish fifty men for manual labor every other day as "it is with great difficulty that we can furnish our daily details . . . without having our men on duty every day." This was granted. But on September 28, the regiment received an order to furnish daily 1 commissioned officer, 3 noncommissioned officers, and 48 privates—16 men on post and 32 in reserve—for detail work near camp. On October 7, the regiment received fresh orders to work on fortifications from 7:00 A.M. to 12 P.M. and from 1:30 P.M. to 5:50 P.M. daily

31. Compiled Service Records of Company E, 73rd USCInf, in RG 15, NA; Muster Roll of Company E, 1st. Regt., Corps d'Afrique, September 1 to October 31, 1863, signed by Lt. Henry C. Nichols, Annual Return of the 1st Infantry Corps d'Afrique, 1863, Descriptive Book, Company C, 1st Regiment, Native Guards (73rd USCInf), Muster Rolls, 73rd USCInf, ser. 57, Regimental Papers, 73rd USCInf, USCT, RG 94, NA.

32. Inspection Report of Companies of the 1st Regiment Corps d'Afrique, September, 1863, ser. 57, Regimental Papers, 73rd USCInf, USCT, RG 94, NA.

until further notice. As a result of the growing desertion rate, a smaller pool of men had to bear an even greater proportion of the load. They also had no fresh or desiccated vegetables or fruit at their meals, ate food prepared in filthy, wet cookhouses, and were prohibited from "loud, boisterous shouting" except for some "proper occasion," such as news of a victory over the enemy.[33]

Major H. R. Perkins, temporarily commanding the regiment at the end of 1863, offered the best explanation for what had happened during the year. He noted that the regiment had devoted much of its time to labor on the fortifications at Fort St. Leon, Baton Rouge, and Port Hudson. Owing to the great amount of this kind of duty, the men had worn out double their allowance of clothing. Most of Company B, for example, were overdrawn on their clothing in the range of $20. Since they received but $7 per month and $3 of that for clothing, Perkins wrote that justice demanded that their clothing account should balance to January 1864. He harked back to Butler's General Order 63, which had authorized the formation of the regiment and had promised it the same pay, equipment, and rations as other volunteer troops of the United States. Noting that "Two-thirds of the Regt when enlisted were Free colored men," and that 25 of the regiment had been killed and 38 injured during the operation against Port Hudson, he attributed the large number of desertions "to the fact that they are not able to maintain their families, and a dissatisfaction . . . that inducements were held out to the soldiers of the 1st Regiment Native Guards to induce them to enlist which have not been lived up to."[34]

A further blow to the pride of the regiment came on February 19 when, as mentioned earlier, General Order 25, which authorized regiments to include upon their colors the words "Port Hudson,"

33. Bassett to Captain G. B. Halstead, September 15, 1863, ser. 57, Regimental Papers, 73rd USCInf, USCT, RG 94, NA; Special Order 68, September 28, 1863, ser. 2112, General Order 3, October 7, 1863, ser. 2110, Capt. R. Desanges to Bassett, November 23, 1863, ser. 2142, Letters Sent, all in U.S. Forces, Port Hudson, Department of the Gulf, RG 393, Pt. 2, NA; Muster Roll of Company B, 1st Regiment, December 31, 1863, ser. 57, Regimental Papers, 73rd USCInf, USCT, RG 94, NA; General Order 2, George B. Halstead by command of Brigadier General George L. Andrews, February 7, 1864, ser. 2111, General Orders, Department of the Gulf, RG 393, Pt. 2, NA.

34. Annual Return of the 1st Infantry, Corps d'Afrique, for 1863, ser. 57, Regimental Papers, 73rd USCInf, USCT, RG 94, NA.

TABLE 6

Desertions from the 1st Regiment, 1863

Companies	Desertions	Apprehensions
Company B	14	0
Company C	32	1
Company E	39	3
Company F	5	0
Company G	13	6
Company H	29	0
Company I	11	0
Company K	21	0

NOTE: Companies A and D were detached and stationed at Fort St. Leon and Fort Jackson.
SOURCE: Annual Return of the 1st Infantry Corps d'Afrique for 1863

failed to include any of the black units. Within six days of that insult, five black officers, including the recently promoted Bourgeau, appeared before the board of examiners to answer charges of "inefficiency" that eventually resulted in their leaving the army. In March, as the regiment moved up the Red River as part of Banks's campaign to capture Shreveport, several officers described their role as that of "an armed fatigue party and semi-military organization." The 1st also experienced another humiliation—one that the men interpreted as an attack on their very identity and legitimacy and which led to a protest.[35]

According to a letter to Banks dated March 28 and signed by the noncommissioned officers, musicians, and privates of the regiment, on March 27, in recently captured Alexandria, brigade commander Colonel William H. Dickey "ordered our flag to be sent to Port Hudson, the flag what we faught [sic] under at Port Hudson and General Banks raised his hat to on the right of Port Hudson." According to the men, Dickey had called the banner "a damn petticoat

35. Special Order 25, in Woodward, *The Negro in the Military*, 2508, RG 94, NA; Col. W. H. Dickey to Capt. George B. Halstead, February 25, 1864, ser. 1990, Letters Sent, 1st Brigade, 1st Division, Corps d'Afrique, Department of the Gulf (Dickey), RG 393, Pt. 2, NA; Muster Rolls of Companies C and I, 1st Regiment, Corps d'Afrique, April 30, 1864, ser. 57, Regimental Papers, 73rd USCInf, USCT, RG 94, NA.

and A disgrace to the brigade." He also allegedly cursed the regiment and referred to the men as "the dam Smart Nigers." The authors of the letter knew they had to tread carefully and so framed it in supplicating and deferential tones. They expressed their regret at having to make such a report but also their hope that they might derive "some good by laying our complaint before the commanding general as we believe thair is no general in the field who will Simpathize with his men when they have been wronged as Genl Banks will." They expressed the hope that they might have their flag returned and "other wrongs Stoped," and they begged pardon if they "were in the wrong." Dickey denied that he had used any such language and attempted to explain away the flag imbrogilio by claiming that the standard brought out by the regiment had been "old, faded and ragged and bore no resemblance to the colors prescribed by regulations." He insisted that the regiment had had "two fine colors" (probably those issued when it became part of the Corps d'Afrique) back at Port Hudson and that he had ordered the commanding officer to return his old banner and have one of the others brought up. The incident obviously rankled the men deeply and pointed up their growing disillusionment and resentment.[36]

On April 4, 1864, as if to underscore the uncertainty regarding their identity, the regiment again received another designation, this time as the 73rd Regiment, United States Colored Infantry. Shortly afterward, during the climactic Red River campaign, General Banks suffered the worst defeat in his less-than-distinguished military career, this time at Mansfield on April 8. As lead elements of his retreating force approached Pleasant Hill the next day, the 73rd formed a line of battle and prepared to engage the pursuing enemy. But before the battle commenced, all black regiments received orders to withdraw to Grand Ecore. The 73rd complied grudgingly. At Grand Ecore from April 10 through April 20, detachments of the regiment guarded transports on the Red River while the remainder occupied itself night and day unloading supplies and guarding stores. Between May 2 and 11, the regiment labored four miles above Alexandria

36. 1st Regt Infty, Corps d'Afrique, to A. A. Genl. G. Norman Lieber, March 28, 1864, with Endorsement of March 29, 1864, ser. 57, Regimental Papers, 73rd USCInf, USCT, RG 94.

building a dam in the Red River to raise the water level to enable gunboats trapped above the falls to escape. During these operations, on May 3, Colonel Bassett was mortally wounded and captured on board the steamer "City Belle." He died the evening of May 10.

The 73rd returned briefly to Port Hudson, where Lt. Col. Henry C. Merriam, a veteran of Antietam and a former officer in the 20th Maine, the 3rd Regiment, Corps d'Afrique, and the 85th United States Colored Troops, joined the regiment on June 3 and became its de facto commander. What he found shocked him. In an inspection report, he noted the condition of arms as bad and accouterments as poor. He found the condition of clothing "unsoldierly," the bearing of the men "indifferent," discipline "lax," military instruction "loose," and officers "inefficient and indifferently informed as to the condition of their command." The 619 men under his command moved upriver to Morganza, where, beginning July 19, they performed guard duty, built fortifications, and drilled.[37]

In early July, the issue of desertions in the regiment reached some-

TABLE 7

Desertions from the 73rd Regiment, 1864

Company	Desertions	Apprehensions
Company A	12	5
Company B	17	6
Company C	13	2
Company D	3	0
Company E	10	7
Company F	8	3
Company G	11	2
Company H	12	4
Company I	8	3
Company K	24	11

SOURCE: Annual Return of the 73rd U.S. Colored Infantry for 1864

37. Annual Return of the 73rd USCInf for 1864, ser. 57, Regimental Papers USCT, RG 94, NA; Henry C. Merriam, ser. 297, Commission Branch File, RG 94, NA; General George B. Drake, Asst. Adj., to Commanding Officer at Morganza, July 5, August 31, 1864, ser. 1820, Letters Sent from the Inspector of the Department of the Gulf, RG 393, Pt. 1, NA; OR, Vol. 41, Pt. 2, 259–60.

thing of a climax; the Regimental Return for the year reported a total of one hundred and nineteen. Merriam chose Sergeant Major John J. Cage, recovered from wounds received at the battle of Port Hudson, to head a detachment of troops bound for New Orleans to apprehend deserters. Sergeants Joseph Fille and Jules Golard would also accompany him. Cage was a mulatto, born in Mississippi, the son of a white man and a black woman. He stood 5'7," had brown eyes and dark hair, spoke English but could not write his name, and eventually married in the Baptist church after the war. Cage had enlisted as a free man at the age of eighteen in September 1862, and had almost immediately become first sergeant of the largely Anglophonic Company I. Promoted to sergeant major of the regiment on June 1, 1864, he harbored hopes of one day becoming an officer.

His mission, however, led to hard feelings and suggested some latent cultural and ethnic tensions as well as pent-up frustration and resentment within the regiment, especially among its original members. On July 4, Sergeant Cage went to the laundress to get his clothes. While there, he sat down for a few minutes with Sergeant Leblanc, Corporal Louis George, and Private James Hooker. Private Léonnel Macarty entered and asked whether Cage was going to New Orleans to arrest deserters. The 5'8" Macarty was about twenty-four years old and probably resented Cage's rise to sergeant major, a post that he had held from September 1862 until January 4, 1863, when he was reduced to first sergeant of D Company. In May 1864, he was demoted again, this time to private in the ranks. Single, light-complexioned like Cage, French-speaking, and a shoemaker (some sources also indicate bricklaying and barbering) by trade, born free in New Orleans, Macarty had also attended school (possibly the Institute Catholique) between 1856 and 1858, and in September 1862, he had enlisted in Captain Sentmanat's company.

When Cage responded affirmatively to Macarty's question, the latter called him "a damned dirty shit ass," accused him of betraying his race and not respecting his color, and allegedly threatened, in so many words, to blow Cage's head off if the sergeant major arrested any of Macarty's relatives. When Cage responded that he had to follow orders, Macarty asserted that he would ignore such an order "and would show them that I could not be forced to arrest and bring back my color to the damned regiment." Macarty lectured Cage about the suffering of the men, including bad treatment and no furloughs and concluded that Cage "ought not to do it and should protect your own color and not see them punished." According to Cage, when he ordered Macarty away, Macarty demanded to know who he thought he was and closed his fists as though to strike him. Cage refused to fight him and Macarty then turned to leave, but not before again calling Cage a "shit ass" and a "cowardly son of a bitch." Cage subsequently reported the incident and Macarty was arrested and charged with disrepectful and seditious language to the prejudice of good order and military discipline and with violation of the 9th U.S. Article of War by threatening to strike a superior. He appeared before a court-martial on September 19.

Macarty, whose membership in a Masonic lodge and the New Orleans police force after the war suggests his sympathy with Afro-Creole radicalism, showed no remorse when he initially appeared before Merriam, but instead boldly reiterated that he would never apprehend deserters because the government had mistreated them. In a letter to the officers composing the court, he claimed that Cage had used provocative language but denied using abusive language or threatening to shoot Cage himself. He did admit to saying that he would not arrest a brother who had deserted from the army if the government had treated that brother as it had treated Macarty. In his ungrammatical English, Macarty went on to explain passionately why he approved the desertions. In the process, he articulated the growing political consciousness and radicalization that the war had spawned among many people of color who had become convinced that only the acquisition of greater political rights would afford them adequate protection and justice. He claimed that he had been among the first to enlist in the regiment both "for the defense of my country and my right," but that the government had broken faith with him and the other men of the regiment. He had received neither the promised $38 bonus nor $13 per month in pay, and after the regiment had labored for nine months in the swamps and woods, "they took away the ration tickets they had give to our families and leave them in a complete state of starvation without no support driven away from they house they had rent on account they couldt pay their rents, half of there families without no shoe, or bread to give to their children, and having their son husband or brother in the United States Service." He asked the officers of his board to consider how they themselves would have reacted to such treatment. Reminding them that *he* had *not* [his emphases] deserted, he wrote, "For my part Gentlemen, I don't require nothing from the government only justice to the poor family that are suffering and their rights." The court-martial found him guilty of seditious speech but innocent of violating Article 9, and sentenced him to six months of hard labor and forfeiture of pay. He served his time at Fort Jefferson in Florida, but remained unbowed. On December 26, he wrote a letter to General Ullman, asking him to look into the case and denying that he was guilty of an offense that merited such severe punishment.[38]

Serving time for desertion in the same prison, seventeen-year-old Warren D. Hamelton of the 73rd repeated Macarty's theme of a broken contract in writing to Secretary of War Stanton of his own experience. Requesting release from incarceration, Hamelton explained that he had felt justified in deserting because of the mistreatment and misrepresentations that he had suffered at the hands of the government. "I though[t] at the time that one breack of enlistment was quite sufficient to justify another perticularly when it was transacted on the part of the govt.," he wrote. Acknowledging that many of the recruits had been free men before the war, he hastened to add that "most of us have nothing more than is required to support our family from day to day as we labor for it." The government's refusal to honor its promises of bounty and equal pay had left his family in dire economic straits. Hamelton reiterated that he would not ordinarily justify desertion if a soldier could receive redress for legitimate grievances "but we tried every way and could get no redress."[39]

The plight of André Cailloux's widow back in New Orleans further exemplified the government's calloused and indifferent treatment of its black troops and their families. Residing uptown in her

38. Annual Return of the 73rd USCInf for 1864, ser. 57, Regimental Papers USCT, RG 94; Service Records of Leonnel McCarty [*sic*] and John J. Cage, Compiled Military Service Records, RG 94, Pension Records of both men, RG 15, NA; Muster Roll of Company I, ser. 57, 73rd USCInf, Regimental Papers, RG 94, NA; Bell, *Revolution, Romanticism, and the Afro-Creole Protest*, 290; Court-Martial of Leonnel McCarty [*sic*], September 19, 1864, in Records of the Office of the Judge Advocate General (Army), Court-Martial Case File, 1809–1890, LL-3106, Pt. 2, RG 153, Leonnel Macarty to Lieut. O. A. Rice, December 26, 1864, Service Record of Leonnel McCarty [*sic*], RG 15, NA.

39. Warren D. Hamelton to Hon. E. M. Stanton, May 1865, in Berlin, Reidy, and Rowland, *Freedom*, II, 384–85.

half-brother Sebastien's house, along with her mother, Feliciana, her two daughters, and one of her sons, Felicie Cailloux endured economic privation following her husband's death. In January 1864, as Maistre left St. Rose of Lima, white radical Thomas Durant interceded on Felicie's behalf, furnishing her with a letter of introduction to General Banks. Reminding Banks that Cailloux had died "gallantly fighting" under the general's command, Durant described Felicie's circumstances as "needy" and commended her to his "powerful aid"—apparently without success. Ten months later, Durant tried to help Felicie recover back pay owed to her husband. Desertion often represented a protest against this general bad faith on the government's part—both its failure to honor its original promises and its indifference to the plight of black families. In the eyes of many black soldiers, the government's breach of contract had freed them from their military obligation to it.[40]

Cage apparently believed otherwise, and proceeded with his detachment to New Orleans, where they netted twenty-seven deserters. Some had absconded while on detail, others while in hospital or camp. Some had fled as early as October 1862, and others as late as April 1864. The sergeants walked the streets of New Orleans checking men for their passes. Sometimes, as in the case of Alcide Joseph of Company E, who had lost a finger at Port Hudson, Cage's men found deserters' mother's and told them to pass word to their sons that it would be better for them to rejoin the regiment. Joseph turned himself in. In other cases, the sergeants apprehended deserters by surprising them at their homes or encountering them on the streets. Most surrendered without much resistance. Philip Sebatier

40. Pension Record of André Caillaux [*sic*], RG 15, NA; Exchange of Property, Bastien Escalado [*sic*] to Louis J. Frederick, November 28, 1868, COB 95-497, Orleans Parish Conveyance Office; Exchange of Property between Bastien Escalado [*sic*] and Louis J. Frederick, November 23, 1868, Act 101, pp. 242–43, in Alcée Ker, Vol. 3, NONA; Thomas J. Durant to Major General N. P. Banks, January 23, 1864, Box 31, Banks Papers, Library of Congress; McTigue, "Forms of Racial Interaction in Louisiana," 63, n. 87; Thomas Durant, October 24, 1864, ser. 1920, Bureau of Civil Affairs, Register of Letters Received, Department of the Gulf, RG 393, Part 2, NA. Mary Maiso, the mother of a soldier in Company E, pleaded for rations in a letter to General Banks, telling him "I . . . am without food or money with a family of five children." See Mary Maiso to General Banks, July 23, 1863, ser. 1920, Letters Received, 1863, Bureau of Civil Affairs, Department of the Gulf, RG 393, Part 1, NA.

of Company G, for example, after briefly trying to elude capture by hiding in his house replied simply, "All right, let me put some clean clothes on." Sergeant Cage encountered Edward Madison of Company A on Common Street and immediately arrested him, forcing him to abandon the cart he was driving right there in the roadway. Other deserters attempted to flee when spotted by the members of the search party, but were captured, sometimes after a chase and at the point of a gun. The apprehension of Edward Joseph of Company E shocked his company commander, Captain Henry C. Nichols, who described him "as one of the best men I had."[41]

Most of the apprehended deserters received sentences of two to three years of hard labor and forfeiture of all pay, but General Banks, aware of manpower needs, agreed to commute most of these, and the deserters returned to service facing an additional year or eighteen months of duty at half pay. General Order 24, ignoring the reality that most of the desertions had occurred after May 1863, asserted in a face-saving gesture that at the early period of enlistment, "when many of the desertions occurred," the men had not received instruction as to the serious nature of that crime. In consideraton of this, and also of their previously demonstrated good character, Banks commuted the sentences of many, "trusting that this act of leniency together with the examples afforded by those whose cases will not justify mercy will be salutary warning to all in this command."[42]

Of course, the government's unjust treatment of the regiment had contributed far more to desertions than had a lack of familiarity with the seriousness of the offense. In the late summer of 1864, white officers at Morganza complained to higher authorities about the situation. Merriam contended that the "poor discipline and efficiency of his regiment "is owing probably to there [sic] being kept, almost constantly at fatigue work." Nevertheless, the commanding officers

41. Courts-Martial of John Nelson, August 26, Alcide Joseph, September 1, Octave Laveau, September 20, Edward Joseph, September 29, Peirre Liruchet, October 1, Philip Sebatier, October 3, and Edward Madison, October 10, all 1864, Records of the Office of the Judge Advocate General (Army), Court-Martial Case File, 1809–1894, LL-3106, Pts. 1 and 2, RG 153, NA.
42. General Order 24, October 30, 1864, ser. 741, General Orders, 1st Brigade, 1st Division, U.S. Colored Troops (Morganza), Department of the Gulf (Dickey, Frisbie), RG 393, Pt. 2, NA.

of each of the four black regiments that constituted the 1st Brigade at Morganza (73rd, 75th, 79th, and 92nd) received an order on August 4 instructing them to detail every enlisted man for labor on the fortifications. After the officers complained, Department Headquarters queried Andrews about "the constant employment of colored troops on fatigue duty beyond and over their fair proportion." Exasperated, the general responded that he had been obliged to employ black troops at Port Hudson on fatigue duty by order of that same department over his "most earnest representations" that disproportionate amounts of fatigue duty had "ill effects" on them. As to the undue employment of colored troops as laborers at Morganza, Andrews noted that "While I have no doubt whatever that they are intentionally so employed, I am not in command of the colored troops of that post except for the purposes of uniform instruction, discipline and inspection. To correct the abuses at that place, those with requisite authority needed to enforce existing orders." By late September, Inspector General Samuel M. Quincy reported that although some commanders at Morganza continued to violate orders restricting the amount of fatigue duty assigned to black soldiers, conditions had improved somewhat and drills had "been undertaken under difficulties." One difficulty was continuing racial hostility. Merriam reported an assault on his men by white troops on the evening of May 27—the anniversary, ironically, of the charge at Port Hudson.[43]

On September 24, 1864, shortly after Quincy's report, Colonel Henry Frisbie, commanding the colored 1st Brigade, weighed in with a slightly different variation on the theme. He reported to the adjutant general's office concerning a recently concluded raid to secure recruits and contrabands in accordance with General Order

43. Notation by Merriam on Muster Roll of Company C, August 31, 1864, ser. 57, Regimental Papers, 73rd USCInf, USCT, RG 94, NA; Circular Order 1, August 4, 1864, ser. 1990, Letters Sent, 1st Brigade, 1st Division, U.S. Colored Troops (Morganza), Department of the Gulf (Dickey, Frisbie), RG 393, Pt. 2, NA; George L. Andrews to Major George L. Drake, September 5, 1864, ser. 57, Regimental Papers, 73rd USCInf, USCT, RG 94; Samuel Quincy to Lt. Col. Wm. S. Albert, September 20, 1864, ser. 1825, Letters Received, Inspector, Department of the Gulf, RG 393, Pt. 1, NA; From Captain Merriam, August 27, 1864, ser. 1993, Register of Letters Received, 1st Brigade, 1st Division, U.S. Colored Troops (Morganza), Department of the Gulf (Dickey), RG 393, Pt. 2, NA.

106, which directed that all able-bodied men of color between 18 and 40 be enlisted for military service. Referring to his black troops, Frisbie contended that, as far as distance, "they march as well as any white troops with which they have come in contact." He suggested, however, that a few officers and a few mounted men to accompany the cavalry would prove more effective than the current practice of breaking up brigades and then mixing white and black regiments to form a new one for raiding purposes. He called such a practice "exceedingly injudicious and productive of much evil and disorganization." "As it is," he explained, "the white soldiers have no interest, and in fact discourage the coming of these persons." On a recent expedition, no white troops lifted an ax or spade while out on the march. Yet, according to Frisbie, the black troops, who marched as far, pulled as much guard duty, and who probably would have fought as hard as the other troops if given the chance, labored at work while the rest lay in the shade.

Frisbie's frustration was apparent. He deplored the constant violation of orders—from the War Department and from Major General Edward R. S. Canby, who had replaced Banks as commander of the Department of the Gulf—prohibiting excessive fatigue duty for black troops. He characterized complaints as so frequent and so ineffective that he had almost "ceased to expect justice from any one." He explained that officers and enlisted men did not object to the work per se, but rather to the "manner and circumstances" of that work, which stigmatized them with the brand of inferiority. Such stigmatization, according to Frisbie, made it "difficult to keep our best officers, for they will not command troops that the Government allows inferiority to become attached to." They wanted only their fair share of common labor, but would do any amount of fighting. Noting that white southerners seemed terror-stricken by black troops despite their soldierly and well-behaved manner, Frisbie urged their use to pacify "this side of Atchafalaya River."[44]

Samuel Quincy, in his role as inspector general, attested to Frisbie's observation about the difficulty of retaining officers. He attributed the acute shortage to the many discharges and resignations (seven officers of the 73rd, only two of them black, had resigned

44. General Order 106, August 2, 1864, ser. 57, 73rd USCInf, Regimental Papers, USCT, RG 94, NA; *OR*, Series 1, Vol. 41, 809–10.

between February and July 1864) and to lengthy delays in promotion and appointments. He urged creation of a permanent board of examiners to expedite matters. Meanwhile, in August and September, the 73rd received infusions of men from two sources: transfers from the disbanded 83rd Colored Infantry and ninety-two recruits from New Orleans, most of them former contrabands and not natives of Louisiana.[45]

As if the regiment did not face enough difficulties, Lieutenant Colonel Merriam became involved in a running dispute with Frisbie, who commanded the 92nd Regiment as well as the entire 1st Brigade. The heavy demand for work details sparked conflict within the brigade between the two officers who had earlier voiced their common outrage over the issue to higher authorities. Apparently to underscore what he considered the unfair burden placed on his men, Merriam formally requested Frisbie to excuse his first sergeant, cooks, and musicians from fatigue detail. In making such a request, Merriam argued that he did not have sufficient manpower to meet the unreasonable levees on his regiment. Frisbie denied that he had given any orders to detail sergeants, cooks, and musicians, and in turn blamed the problem on Merriam's failure to submit timely and accurate morning reports of the number of men available for duty. He then accused Merriam of falsifying a subsequent report by understating the actual number of men available. Frisbie contemptuously remarked, "There does not seem to be sufficient brains in that regiment for its proper management. It has a hundred aggregate more than the 92nd, yet cannot furnish as many within a hundred men for active duty." The conflict was probably rooted in both clashing

45. See the following entries of discharged officers: Capt. Joseph Follin, no. 34, February 18, 1864, 1st Lt. Abram E. Garrison, nos. 4 and 21, May 27, 1864, Capt. George Guest, no. 17, July 17, 1864, James H. Ingraham, no. 4, March 11, 1864, Capt. James Sears, no. 2, March 10, 1864, 2d Lt. Amos R. Ladd, no. 4, July 16, 1864, Lt. Howard Morton, no. 25, July 17, 1864, Lt. Sam Ryna, no. 12, July 17, 1864, all in ser. 1993, Register of Letters Received, 1st Brigade, 1st Division, U.S. Colored Troops (Morganza), RG 393, Pt. 2, NA; S. M. Quincy to Lt. Col. Wm. S. Albert, September 10, 1864, ser. 1825, Letters Received, Inspector, Department of the Gulf, RG 393, Pt. 1, NA; Henry C. Merriam to Headquarters, September 22, 1864, Muster and Descriptive Roll of a Detachment of Men Drafted, n.d., [but obviously August 1864], Report of the Extension of the Time of Service of the 73rd Colored Infantry, ser. 57, 73rd USCInf, Regimental Papers, USCT, RG 94, NA; OR, Vol. 41, Pt. 2, 118, 581.

personalities and professional rivalry, but it may also have stemmed in part from confusion about the number of men available for duty because of the tendency of some officers to carry troops on the roster even though they had deserted.[46]

The animosity between the two men escalated into public view, with Frisbie eventually ordering the arrest of Merriam on charges of gross neglect, falsehood, inefficiency, and insubordination. In forwarding his charges, Frisbie described Merriam as "only the exponent of a small combination of scheming officers . . . who approve of his doings and 'glory in his spunk.' " Frisbie insisted that this "spirit of insubordination . . . be promptly checked" by a general court-martial. Such did not convene, however, and Merriam was released from arrest as of December 21, 1864, under terms of an act of Congress limiting such arrests.[47]

While their officers sparred with one another, some of the men of the regiment also continued to push at the boundaries restricting them. In October, Joseph Bazile of Company C, a free man before April 1861 who had joined the regiment in September 1862, pressed his claim for a hundred-dollar bounty as he left the army because of a disability incurred by wounds. The paymaster declined to pay it under various pretexts, finally taking the position that no law authorized him to give such a payment. Bazile took his case to Frisbie, who thereupon wrote to the adjutant general's Office. Frisbee carefully

46. Endorsements on report forwarded by Lt. Colonel Henry C. Merriam, October 20, 1864, ser. 1991, Endorsements Sent, 1st Brigade, 1st Division, U.S. Colored Troops (Morganza), Department of the Gulf (Dickey, Frisbie), RG 393, Pt. 2, NA; Col. and A. A. Inspector General, Dept of the Gulf, Inspection Report of Companies of the 1st Regiment Corps d'Afrique, September 27, 1863, ser. 57, Regimental Papers, 73rd USCInf, USCT, RG 94; Special Examiner M. Whitehead to S. A. Cuddy, Chief of Law Division, August 18, 1905, Pension File of Joseph Fille, RG 15, NA.

47. Endorsement of Demand by Lt. Col. Henry C. Merriam, October 21, 1864, ser. 1993, 1st Brigade, 1st Division, U.S. Colored Troops (Morganza), Register of Letters Received, Department of the Gulf (Dickey, Frisbie), RG 393, Pt. 2, NA; Endorsement on Special Order 25, forwarded by Col. Frisbie, Cmdg 1st Brigade, November 6, 1864, ser. 1991, Endorsements Sent, 1st Brigade, 1st Division, U.S. Colored Troops (Morganza), Department of the Gulf (Dickey, Frisbie), RG 393, Pt. 2; Frisbie to Hdqtrs, November 9, 1864, Wm. H. Dickey to Lieut O. A. Rice, Acting Ast. Adj General, December 21, 1864, ser. 1990, Letters Sent, 1st Brigade, 1st Division, U.S. Colored Troops (Morganza), Register of Letters Received, Department of the Gulf (Dickey, Frisbie), RG 393, Pt. 2, NA.

laid out his argument, noting that Bazile had been free prior to April 6, 1861; that Congress had provided in March 1863 that all who received a discharge by reason of wounds received in battle would be entitled to receive the same bounty as granted to those discharged after two years of service; that Congress had provided in June 1864 that persons of color would receive any such bounty up to one hundred dollars as the president directed; and that the same act provided that all persons of color free on April 19, 1861, would receive the same bounty allowed to any persons by the law existing at the time. The case eventually went to the attorney general's office, but its ultimate disposition remains unclear.[48]

The ferment within the regiment had its counterpart in the national political arena, and once again black New Orleans radicals brandished the name of André Cailloux and the symbol of Port Hudson to good effect. On Octrober 4, 1864, the last of the National Negro Conventions that had first begun meeting in 1830 convened in Syracuse, New York. Former captain of the 1st Regiment James Ingraham, who had briefly taken command of Cailloux's Company E and who had recently resigned from the army under pressure, served as Louisiana's delegate. A native of Mississippi, Ingraham was the son of a slave woman and a white slave owner who freed him at the age of six. English-speaking and a Methodist, Ingraham allied himself with the political agenda of Afro-Creole radicals and both literally and figuratively took up Cailloux's standard at the convention.[49]

Encouraged by the performance of black troops and by conservative attorney general Edward Bates's publicized opinion that all free persons born in the United States were citizens, and meeting on the eve of the crucial 1864 presidential election, Ingraham vigorously advocated the integrationist-suffrage agenda of Afro-Creole radical-

48. Col. H. N. Frisbie to Adj. General, October 24, 1864, ser. 1990, Letters Sent, 1st Brigade, 1st Division, U.S. Colored Troops (Morganza), Department of the Gulf (Dickey, Frisbie), RG 393, Pt. 2, NA; Endorsements on Frisbee's letter, ser. 264, Letters Received by the Adjutant General's Office, 1864, and Endorsement Book 2, p. 125, RG 94, NA.
49. "Proceedings of the National Convention of Colored Men, Held in the City of Syracuse, N. Y., October 4, 5, 6, 7, 1864," in Howard Holman Bell, ed. *Minutes of the Proceedings of the National Negro Conventions, 1830–1864* (New York, 1969), 62; Hollandsworth, *The Louisiana Native Guards*, 105.

ism, joining with like-minded delegates, including Frederick Douglass, to vanquish the last vestiges of the emigrationist wing of the convention movement, formerly associated with the imposing figure of Henry Highland Garnet. To that end, Ingraham skillfully and dramatically used the tattered banner of the 1st Regiment that Colonel Dickey had reviled earlier that year. On leaving the army, Ingraham had apparently taken the original, blood-stiffened standard with him, and now, in a dramatic gesture, he appeared with it at the convention. On the afternoon of the second day, a committee of two, including Garnet—who had, during the war, abandoned his earlier emigrationist stance—was appointed to "borrow the battle-flag of the First Louisiana Colored Troops and to suspend it across the platform." Garnet presented "the beautiful flag" to the convention and explained that "it was borne over the ramparts of Port Hudson, and is even now stained with the blood of the brave Captain Cailloux," though the blood was actually Planciancios's. He then recognized Ingraham, who had helped lead the attack in which Cailloux fell and who was himself subsequently wounded in the battle. The convention exploded in applause while Ingraham rose and bowed his acknowledgment of the warm reception. The crowd repeatedly saluted the flag, such was the power of its symbolism. Ingraham then took the stage and emotionally recounted the events connected with the banner. Then Frederick Douglass, the president of the convention, led the audience in three rousing cheers for Ingraham, his comrades at Port Hudson, and the battle flag.[50]

Time and again, delegates to the convention alluded to Ingraham as the heir to Cailloux's legacy. Garnet declared that soldiers had the right to enfranchisement and urged the convention to say so. He went on, "I see before me a gallant captain . . . who bears a wound in his side—who fought side by the side of the brave Cailloux, and now bears the battle-flag all stained with Cailloux's blood and brains as he fell." Ingraham was subsequently elected a vice-president of the convention and pushed relentlessly for black suffrage. The convention went on to call for the creation of a National Equal Rights League, an organization dedicated to securing black voting rights throughout the nation. The League held its first meeting immedi-

---

50. Cox, *Lincoln and Black Freedmen*, 79; Bell, *Minutes of the Proceedings*, 12–13; *Weekly Anglo-African*, October 15, 1864.

ately after the adjournment of the convention, and Ingraham promised to send $300 from Louisiana within thirty days to support it.[51]

Back home in New Orleans, Ingraham helped organize mass meetings in December to demand black suffrage. One of his fellow organizers, grand master of the Prince Hall Masonic Lodge Oscar J. Dunn, asserted, "We regard all black and colored men as fellow sufferers." On January 9, 1865, a Louisiana State Colored Convention convened with Ingraham presiding. Shortly after it got under way, the convention created an Equal Rights League of Louisiana. On January 11, the convention publicly recognized the attendance of Maistre and invited him to take a seat. The next morning, Maistre delivered the opening prayer for the session, and on the final day he received the convention's public thanks for his discourse at Cailloux's funeral. Although free people of color, including a number of former officers, constituted a majority of the delegates, the *Tribune*, trumpeting black unity, pointed out that poor, illiterate laborers only recently removed from slavery also served. The convention's resolutions demanded black suffrage and equal access to streetcars. Ingraham, once again drawing on the name of Cailloux, took the initiative in forming auxiliary "Cailloux Leagues" throughout the city to support the objectives of the Equal Rights League, particularly by raising money.[52]

News of the electrifying political developments no doubt filtered back to the men in the field and may have helped to lift their spirits. Morale certainly received a boost in November 1864 when Secretary of War Stanton, responding to entreaties from the regiment's officers, authorized that the words "Port Hudson" be inscribed on the colors of the 73rd "in consideration of the distinguished part borne by it in the siege and capture of that place." Following closely on that decision, several black noncommissioned officers—Sergeant Major Cage, who had led the search party for deserters in New Orleans,

51. Philip S. Foner and George E. Walker, *Proceedings of the Black State Conventions, 1840–1865*, (Philadelphia, 1980), II, 247, 251; *Weekly Anglo-African*, October 15, 22, 1864.

52. Bell, *Revolution, Romanticism, and the Afro-Creole Protest*, 250–56; Eric Foner, *Reconstruction: America's Unfinished Revolution, 1863–1877* (New York, 1988), 64; *Tribune*, January 10–15, February 18, March 3, April 23, September 22, 1865; *Weekly Anglo-African*, October 22, 1864.

First Sergeant Célestin Dupin of Company H, and Private Solomon Moses, a two-year veteran of the 76th Regiment—applied for commissions as officers in newly authorized black units. General Andrews indicated the fate of those applications in the endorsement he penned on the letter of Solomon Moses on November 28: "if colored officers are to be allowed in the new organizations—I see no objection to this man's applicaton being granted. So far as my own opinion . . . as to the advisability of admitting colored commissioned officers, I am for the present opposed thereto." He explained that because of existing prejudices few or no good white officers would enter a regiment with black officers. Besides, based at least on his observations, which had revealed few efficient black officers, he did not believe that enough qualified colored men existed to fill all the positions. Filling slots for noncommissioned officers had proved difficult enough. "All well-qualified colored men are greatly needed in the non-commissioned staff of regiments," he added.[53]

From the chaplain's point of view, the regiment also needed better white officers. On December 19, 1864, after accompanying a combined force of the 73rd and 92nd on a scouting mission, a disturbed Samuel Gardner, who had replaced Asa Barnes as chaplain in September, wrote "unofficially" to the brigade commander. He told of officers abusing their men by cursing and vilifying them in the most shameful language, and striking and kicking them in a manner that indicated that such was commonplace. Gardner noted that such behavior violated military order, and "would not be practiced upon white soldiers." Viewing black soldiers as in a state of tutelage and military service as an excellent school to lead them from enforced degradation to manhood and citizenship, Gardner deplored tactics and discipline that reproduced rather than contrasted with the irre-

53. S. M. Quincy to Dear Mother, March 12, 1864, Quincy, *et. al.* Family Papers, LC; Special Order 42, November 11, 1864, War Department, AGO, E. D. Townshend, AA General, in Woodward, *The Negro in the Military*, 2833, RG 94, NA; Letters from Sgt. Major John P. Cage, November 3, 1864, and 1st Sgt. Celesta Dupin, November 7, 1864, entries 50 and 16 respectively, ser. 1993, 1st Brigade, 1st Division, U.S. Colored Troops (Morganza), Register of Letters Received, Department of the Gulf (Dickey, Frisbie), RG 393, Pt. 2, NA; Andrews's endorsement on the letter of Solomon Moses to George B. Drake, November 19, 1864, Service Record of Solomon Moses, Sgt. Major John J. Cage to Asst. Adj. General, Department of the Gulf, January 26, 1865, Service Record of John J. Cage, Compiled Military Service Records, RG 94, NA.

sponsible cruelties of slavery. Such treatment as he referred to would only add to their former degradation the humiliating thought that it came from those who professed friendship. After such proof of bad faith, Gardner asked rhetorically, "what hope or ambition can be left in them? . . . all effort towards their elevation in this generation or the next, will be futile, unless there is an end to the plantation style of government; that is, so far as the army is their school." He ended by expressing uncertainty whether those in authority possessed the disposition and commitment to enforce better behavior.[54]

The year thus ended on a mixed note. The regiment had lost thirty-eight men, mostly from disease, connected in no small part to unsanitary and inadquate preparation and cooking of food. It also still lacked an adequate number of officers. On Janaury 1, it had only four captains and three lieutenants for duty on the line. Another officer, Captain Henry Nichols, who commanded Cailloux's old company, would face an examining board on charges of "general inefficiency and immorality rendering him unbecoming of respect." Unlike some other regiments, the chaplain of the 73rd did not maintain a school in which the men might pursue educations. In fairness to Gardner, many of those from New Orleans who had been free before the war could already read. Most of the new recruits, however, could not. During 1864, one hundred and twenty-one men had deserted, though search parties had apprehended forty-three. Still, amidst the difficulties, Merriam detected some hopeful signs. The new recruits, most of them recent slaves, had higher morale and less reason than the veterans to resent the government, espcially following Congress's decision in June 1864 to pay black and white soldiers equally, retroactive to January 1, 1864. The regiment performed well in company and battalion drill and fair in school of soldiers. Only Company E, Cailloux's old unit, received a "bad" rating for drill; its discipline also rated only a "fair." On February 9, 1865, in a move that boosted morale as well as manpower, Merriam recommended the return of thirteen former deserters to their companies, explaining that "there are many circumstances connected with the desertions from this regiment prior to May, 1864, which tend to palliate the offense." Even more deserters would take advantage of President Lincoln's offer of amnesty in March 1865. In all, eighty returned to

54. Berlin, Reidy, and Rowland, *Freedom*, II, 417–18.

the regiment. Most had to make good for time lost and forfeit all pay and allowances during their absences.[55]

Merriam managed to improve the spirit as well as the training of his men during early 1865, and as the war neared its end the regiment got the opportunity to make one more charge in combat. In March, the 73rd received orders to join General John P. Hawkins's division of colored troops as part of a Union operation against Fort Blakely outside Mobile, Alabama. Confederate brigadier general St. John R. Liddell commanded the fort, which lay on the east side of the Appalachee River, on the eastern side of Mobile Bay about ten miles from the city. The regiment moved from Morganza to Metairie and then to Lake Ponchatrain where it embarked on board the steamer *General Banks* for Barrancas, Florida. Proceeding on foot from Barrancas toward Pensacola, the troops had to wade, often up to their armpits, across an inlet of the Gulf that stretched from one to three miles wide. On March 20, a week after its arrival at Pensacola, the 73rd, now part of a brigade commanded by General William Anderson Pile, set out for Fort Blakely via northwest Florida and southern Alabama, approaching the fort from the rear. The roads proved especially difficult for moving wagons and artillery. A heavy storm during the night of the twentieth reduced the camp to a swamp in which the pieces sank to their hubs and animals became mired in the quicksand. Company E was detailed to help the wagons trapped in the mud and miasma. They used dragropes to assist the horse teams and then went on to lay miles of corduroy road. Because supply wagons could not keep pace with the main force, the men ran short of rations and for four days had to subsist on ears of corn, which they had time to roast only during the night. One lieutenant recalled that he went forty-eight hours without food and that at the same time his men were on half rations. The Reverend Mr. Gardner praised the "manly and patient" spirit exhibited by the regiment during the difficult march. In stark contrast to his report of the previous December, he commended the officers for their interest in the welfare of their men and noted that in the contact between white and

55. Inspection by Henry C. Merriam, January 1, 1865, and Annual Return of the 73rd USCInf for 1864, ser. 57, Regimental Papers, 73rd USCInf, RG 94, USCT, NA; Berlin, Reidy, and Rowland, *Freedom*, II, 367; Merriam to Lt. A. A. Rice, AAG, February 9, 1865, ser. 360, Letters Received by the Office of the Adjutant General, RG 94, NA.

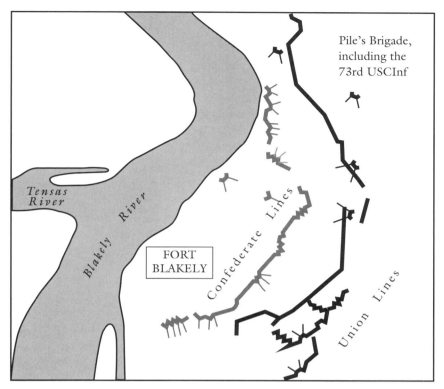

Union and Confederate Lines at Ft. Blakely, Ala. The fort was captured
by the Army of West Mississippi, April 9, 1865.

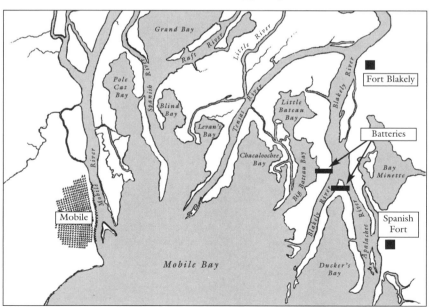

Fort Blakely and the Defenses of Mobile

black soldiers "a gratifying respect has been manifested, and full acknowlegment of their [black troops'] soldierly qualities rewarded." He added, "The future of the colored soldier seems to open more and more auspiciously, both for himself and this country." Arriving at the site of Blakely on April 2, the regiment took part in the weeklong siege that began the next day and culminated on April 9, one of the last major engagements of the war.[55]

About 3 P.M. on the same day that Lee surrendered at Appomattox, the 73rd came full circle, reprising its charge at Port Hudson, but this time, under better circumstances and with a successful result. In doing so, it recaptured the spirit of the fallen Cailloux and helped redeem the bitter experience of the two years since his death. Elements of the regiment dashed to the outer line of Confederate defenses, penetrating the abatis and capturing the rifle pits. Merriam, who was promoted to full colonel and eventually received the Medal of Honor for his "meritorious service" that day, then volunteered to storm the enemy's works with his regiment in advance of orders for the general assault. Upon obtaining permission, he led an attack on the main line, quickly capturing seven pieces of artillery and some prisoners. The black troops carried all before them, planting their colors on the enemy's parapet. The 73rd had been the first in position in front of Fort Blakely, the first to storm the rampart, and the first to enter the works. Many of the Confederate troops, fearing retribution from black troops for Confederate massacres of black soldiers, threw down their arms and ran to their right toward the advancing white forces to avoid capture by the black troops. Augustin Carriere later recalled, "We advanced in a stooping position and the enemy's fire went over our heads. I was fourth man to enter the fort. The enemy was frightened and did not a man resisted us as we

56. Dyer, *A Compendium of the War of the Rebellion*, 1734–35; John M. Wilson, "The Campaign Ending with the Capture of Mobile," *Military Order of the Loyal Legion of the United States: War Papers Read Before the Commander of the District of Columbia*, XVII (1894), 13, 21, 22–23; Philip S. Foner and George E. Walker, eds., *Proceedings of the Black State Conventions*, 1840–1865, II, 247, 251; *Tribune*, April 19, July 14, 1865; Samuel S. Gardner to Adjutant General, April 15, 1865, no. 6339, ser. 360, Letters Received by the Office of the Adjutant General, 1863–1888, RG 94, NA; Deposition C, Augustin Carriere, May 3, 1895, Deposition F, Stanislaus Coiron, May 7, 1895, Pension Records of Basil Ulgère, RG 15, NA. See also the Pension Records of Basil S. Dede, John Durand, and Eugene Bonhomme, all in RG 15, NA.

crawled over the wall. Not a man of our company was clubbed by a rebel soldier that day." Stanislaus Coiron affirmed, "The enemy . . . didn't resist us as we scaled the fort." Within thirty minutes, Ft. Blakely, with thirty-five hundred men and forty pieces of artillery, had fallen. The regiment had two enlisted men killed and two wounded. One of the latter, Eugene Bonhomme, was a former slave who had enlisted in September 1862, deserted in September 1863 at Port Hudson, and then returned on February 26, 1865. Struck by a torpedo fragment, his left foot was amputated in the field.[57]

Chaplain Gardner observed in his report that "the troops . . . appeared comparatively free from the spirit of violence and nastiness . . . and while some individuals have expressed sentiments of inhuman cruelty as might be expected from the relations they formerly had with many, no acts of outrage have been committed." Col. Samuel Quincy, the titular commander of the 73rd since May 29, 1864, wrote to his mother on April 19, 1865, in the wake of the capture of Fort Blakely and Lincoln's assassination, "Our Negro troops . . . feel as if they had lost their father [Lincoln] in the President. . . . If the murder of the President had then taken place and been known [at the time of Blakely] they would have charged with Lear's famous cry of 'kill, kill, kill, kill,' and nothing human could then have saved the garrison." In New Orleans, the *Tribune* thrilled to the exploits at Fort Blakely. The paper praised the 73rd's "prodigies of valor" and claimed that the impetuosity of its charge had left its white officers far behind. The *Tribune* also hotly disputed an account in the New Orleans *Times* that incorrectly identified the 11th Wisconsin as the first to plant its banner on the parapet of Fort Blakely. "The conquerors of Ft. Blakely," the *Tribune* intoned, "is a new title that our soldiers of color have acquired in recognition of their patriotism."[58]

57. *OR*, Vol. 49, Pt. 1, 288–90; Service Record of Henry C. Merriam, RG 15, NA; Henry C. Merriam to Adjutant General, February 7, 1894, William A. Pile to Hon. Henry Wilson, February 9, 1867, John P. Hawkins to Hon. Henry Wilson, April 19, 1866, all in Commission Branch File of Henry C. Merriam, RG 15, NA; *Tribune*, April 19, June 20, July 14, 1865; Hollandsworth, *The Louisiana Native Guards*, 102; Pension Records of Augustin Carriere and Stanislaus Coiron, RG 15, NA; Wilson, "The Campaign Ending with the Capture of Mobile," 23–24; Pension Record of Eugene Bonhomme, RG 15, NA.

58. Samuel S. Gardner to Adjutant General, May 2, 1865, G 436, ser 360, Letters Received by the Office of the Adjutant General, RG 94, NA,; S. M. Quincy

After the fall of Ft. Blakely, the 73rd encamped in the woods about a mile distant for a week, drilling twice a day. On the eighth day, the regiment embarked onboard the steamer *Iberville* for Selma, Alabama. The men loaded the steamboat with cotton and went up the Alabama River to Selma, where they remained only two days before returning on the same steamer to Mobile. There they worked for three weeks on the fortifications and unloaded government transports. Then they marched to Mississippi to rebuild railroads that Union forces had recently destroyed. The *Tribune* bemoaned, "They had again to labor, as they had before at English Turn, at Baton Rouge, at Port Hudson and at Morganza." Sensitive to critics who called the regiment a glorified labor unit, the paper recalled both "our immortal compatriot, Captain André Cailloux" at Port Hudson and the storming of Fort Blakely. It asked rhetorically, "Was it not fighting as hard and as gallant as has been done anywhere?" The bitterness in the Afro-Creole community prompted the *Tribune* to recall, "At the same time that this regiment was working in both ways—by actual fighting and by hard labor—they saw every favor and advantage granted to white troops who had never seen any battle. The heroes of Port Hudson and Fort Blakely were kept on the hardest work on railroads, while white regiments that were never in an actual fight enjoyed rest and comfort or were simply employed on provost guard duty." It went on to say that "if our colored brethren exacted the respect of our countrymen, they did not reap the just tribute of consideration and regard they had a right to expect from the country they . . . so gallantly and so faithfully served." Calling the 73rd "the pet regiment of New Orleans," the paper asserted that men who placed patriotism above distinctions of color appreciated their courage and devotion.[59]

Demobilization for the regiment came on the afternoon of September 23, 1865, only days after the Afro-Creole leadership, frustrated in its efforts to secure the franchise yet zealous as ever to demonstrate both the fitness and determination of blacks to gain that right, had

to Mother, April 19, 1865, Quincy *et al.* Family Papers, LC; *Tribune*, April 15, 16, 22, 1865.

59. Dyer, *A Compendium of the War of the Rebellion*, 1734–35; *Tribune*, June 14 and July 14, 1865 (English).

organized a mock ("shadow") election to coincide with the official election day. On the evening of the 23rd, about 250 former members of the 73rd marched down Conti Street with fife and drum, stopped in front of the offices of the *Tribune*, and gave rousing cheers. The editor promised that "in the full measure of our power, we'll battle with pen in hand, for the same noble cause" for which so many had suffered, fought, bled, and died. About a month later, at the conclusion of another march and rally by about 100 veterans, the men donated $500 to help defray expenses for the Friends of Universal Suffrage, an interracial political coalition of former soldiers and other loyalists organized in June 1865. Chapters of the Cailloux League, swollen in membership (no doubt by returning veterans), also donated money to the Friends of Universal Suffrage, while spiritualist mediums linked to the Afro-Creole leaderhip continued to contact Cailloux's spirit for inspiration.[60]

Fourteen former members of the 73rd Regiment would eventually go on to fill leadership roles during Reconstruction. As the war ended, the men of the regiment looked forward to that triumph of "justice and principle" for which Cailloux had given his life and for which Fr. Maistre continued to pray and preach publicly in New Orleans.[61]

60. Bell, *Revolution, Romanticism, and the Afro-Creole Protest*, 250–56; Hollandsworth, *The Louisiana Native Guards*, 103–104; *Tribune*, September 19, 22, October 24, 1865. See Séances, July 17, 1863, 85–30, p. 156, and February 6, 1869, 85-31, p. 266, Spiritualist Registers, Grandjean Collection, UNO.

61. Rankin, "The Politics of Caste," in MacDonald, Kemp and Haas, *Louisiana's Black Heritage*, 109, 139–45. Rankin identified men as leaders if they served as ward officers and/or spokesmen of the major political organizations of the city: Club Unioniste Republican, Société de Bienfaisance de Frères Unis, Union Political Association, National Equal Rights League, Friends of Universal Suffrage, and the Republican Party.

8

REPENTANT RADICAL

The stalemate between Father Claude Paschal Maistre and Archbishop Jean-Marie Odin continued after the war, constituting one act in the larger drama of Reconstruction in the city and state. During that time, Maistre continued his ministry to blacks and his high-profile support of Afro-Creole radicals, who gladly returned the favor. When Maistre had buried Cailloux back in 1863, he had eloquently predicted the triumph of equality and justice. The postwar years would determine the accuracy of that prediction.

In the final months of the war, Maistre remained the Catholic clerical mainstay at radical gatherings. In January 1865, he had played a highly visible role at the founding convention of the Equal Rights League, receiving in the process its public thanks. At a mass meeting of ten thousand blacks on April 23, at Congo Square to mourn President Lincoln's assassination, Maistre marched at the head of what the *Tribune* called his "vast congregation," along with members of over one hundred benevolent societies. Some of them, such as the Society of St. Michael, which maintained close ties with Maistre, donated small sums to aid the campaign of the Friends of Universal Suffrage.[1]

Still, even as he identified himself with radicalism, in the late spring and summer of 1865, Maistre quietly attempted to negotiate an end to the impasse with Odin, so that he might remain in the archdiocese. Three times he sent to Odin the same group of three emissar-

1. *Tribune,* January 14, April 23, September 22, 1865.

ies—all practicing Catholics, including two prominent persons of color who had been free before the war and one white, Jesuit-educated gentleman—bearing petitions for his reinstatement. Each time the archbishop replied that Maistre would have to abandon his sacrilegious ministry, repair the scandal, apply to Rome to lift the ecclesiastical censure, and accept measures that Odin would impose to ensure the salvation of his soul. After the third failed meeting, Maistre received advice from yet another clerical maverick drawn to his side, itinerant Capuchin priest Josaphat Kleiber, whom Maistre had befriended and with whom he shared his quarters. Restless and volatile, the forty-five-year-old Fr. Josaphat belonged to the Bavarian Province of Capuchins (an independent reform branch of the Franciscans), which he had entered twenty-seven years earlier. He had served for nine years as a missionary in India, and then in 1860 had come to the Capuchin community in Detroit. He evidently made arrangements to solicit funds for missionary work in the diocese of Louisville but ran into difficulties with Bishop Martin Spalding. Indeed, Kleiber possessed a knack for alienating others. His fellow Capuchins viewed him as something of a blustering braggart and "less than devout." He became a source of friction and controversy in the Capuchin parish in Milwaukee, practically coming to blows with his confreres, who eventually had him physically removed from the monastery by one of the brothers. He traveled to Immaculate Conception Parish in Fountain City, Wisconsin, and finally found his way to New Orleans and Maistre.[2]

In May 1865, Kleiber convinced Maistre, who had doubted that he could get a hearing in Rome, to take the archbishop at his word and appeal his case to the Propaganda. In his letter to Barnabó, Mais-

2. Claude Paschal Maistre to Cardinal Alessandro Barnabó, February 20, 1866, Vol. 21, fol. 151rv, May 15, 1865, Vol. 20, fol. 1658rv, and Archbishop Jean-Marie Odin to Barnabó, April 12, 1866, Vol. 21, fol. 216rv, *Scritture Riferite nei Congressi: American Centrale*, PA; Fr. Josaphat to Dear Superior, May 1, 1860, in Archives of the Province of St. Joseph of the Capuchin Order, Detroit; Celestine Bittle, OFMCap., *A Romance of Lady Poverty: The History of the Province of St. Joseph of the Capuchin Order in the United States* (Milwaukee, 1933), 123–36; *The Rise and Progress of the Province of St. Joseph of the Capuchin Order in the United States, 1857–1907* (New York, 1907), 84–89; "Daten zur Person des P. Josaphat Kleiber, Kapuziner der Bayerischen Kapüzinerprovinz, 1839–1869," in Bavarian Province Archives of the Capuchins, furnished by J. Alphonsus Sprinkart, OFMCap., April 30, 1995.

tre charged bluntly that "the blacks emancipated by the war and by the proclamation of the President of the United States" were "the innocent but direct cause" of the difficulties between him and the archbishop, and that Odin had punished him for ministering to blacks in distress. He described the local clergy as overtly pro-Confederate and charged that following the capture of the city by the Federals, priests had refused absolution and the last rites to blacks unless they consented to return to their former masters. Turning to Odin's charge that he had sown discord, Maistre claimed that despite intense, widespread, and almost lunatic opposition from whites, he had extended his ministry to black refugees because he viewed their liberty as a gift from God and the sacraments as meant for all persons.

Maistre asserted that at the beginning of the contretemps his ecclesiastical superiors had enjoined him to leave both St. Rose and the archdiocese and had promised him positive letters of recommendation and protection that would enable him to find another diocese in which to work. Maistre somewhat disingenuously said that he had attempted to comply with Odin's initial order to leave the archdiocese but that military authorities had prevented him from doing so. He had reported the dilemma to Odin and prayed him to delay, but Odin had responded to his "supplication" with a written notice suspending and interdicting him. In lawyerlike fashion, Maistre disputed the validity of the suspension and interdict, arguing that it violated formalities and procedures by failing to specify cause or to reproach him for the administration of his parish, and by bearing the erroneous date of May 16, 1862, rather than 1863. He further claimed that the political motivation behind the archbishop's actions rendered the suspension and interdiction null and void. Maistre insisted that, desirous of peace, he stood ready to submit, but had disinterestedly stayed at his post in order to preserve the Catholicism of vast numbers of restive black Catholics whom the archbishop had scandalized by his behavior and who had threatened to leave the church and join Protestant sects such as the Methodists. In addition, Maistre repeated his implausible story that military authorities had refused to allow him to leave. After Odin had regained possession of St. Rose, Maistre claimed that "the faithful" (rather than he) had bought a piece of land and built a church (Holy Name) whose size could still not accommodate the large numbers who attended. Maistre characterized himself as the victim of a clerical conspiracy intent on defaming him and ruining his reputation by feeding the Holy See a mass of lies that offended Christian charity. He pleaded with Barnabó for a decision from Rome that would incline the heart of the archbishop "toward his children of African descent," and appended a note of support from Fr. Josaphat, who testified that Maistre had acted "without guile" and that he had administered the sacraments to blacks at a time when other priests had abandoned them.[3]

While Maistre's appeal was on its way to Rome, Odin and his vicar general, Étienne Rousselon, had to deal with the continuing realities of the schismatic parish. Although the archbishop had declared that any Catholic who patronized Maistre would incur a penalty that only the archbishop could remove, in actual cases, Rousselon dealt more leniently and pastorally. In August 1865, for example, he permitted priests from St. Augustine's to officiate at the burial of a young black woman who had regularly confessed to Maistre and who had received the last rites from him. Maistre viewed this decision as something of a vindication and profusely thanked Rousselon, especially since some had attempted to forestall the burial because of her association with Maistre and had written to Rousselon informing him of the planned interment. Seeking, perhaps, to drive a wedge between Rousselon and Odin, Maistre expressed joy that Rousselon did not share Odin's notion of the reprobation attached to his ministry. "I have never doubted the validity of the sacraments that I administer," he wrote, "but I am particularly edified to see that you . . . in your heart of hearts have the same conviction. Thank you dear monsignor for your agreement."[4]

Clergy outside the city also faced repercussions from Maistre's schism. On August 17, 1865, Father Hyacinthe Marie LeCozic of Bonfouca, Louisiana, reported to Odin that several parishioners who had been in New Orleans had dealt with Maistre in spiritual matters. Averring to the archbishop's pastoral that required them to have recourse to him in order to obtain absolution "for their crime," and attesting that these persons could make their way back to the arch-

3. Maistre to Barnabó, May 15, 1865 (Fr. Josaphat note appended),Vol 20, fols. 1461rv–1462rv, Odin to Barnabó, November 8, 1865, Vol. 20, fols. 1658rv–1659rv, *Scritture Riferite nei Congressi: American Centrale,* PA.
4. Widow Charpolet to Étienne Rousselon, August 10, 1865, 1-c-6, ANOC; Maistre to Rousselon, August 11, 1865, Rousselon Papers, AANO.

bishop only with great difficulty, he asked for, and apparently received, permission to absolve them.[5]

In September 1865, Barnabó addressed himself to Maistre's appeal. Although he found Maistre's statements "so fantastic as to be unbelievable," he informed Odin of the appeal and of the charges that Maistre had lodged against the archbishop. The cardinal asked Odin to respond, and the latter did so vigorously, indignantly denying what he characterized as Maistre's and Josaphat's calumnies. He recapitulated his version of the origins of the case and declared that most of Maistre's followers had deserted him and returned to the Church. He insisted that cupidity had always motivated Maistre, and he cited his own personal experience with the priest in the matter of the lot and the church of St. Rose. He also dredged up the earlier accusations against Maistre from other dioceses, including that of extorting money in return for administering the sacraments. Odin insisted that Catholic churches had always remained open to blacks and that Communions among them, far from diminishing, had actually increased. He attributed Maistre's letter to Barnabó to the promptings of Josaphat, whom he characterized as "a dangerous man and an enemy to all authority."[6]

Maistre's checkered past almost certainly undermined his credibility with the Propaganda. On January 5, 1866, Barnabó dispatched letters to each of the principals in the case. Assuring Maistre that he had read his appeal and the archbishop's rebuttal, he urged the priest to submit to Odin "with complete docility of spirit," and implied that he would then receive mercy from the archbishop. He noted, however, that should Maistre desire a new hearing, he should signify such in a letter to Barnabó and the cardinal-prefect would submit the case to the full Congregation for deliberation. To Josaphat, he wrote a curt note, directing him, in effect, to mind his own business. (That year, Fr. Josaphat returned to Europe. He later left the Capuchin order, became a layman, and returned to the United States in 1869.) Barnabó forwarded the two letters for Odin to peruse and then to pass on to Maistre and Josaphat.[7]

5. Hyacinthe LeCozic to Odin, August 17, 1865, 1-c-6, AANO, AUND.

6. Barnabó to Odin, September 21, 1865, Vol. 356, fols. 448v, 449r, in *Lettere Di S. Congregazione,* Odin to Barnabó, November 8, 1865, Vol. 20, fols. 1658rv–1659rv, *Scritture Riferite nei Congressi: American Centrale,* PA.

7. Barnabó to Maistre, and to Father Josaphat, both January 5, 1866, Vol. 357, fols. 7v, 7r, 7rv, in *Lettere Di S. Congregazione,* PA; "Daten zur Person des P. Josaphat Kleiber"; Barnabó to Odin, January 5, 1866, VI-2-k, ANOC.

After receiving Barnabó's missive, Maistre attempted to comply, but only on the condition that Odin allow him to remain in the archdiocese. In a letter to the archbishop on February 13, 1866, he referred to Barnabó's injunction that he submit and the accompanying implication that in return, he could expect from the archbishop the favor he sought. Maistre assured Odin that, but for an illness that had indisposed him for two weeks, on receiving Barnabó's letter he would have come to see the archbishop immediately in order to place himself at his disposal and to pray him humbly to receive him in grace and mercy. Instead, he sent the same intermediaries to the archbishop who had borne his petitions of the previous summer. In keeping with Barnabó's recommendation, Maistre besought the archbishop "on both knees and prostrate" to lift the interdict and to extend his grace and gentleness to Maistre and Maistre's flock. He also begged Odin's pardon "for the pain that I have given you" and he promised to obey docilely his orders and to defer to his advice.[8]

Odin remained unyielding, rejecting Maistre's peace feelers and demanding unconditional surrender. Convinced of Maistre's duplicity, Odin regarded the letter not as a humble submission but as an attempt to discover terms according to which Maistre could regain his faculties in the archdiocese. Odin informed Maistre's emissaries that under no circumstances would he allow the priest to remain in the archdiocese and that for the rest, he would have to come to speak directly with him. That meeting took place on February 19, at the archevêque, the archiepiscopal residence in the old Ursulines convent. Odin minced no words, calling Maistre a wretched soul who had given horrible scandal. He ordered him to close his church, leave the city, and commit himself to a monastery to make a long penance; Rome would then decide what he must do next. As for himself, he could not and would not do anything else. Odin closed by angrily reproaching Maistre for his "calumnious" letter to Barnabó. Hearing in Odin's words a sentence of perpetual exile, Maistre lashed back, ending the audience by accusing Odin of tyranny and despotism.

As Maistre's prospects for reconciliation with Odin looked bleak, so too did those of his radical black and white backers. In late 1865 and early 1866, as a result of President Andrew Johnson's lenient policy of Reconstruction, former Confederates swept back into

8. Maistre to Odin, February 13, 1866, VI-2-k, ANOC.

power in Louisiana and in New Orleans. As in other southern states, they passed a series of Black Codes intended to keep freedmen in a subordinate position, and on July 30, white militants attacked a convention at Mechanic's Institute that was meeting to demand the disfranchisement of ex-Confederates and the extension of the suffrage to blacks. Although Afro-Creole leaders had thought the meeting unwise, many attended as observers. The carnage from the riot included forty-four dead and another hundred wounded.[9]

Afro-Creole radicals and their white allies appealed to Congress for protection while Maistre turned back to Rome. Hoping to garner support from the hitherto unsympathetic Barnabó, the priest presented himself as "sweet reasonableness" and as indispensable to the Church's future among black people in the city, especially the freedmen. Attempting to appeal to the cardinal's missionary zeal, he pointed to blacks as a potentially rich harvest for Catholicism—he had baptized 138 in 1866—and underscored the need for more churches and schools among them. "All of this," he wrote, "is temporarily suspended because of the dispute with the archbishop." Maistre promised that "If your Eminence wished to encourage us, I do not doubt that with the influence and confidence that I believe I have among blacks, we would successfully build the necessary buildings." He also blamed the continuing impasse on the archbishop's unwillingness to make the least concession. Maistre expressed his hope for better from the Propaganda and Barnabó's benign and favorable intervention.

The account of the meeting that Odin sent to Barnabó agreed in details with Maistre's, except that he omitted mention of his insistence that the priest leave the archdiocese. Odin reiterated to Barnabó his demand for unconditional submission, after which time he would determine Maistre's fate, and he excoriated Maistre for what he considered the latter's falsehoods to the Perfect. Barnabó who had throughout the dispute supported Odin in what he viewed as a disciplinary matter, could not tolerate priestly defiance of episcopal authority and acceded to the archbishop, leaving matters completely in his hands. That Odin regularly sent money from his strapped archdiocese to the hard-pressed Holy See ($5,500 on April 16, 1866, for example) probably did not hurt his cause with Barnabó.[10]

9. Bell, *Revolution, Romanticism, and the Afro-Creole Protest,* 261–63.
10. Maistre to Barnabó, February 20, 1866, Vol. 21, fol. 151rv, Odin to Barnabó, April 12, 1866, Vol. 21, fol. 216rv, *Scritture Riferite nei Congressi: American Centrale,* PA. Barnabó to Odin, April 16, 1866, VI-2-i, ANOC.

From Odin's point of view, impertinence doubtless seemed the order of the day. In addition to Maistre and his renegade congregation, Odin had to deal with other black Catholics exploring the boundaries of protest. In January 1866, he received another petition from another group, this one led by Achille and P. F. Glaudin—members of the Glaudin cigar-making clan who were in their late twenties and were active figures in Unionist and Republican politics—and Joseph Blanchard. Their petition displayed more race consciousness than had that of the Congregation Unioniste almost three years earlier. Probably influenced by the proliferation of Protestant churches in the city headed by black ministers, the petitioners reflected the desire of some black Catholics to exercise greater leadership in their church. Emphasizing their *bona fides* by identifying themselves as Catholics from birth who had been "deprived of a church" specifically for their race, the petitioners asked the archbishop to erect a black parish under his protection. They then requested that he lend his assistance in obtaining a priest "of the African race," a request that contained another implied rebuke, since only three priests of African heritage lived in the United States. Perhaps alluding to the earlier petition of the Congregation Unioniste, they also asked pointedly but politely for a response as soon as possible. Odin may well have attributed at least some of the growing assertiveness of black Catholics to Maistre's rebellious bad example. The archbishop's reply, if any, to the petitioners did not survive, nor did they get a parish or black priest.[11]

Nevertheless, some of the issues raised by black Catholics and Maistre resonated with Barnabó and American prelates who worried about the condition of blacks in the South. As early as October 1863, in a letter to Odin, Bishop Spalding of Louisville had referred to an

11. P. F. Glaudin *et al.* to Monsignor Odin, January 23, 1866, VI-2-k, ANOC; Rankin, "The Politics of Caste," in Macdonald, Kemp, and Haas, *Louisiana's Black Heritage*, 109, 142. The black priests were the three Healy brothers: James Augustine, Alexander Sherwood, and Patrick. They were the sons of Michael Morris Healy, an Irishman who had settled in Georgia, and María Eliza, his mulatto slave whom he regarded as his wife. All three brothers attended seminary and were ordained in Europe—James in 1854, Alexander in 1858, and Patrick in 1864. James, who would become Bishop of Portland, Maine, in 1875, and Alexander were priests of the Diocese of Boston; Patrick entered the Jesuits and eventually served as rector of Georgetown University. While making no secret of their African heritage, the light-skinned Healy brothers appeared to identify more with their Irish than their African ancestry. See Davis, *The History of Black Catholics*, 146–52.

appeal from William Henry Elder of Natchez that abolitionist archbishop John Baptist Purcell of Cincinnati had forwarded to him. Elder asked Spalding for priests and sisters to provide spiritual aid to poor black refugees who had come into Union lines and were dying in frightful numbers from disease and malnutrition in Vicksburg and Natchez. Spalding doubted that he could find suitable clergy or sisters able and willing. Echoing sentiments first expressed by Archbishop Peter Kenrick of St. Louis, Spalding bitterly observed to Odin that those like Purcell who had sympathized with and encouraged the abolition that had led to "this frightful result" should consider it their duty to volunteer to aid in repairing the mischief. Little came of Elder's appeal. Almost two years later, on June 14, 1865, Spalding, now archbishop of Baltimore, broached the idea of a plenary council, or general meeting of the archbishops and bishops of the United States, to Cardinal Barnabó and suggested as one of the topics the problem of the freedmen, whose fate increasingly weighed on Spalding's mind. He wrote, "Four millions of these unfortunates are thrown on our charity and they silently but eloquently appeal to us for help. It is a golden opportunity to reap a harvest of souls. . . . It is imperative on us to see immediately what is the most practical means." When the Propaganda approved a council in late 1865, Barnabó directed the council fathers to include the spiritual care of black Americans on the agenda.[12]

Spalding wrote to Odin telling him that the council would especially want "the benefit of Odin's experience in devising the most effectual means for saving the emancipated Negroes" and assigned to him the task of preparing the council decrees under Title X: "On the Care of Souls." Odin, however, who in his appeals for funds during the war to the Lyon Society for the Propagation of the Faith in France had drawn a pitiful picture of the dire condition of indigent black refugees suffering from hunger and disease, and who earlier in the year had received the petition from black Catholics calling for a priest of their own race, did not mention blacks in his first draft. This led Spalding to ask him specifically to address himself to Spalding's

12. Pastoral Letter of the Most Rev. Archbishop of New Orleans, January 24, 1864, *Pastorals*, Vol. 1 (1844–1887), AANO; Martin John Spalding to Odin, October 22, 1863, VI-2-h, ANOC; entry for August 20, 1863, in Gerow, ed., *Civil War Diary (1862–1865) of Bishop William Henry Elder*, copy in ADJ.

idea of appointing a priest administrator, or prefect apostolic, for missionary work among blacks, who would find staff, raise money, organize projects, and eventually, perhaps, exercise episcopal powers. When the council debated the Negro question on October 22 at a stormy extraordinary session that convened after the council had formally adjourned, Odin and Archbishop Peter Kenrick, sensitive to implications that they had neglected the care of blacks and concerned about potential jurisdictional disputes, led the opposition to a priest administrator and insisted several times that they had done everything possible for blacks in their jurisdictions. Except for an increase in the number of missionaries, they wanted no further innovations. Convinced that the tradition of racially mixed parishes in southern Louisiana best met the needs of both Afro-Creoles and freedpeople and aware that many of his French-speaking pastors depended financially on black parishioners, Odin also opposed the notion of separate churches for blacks, though he urged providing more Catholic schools for blacks. (Sensitive to the socially volatile issue of mixing white and black schoolchildren, however, the archdiocese maintained segregated Catholic schools.) After more debate, the prelates rejected the idea of a prefect apostolic and accepted a motion, seconded by Odin, to leave specific measures on behalf of blacks to the determination of each bishop in his own diocese, thereby scuttling a more coordinated effort.[13]

The council settled on a policy of exhortation. The published decrees urged greater efforts on behalf of black evangelization but reflected the ambivalence of the bishops toward the abolition of slavery, expressing regret that a more gradual process had not been adopted that would have prepared blacks to make better use of their

13. Thomas Spalding, *Martin John Spalding: American Churchman* (Washington, D.C., 1973), 194–95, 199–200, 202, 204–209, 221–222; Jean-Marie Odin to Lyon Society for the Propagation of the Faith, July 20, 1863, F02855, in Lyon Society Collection, AANO; Glaudin *et al.* to Odin, New Orleans, January 23, 1866; Martin J. Spalding to Odin, March 4, 1866, VI-2-k, ANOC; Peter E. Hogan, S.S.J., "Filling in the Background," *Josephite News Letter* (November–December, 1966; January 1967) in JA; Edward J. Misch, "The Catholic Church and the Negro, 1865–1884," *Integrateducation*, XII (November–December, 1974), 37; Diary of Canon Peter Benoit, 1875, typescript copy in Mill Hill Fathers Collection, JFA; John B. Alberts, "Origins of Black Catholic Parishes in the Archdiocese of New Orleans, 1718–1920" (Ph.D. dissertation, Louisiana State University, 1998), 151–53.

freedom. The council divided over the question of separate churches for blacks versus their continued worship in parish churches that often segregated them in seating and in the reception of the sacraments, thereby alienating many. Again, this matter was left to the discretion of the bishop of each diocese. The decrees emphasized the grave obligation of priests and bishops to make the sacraments available to Negroes and pleaded for priests "through the bowels of the mercy of . . . God," to devote themselves to the evangelization of blacks.[14]

Spurred by the debate at the council and by one of its preliminary recommendations for more orphanages and schools, and no doubt stung by Maistre's charges to Barnabó, Odin sought to enlist white religious communities of sisters in the work, but for months he did not receive a single affirmative reply. (In 1866, four hundred sisters belonging to nine orders ran seven orphanages, three hospitals, and twenty schools in the New Orleans archdiocese.) "The initial difficulties would be greatest," Odin warned, and would require tact, prudence, and intrepidity in the face of the opposition that would almost certainly arise. Several demurred for fear of damaging their already existing institutions. Meanwhile, in November 1866, Odin invited the Oblate Sisters of Providence from Baltimore, a black congregation founded in 1829, to send three sisters to open a day school and take charge of an orphanage particularly intended to care for the children of black Civil War soldiers and sponsored by L'Association Louisianaise pour l'Assistance des Orphelins de Couleur, or the Institution des Orphelins Indigents. L'Association members included Hortense Trévigne (the wife of *L'Union* and *Tribune* editor Paul Trévigne) and Dr. Louis Charles Roudanez, both outspoken critics of the archbishop. In December 1866, Odin sent $200 to the sisters to cover the cost of their passage to New Orleans and purchased a house for them for $2800. L'Association pledged that it would furnish the funds necessary to provide for the orphanage. In a letter dated December 15, 1866, Hortense Trévigne fulsomely praised Odin on behalf of the institution for his generous charity, "so universally recognized," and for his offer to send the three Oblate Sisters of Providence there.[15]

14. Davis, *The History of Black Catholics,* 118–21; Hennesey, *American Catholics,* 161–62.
15. Grace Sherwood, *The Oblates' Hundred and One Years* (New York, 1931), 143, 159; statistics on the number of sisters in the Archdiocese of Louisiana are

* * *

Trévigne's letter reflected the often conflicted relationship between some elite Afro-Creoles and the institutional Church. The board of the Institution des Orphelins of which Trévigne was a member, had allowed its director, Madame Louise de Mortie, to invite Protestant preachers to conduct services on Sunday afternoons with the avowed purpose of promulgating "Christian spirit, not dogma." Indeed, some black Creole radicals rejected institutional Catholicism altogether, regarding it as dogmatic, narrow, reactionary, and sectarian. Instead, they embraced Freemasonry and spiritualism for their ideals of universal brotherhood—ideals which, according to radicals, the Catholic Church proclaimed but did not practice. In 1867, French-speaking Scottish-rite Masonic lodges in the city, on orders from the Grand Master in Lyon, officially opened their ranks to blacks, though apparently some free persons of color had belonged to lodges during the antebellum years. Yet Afro-Creole radicals continued to admire and support the philanthropic activities associated with the Church and its religious orders, and Catholic saints noted for their charity, such as St. Vincent DePaul, occupied a place of honor among spiritualists. Some Afro-Creole Freemasons and spiritualists considered themselves genuine Catholics and, while bitterly assailing the policies of the Church and ignoring its prohibitions against membership in secret societies, raised their children as Catholics and died with the sacraments.[16]

---

found in Odin to "Messieurs," January 26, 1866, F02861, in Lyon Society Collection, AANO; *Annals,* December 10, 1866, copy of a letter from Peter L. Miller, S.J., spiritual director of the Oblate Sisters, to Monsignor [Archbishop Jean Marie Odin], December 14, 1866, Archives of the Oblate Sisters of Providence, Baltimore, Md.; Notes on Oblate Sisters of Providence and transcriptions from Diary of the Oblate Sisters of Providence, II and III, 1843–1874, Sisters of the Holy Family Archives (hereafter, SHFA), New Orleans; Sale of Property, Michael Comford to Jean-Marie Odin, January 3, 1867, Act before Octave de Armas (copy), Diocesan Account Book, 1865–1869, AANO; Houzeau, *My Passage at the New Orleans Tribune,* 19–25; Hortense Trevigne to Odin, December 15, 1866, VI-2-1, ANOC; McTigue, "Forms of Racial Interaction," n. 59, p. 24.

16. Bell, *Revolution, Romanticism, and the Afro-Creole Protest,* 182, 245–46, 264–65. See Archbishop Janssens' account of Thomy Lafon's death in the Diary of Archbishop Francis Janssens, pp. 105, 111, 122, typescript copy in Notes from the New Orleans Archdiocesan Archives, JA. The entry of December 22, 1893 reads: "Died, Mr. Thomy Lafon, a light mulatto, the founder of the Lafon Asylum for col. boys & the addition to the Asylum for co. old men. He rec'd devoutly the last sacr. & I pronounced the absolution at his funeral in St. Augustine's Church."

In fact, the majority of ordinary Creoles of color showed themselves more radical in politics than religion and therefore remained Catholic—a reality that *L'Union* both acknowledged and bemoaned. Acquiescence to the church, however, did not necessarily characterize them, as their participation in Cailloux's funeral, their petitions to Odin for separate black churches in 1863 and 1866, and even their attendance at Maistre's Holy Name of Jesus parish demonstrated. Maistre and his congregation did not aspire to doctrinal and/or institutional separation from the Church, although they clearly had a racial agenda different from the archbishop's. They had created the schismatic church in reaction to Odin's disciplinary moves against Maistre for his abolitionism and then played for time until the archbishop or his successor would relent and remove the suspension and interdict. Ties of family, history, tradition, culture, and belief—not to mention sometimes close personal connections with priests and nuns, some of whom may have tacitly sympathized with their political and social aspirations—kept black Creoles Catholic, a factor again grudgingly recognized by *L'Union*. The Afro-Creoles' inherited Latin Catholicism, with its somewhat relaxed approach to doctrine and rules and its aroma of anticlericalism, allowed them broad latitude in belief and practice. With regard to race, they knew of another French Catholic Universalist tradition, personified by Bishop Dupanloup and Fr. Maistre, that had condemned slavery and supported egalitarian ideals. They understood far better than most of their white counterparts that "catholic" meant universal and that the logic of Church teachings on the common fatherhood of God implied equality, not subordination. Their persistent adherence to an inclusive interracial ideal probably kept many Afro-Creoles in the Church and in their own traditional parishes rather than Holy Name. They were not about to abandon and leave to whites the interracial parishes that they had helped build, despite their admiration of Maistre. Indeed, they recognized that Maistre's pursuit of a genuine interracialism had led to his exile at Holy Name.[17]

The liturgical-sacramental nature of the Catholic Church, which gave rise to what modern scholars call a "sacramental imagination,"

17. *L'Union*, May 31, 1864. John B. Alberts develops the concept of a Catholic universal ideal and applies it to Maistre's case in "Origins of Black Catholic Parishes in the Archdiocese of New Orleans," 19–20.

may also have operated to keep Afro-Creoles in the Church. The mediating role between God and human beings played by rituals, saints, sacramentals, art, and the seven sacraments perhaps rendered the racial views of priests and bishops less critical to Afro-Creole Catholics than would otherwise have been the case had they belonged to an evangelical Protestant tradition with its emphasis on the role of the minister as preacher. According to Catholic theology, which also translated into popular belief, the efficacy of a sacrament did not depend on the moral state of the priest *(ex opere operato)*. Afro-Creole Catholics, therefore, could take part in the liturgical life of the church, petition the saints and Mary in their popular devotions, light candles, and receive the sacraments that marked life's special passages for them and their children despite the temperament or views of a particular priest. For Creole Catholics, what the priest did in administering the sacraments counted as much or more than what he said in a sermon or how he acted outside of his sacramental role. Of course, some Afro-Creoles simply respected the office of the priest too much to question what he said or did, and others remained Catholic in name only. Still, despite defections to Protestant sects, especially among some nominally Catholic freedmen, and notwithstanding the prevalence of Freemasonry and spiritualism among Creoles of color, the "mystic chords of memory," tradition, and piety, as well as the sacramental imagination may have acted as psychological shields, enabling the majority of Afro-Creoles to maintain their Catholic identities. Whatever Hortense Trévigne's personal views on the Church, then, she was able to look forward to the arrival of the Oblates and appreciate Odin's efforts to secure their services on behalf of blacks and to generally increase the number of schools available for black children.[18]

On arriving in New Orleans, the Oblates found that their house still needed repairs, so they stayed briefly with the Sisters of the Holy Family. The three sisters from Baltimore, all of whom shared a San Dominguan heritage, started a boarding school in 1867 and took

18. For an explanation of the "sacramental imagination" among modern Catholics, see Andrew M. Greeley, *The Catholic Myth: The Behavior and Beliefs of American Catholics* (New York, 1990); Alberts, "Origins of Black Catholic Parishes in the Archdiocese of New Orleans," 155, 161.

charge of the orphanage when it opened in 1869, but they found
that they could not win the confidence of black New Orleanians,
who regarded them as alien. Conflicts with the Sisters of the Holy
Family and with Methodist leader Rev. J. T. Newman, who withdrew
Protestant children, and loss of financial support from the Freedmen's Bureau, further plagued the Oblates, who found themselves
hard pressed to procure the necessities of life for themselves and their
charges. In 1873, in the midst of hard times made still worse by the
Panic of 1873, they closed both the school and the orphanage and
left New Orleans.[19]

Meanwhile, the Religious of the Sacred Heart under Mother
Shannon proved receptive to Odin's urgent pleas to open a school
for black children, especially after his reassurance that he would not
insist on continuation of the project if it proved detrimental to the
convent. Mother Shannon authorized a small school in St. Michael's
parish under the direction of a young Catholic mulatto woman and
gradually introduced sisters into the faculty. The Sisters of Mt. Car-
mel continued to operate the St. Claude Street School for blacks near
St. Augustine's Church that they had taken over from the Ursulines
in 1838 and Medard H. Nelson, a highly educated man who spoke
seven languages, opened a private Catholic academy within the
boundaries of St. Louis Cathedral parish. In a written request for
money, dated June 16, 1867, to the Lyon Society for the Propagation of the Faith, Odin reported the opening of the Oblates' school,
but insisted that many more were needed in the face of a Protestant
onslaught. He decried the inroads made by Protestants, especially
the establishment of churches and schools for the freedmen, and described their motivation as largely political. Recalling nostalgically
how masters and mistresses had taken care of the spiritual instruction
of slaves, Odin emphasized his unhappiness at recent developments.[20]

19. Notes on Oblate Sisters of Providence, Journal of Mother Bernard Diggs,
March, 1894, copies from Diary of the Oblate Sisters of Providence, II and III,
1843–1874, SHFA; Joseph Logsdon, "A History of Gilbert Academy," (unpub-
lished manuscript, in Professor Logsdon's possession).

20. Sr. M. Florita Lee, C.C.V.I., "The Efforts of the Archbishops of New Orleans to Put into Effect the Recommendations of the Second and Third Plenary
Councils of Baltimore with Regard to Catholic Education (1860–1917)," (Ph.D.
dissertation, Catholic University of America, 1946), 50–52; Alberts, "Origins of

* * *

On the political scene, these troubling developments doubtless included the Reconstruction Acts of 1867, which returned Federal troops to the South, abolished the state governments dominated by former rebels, mandated black suffrage and new state constitutions, required ratification of the Fourteenth Amendment, and brought Radical Republicans into power in most southern states, including Louisiana. In the spring of 1867, the *Tribune* spearheaded a drive for not only the ballot, but also equal access to juries, public schools, and public conveyances. The next year, Maistre and his radical allies took heart from the Louisiana state constitution of 1868, which, among other things, guaranteed universal manhood suffrage, prohibited segregated public schools, and outlawed discrimination in public accommodations. An ecstatic Henry Rey reported a spirit message from André Cailloux: "I have fallen but my principle, doesn't it live? Don't you see the realization of my dreams today? Aren't I the conqueror today?" Emboldened Afro-Creoles in the Catholic church in St. Landry Parish demanded their right to rent seats anywhere in the church, which meant encroaching on the steadfast privileges of whites.[21]

Yet despite progress on the political front, churches, like other social institutions in the city resisted racial change. Predominantly white Protestant denominations continued to relegate their black members to galleries, and Catholics also experienced turmoil. In December 1867, the *Tribune* bitterly denounced the treatment of blacks who had gathered at St. Louis Cathedral for a reception for Archbishop Odin, an event the *Tribune* had urged its readers to avoid because it feared results more political than religious. The *Tribune* reported that, upon the complaint of a white woman who declared

Black Catholic Parishes in the Archdiocese of New Orleans," 157; Odin to the Lyon Society for the Propagation of the Faith, June 16, 1867, F02864, copy in Lyon Society Collection, AANO; Odin to Martin John Spalding, March 6, 1868, Martin J. Spalding Papers, Archives of the Archdiocese of Baltimore (hereafter, AAB).

21. Bell, *Revolution, Romanticism, and the Afro-Creole Protest,* 264, 272; Spiritualist Registers, 85–31, February 6, 1869, Grandjean Collection, UNO; I. L. Estorge and other wardens of the Catholic Church of St. Landry Parish to General Philip S. Sheridan, "Soon after Easter Sunday," 1867, ss 2084, in ser. 4498, 5th Military District, Division of the Southwest, Department of the Gulf, RG 393, Pt. 1, NA.

that the ceremony was intended only for whites, a policeman drove out some black children. White women also demanded that black women who owned pews should surrender them for the use of their servants. Avowing that "it is not our desire to find fault with the Roman Catholic religion," the paper characterized the cathedral as "only a place where incense is burned in honor of the god of prejudice," and charged that the foreign-born "priests . . . more than any other class of men imbibed the [racial] prejudices of the country."[22]

In the eyes of the *Tribune,* Maistre represented the exception to the rule. His renegade parish, based as it was on his standing among blacks, gave him something of a power base and remained his chief bargaining chip with ecclesiastical authorities. He recorded a high of 98 baptisms at Holy Name in 1867, and in December presided at a commemorative celebration at the church on the occasion of the anniversary of John Brown's death. His parish also counted many former Native Guards and other black Union veterans, who constituted almost a third of the names in the marriage registers. Approximately one third of the baptisms Maistre performed also involved the children of Union veterans. The majority of black Creoles, however, whatever their political sympathies, remained in their own territorial parishes while chagrined Afro-Creole radicals lamented the persistent influence of the conservative Catholic clergy over pious people of color.[23]

Those radicals also bemoaned their temporary defeat in a contest for control of the Republican Party against the faction of white Republicans led by the more conservative and increasingly corrupt Henry C. Warmouth, the state's governor. The wily Warmouth had allied himself with the rising leaders of the Anglophonic and Protestant freedmen such as Oscar Dunn and P. B. S. Pinchback and had successfully secured his party's nomination for governor in 1868 by one vote over the Afro-Creole candidate, Francis Dumas. The un-

22. Blassingame, *Black New Orleans,* 116–21, 182–197, 199; *Tribune,* December 3, 1867.

23. Bell, *Revolution, Romanticism, and the Afro-Creole Protest,* 264–65; Holy Name Register, AANO; *Tribune,* December 1, 1867; *L'Union,* May 31, 1864. The author compared the names of the men in the Holy Name register of baptisms and marriages to those in the muster rolls of the 73rd, 74th, and 75th USCInf, the 6th and 7th La. Regiments (col.), and in the Compiled Military Service Records at the National Archives.

TABLE 8

Baptisms at Holy Name of Jesus Parish, 1864–1871

1864	1865	1866	1867	1868	1869	1870	1871
97	72	97	98	72	73	38	3

SOURCE: Baptismal and Marriage Registers, Holy Name of Jesus Schismatic Parish, Archives of the Archdiocese of New Orleans

TABLE 9

Marriages at Holy Name of Jesus Parish, 1864–1871

1864	1865	1866	1867	1868	1869	1870	1871
30	48	26	25	24	16	13	0

SOURCE: Baptismal and Marriage Registers, Holy Name of Jesus Schismatic Parish, Archives of the Archdiocese of New Orleans

wise decision of the Afro-Creole radical leadership to support an alternative ticket further weakened them within the party. Warmouth attempted to ensure his subsequent control by nurturing political rivalries between Afro-Creole and Anglophonic black leaders—rivalries exacerbated by ethnic differences: linguistic, cultural, and religious. This bitter intraparty contest strained the wartime and immediate postwar bi-ethnic coalition between Afro-Creoles and freedmen, opened a breach between their leaders, and weakened the Republican party internally.[24]

Maistre, of course, followed political developments closely. But he also faced the daunting challenge of operating and maintaining a parish independent from the archdiocese, whose congregation consisted primarily of working class Afro-Creoles struggling in the midst of a generally depressed economy. A dip in the number of baptisms and marriages in 1868 and 1869 suggests a modest decline in parish membership. Satisfied that Holy Name had played its role in stimulating and supporting social and political change, perhaps a number of Holy Name's members simply returned to their traditional par-

24. Holy Name Register, AANO; Logsdon and Bell, "The Americanization of Black New Orleans," 245–51; Bell, *Revolution, Romanticism, and the Afro-Creole Protest,* 274–75.

ishes. Their departure would probably have translated into a decline in parish revenue. Needing cash, and anticipating the eventual resolution of the schism after the aging and ill Odin departed New Orleans for France on his way to the First Vatican Council in May 1869, Maistre executed a mortgage on September 22, 1869, for $5,000 on two of the three lots that he owned, including the church property. He also agreed to pay 8 percent interest per year on the unpaid balance of the note.[25]

In his efforts to maintain his parish, Maistre continued to enjoy the faithful support of his long-time collaborator, Felicie Caillau, who continued to serve as his housekeeper, a witness at weddings, a godmother at baptisms, and perhaps as a teacher of children in the parish and contributor of funds. In April 1866, she possessed enough money of her own to pay $1,500 cash for two lots located on Johnson Street about five blocks from Holy Name. In December 1867, she turned a nice profit by selling the two lots for $3,300. Six months later, on June 18, 1868, she purchased property for $1,500 at the corner of Roman and St. Phillip Streets, only a block from Holy Name. Beginning a pattern of similar transactions that would emerge over the following two years, Felicie followed Maistre's lead by partially mortgaging her property for a far more modest sum of four hundred dollars.[26]

The new year found Maistre teaching at recently established Straight University, where he served as one of the charter faculty members of the nondenominational institution, which opened in

25. Holy Name Register, AANO; Schweninger, "Prosperous Blacks in the South," 47–49; Rankin, "The Impact of the Civil War on the Free Colored Community of New Orleans," 396–99; Baudier, *The Catholic Church in Louisiana*, 434; Mortgage, P. Maistre fav'r Leon Destez, September 22, 1869, Act 197, in Ernest Eude, Vol. 9, NONA.

26. See, for example, entries on August 11, 1858, October 4, 1862, April 7, 1863, October 12, 1865, July 23, 1866, March 17, 1867, March 3, 1868, March 19, 1870, all in Registre des Marriages et Baptêmes, Holy Name of Jesus, AANO; Ninth United States Census, 1870, New Orleans, 251; SLC, Bk. 25, May 29, 1837, p. 196, Act 597, June 25, 1838, p. 353, Act 1002, AANO; Bell, *Revolution, Romanticism, and the Afro-Creole Protest*, 216–17; Desdunes, *Our People and Our History*, 104; COB 91-193, COB 93-492, Orleans Parish Conveyance Office; Vente de Propriete par Mme. Adele Asmar et Amadee Gardere à Mlle. Felicie Caillau, June 18, 1868, in A. Ducatel, Vol. 92, NONA; Mortgage, F. Caillau fav'r C. B. LeCarpenter, October 20, 1869, in Octave DeArmas, Vol. 89, NONA.

New Orleans in February 1870 under the auspices of the Congrega-
tionalist-affiliated American Missionary Association. The New Orleans *Republican* described the school's mission as that of aiding
"the colored element in the South in their efforts to obtain complete
emancipation by placing within easy reach the power of knowledge."
One of five faculty members in the collegiate department, Maistre
held the post of professor of modern languages and literature. The
presence of a Catholic priest, even a suspended one, at an AMA-
sponsored institution was unique. The AMA, which had founded
forty schools in the south by 1870, regarded the Catholic Church
with deep suspicion if not outright hostility, sentiments reciprocated
by Catholic authorities and publications. A renegade priest on its
faculty represented something of a coup for the school, making it a
haven for refugees from Catholic authoritarianism and racial neglect.
For his part, Maistre had throughout his priestly life shown himself
far less sectarian than most Catholic clergy. During the war he had
cooperated and collaborated with a range of Protestant abolitionists,
ministers, and military officials, not to mention the freethinking Creoles of color grouped around *L'Union* and the *Tribune*. In addition,
as the Reverend J. W. Healy, the first president of Straight, acknowledged, French-speaking Catholic Creoles composed three-quarters
of the student population and were "not easily approached by the
English tongue." Healy probably saw Maistre as a bridge to those
students, perhaps making the institution seem a less alien place to
Afro-Creole Catholics. Maistre's acceptance of the position certainly
meshed with his previous twelve years of ministry to blacks. The
Catholic Church sponsored no high school or college for blacks in
New Orleans, and he probably viewed his service at Straight as another of his contributions to racial uplift and to the maintenance of
Catholicism among blacks. Since the AMA paid so poorly and so
irregularly, however, he could not count on much money from the
job.[27]

27. Straight University Charter, Board of Trustees, Faculty, 1870, no. 45869
in American Missionary Association Archives (hereafter, AMA), Amistad Research
Center, Tulane University, New Orleans; Joe M. Richardson, *Christian Reconstruc-
tion: The American Missionary Association and Southern Blacks, 1861–1890* (Athens,
Ga., 1986); Joe M. Richardson, "The American Missionary Association and Black
Education in Louisiana, 1862–1878," in Macdonald, Kemp, and Haas, *Louisiana's
Black Heritage,* 148, 155–56; Rev. John L. Spalding, quoted in "Catholic Collec-

The university chose to showcase Maistre as one of three speakers at the first commencement exercises of the collegiate department on June 30, 1870. He delivered his address in French, emphasizing the interrelationship between freedom and responsibility—key concepts of republican radicalism. Speaking at a time when Reconstruction had apparently reached a victorious climax with the March ratification of the Fifteenth Amendment to the Constitution and the earlier ratification of the Fourteenth Amendment and adoption of the Louisiana state constitution in 1868, Maistre cautioned his audience that the great revolution that had endowed blacks with "all the rights that belong to men and to citizens," brought with it corresponding duties. No human power had wrought the wondrous change, he reminded them: "It was the power of God." He urged the newly enfranchised race to perform its civil duties so as to garner the blessings of God. The *American Missionary,* the journal of the AMA, while noting Maistre as one of the commencement speakers, omitted any account of his remarks, although it published those of the other two.[28]

As it turned out, Maistre's commencement address also served as his valedictory to blacks in New Orleans, for within two weeks of his speech, he finally submitted to the archbishop. Odin's death on May 25, 1870, and the succession of Maistre's old friend and Odin's coadjutor, Napoleon J. Perché, made possible the resolution of the schism that had become as much a test of wills as a clash of principles. Unlike Odin, Perché had no vested personal interest in the controversy and wanted to resolve it in a manner consistent with the maintenance of episcopal supremacy. For Maistre, the time also seemed ripe to leave the field of politics and polemic, because it appeared—mistakenly as it turned out—that the forces of progress had triumphed. Odin had departed the scene, the church had increased its efforts on behalf of blacks (particularly in providing additional parish

tions for Freedmen," *American Missionary,* XIII (1869), 227–28, AMA Papers (see also Romanist Schools," XIII (1869), 250; J. W. Healy to My Dear Brother, June 18, 1870, no. 45839, William L. Johnson to Dear Brother Smith, care of Rev. J. W. Healy, July 13, 1870, no. 45841, Seymour Straight to Rev. George M. Whipple, April 5, 1870, no. 4582, all in AMA Papers.

28. New Orleans *Republican,* June 30, 1870; William Gillette, *Retreat from Reconstruction, 1869–1879* (Baton Rouge, 1980), 23–24; *American Missionary,* XIV, (1870), 170.

schools, a development which gained momentum during the decade), the Republicans were poised to win their most sweeping victory
yet in state elections that fall, and both the United States and Louisiana state constitutions finally recognized African American men as
free, citizens, and voters. Numerous antislavery societies in the North
disbanded in the wake of the Fifteenth Amendment, believing their
work finished. Maistre, like other radicals of the time such as William
Lloyd Garrison and Jean Charles Houzeau and Charles Roudanez of
the *Tribune,* chose to return to his original calling, taking solace from
the role that he had played in promoting emancipation and equal
political and civil rights for African Americans and in highlighting to
Rome the plight of black Catholics in New Orleans.[29]

Growing older, perhaps suffering pangs of conscience about his continued estrangement from the Church, and concerned about his economic security, Maistre negotiated an agreement with Perché whereby
he publicly humbled himself and terminated his schism, but avoided
becoming a clerical exile. On July 12, 1870 (the same year in which
black New Orleanians temporarily restored their bi-ethnic coalition
and forced Governor H. C. Warmouth and Superintendent Thomas
W. Conway to institute desegregation of the city's public schools,
albeit for a relatively short time), Maistre sent Perché an open and
abject letter of regret and repentance—the price for his remaining in
the archdiocese. In it, he disavowed without specification all that had
"been irregular and condemnable" in the exercise of his ministry
while under ecclesiastical censure. He admitted to having caused evil
by his defiance of episcopal authority, and agreed to submit to conditions for his rehabilitation as prescribed by Perché according to
canon law, not simply the archbishop's whim. Maistre thus apologized for his disobedience and for the scandal that had ensued but
not for his advocacy of emancipation, black equality, and greater justice for blacks within the Church. At Maistre's request, the *Morning
Star and Catholic Messenger* reprinted the letter from the pages of *Le
Propagateur Catholique* on July 17. It read in full:

> Monsignor.— You have been good enough to receive with
> charity the earnest prayer which I have addressed to you,

29. Baudier, *St. Rose of Lima,* 24; Gillette, *Retreat from Reconstruction,* 23–24;
Alberts, "Origins of Black Catholic Parishes in the Archdiocese of New Orleans,"
160–161; Ted Tunnell, *Crucible of Reconstruction,* 164.

to assist me in leaving a false and irregular position which I have too long occupied. Wishing to testify to you my acknowledgment, and at the same time to commence to repair the evil of which I have been the occasion, I publicly declare that I submit to the conditions which you have prescribed in order to [*sic*] my rehabilitation. I regret and disavow all that has been irregular and condemnable in the exercise of the ministry while laboring under ecclesiastical censures. I submit to the canons and laws of the Church, and to its authority, of which you are the depository in this diocese. My greatest desire is to efface the bad example which I have given, and to remove the unhappy consequences which they might have made. I hope, with the grace of God, that my good example, and later, when you may judge proper, my labors and efforts, will contribute to bring back those, who, through my lead, strayed from the fold. And as an evidence of the sincerity of my sentiments, I desire that this letter may be made public, and that these retractions may rejoice all those to whom my unhappy estrangement has caused sorrow.

Apparently with Perché's permission, Maistre continued his ministry at Holy Name of Jesus Parish until early 1871, which represented something of a public vindication for his efforts there and perhaps was seen by the archbishop as a way by which Maistre could honor his promise to "bring back those, who, through my lead, strayed from the fold." In March 1871, the parish closed its doors for good and its members presumably returned to their territorial parishes.[30]

Following his public submission, Maistre and Felicie Caillau prepared for the changes that would invariably flow from it. One month after the publication of the letter, Felicie Caillau sold her four-room Creole cottage at auction for $700 in cash plus a promissory note of $700 and moved into Maistre's house. According to the 1870 census, she resided there along with Aimée Pavageau, Maistre's seventy-

30. Bell, *Revolution, Romanticism, and the Afro-Creole Protest*, 277; Logsdon and Bell, "The Americanization of Black New Orleans," in Hirsch and Logsdon, *Creole New Orleans*, 250; *Morning Star and Catholic Messenger*, July 17, 1870; Holy Name Register, AANO.

year-old mulatto cook. Still juggling his finances and having paid $1500 on his mortgage, on February 8, 1871, Maistre took out a new one for the balance of $3,500, evidently hoping to reduce the amount he would pay in interest. He then spent some months in retreat and penance, after which Perché named him pastor of the remote little parish of St. Lawrence in Chacahoula, about sixty miles southwest of New Orleans in Terrebonne civil parish. Maistre's first baptism there took place on October 16, 1871. Felicie Caillau's signature as a witness at some weddings indicates that she accompanied Maistre to St. Lawrence. In March 1872, Maistre again turned his attention to financial matters, negotiating a new mortgage on the same lots for $4,350, thus leaving him with an extra $850. Finally, on June 12 of the same year, he sold the property in New Orleans that had included Holy Name of Jesus Church for $5,000. The purchaser paid Maistre $650 in cash and assumed his outstanding note of $4,350. Maistre remained at St. Lawrence until 1874, when illness forced him to return to New Orleans where, ironically in light of all that had happened between him and Odin, he resided at the archbishop's residence.[31]

During the previous year, on September 16, 1873, Felicie Cailloux, who had turned to Maistre at the time of her husband's funeral, died of a stroke. The years after her husband's death had continued to be difficult for her. In 1867, the government had denied her a widow's pension because of a clerical error in her application related to her inability to read English. In November 1868, her half-brother, Sebastien, evidently unable to pay taxes on his property, exchanged his lot, purchased in 1842 in partnership with his mother Feliciana, for one at Philipps and St. Denis Streets owned by Louis Jefferson Frederic St. Ferol. The latter agreed to pay all taxes on both properties and to build a four-room Creole cottage on the lot that Sebastien would receive. Thus Feliciana, through the investments that she had

31. Sale of Property, F. Caillau to A. Marrero, August 16, 1870, Act 97, in O. Drouet, Vol. 1, NONA; COB 90-428, in Orleans Parish Conveyance Office; Mortgage by C. P. Maistre to St. Leon Destez, February 8, 1871, in Ernest Eude, Vol. 5, NONA; Baudier, *St. Rose of Lima,* 21–23; Baptismal and Marriage records of St. Lawrence Parish, microfilm, AANO; Mortgage by C. P. Maistre fav'r of Juste Fontaine, March 15, 1872, pp. 160–161, in A. Ducatel, Vol. 100, NONA; Sale of Property, C. P. Maistre to V. Fontaine, June 12, 1872, Act 119 in O. L. Kernion, Vol. 1, NONA.

made in property a quarter century earlier, continued to provide for her family even in straitened circumstances. The family's old friend Meurice Glaudin witnessed the agreement, as Felicie, Feliciana, and Bastien made their marks on the notarial act. Three years later, in 1871, Felicie at last secured a pension from the United States government which provided her with $20 per month. Her sons, Jean Louis, a carpenter and journeyman, and Eugene, a cigar maker like his father, also resided in the city (Eugene in the same house as his mother), attempting to earn their livings in an economic environment that Odin, in a letter shortly before his death, described as "terrible." Neither Jean Louis nor Eugene would acquire real estate as their father had done before the war. In September 1875, the state of Louisiana seized their uncle Sebastien's property for nonpayment of taxes and sold it at auction.[32]

The Cailloux family's situation reflected the fraying economic fortunes of Afro-Creoles in New Orleans. Their position had begun to erode in the 1850s when political pressure and legal enactments had impinged on their economic activities. Subsequently, the dislocations caused by the war, the relative economic decline of postwar New Orleans, and especially the depression that began with the Panic of 1873 and which saw the collapse of the Freedmen's Savings and Trust Company in 1874, exacerbated the economic difficulties of Afro-Creoles and blacks in general. The denial of vocational, educational, and political opportunities in the post-Reconstruction era compounded their difficulties, though some working-class black Creoles, such as Eugene Cailloux, managed to overcome the daunting obstacles and raise, support, and educate their families in dignity and decency, laying the groundwork for future gains for their children.[33]

32. Death Index, Orleans Parish, Vol. 59, p. 371, microfilm, Louisiana State Archives, Bureau of Vital Statistics, Baton Rouge, La.; St. Louis Cemetery Burial Register, 1870–73, p. 339, AANO; Pension Records of André Caillaux [sic] RG 15, NA; Exchange of Property, Bastien Escalado [sic] to Louis J. Frederick, November 28, 1868, COB 95-497, Orleans Parish Conveyance Office; Exchange of Property between Bastien Escalado [sic] and Louis J. Frederick, November 23, 1868, Act 101, pp. 242–43, in Alcee Ker, Vol. 3, NONA; New Orleans City Directories, 1867, 1872, 1873, microfiche, Louisiana Collection, NOPL; Odin to Martin John Spalding, April 6, 1869, Spalding Papers, AAB; COB 105-958, Orleans Parish Conveyance Office.

33. Schweninger, "Prosperous Blacks in the South," 47–49; Loren Schweininger, *Black Property Owners in the South, 1790–1915* (Urbana, 1990), 192–96,

As the Cailloux brothers struggled in the early 1870s, Maistre's physical condition also continued to deteriorate. On January 26, 1875, he executed a will which underlined his submission to episcopal authority. He named Perché his executor and bequeathed to him $2,000 in cash. To the archdiocese of New Orleans he left the small amount of foreign currency that he possessed. To Felicie Caillau, in return for the services that she had rendered and continued to render to him, he left his personal effects: silverware, some worn furniture, and linens amounting in value to $125. Whether he had also given her money independent of his will prior to his death remains unknown but certainly possible. The fifty-five year-old Maistre died three days later (January 29, 1875) in his room at the archevêque. Perhaps he drew consolation from the hope that, despite waning national interest in and commitment to Reconstruction, continuing factionalism within the Republican party in Louisiana and increasing defections of whites from its ranks, and growing challenges from white supremacists in both state and church, justice would prevail. After all, in September 1874 federal troops had suppressed an attempted coup by the militia of the White League against the Republican state government in New Orleans. That government remained in power, and despite its corruption and shortcomings, still provided African Americans with the venue for exercising their political and civil rights. The public schools in New Orleans continued to operate on an integrated basis, and Afro-Creoles stood ready to resist further encroachments of racism in the Catholic Church. Maistre's death certificate specified cause of death as "Cerebral fever complicated." In a gesture of racial solidarity reminiscent of Thaddeus Stevens, Maistre was interred in the tomb of the Society of Our Lady of Vic-

---

114–15; Rankin, "The Impact of the Civil War on the Free Colored Community of New Orleans," 396–99; New Orleans City Directory 1899, microfilm, NOPL; Eleventh United States Census, 1900, New Orleans; Obituary of Andrew Cailloux III, Box 17, Marcus Christian Collection; Eric Foner, *Reconstruction: America's Unfinished Revolution*, 531–32. By 1900, Eugene Cailloux, still a cigar maker and now a married man with four children, lived in a rented house on Howard Street. His two younger sons, Eugene and George, moved to Long Island, New York, and became successful businessmen. George in particular acquired wealth and prominence and helped other blacks seeking to go into business. The oldest son, Andrew Cailloux, named after his famous grandfather and popularly known in New Orleans circles as "Cap Cailloux," died in 1960. For many years, he reportedly carried in his wallet a letter written to his grandfather by General Benjamin Butler, thanking him for raising E Company.

tory in square number 3 of St. Louis Cemetery No. 2—the square reserved for blacks and housing the vaults of many black societies and probably the remains of André Cailloux.[34]

To the end, Maistre remained an enigmatic and paradoxical figure whose life raised many questions. Rebellious throughout his priestly career and trailing the scent of scandal, he nevertheless died submissive and dependent on the archbishop. His dealings with political radicals and blacks suggested his embrace of a more liberal French Catholicism than prevailed among most whites in New Orleans. In some respects, Maistre seemed a latter-day Antonio de Sedella, in his ministry to slaves and free people of color, his tolerance of Freemasons, and his anti-authoritarianism. Unlike Sedella, however, who lived a life of poverty, Maistre showed a penchant for acquiring at least modest amounts of money, though in most cases pastors who build churches and show themselves proficient in managing finances are highly regarded. His relationship with Felicie Caillau also raises intriguing questions. Their similar ages, continuous association over twenty-five years (including her accompanying him to St. Lawrence Parish), and the terms of his will suggest the possibility that their relationship might have gone beyond that of priest and loyal housekeeper, a not uncommon occurrence in some traditions of Latin Catholicism. Still, if it did, rumors probably would have circulated and Odin would have included them along with the others that he reported to Barnabó. Whatever the true nature of their relationship, this literate, property-owning, and independent woman clearly played a vital role in Maistre's life and ministry and he in hers.

Finally, although Maistre forthrightly championed the cause of abolition and equal rights at considerable risk to himself and showed

34. Copy of Testament of Rev. Claude P. Maistre or Maitre, January 26, 1875, Act 16, Octave de Armas, Inventory of the Estate of the Rev. C. P. Maitre or Maistre, April 3, 1875, both in Succession of Claude Paschal Maistre, no. 37895, Second District Court for the City of New Orleans, Microfilm, Louisiana Collection, NOPL; Death Certificate of Claude Paschal Maistre, New Orleans Health Department Death Certificates as kept by the Recorder of Births, Marriages and Deaths, vol. 62, 1874–1875, microfilm, Louisiana Collection, NOPL; Liva Baker, *The Second Battle of New Orleans: The Hundred-Year Struggle to Integrate the Schools* (New York, 1996), 23–24; Burial Records of the Clergy, 1866–1896, AANO; St. Louis Cemetery No. 2, Burials, 1873–1875, part II, map of vaults in Square No. 3 of St. Louis Cemetery No. 2, AANO.

genuine concern for the spiritual welfare of African Americans, relatively early in his dispute with the archbishop he indicated his willingness to abandon his irregular parish in return for Odin's guarantee that he could remain in the archdiocese. Once Odin passed from the scene, Maistre almost immediately bowed to Perché, indicating his desire to reconcile with the Church—a Church he never seriously considered abandoning during his years of schism. He viewed his schismatic status as the result of one archbishop's vindictiveness, not of fundamental incompatibility between him and the holy institution. Odin's implacability and Maistre's devotion to the spiritual and political well-being of African Americans compelled him to create an independent power base from which to deal. In the end, though, he returned in obedience to his priestly status vis-à-vis the archbishop of New Orleans.

Despite Maistre's hopes to the contrary, his death and that of Felicie Cailloux coincided with the beginning of the end of Reconstruction in Louisiana. On September 14, 1874, the militia of the White League, a white supremacist organization made up of ex-Confederates and the white business elite dedicated to restoring Democratic Party rule in the state, staged a coup in New Orleans. The League's numerically superior militia defeated five hundred Metropolitan Police and three thousand black militia loyal to the biracial Republican state government in a battle on Canal Street in New Orleans. They temporarily ousted inept governor William Pitt Kellogg and controlled New Orleans for three days. Although President Ulysses S. Grant ordered five thousand federal troops to restore order and to reinstate Kellogg's government, the so-called Battle of Canal Street, or of Liberty Place, as it came to be known after 1877, and continuing violence and intimidation directed against blacks in rural areas highlighted the precarious position of Reconstruction in the state. As the situation deteriorated, Afro-Creoles could still draw inspiration from their fallen hero, André Cailloux. Combining a play on words involving Cailloux's last name with a biblical allusion to St. Peter, spiritualist mediums described the captain as "the rock of the spiritual world." Cailloux's spirit messages urged Afro-Creoles to remain vigilant, to march forward courageously as he had done, to challenge injustice, and to work diligently in the cause of liberty and truth, which would ultimately triumph.[35]

35. Stuart Omer Landry, *The Battle of Liberty Place: The Overthrow of Carpet-*

In the same year that Maistre died, the New Orleans *Louisianian* reported attempts at St. Louis Cathedral to segregate seating. It declared that St. Louis "is so very anti-Catholic in its direction that numbers of the most respected colored communicants hitherto, now fail in attendance because of the foolish caste or color distinctions sought to be made." The *Louisianian* also accused church authorities not only of attempting to draw invidious distinctions between black and white communicants, but also of blatantly allying themselves with the White League. It reported that one priest openly espoused the cause of the League in a sermon at the cathedral. After a visit to the city in 1872, Archbishop Herbert Vaughan, the founder of the English Mill Hill Josephite Fathers, a congregation devoted to missionary work among blacks, noted growing segregation in seating throughout the city's Catholic churches and unhappiness among black Catholics over the refusal of priests to allow their children to make their First Holy Communion with white children. Yet he also recorded Archbishop Perché's request that he establish an industrial school for blacks in the city, a request consistent with Perché's energetic policy of providing segregated grammar schools for them in the racially mixed parishes that continued to predominate in New Orleans for the remainder of the century. And paradoxically, given widespread white Catholic opposition to the very notion, in April of the same year, Perché asked Vaughan to accept a young black man, Medard Nelson, into his English seminary to study for the priesthood. Vaughan agreed, but stipulated that Nelson would have to pay his own passage and his first year's tuition. He did not enroll.[36]

Conflict over the treatment of blacks increasingly surfaced among priests at the cathedral. There, according to Adrien Rouquette, Gil-

---

Bag Rule in New Orleans, September 14, 1874 (New Orleans, 1955); Gillette, *Retreat from Reconstruction,* 119–20; Tunnell, *Crucible of Reconstruction,* 1–2, 202–204; Séance, October 5, 1871, 85-32, March 2, 1872, 85-39, Spiritualist Registers, Grandjean Collection, UNO.

36. New Orleans *Louisianian,* May 10, 20, 29, December 4, 1875; Herbert Vaughan Diary, 1871–1872, pp. 14–20, copy in JA; J. G. Snead-Cox, *The Life of Cardinal Herbert Vaughan,* 2 vols. (London, 1910), II, 267; John Alberts argues that the construction of these schools, even though they operated on a segregated basis, provided an essential service for black Catholics and helped to staunch their exodus from the Church. See Alberts, "The Origins of Black Catholic Parishes," 160–62 and 163–272 *passim;* Stephen J. Ochs, *Desegregating the Altar: The Josephites and the Struggle for Black Priests, 1871–1960* (Baton Rouge, 1990), 53.

bert Raymond, the vicar general of the archdiocese, at the request of Fr. Gustave Rouxel, removed Fr. Pierre LaPorte, another priest of the cathedral, not because of the latter's hot-headed language, as claimed, but because of LaPorte's "devotion to the colored population." In December 1875, Rouquette observed that Raymond "is not able to forget the past." The boycott organized by black parishioners that year, however, proved effective, and the cathedral quietly returned to its traditional nondiscriminatory policy. The tradition of racially mixed Catholic congregations would persist, despite growing pressures, into the second decade of the twentieth century.[37]

Still, Archbishop Perché, to borrow Rouquette's phrase, could not forget the past. The old unreconstructed rebel lent his support to the efforts of Louisiana white conservatives to regain control of the state. In that endeavor, they drew encouragement from the waning commitment of the Federal government to Reconstruction and from the successful use of violence, fraud, and intimidation by white supremacists in other southern states intent on ousting Republican state governments. Following the disputed legislative election in late 1874, Democrats kidnapped Republican legislators in an attempt to take control of the lower chamber. In January 1875, General Philip H. Sheridan, the commander of the Department of the Gulf whom Grant had authorized to investigate the situation, instructed troops to march into the legislature, eject Democrats not recognized by the Republican election return board, and restore control of that body to the Republicans. Sheridan justified his actions in telegrams to the Secretary of War in which he warned that white Louisianians openly defied the law and supported the violence and terror of the White League. Perché, joined by Protestant and Jewish clergy, published a letter in the *Morning Star* condemning the charges as unwarranted, unfounded, erroneous, and lodged by self-serving, corrupt politicians attempting to perpetuate their power. A little more than two years later, following the fraudulent, violence-marred, and disputed election of 1876 and the Compromise of 1877 that saw the South accept the election of Republican Rutherford B. Hayes as President in return for his promise to withdraw the last federal troops from their region, Reconstruction came to an end in Louisiana. In a pasto-

---

37. Adrien Rouquette to Napoleon Perché, December 25, 1875, VI-2-o, ANOC; Alberts, "The Origins of Black Catholic Parishes," 143–312 *passim*.

ral letter dated May 6, 1877, Perché prescribed that a *Te Deum* be sung in all of the churches of the archdiocese in thanksgiving for the "pacification" of the state.[38]

The patriot had fallen, the priest had submitted, Reconstruction had ended, and the dark night of racism that would culminate in Jim Crow, disfranchisement, and widespread lynchings had begun, though blacks continued to vote in Louisiana in considerable numbers until passage of the Constitution of 1898. Still, Cailloux and Maistre had not struggled in vain, for each in his own way had contributed to the final victory over slavery and to the emergence of a compelling, racially egalitarian ideology among blacks and whites, thus transforming the dream of racial equality into a realistic ideal for America's future. Maistre had preached against the hated institution, provided a haven in his parish for contrabands, encouraged black enlistments in the Union army, given solace and support to the families of black soldiers, including that of André Cailloux, and abetted the Afro-Creole drive for suffrage and equal rights. In the process, he had espoused a racially inclusive vision of Catholicism that incurred his ecclesiastical censure but had also spurred church authorities to greater efforts on behalf of black Catholics. Cailloux's valor at Port Hudson had helped to legitimize the use of black combat troops and, as *L'Union* observed, to vindicate his race from the charge that it lacked manliness and martial spirit. This was a particularly important contribution in light of defiant attitudes among Confederate leaders such as Georgia Governor Brown, who had, as mentioned above, admitted bitterly that proof of African American military fitness would "destroy our whole theory that they are unfit to be free." Cailloux had served in the vanguard of the approximately 180,000 black Union troops, who—according to both President Lincoln and

38. Gillette, *Retreat from Reconstruction,* 122–23; General Philip Sheridan to the Honorable W. W. Belknap, Secretary of War, January 4, 1875 (transcription of telegram) Civil War Miscellaneous, Baudier Collection, AANO; New Orleans *Morning Star,* January 5, 1875, May 6, 1877. For a single-volume treatment of Reconstruction, see Foner, *Reconstruction.* On Reconstruction in Louisiana, see Joe Gray Taylor, *Louisiana Reconstructed, 1863–1877* (Baton Rouge, 1974), and Tunnell, *Crucible of Reconstruction.* On the end of Reconstruction throughout the South, see William Gillette, *Retreat from Reconstruction,* and Michael Perman, *The Road to Redemption* (Chapel Hill, 1984), and Foner, 512–612.

modern scholars—had tipped the scale of war in favor of the Union, thereby sealing the death of slavery and providing African Americans with a convincing claim to citizenship. During the war and Reconstruction, the image of Cailloux as an American Spartacus remained a potent rallying symbol among both Creole and English-speaking blacks and their white allies, who regularly invoked his name as part of their campaign for suffrage and equal civil rights.[39]

In the years after Reconstruction, black Creole activists such as C. C. Antoine, Rodolphe Desdunes, Arthur Esteves, Thomy Lafon, Louis Martinet, Aristide Mary, Homer Plessy, and Paul Trévigne, strengthened in part by the Cailloux legend, refused to go quietly into that evil night of Jim Crow. They rejected the call of P. B. S. Pinchback (a key African American leader and rival of the Creoles in the Republican Party) for racial accommodation with the more moderate white southern leaders. Instead, over the ensuing twenty years, they strenuously resisted segregation and disenfranchisement in state and church, counterattacking by filing state and federal court challenges to segregated schools, creating a new national civil rights organization, the American Citizens' Equal Rights Association (ACERA), and founding a newspaper, the *Daily Crusader*. In the Supreme Court case of *Plessy v. Ferguson* (1896) they would, like both the black captain at Port Hudson and the white priest in New Orleans in 1863, assault what had become a seemingly impregnable fortress of racism. Like Cailloux and Maistre, they would fail in their attempts, but not for lack of persistence or courage.[40]

39. *L'Union*, quoted in *Harper's Weekly*, August 29, 1863; Glathaar, "Black Glory," in Boritt, *Why the Confederacy Lost*, 138–40; Desdunes, *Our People and Our History*, 125.

40. Henry C. Dethloff and Robert R. Jones, "Race Relations in Louisiana, 1877–98," *Louisiana History*, IX (1968), 304–309; Logsdon and Bell, "The Americanization of Black New Orleans," in Hirsch and Logsdon, *Creole New Orleans*, 251–61; Baker, *The Second Battle of New Orleans*, 12–48. For the *Daily Crusader* and the campaign waged against Jim Crow in the Catholic Church, see the scrapbook of clippings of the *Daily Crusader* in the Charles B. Rousseve Papers, Xavier University Archives, New Orleans. See also Lester Sullivan, "The Unknown Rodolphe Desdunes: Writings in the New Orleans *Crusader*," *Xavier Review*, X (1990), 17, Alberts, "The Origins of Black Parishes," 192–382, Dolores Egger Labbe, *Jim Crow Comes to Church: The Establishment of Segregated Catholic Parishes in South Louisiana*, 2nd. ed. (Lafayette, La., 1971), and Annemarie Kasteel, *Francis Janssens, 1843–1897: A Dutch-American Prelate* (Lafayette, La., 1992). Adam Fair-

In a séance on June 2, 1877, shortly after Archbishop Perché's proclamation of the *Te Deum* celebrating the end of Reconstruction, a black spiritualist medium turned once again for inspiration to the hero of Port Hudson and reported the following message from Cailloux in words strikingly similar to Maistre's peroration at the end of his 1863 sermon celebrating the Emancipation Proclamation: "Man falls! Principles persist!"[41]

At a later time, in the next century, during the Second Reconstruction, the principles that led Maistre to defy an archbishop and Cailloux to sacrifice his life would be vindicated. In October 1957, at the height of the Little Rock High School desegregation crisis, New Orleans civil rights activist and historian Marcus Christian would again draw on Cailloux's example to inspire resistance to injustice and persistence in the face of apparently implacable opposition. Playing on the French meaning of the Captain's last name, he appropriately titled a piece in the *Louisiana Weekly,* "Andre Cailloux—The Rock."[42]

---

clough, *Race and Democracy: The Civil Rights Struggle in Louisiana, 1915–1972* (Athens, Ga., 1995), and Baker, *The Second Battle of New Orleans,* provide good overviews of events that followed Maistre's death and emphasize the continuity between Afro-Creole radicals and the modern civil rights movement.

41. Séance, June 2, 1877, no. 64, pp. 21d–22a, Spiritualist Registers, Grandjean Collection, UNO.

42. Christian, "Captain Andre Cailloux: The Rock," Parts I and II, typescript copies in Box 17, Marcus Christian Collection, Earl K. Long Library.

Appendix: Muster Rolls of
Two Companies of Louisiana Native Guards

PART A: Muster Roll of Order Company, Louisiana Native Guards (Louisiana Militia, in Confederate Service 1861–62)

Name	Rank	Eventual Service in U.S. Forces
Sentmanat, Charles	Captain	1st Regt. La. Native Guards
Cailloux, André	1st Lieutenant	1st Regt. La. Native Guards
Derbigny, Théophile	2nd Lieutenant	
Lavigne, V. S. L.	Sergeant Major	
Petit, Louis	1st Sergeant	
Ferrand, Baptiste, Sr.	2nd Sergeant	1st Regt. La. Native Guards
Glapion, Joseph	3rd Sergeant	
St. Cyr, Clement	4th Sergeant	3rd Regt. La. Native Guards
Washington, Maurice	Corporal	
Francois, Joseph	Corporal	
Ferrand, Baptiste, fils	Corporal	1st Regt. La. Native Guards
Jolibois, Joseph	Corporal	
St. Amand, Joseph	Corporal	
Lavigne, Henry	Corporal	
Alcide, Joseph	Private	1st Regt. La. Native Guards, Co. E
Alcine, Louis	Private	
Allougas, Gustave	Private	
Armstrong, Joseph	Private	
Ascendio, Joseph	Private	
Athénos, Ernest	Private	1st Regt. La. Native Guards, Co. E
Bébelle, Joseph	Private	1st Regt. La. Native Guards
Benjamin, Antoine	Private	1st Regt. La. Native Guards
Bercy, Edouard	Private	1st Regt. La. Native Guards
Bernard, Joseph	Private	1st Regt. La. Native Guards
Bernard, Jules	Private	1st Regt. La. Native Guards
Blancand, B.	Private	1st Regt. La. Native Guards
Borée, Louis	Private	1st Regt. La. Native Guards
Boustillos, Antoine	Private	1st Regt. La. Native Guards, Co. E
Calliole, Jean	Private	
Cannelle, Pierre, Jr.	Private	
Casimir, Lucien	Private	

Caspian, Joseph	Private	1st Regt. La. Native Guards
Cassenave, R. C.	Private	
Cassino, A.	Private	2nd La. Native Guards
Castille, R.	Private	3rd Regt. La. Native Guards
Cerrere, Etienne	Private	1st Regt. La. Native Guards, Co. E
Clément, Louis	Private	
Delpit, Louis	Private	
Dumas, Charles	Private	6th La. Regiment (Colored)
Durand, Jean	Private	1st Regt. La. Native Guards
Duvernay, Jean	Private	
Eugene, Elie Joseph	Private	6th La. Regt. (Colored)
Farrar, Emile	Private	1st Regt. La. Native Guards
Ferbos, Victor	Private	
Ferrand, Joseph, III	Private	1st Regt. La Native Guards
Ferrand, Joseph, Jr.	Private	1st Regt. La. Native Guards
Ferrand, Louis	Private	1st Regt. La. Native Guards
Fleury, Joseph	Private	2nd Regt. La. Native Guards
Forégane, Oscar	Private	
Forestier, Jean	Private	
Germain, Jean	Private	1st Regt. La. Native Guards, Co. E
Glapion, Télesphore	Private	
Guillaume, Georges	Private	1st Regt. La. Native Guards
Guillaume, Joseph, fils	Private	1st Regt. La. Native Guards
Handy, Etienne	Private	1st Regt. La. Native Guards
Hippolyte, Francois	Private	1st Regt. La. Native Guards, Co. E
Hippolyte, Louis	Private	1st Regt. La. Native Guards, Co. E
Jacques, Arthur	Private	
Jannieau, Baptiste	Private	
Jean Baptiste, Etienne	Private	6th La. Regt. (Colored)
Lavigne, Louis	Private	
Lazare, Louis	Private	1st Regt. La. Native Guards, Co. E
Legra, Jacques	Private	
Legros, Lous	Private	
Lépine, Joseph	Private	1st Regt. La. Native Guards
Lopes, Alphonse	Private	
Louis, Charles	Private	3rd Regt. La. Native Guards
Magloire, Casimir	Private	
Manuel, Louis	Private	2nd Regt. La. Native Guards
Marcelin, John	Private	1st Regt. La. Native Guards
Marie, Murville	Private	
Maurice, Augustin	Private	91st Regt. USCInf
Montiague, Jules	Private	1st Regt. La. Native Guards
Morphy, Jules	Private	91st Regt. USCT
Morray, Millien	Private	
Page, Louis	Private	1st Regt. La. Native Guards
Pepe, Hippolyte	Private	1st Regt. La. Native Guards

Ribaud, Jean	Private		
Theverette, Simon	Private		
Thomassin, Benjamin	Private	6th La. Regt. (Colored)	
Toregane, Michel	Private		
Toussaint, Auguste	Private	1st Regt. La. Native Guards, Co. E	
Trépagnier, Francis	Private		
Ursin, Francois	Private	1st Regt. La. Native Guards, Co. E	
Victor, Arthur Joseph	Private	1st Regt. La. Native Guards	

SOURCES: Data is based on muster rolls of Confederate units in the War Department Collection of Confederate Records in the National Archives and on the Soldiers and Sailors System also maintained by the Archives.

PART B: First Muster Roll of Company E, 1st Louisiana Native Guards (Union)

NAME	RANK	AGE	DESERTED
Cailloux, Andre*	Captain	38	
Poree, Paul	1st Lieutenant	35	
Hyppolite, St. Louis	2nd Lieutenant	36	
Dede, Francois	Sergeant	29	X
Bacchus, Noel	Sergeant	42	
Planciancios, Anselmo*	Sergeant	40	
Urquhart, Victor	Sergeant	30	
Gros, Joseph	Sergeant	21	X
Boree, Louis	Corporal	30	X
Esquiano, Francis	Corporal	23	X
File, Joseph	Corporal	36	
Leveiller, Louis	Corporal	45	X
Durand, Jean	Corporal	28	X
Carriere, Augustin	Corporal	41	X
Laurent, Joseph	Corporal	42	
Glapion, Pierre	2nd Corporal	23	
Glenis, Joseph	Music	28	X
Thelemaque, Joseph	Music	17	X
Fazinde, Atanas	Teamster	26	X
Adolphe, Gustave	Private	25	X
Athenos, Ernest	Private	22	X
Baptiste, John	Private	19	

Barthelemy (?) Henry	Private	22	
Bastille, Antoine	Private	39	
Belzin, Jean Baptiste	Private	19	X
Banjamin, A. T. (?)	Private	24	
Bernard, Tzebo	Private	24	
Bonome, Eugene	Private	23	X
Brune, Pierre	Private	39	X
Butler, Robert	Private	28	
Carrere, Edouard**	Private	43	
Carrere, Etienne**	Private	20	
Carrere, Joseph	Private	24	X
Celestin, Joseph	Private	18	
Charles, Joseph	Private	36	X
Charles, Pierre	Private	36	X
Christophe, Eugene	Private	35	
Chucchow, Alexander	Private	28	
Compagnon, J. Pierre	Private	30	
Cordoba, Pedro	Private	24	X
Dede, Basile	Private	30	
Esquiver, Francois	Private	47	X
Fermon, Charles	Private	48	
Foreil, Edouard	Private	24	X
Francois, Edouard	Private	24	
Francois, Ursin	Private	24	
Garcy, Peter	Private	23	X
George, Edouard	Private	26	X
George, Ginkin	Private	39	X
Germain, Anatole	Private	22	X
Germain, John	Private	42	
Gros, Peter	Private	27	X
Henderson, Charles	Private	23	
Henry, Patrick**	Private	53	
Henry, Robert	Private	26	
Hippolyte, Louis	Private	32	X
Jacques, Augustin	Private	26	
Jeffre, Goulon	Private	42	
John Baptist, Gustave	Private	21	X
John Baptiste, Nicholas	Private	24	X
John Louis, A. A.	Private	35	
Jolly, Francois	Private	41	X
Joseph, Alcide	Private	18	X
Joseph, Edouard	Private	22	X
Joseph, Zenon	Private	38	
Kama, Albert	Private	22	X
Kingsbury, Daniel	Private	19	X
Ladner, Sylvester	Private	42	

Laffone, Charles	Private	38	
Laveau, Octave	Private	20	X
Lazare, Louis	Private	28	X
Legis, John	Private	39	
Legis, Louis	Private	42	
Leveiller, Louis*	Private	18	
Louis, Peter	Private	45	X
Madere, Jean Baptiste**	Private	24	
Miller, Joseph*	Private	24	
Moniack, Jules	Private	30	X
Narcisse, Louis	Private	53	X
Nicoles, Azore	Private	45	X
Noel, Alfred	Private	18	X
Norbert, Joseph	Private	35	X
Novay, Aleck	Private	25	
Paole, Gabriel	Private	19	X
Raymond, Antoine	Private	40	
Reboul, Henry	Private	26	
Regis, Arthus J.	Private	28	
Richard, Aurest	Private	40	X
Robertson, William	Private	24	X
Saulee, Laurent	Private	42	
St. Cyr, Thomas	Private	23	
Stanislas, Quoiron	Private	24	
Sylvestre, Pierre	Private	26	X
Theodule, Peter	Private	21	
Theophile, Joseph**	Private	38	
Theophile, Victor	Private	45	X
Toussaint, August**	Private	38	
Ulgere, Athanas	Private	24	
Ulgere, Bazile	Private	20	
Victor, Arthur	Private	19	X
Victor, Cheneum	Private	20	
Victor, John	Private	27	
Victor, Theopile	Private	45	
Victor, Zenon*	Private	39	

*Killed in action
**Died of disease

SOURCES: The names were transcribed from the original muster roll of Company E in the National Archives. A number of them were anglicized and no French accent marks were included. Notations on desertions come from Compiled Service Records in the National Archives. The spelling of names on the service records differs at times from that on the muster roll.

BIBLIOGRAPHY

PRIMARY SOURCES

MANUSCRIPT COLLECTIONS

Allen J. Ellender Archives, Nicholls State University, Thibodaux, Louisiana
    Lafourche Parish Historic Records Preservation Project Collection
Amistad Research Center, Tulane University, New Orleans
    American Missionary Association Archives
Archives of the Archdiocese of Baltimore, Baltimore
    Spalding, Archbishop Martin J. Papers.
Archives of the Archdiocese of Chicago, Chicago
    O'Regan, Bishop Anthony. Papers.
    Van de Velde, Bishop James Oliver. Papers.
Archives of the Archdiocese of New Orleans, New Orleans
    Baudier, Roger. Collection.
    Blanc, Archbishop Antoine. Papers.
    Burial Records of the Clergy, 1866–1896.
    Catholic Institution English Composition Copybook, First Class, begun on the 13th of March, 1861, Wm. Vigers, Teacher.
    Diocesan Account Book, 1865–1869.
    Journal des Séances de la Direction de l'Institution Catholique pour les Orphelins dans l'Indigence, 1850–1914.
    Lyon Society for the Propagation of the Faith Collection.
    Marriages and Funerals: St. Rose of Lima, 1857–1864, and Holy Name of Jesus, 1864–1871.
    Odin, Archbishop Jean-Marie. Papers.
    Pastoral letters of the Archbishops of New Orleans, Vol. 1 (1844–1887).
    Perché, Archbishop Napoleon. Papers.
    Registre des Marriages et Baptêmes depuis 17 Décembre 1857 jusqu'à 22 Avril 1871, Book III, Holy Name of Jesus Parish [St. Rose of Lima Registers].
    Rousselon, Étienne. Papers.
    St. Lawrence (Chacahoula) Baptism and Marriage Records (microfilm).
    St. Rose of Lima Baptisms, Marriages, and Funerals of People of Color, Vol. 1.
    St. Louis Cathedral Book of Baptisms of Free Persons of Color and Slaves.
    St. Louis Cemetery No. 1, Burial Register, 1870–1873.
    St. Louis Cemetery No. 2, Burial Register, 1843–1847.
    St. Theresa of Avila Baptismal Book for Mulattos and Negroes, Bk. 1.
Archives Départmentales, Départment de l'Aubé, France
    Biographical information on Claude Paschal Maistre.

Archives of the Diocese of Jackson, Jackson, Mississippi
  R. O. Gerow, ed., *Civil War Diary (1862–1865) of Bishop William Henry Elder, Bishop of Natchez* (Private printing, n.d.).
Archives of the Oblate Sisters of Providence, Baltimore, Md.
  Annals, 1966.
Archives of the Province of St. Joseph of the Capuchin Order, Detroit
  Kleiber, Rev. Josaphat, OFMCap. Biographical File.
Archives of the Sisters of the Holy Family, New Orleans
  Journal of Mother Bernard Diggs.
  Notes on Oblate Sisters of Providence.
  Transcriptions from Diary of the Oblate Sisters of Providence, II and III, 1843–1874.
Archives of the University of Notre Dame
  Archdiocese of New Orleans Collection.
  Congregation of the Propaganda Fide Archives (microfilm).
  Odin, Jean-Marie. Diary. Vincentian Collection.
Capuchin Provincial Archives, Bavaria, Munich, Germany
  Kleiber, Josaphat P. *Daten zur Person des P. Josaphat Kleiber, Kapüzinerder-Bayerischen Kapüzinerprovinz, 1838–1869.*
Colgate University Library
  Civil War Letters of Galutia York.
Earl K. Long Library, University of New Orleans
  Christian, Marcus B. Collection.
  Grandjean, René. Collection.
  Supreme Court of Louisiana Collection.
  Supreme Court of Louisiana Collection of Legal Archives.
Historic New Orleans Collection, New Orleans
  Spanish Louisiana Slave Records.
Howard Tilton Memorial Library, Tulane University, New Orleans
  Prospectus de L'Institution Catholique des Orphelins Indigents. New Orleans, 1847.
John Hay Library, Brown University, Providence, Rhode Island
  Perry, Henry. "Dirge of Andre Squash Cailloux: Killed before Port Hudson, May 27th, 1863, while in the act of slaughtering Southerons," July 29, 1863.
Josephite Archives, Baltimore
  Benoit, Canon Peter. Diary of a Trip to America, 1875. Typescript copy of original in Mill Hill Archives, London.
  Janssens, Francis. Diary. Typescript copy of original in Archdiocesan Archives of New Orleans.
  Spalding, Martin J. Collection.
  Vaughan, Herbert. Diary, 1871–1872. Copy of original in Mill Hill Archives, London.
  Josephite News Letter, 1966, 1967.
Library of Congress, Washington, D.C.
  Banks, Nathaniel P. Papers.

Quincy, Wendell, Holmes, Upham Family Papers (microfilm).
New Orleans City Directories, 1858–1861, Microform Reading Room.
Louisiana State Archives, Baton Rouge
   Birth and Death Certificates.
Masonic Temple Archives, New Orleans
   Directories.
National Archives, Washington, D.C.
   Record Group 15: Records of the Veterans Administration.
      Commission Branch File.
      Pension Records.
   Record Group 94: Records of the Adjutant General's Office, 1780s–1917.
      Civil War Soldiers and Sailors System online at http://www.itd.nps.gov/cgi-bin/dualz.test.
      Compiled Military Service Records, Showing Service of Military Units in Volunteer Union Organizations, Civil War.
      Endorsements.
      Generals' Papers and Books.
      Generals' Reports of Service.
      Letters Received by the Office of the Adjutant General, 1863–1888.
      Miscellaneous Papers, United States Colored Troops.
      Regimental Books, 73rd. United States Colored Infantry, United States Colored Troops.
      Regimental Muster Rolls and Papers, 73rd. United States Colored Infantry, United States Colored Troops.
      Special Orders.
      Woodward, Elon A., comp. *The Negro in the Military Service of the United States, 1639–1886: A Compilation,* M-858.
   Record Group 109: War Department Collection of Confederate Records.
      Compiled Service Records, Confederate Soldiers who served in units from Louisiana in Records of the Louisiana State Government, 1850–1888.
   Record Group 153: Records of the Office of the Judge Advocate General (Army).
      Court Martial Case File, 1809–1894, Parts 1 and 2.
   Record Group 233: Records of the United States House of Representatives.
   Record Group 393: Records of the U.S. Army Continental Commands, 1821–1920.
      Part 1
         Department of the Gulf
            General Orders.
            Letters Received, 1862–1865.
            Letters Received, 1863, Bureau of Civil Affairs
            Letters Received, 1867, 5th Military District, Division of the Southwest.
               Kennedy, John A., Co. H. 1st Arkansas Regiment. Diary.
            Letters Received, Inspector.
            Letters Sent, Inspector.
            Provost Marshall General Records, Department of the Gulf.

Letters Received, 1863–1865, Inspectors of the Department of the Gulf.

Letters Sent, 1862–1865.

Letters Received, 1862–1865.

Special Orders, Department of the Gulf.

Part 2

Department of the Gulf

General Orders.

1st Brigade, 1st Division, Corps d'Afrique, January to April 1864.

1st Brigade, 1st Division, U.S. Colored Troops, April 1864–February 1865.

U.S. Forces, Port Hudson, 1863–1866.

Letters Received.

1st Brigade, 1st Division, Corps d'Afrique, January–April 1864.

Letters Sent.

1st Brigade, 1st Division, Corps d'Afrique, January–April 1864.

1st Brigade, 1st Division, U.S. Colored Troops, April 1864–February 1865.

U.S. Forces, Port Hudson, 1863–1866.

Register of Letters Received.

1st Brigade, 1st Division, Corps d'Afrique, January–April 1864.

1st Brigade, 1st Division, U.S. Colored Troops, April 1864–February, 1865.

U.S. Forces, Port Hudson, 1863–1866.

Special Orders.

1st Brigade, 1st Division, Corps d'Afrique, January–April 1864.

1st Brigade, 1st Division, U.S. Colored Troops, April 1864–February 1865.

U.S. Forces, Port Hudson, 1863–1866.

Part 4

Letters Received, Provost Marshall General, Parish of Orleans.

New Orleans Public Library

Louisiana Collection.

City Directories, 1832–1833, 1846, 1852–1861, 1866, 1870, 1872–1873, 1899.

Muster Rolls of the Native Guards (Confederate), Louisiana Troops (microfilm).

New Orleans Health Department Death Certificates as kept by the Recorder of Births, Marriages and Deaths.

Wills and Successions.

City Archives.

Board of Assessors: Records, 1856–1869.

Municipality Record Book, 1842–1844.

Mayor's Office Records.

Indenture Book 5.

Oaths and Bonds for City Licenses on Vehicles, 1834–1866.

Orleans Parish Policy Jury, Petitions for the Emancipation of a Slave, Book
C (vol. 3).
Orleans Parish, Court of Probate, Succession and Probate Records.
Parish Court Petitions for Emancipation.
Records of the Second Municipality: Tax Registers, 1836–1851.
Sixth District Court of New Orleans, Docket Book C.
Treasurer's Office: Tax Ledgers, 1852–1861.
Oneida County Historical Society, Utica, New York
Stafford, Spencer H. Papers.
Port Hudson State Commemorative Area Museum, Zachary, Louisiana
P. F. DeGournay. "The Siege of Port Hudson," *New Orleans Times Weekly,* in
Annals of War: Chapters of Unwritten History, copy.
William T. Rogers. Brandon, Mississippi
Turner, Walter Stephens. Diary.
Woodstock Theological Center Library, Georgetown University, Washington, D.C.
Annales de la Propagation de la Foi.
Xavier University Archives, New Orleans
Rousseve, Charles B. Papers.
Daily Crusader clippings.
*Constitution De La Société Catholique Pour L'Instruction Des Orphelins Dans
L'Indigence, June 20, 1849.*

PUBLIC DOCUMENTS

Federal
U.S. Bureau of the Census. 4th, 5th, 6th, 7th, 8th, 9th Censuses.
*Official Army Register of the Volunteer Force of the United States Army, 1861, '62,
'63, '64, '65.* Washington, D.C., 1867. Vol. VIII of 8 vols.
U.S. War Department. *U.S. Infantry Tactics for the Instruction, Exercise, and Ma-
neuvres of the United States Infantry.* Philadelphia, 1862.
U.S. War Department. *The War of the Rebellion: A Compilation of the Official
Records of the Union and Confederate Armies.* Washington, D.C., 1880–1901.
128 vols.

State and Municipal
Louisiana State Archives
Bureau of Vital Statistics, Baton Rouge, Louisiana
Death Index, 1873. Orleans Parish.
Jefferson Parish Conveyance Office, Gretna, Louisiana
Conveyance Books, Vendor.
Office of Mortgages, Orleans Parish, Louisiana
Mortgage Books.
Society Book #3, folio 508.
New Orleans Notarial Archives
Original Acts of Orleans Parish

J. Cuvillier.
Michael de Armas.
Octave de Armas.
Narcisse Broutin.
L. T. Caire.
H. B. Cenas.
Achille Chiapella.
William Christy.
O. Drouet.
A. Ducatel.
Ernest Eude.
C. V. Foulon.
O. L. Kernion.
Paul Emile Laresche.
Pedro Pedesclaux.
Philippe Pedesclaux.
T. Seghers.
CHD13, Plan Book A, Folio B, "Plan of 1 Lot of Ground with Buildings Situated in the 4th District," New Orleans, A. Chastang.
Recorder of Conveyances, Orleans Parish, Louisiana
Vendor and Vendee Books.
Plaquemines Parish, Notarial Acts, Books 3 and 4, Clerk of Court, Pointe-à-la-Hâche, Louisiana.
Probate Records, Clerk of Court.

PUBLISHED MEMOIRS, LETTERS, ARTICLES, DOCUMENTS, LITERARY WORKS, AND HISTORICAL NARRATIVES
Bacon, Edward. *Among the Cotton Thieves.* Detroit, 1867.
Bell, Howard Holman, ed. *Minutes of the Proceedings of the National Negro Conventions, 1830–1864.* New York, 1969.
Bosson, Charles P. *A History of the 42nd Regiment Infantry, Massachusetts.* Boston, 1886.
Brasseaux, Carl A., Keith P. Fontenot, and Claude F. Oubre. *Creoles of Color in the Bayou Country.* Jackson, Miss., 1994.
Butler, Benjamin F. *Butler's Book: A Review of his Legal, Political and Military Career.* Boston, 1892.
———. *Private and Official Correspondence of General Benjamin Butler During the Period of the Civil War.* Edited by Jessie Ames Marshall. Vol. II of 5 vols. Norwood, Mass., 1917.
Carpenter, George N. *A History of the Eighth Vermont Volunteers, 1861–1865.* Boston, 1886.
"Catholic Collections for Freedmen." *American Missionary,* XIII (October, 1869), 227–28.
Corsan, W. C., *Two Months in the Confederate States: An Englishman's Travels through the South.* Ed. Benjamin H. Trask. Baton Rouge, 1996.

Crété, Liliane. *Daily Life in Louisiana, 1815–1830*. Trans. Patrick Gregory. Repr. Baton Rouge, 1981.

Dupanloup, Félix-Antoine-Philibert. *Lettre De Monseigneur L'Evêque D'Orléans Au Clergé De Son Diocese, Sur L'Esclavage*. Orleans, France, 1862.

Fitts, James Franklin. "The Negro in Blue," *Galaxy*, III (1867): 249–55.

Foner, Philip S., and George E. Walker. *Proceedings of the Black State Conventions, 1840–1865*. Vol. II of 2 vols. Philadelphia, 1980.

Garcia, Céline Fremaux. *Céline: Remembering Louisiana, 1850–1871*. Athens, Ga., 1987.

Hamilton, Thomas. *Men and Manners in America*. London, 1848.

Hebert, Donald J. Genealogical Research Society of New Orleans, *First Book of Confirmations of the Parish of St. Louis of New Orleans*. New Orleans, 1967.

Higginson, Thomas Wentworth, ed. *Harvard Memorial Biographies*. Vol. 1 of 2 vols. Cambridge, Mass., 1866.

Houzeau, Jean-Charles. *My Passage at the "New Orleans Tribune": A Memoir of the Civil War Era*. Edited by David C. Rankin and translated by Gerard F. Denault. Baton Rouge, 1984.

Irwin, Richard B. *History of the XIXth Army Corps*. 1892; repr. Baton Rouge, 1985.

Johns, Henry T. *Life with the Forty-Ninth Massachusetts Volunteers*. Pittsfield, Mass., 1864.

Kautz, August V. *Customs of Service for the Non-Commissioned Officers and Soldiers*. Philadelphia, 1864.

Latrobe, Benjamin Henry. *Impressions Respecting New Orleans: Diary and Sketches, 1818–1820*. New York, 1951.

Latrobe, John H. B. *Southern Travels: Journal of John Latrobe, 1834*. Edited by Samuel Wilson, Jr. New Orleans, 1986.

Merriam, Henry C. "The Capture of Mobile." *War Papers Read before the Commandery of the State of Maine, Military Order of the Loyal Legion of the United States*. Portland, Maine, 1908.

Metropolitan Catholic Almanac and Laity Directory. Baltimore, 1851–55.

Moors, J. F. *History of the 52nd Regiment, Massachusetts Volunteer Militia*. Boston, 1893.

"Romanist Schools." *American Missionary*, XIII (1869), 250.

Rowland, Kate Mason, and Mrs. Morris L. Croxall, eds. *The Journal of Julia Le-Grand*. Richmond, 1911.

Smith, M. J., and James Freret, "Fortification and Siege of Port Hudson." *Southern Historical Papers*, XIV (1886), 305–48.

Southwood, Marion. *Beauty and Booty: The Watchword of New Orleans*. New York, 1867.

"Straight University." *American Missionary*, XIV (May, 1870), 105.

———. *American Missionary*, XIV (August, 1870), 170.

Wiley, Nathan. "Education of the Colored Population of Louisiana." *Harper's New Monthly*, XXXIII (1866), 244–50.

Wilson, John M. "The Campaign Ending with the Capture of Mobile," *Military Order of the Loyal Legion of the United States: War Papers*, XVII (1894), 3–29.

Wright, Lt. Howard C. *Port Hudson: Its History from an Interior Point of View.* 1863; repr. Baton Rouge, 1961.

NEWSPAPERS

Frank Leslie's Illustrated Weekly, 1863.
Harper's Weekly, 1862–1863.
National Antislavery Standard, 1862.
New Orleans *Bee* (L'Abeille de la Nouvelle Orléans), 1843–1859.
New Orleans *Daily Picayune,* 1862–1863.
New Orleans *L'Orléanais.*
New Orleans *Louisiana Courier (Le Courrier de la Louisiane),* 1843–1859.
New Orleans *Louisiana Weekly Newspaper,* 1957.
New Orleans *Louisianian,* 1875.
New Orleans *L'Union,* 1862–1864.
New Orleans *Morning Star and Catholic Messenger,* 1870, 1912.
New Orleans *Le Propagateur Catholique,* 1850–1862.
New Orleans *Republican,* 1870.
New Orleans *Times Weekly,* 1863.
New York *Herald,* 1863.
New York *Times,* 1862–1863.
New York *Weekly Anglo-African,* 1863–1865.
Richmond *Enquirer,* 1863.

SECONDARY SOURCES

BOOKS AND PAMPHLETS

Arms and Equipment of the Union. By the editors of Time-Life Books. Morristown, N.J., 1991.
Baker, Liva. *The Second Battle of New Orleans: The Hundred Year Struggle to Integrate the Schools.* New York, 1996.
Baudier, Roger. *The Catholic Church in Louisiana.* New Orleans, 1939.
———. *St. Rose of Lima Parish: Centennial, 1857–1957.* New Orleans, 1957.
———. *St. Theresa of Avila Parish: Historical Sketch.* New Orleans, 1948.
Bell, Caryn Cossé. *Revolution, Romanticism, and the Afro-Creole Protest Tradition in Louisiana, 1718–1868.* Baton Rouge, 1997.
Bell, Howard Holman. *Minutes of the Proceedings of the National Negro Conventions, 1830–1864.* New York, 1969.
Berlin, Ira. *Many Thousands Gone: The First Two Centuries of Slavery in North America.* Cambridge, Mass., 1998.
———. *Slaves Without Masters: The Free Negro in the Antebellum South.* New York, 1974.
Berlin, Ira, Joseph Reidy, and Leslie S. Rowland, eds. *Freedom: A Documentary History of Emancipation, 1861–1867.* Ser. II, *The Black Military Experience.* New York, 1982.

Blassingame, John W. *Black New Orleans, 1860–1880*. Chicago, 1973.

Blied, Benjamin J. *Catholics and the Civil War*. Milwaukee, 1945.

Boles, John B., ed. *Masters and Slaves in the House of the Lord: Race and Religion in the American South, 1740–1870*. Lexington, 1988.

Boles, John B., and Evelyn Thomas Nolen, eds. *Interpreting Southern History: Historiographical Essays in Honor of Sanford W. Higginbotham*. Baton Rouge, 1987.

Bony, Abbé. *Vie de Mgr. Jean-Marie Odin, Missionaire Lazarist de la Nouvelle-Orléans par L'Auteur de L'Initiateur du Voeu National Paris*. Paris, 1896.

Bittle, Celestine, OFMCap. *A Romance of Lady Poverty: The History of the Province of St. Joseph of the Capuchin Order in the United States*. Milwaukee, 1933.

Borritt, Gabor S., ed. *Why the Confederacy Lost*. New York, 1992.

Brown, William Wells. *The Negro in the American War of the Rebellion: His Heroism and His Fidelity*. Boston, 1867.

Campbell, Edward D. C., Jr., and Kym S. Rice, eds. *Before Freedom Came: African-American Life in the Antebellum South*. Charlottesville, 1991.

Capers, Gerald M. *Occupied City: New Orleans under the Federals, 1862–1865*. Lexington, 1965.

Castaneda, Carlos E. *Our Catholic Heritage in Texas, 1519–1936. Supplement, 1936–1950*. Austin, 1936–1958. Vol. VII of Castaneda, *The Church in Texas Since Independence, 1836–1850*. 7 vols.

Christovich, Mary Louise, and Toledano Roulhac, eds. *Faubourg Tremé and Bayou Road*. Gretna, La., 1980. Vol. VI of Christovich, ed., *New Orleans Architecture*. 6 vols.

Conrad, Glenn R., ed. *Cross, Crozier, and Crucible: A Volume Celebrating the Bicentennial of a Catholic Diocese in Louisiana*. Lafayette, La., 1993.

―――――. *The German Coast: Abstracts of the Civil Records of St. Charles and St. John the Baptist Parishes, 1804–1812*. Lafayette, La., 1981.

―――――. *Readings in Louisiana History*. New Orleans, 1978.

Conrad, Glenn R., and Ray F. Lucas. *White Gold: A Brief History of the Louisiana Sugar Industry, 1795–1995*. Lafayette, La., 1995.

Cornish, Dudley Taylor. *The Sable Arm: Negro Troops in the Union Army, 1861–1865*. New York, 1996.

Cox, Lawanda. *Freedom, Racism, and Reconstruction: Collected Writings of Lawanda Cox*. Ed. Donald G. Nieman. Athens, Ga., 1998.

Dansette, Adrien. *Religious History of Modern France: From the Revolution to the Third Republic*. Vol I of 2 vols. Edinburgh, 1961.

Davis, Cyprian, O.S.B. *The History of Black Catholics in the United States*. New York, 1990.

Desdunes, Rodolphe Luciene. *Our People and Our History*. Trans. and ed. Sister Dorothea Olga McCants. Baton Rouge, 1973.

Detiege, Sister Audrey Marie. *Henriette Delille, Free Woman of Color: Foundress of the Sisters of the Holy Family*. New Orleans. 1976.

De Ville, Winston. *The 1795 Chimney-Tax of New Orleans: A Guide to the Census of Proprietors and Residents of the Vieux Carré*. Ville Platte, La., 1994.

DeVore, Donald E., and Joseph Logsdon. *Crescent City Schools: Public Education in New Orleans, 1841–1891*. Lafayette, La., 1991.

Diamond Jubilee of the Archdiocese of Chicago: Antecedents and Developments. Chicago, 1920.

Dorman, James H. ed. *Creoles of Color of the Gulf South.* Knoxville, 1996.

Duncan, Russell. *Blue-Eyed Child of Fortune: The Civil War Letters of Robert Gould Shaw.* Athens, Ga., 1992.

Dyer, Frederick H. *A Compendium of the War of the Rebellion.* Dayton, 1908.

Edmonds, David C. *The Guns of Port Hudson: The Investment, Siege, and Reduction.* 2 vols. Lafayette, La., 1984.

Ellsworth, Lucius F. *The Americanization of the Gulf Coast, 1803–1850.* Pensacola, 1972.

Evans, Sally Kittredge, Frederick Stielow, and Betsy Swanson. *Grand Isle on the Gulf: An Early History.* Metarie, La., 1979.

Fairclough, Adam. *Race and Democracy: The Civil Rights Struggle in Louisiana, 1915–1972.* Athens, Ga., 1995.

Ferrar, H., J. A. Hutchinson, and J. D. Baird, eds. *The Concise Oxford French Dictionary.* 2nd ed. New York, 1980.

Fischer, Roger A. *The Segregation Struggle in Louisiana, 1862–1877.* Urbana, Ill., 1974.

Foner, Eric. *Reconstruction: America's Unfinished Revolution, 1863–1877.* New York, 1988.

Fortier, Alcée. *Louisiana Folklore.* Baltimore, 1888.

Gannon, Michael. *Rebel Bishop: The Life and Era of Augustin Verot.* Milwaukee, 1964.

Gibson, Ralph. *Social History of French Catholicism, 1789–1914.* New York, 1989.

Gillard, John T., S.S.J., *The Catholic Church and the American Negro.* Baltimore, 1929.

Gillette, William. *Retreat from Reconstruction, 1869–1879.* Baton Rouge, 1980.

Glatthaar, Joseph T. *Forged in Battle: The Civil War Alliance of Black Soldiers and White Officers.* New York, 1990.

Gould, Virginia Meacham, and Charles E. Nolan. *Henriette Delille: "Servant of Slaves."* New Orleans, 1998.

Greeley, Andrew M. *The Catholic Myth: The Behavior and Beliefs of American Catholics.* New York, 1990.

Hanger, Kimberly S. *Bounded Lives, Bounded Places: Free Black Society in Colonial New Orleans, 1769–1803.* Durham, 1997.

Hall, Gwendolyn Midlo. *Africans in Colonial Louisiana: The Development of Afro-Creole Culture in the Eighteenth Century.* Baton Rouge, 1992.

———. *Slave Control in Plantation Societies.* Baltimore, 1971.

Harris, William C. *With Charity for All: Lincoln and the Restoration of the Union.* Lexington, 1997.

Hart, Sister Mary Francis Borgia, S.S.F. *Violets in the King's Garden: A History of the Sisters of the Holy Family of New Orleans.* New Orleans, 1976.

Hennesey, James, S.J. *American Catholics: A History of the Roman Catholic Community in the United States.* New York, 1981.

Hewitt, Lawrence Lee. *Port Hudson: Confederate Bastion on the Mississippi.* Baton Rouge, 1987.

Hirsch, Arnold R., and Joseph Logsdon, eds. *Creole New Orleans: Race and Americanization*. Baton Rouge, 1992.

Hollandsworth, James G., Jr. *The Louisiana Native Guards: The Black Military Experience During the Civil War*. Baton Rouge, 1995.

————. *Pretense of Glory: The Life of General Nathaniel P. Banks*. Baton Rouge, 1998.

Kasteel, Annemarie. *Francis Janssens, 1843–1897: A Dutch-American Prelate*. Lafayette, La., 1992.

Kauffman, Christopher J. *Tradition and Transformation in Catholic Culture: The Priests of Saint Sulpice in the United States from 1791 to the Present*. New York, 1988.

Labbé, Dolores Egger. *Jim Crow Comes to Church: The Establishment of Segregated Catholic Parishes in South Louisiana*, 2nd ed. Lafayette, La., 1971.

Landers, Jane G., ed. *Against the Odds: Free Blacks in the Slave Societies of the Americas*. London, 1996.

Landry, Stuart Omer. *The Battle of Liberty Place: The Overthrow of Carpet-Bag Rule in New Orleans, September 14, 1874*. New Orleans, 1955.

Le Breton, Dagmar Renshaw. *Chahta-Ima: The Life of Adrien-Emmanuel Rouquette*. Baton Rouge, 1947.

Linderman, Gerald F. *Embattled Courage: The Experience of Combat in the American Civil War*. New York, 1987.

Macdonald, Robert R. John R. Kemp, and Edward F. Haas, eds. *Louisiana's Black Heritage*. New Orleans, 1979.

McConnell, Roland C. *Negro Troops in Antebellum Louisiana: A History of the Battalion of Free Men of Color*. Baton Rouge, 1968.

McPherson, James M. *For Cause and Comrades: Why Men Fought in the Civil War*. New York, 1997.

————. *Ordeal by Fire: The Civil War and Reconstruction*. New York, 1982.

Maduell, Charles R., Jr., comp. *Marriages and Family Relationships of New Orleans, 1820–1830*. New Orleans, 1969.

Miller, Randall, and Jon C. Wakelyn, eds. *Catholics in the Old South: Essays on Church and Culture*. Macon, Ga., 1983.

Mills, Gary B. *The Forgotten People: Cane River's Creoles of Color*. Baton Rouge, 1977.

Moore, James Talmadge. *Through Fire and Flood: The Catholic Church in Frontier Texas, 1836–1900*. College Station, Tex., 1992.

Nevins, Albert J. *The Maryknoll Catholic Dictionary*. New York, 1965.

Ochs, Stephen J. *Desegregating the Altar: The Josephites and the Struggle for Black Priests, 1871–1960*. Baton Rouge, 1990.

Perman, Michael. *The Road to Redemption*. Chapel Hill, 1984.

Poole, Stafford, C.M., and Douglas J. Slawson, C.M. *Church and Slave in Perry County, Missouri, 1818–1865*. Lewiston/Queenstown, Mo., 1986.

Quarles, Benjamin. *The Negro in the Civil War*. 1953; repr. New York, 1968.

Rice, Madeleine Hooke. *American Catholic Opinion in the Slavery Controversy*. Gloucester, N.Y., 1964.

Richardson, Joe M. *Christian Reconstruction: The American Missionary Association and Southern Blacks, 1861–1890.* Athens, Ga., 1986.

The Rise and Progress of the Province of St. Joseph of the Capuchin Order in the United States, 1857–1907. New York, 1907.

Rousseve, Charles Barthelemy. *The Negro in Louisiana: Aspects of His History and His Literature.* 1937; repr. New York, 1969.

Schafer, Judith Kelleher. *Slavery, the Civil Law, and the Supreme Court of Louisiana.* Baton Rouge, 1994.

Schweninger, Loren. *Black Property Owners in the South, 1790–1915.* Urbana, Ill., 1990.

Sherwood, Grace. *The Oblates Hundred and One Years.* New York, 1931.

Snead-Cox, J. G. *The Life of Cardinal Herbert Vaughan.* Vol. II of 2 vols. London, 1910.

Soulé, Leon Cyprian. *The Know Nothing Party in New Orleans: A Reappraisal.* Baton Rouge, 1962.

Spalding, Thomas. *Martin John Spalding: American Churchman.* Washington, D.C., 1973.

Steans, Peter N. *Priest and Revolutionary: Lamennais and the Dilemma of French Catholicism.* New York, 1967.

Sterkx, H. E. *The Free Negro in Ante-bellum Louisiana.* Rutherford, N.J., 1972.

Taylor, Joe Gray. *Louisiana Reconstructed, 1863–1877.* Baton Rouge, 1974.

Tinker, Edward Larocque. *Les Écrits de Langue Française en Louisiana Au XIXe Siécle.* Paris, 1932.

Trudeau, Noah Andre. *Like Men of War: Black Troops in the Civil War, 1862–1865.* New York, 1998.

Tunnell, Ted. *Crucible of Reconstruction: War, Radicalism, and Race in Louisiana, 1862–1877.* Baton Rouge, 1984.

Uya, Okon E. *From Slavery to Public Service: Robert Smalls, 1839–1915.* New York, 1971.

Vella, Christina. *Intimate Enemies: The Two Worlds of the Baroness de Pontalba.* Baton Rouge, 1997.

Vidler, Alec R. *The Church in an Age of Revolution: 1789 to the Present Day.* Harmondsworth, England, 1971. Vol. V of Owen Chadwick, *The Pelican History of the Church,* 6 vols.

Vincent, Charles. *Black Legislators in Louisiana During Reconstruction.* Baton Rouge, 1976.

Voorhies, Jacqueline, comp. and trans. *Some Late Eighteenth Century Louisiana Census Records, 1758–1796.* Lafayette, 1973.

Wade, Richard C. *Slavery in the Cities: The South, 1820–1860.* New York, 1964.

Weaver, C. P. ed. *Thank God My Regiment an African One: The Civil War Diary of Colonel Nathan W. Daniels.* Baton Rouge, 1998.

Westwood, Howard C. *Black Troops, White Commanders, and Freedmen During the Civil War.* Carbondale, Ill., 1992.

Williams, George Washington. *A History of the Negro Troops in the War of the Rebellion, 1861–1865.* 1888; repr. New York, 1969.

Wilson, Joseph T. *The Black Phalanx.* 1890; repr. New York, 1968.

Wilson, Samuel, Jr. *The Creole Faubourgs.* Comp. Mary Louise Christovich, Sally Kittredge Evans, and Roulhac Toledano. Gretna, La., 1974. Vol. IV of Mary Louise Christovich, ed., *New Orleans Architecture.* 6 vols.

Wilson, Samuel, Jr., and Leonard V. Huber. *The St. Louis Cemeteries of New Orleans.* New Orleans, 1963.

Winters, John D. *The Civil War in Louisiana.* Baton Rouge, 1963.

Whitten, David O. *Andrew Durnford: A Black Sugar Planter in the Antebellum South.* New Brunswick, 1995.

Zanca, Kenneth J., comp. and ed. *American Catholics and Slavery: 1789–1866: An Anthology of Primary Documents.* Lanham, Md., 1994.

ARTICLES

Alvarez, David J. "The Papacy in the Diplomacy of the American Civil War." *Catholic Historical Review,* LXIX (1983), 227–48.

Bergeron, Arthur W., Jr. "Free Men of Color in Grey." *Civil War History,* XXXII (1986), 247–55.

Berry, Mary F. "Negro Troops in Blue and Gray: The Louisiana Native Guards, 1861–1863." *Louisiana History,* VIII (1967), 165–90.

Berlin, Ira. "The Structure of the Free Negro Caste." *Journal of Social History,* IX (1976), 297–318.

Carriere, Jr., Marius M. "Anti-Catholicism, Nativism, and Louisiana Politics in the 1850s." *Louisiana History,* XXXV (1994), 455–74.

Caravaglios, Maria Genoino. "A Roman Critique of the Pro-Slavery Views of Bishop Martin of Natchitoches, Louisiana." *Records of the American Catholic Historical Society of Philadelphia,* LXXXIII (June, 1972), 67–81.

Clark, Emily. " 'By All the Conduct of Their Lives,': A Laywomen's Confraternity in New Orleans, 1730–1744." *William and Mary Quarterly,* LIV (1997), 769–94.

Connor, William P. "Reconstruction Rebels: The *New Orleans Tribune* in Post-War Louisiana." *Louisiana History,* XXI (1980), 159–81.

Dethloff, Henry C., and Robert R. Jones. "Race Relations in Louisiana, 1877–98." *Louisiana History,* IX (1968), 301–23.

Dorman, James H. "Louisiana's 'Creoles of Color': Ethnicity, Marginality, and Identity." *Social Science Quarterly,* LXXIII (1992), 615–26.

Dunbar-Nelson, Alice. "People of Color of Louisiana." Part I. *Journal of Negro History,* I (1916), 361–76.

———. "People of Color of Louisiana." Part II. *Journal of Negro History,* II (1917), 51–78.

Ellison, Mary. "African-American Music and Muskets in Civil War New Orleans." *Louisiana History,* XXXV (1994), 285–319.

Everett, Donald E. "Demands of the New Orleans Free Colored Population for Political Equality, 1862–1865." *Louisiana Historical Quarterly,* XXXVIII (1955), 43–64.

———. "Ben Butler and the Louisiana Native Guards, 1861–1862." *Journal of Southern History,* XXIV (1958), 202–17.

Foley, Patrick. "Jean-Marie Odin, C.M., Missionary Bishop Extraordinaire of Texas." *Journal of Texas Catholic History and Culture* (March, 1990), 42–60.

Foner, Laura. "The Free People of Color in Louisiana and St. Domingue: A Comparative Portrait of Two Three Caste Slave Societies." *Journal of Social History,* III (1970), 406–30.

Glatthaar, Joseph. "The Civil War Through the Eyes of a Sixteen-Year-Old Black Officer: The Letters of Lieutenant John H. Crowder of the 1st Louisiana Native Guards." *Louisiana History,* XXXV (1994), 201–16.

Gould, Virginia Meacham. " 'The House that Never Was a Home': Slave Family and Household Organization in New Orleans, 1820–1850." *Slavery and Abolition,* XVIII (1997), 90–103.

Heisser, David C. R. "Bishop Lynch's Civil War Pamphlet on Slavery." *Catholic Historical Review,* LXXXIV (1998), 681–96.

Hollandsworth, James G. "The Execution of White Officers from Black Units by Confederate Forces During the Civil War." *Louisiana History,* XXXV (1994), 475–89.

Ingersoll, Thomas N. "Free Blacks in a Slave Society: New Orleans, 1718–1812." *William and Mary Quarterly,* XLVIII (1991), 173–200.

Joshi, Manoj K., and Joseph P. Reidy. " 'To Come Forward and Aid in Putting Down this Unholy Rebellion': The Officers of Louisiana's Free Black Native Guard During the Civil War Era." *Southern Studies,* XXI (1982), 326–42.

Kinzer, Charles E. "The Band of Music of the First Battalion of Free Men of Color and the Siege of New Orleans, 1814–1815." *American Music,* X (1992), 348–69.

Klement, Frank L. "Catholics as Copperheads During the Civil War." *Catholic Historical Review,* LXXX (1994), 36–57.

Kotlikoff, Laurence J., and Anton J. Rupert. "The Manumission of Slaves in New Orleans, 1827–1846." *Southern Studies,* XIX (1980), 172–81.

Kynoch, Gary. "Terrible Dilemmas: Black Enlistment in the Union Army during the American Civil War." *Slavery and Abolition,* XVIII (1997), 104–27.

Lachance, Paul. "The Formation of a Three-Caste Society." *Social Science History,* XVIII (1994), 211–42.

Labbé, Dolores Egger. " 'Helpers in The Gospel': Women and Religion in Louisiana, 1800–1830." *Mid-America,* LXXIX (1997), 153–75.

———. "Index to the Black Books." *New Orleans Genesis,* XII, no. 45, (June 1973), 24.

Miller, Randall M. "The Enemy Within: Some Effects of Foreign Immigrants on Antebellum Cities." *Southern Studies,* XXIV (1985), 30–53.

Misch, Edward J. "The Catholic Church and the Negro, 1865–1884." *Integrateducation,* XII (November–December, 1974), 36–40.

O'Neill, Charles Edwards. " 'A Quarter Marked by Sundry Peculiarities': New Orleans, Lay Trustees, and Père Antoine." *Catholic Historical Review,* LXXVI (1990), 235–77.

Prevos, André. "Afro-French Spirituals about Mary Magdalene." *Louisiana Folklore Miscellany,* IV (1980), 41–53.

Rankin, David C. "The Impact of the Civil War on the Free Colored Community of New Orleans." *Perspectives in American History,* XI (1977–1978), 379–416.

———. "The Origins of Black Leadership in New Orleans During Reconstruction." *Journal of Southern History,* XL (1974), 417–40.

Reinders, Robert C. "The Churches and the Negro in New Orleans, 1850–1860." *Phylon,* XXII (1961).

———. "The Decline of the New Orleans Free Negro in the Decade Before the Civil War." *Journal of Mississippi History,* XXIV (1962).

———. "The Free Negro in the New Orleans Economy, 1850–1860." *Louisiana History,* VI (1965), 273–85.

———. "Slavery in New Orleans in the Decade Before the Civil War." *Mid-America,* XLIV (1962), 211–21.

Reeves, Sally K. "The Plan Book Drawings of the New Orleans Notarial Archives: Legal Background and Artistic Development." *Proceedings of the American Antiquarian Society,* CV (Part I, 1995), 105–25.

Root, William H. "The Experiences of a Federal Soldier in Louisiana, 1863." Ed. L. Carroll Root. *Louisiana Historical Quarterly,* XIX (1936), 635–67.

Schweninger, Loren. "Prosperous Blacks in the South, 1790–1880." *American Historical Review,* LXXXV (1990), 31–56.

Spalding, David. "Martin J. Spalding's 'Dissertation on the American Civil War.'" *Catholic Historical Review,* LII (1966), 66–85.

Sullivan, Lester. "The Unknown Rodolphe Desdunes: Writings in the New Orleans *Crusader.*" *Xavier Review,* X (1990), 1–17.

Tregle, Joseph G., Jr., "Early New Orleans Society: A Reappraisal." *Journal of Southern History,* XVIII (1952), 20–36.

Manuscripts and Unpublished Papers

Baudier, Roger. "Memorandum for Rev. Robert Guste on White and Negro Relationships After War between the States." Typescript, August 22, 1956, Roger Baudier Collection, Archives of the Archdiocese of New Orleans.

———. "The Story of St. Louis School of Holy Redeemer Parish, New Orleans, formerly St. Louis School for the Colored, l'Institution Catholique pour l'Instruction des Orphelins dans l'Indigence, Widow Couvent's School." Typescript, 1956, Roger Baudier Collection, Archives of the Archdiocese of New Orleans.

Belsom, Jack. "Duvernay Genealogy." In possession of Jack Belsom, New Orleans, Louisiana.

Christian, Marcus B. "Genealogy: The Beginnings of the Free Colored Class." Typescript, n.d., Marcus B. Christian Collection, Earl K. Long Library, University of New Orleans.

Clark, Emily. "Evangelizing and Empowering Free Women of Color in New Orleans, 1727–1862: The Early Ursulines." Paper delivered at the annual meeting of the American Historical Association, Washington, D.C., January 9, 1999.

Evans, Sally Kittredge. "Some 18th and 19th Century Families of Grand Isle, Louisiana, and their Migrations." Paper delivered at the 1984 Nicholls State University Symposium.

Foley, Patrick. "Odin of Texas: First Bishop of Galveston." Manuscript in possession of Patrick Foley, Azle, Texas.

Nolan, Charles E. "New Wine in Old Wineskins: Religious Women and the Revitalization of Louisiana Catholicism, 1803–1836." Paper delivered at the annual meeting of the American Historical Association, Washington, D.C., January 9, 1999.

DISSERTATIONS AND THESES

Alberts, John B. "Origins of Black Catholic Parishes in the Archdiocese of New Orleans, 1718–1920." Ph.D. dissertation, Louisiana State University, 1998.

Bru, Hubert Joseph. "Archbishop Odin: Reformer and Disciplinarian." Master's thesis, Notre Dame Seminary, New Orleans, 1938.

Doorley, Michael. "The Irish and the Catholic Church in New Orleans, 1835–1918." Master's thesis, University of New Orleans, 1987.

Doyle, Elisabeth. "Civilian Life in Occupied New Orleans, 1862–1865." Ph.D. dissertation, Louisiana State University, 1955.

Gould, Lois Virginia Meacham. "In Full Enjoyment of Their Liberty: The Free Women of Color of the Gulf Ports of New Orleans, Mobile, and Pensacola, 1769–1860." Ph.D. dissertation, Emory University, 1991.

Lee, Sr. M. Florita, C.C.V.I. "The Efforts of the Archbishops of New Orleans to Put into Effect the Recommendations of the Second and Third Plenary Councils of Baltimore with Regard to Catholic Education, 1860–1917." Ph.D. dissertation, Catholic University of America, 1946.

McTigue, Geraldine. "Forms of Racial Interaction in Louisiana, 1860–1880." Ph.D. dissertation, Yale University, 1975.

Walker, Harry Joseph. "Negro Benevolent Societies in New Orleans: A Study of Their Structure, Function, and Membership." Master's thesis, Fisk University, 1937.

PERSONAL COMMUNICATIONS

Joseph Logsdon to author, telephone conversation, August 27, 1993.

Peter Caron to author, e-mail, June 23, 1997.

INDEX

Abolitionism: of Maistre, xv, 1–2, 100–101, 111, 114–15, 190, 200–201, 261, 266; and Catholic Church, 100–101, 109, 242, 243–44; and newspaper tributes to Cailloux following his death, 156–58; and free people of color, 186–87; and Union Association in New Orleans, 186

ACERA. *See* American Citizens' Equal Rights Association (ACERA)

African Americans. *See* Free people of color; Freedpeople; Louisiana Native Guards; Slaves; and headings beginning with Black troops

Afro-Creoles. *See* Free people of color

Alberts, John, 262n36

Alcès, Georges, 59, 167

Alexandria, La., 211, 212–13

Alexis, J. B., 198

Aliquot, Marie Jeanne, 51, 52

AMA. *See* American Missionary Association (AMA)

American Citizens' Equal Rights Association (ACERA), 265

American Freedman's Inquiry Commission, 186

American (Know-Nothing) Party, 49, 104, 105

American Missionary Association (AMA), 253–54

Anderson, William, 228

Andrews, George L., 150, 201, 202–08, 219, 226

Antietam, battle of, 202, 213

Antoine, C. C., 265

Antonia (sister of the senior André), 11

Appomattox, surrender at, 230

Aquinas, Thomas. *See* Thomas Aquinas, St.

Arkansas 1st Regiment, 144

Arkansas 17th Mounted Infantry, 204–05

Association Louisianaise pour l'Assistance des Ophelins de Couleur, 244

Auger, Marie Magdelaine Clemence, 43

Augur, Christopher, 129

Babcock, Willoughby M., 152

Bacchus, Noel, 79, 145

Bailey (Lartet), Aimée Duvernay. *See* Lartet, Aimée

Bailey, William, 15, 16–17

Banks, Nathaniel: Cailloux at headquarters of, 80; and white opposition to black troops, 117; appointment of, as commander of Department of the Gulf, 122, 137; opposition to black officers by, 122–25, 156, 163–64, 202, 207; aide of, on fatigue duty for black troops, 127; military defeats during Civil War, 137, 139; political career of, 137; nickname of, 139; and Port Hudson battle, 139–40, 147, 148, 150, 151; and burial of dead after Port Hudson battle, 148; and black troops for defense of New Orleans, 156, 156n32; and Cailloux's funeral, 156; and Lincoln's "Ten Percent Plan," 188; and black suffrage, 190; and Odin, 191–94, 197; and eviction of Maistre from St. Rose of Lima Church, 197; Maistre on, 200; and dismissal of Stafford, 201; and wages of officers, 207; protest by black troops of 1st Corps d'Afrique to, 211–12; and Red River campaign, 211, 212–13; and economic distress of widows of black troops,

ficer's pay, 82, 127; at Bayou Lafourche, 117–18; construction duty at Fort Jackson, 121, 123; at Baton Rouge, 126–29; Port Hudson battle, 130–31, 137–44, 264

Cailloux, André (father), 9–17, 22–23, 25–26

Cailloux, Andrew "Cap," 259n33

Cailloux, Athalie Clemence, 45

Cailloux, Eugene, 37, 53, 258, 259n33

Cailloux, Felicie: at husband's funeral, 4, 155; manumission of, 9, 33, 35, 36; ancestry and parents of, 30–36, 45–46; birth of, 31; children of, 34–37, 43, 45, 48, 53, 258; marriage of, 36–37; homes of, 46–47, 73, 169; and Institute Catholique, 55–56; economic problems after husband's death, 216–17, 257–58; death of, 257

Cailloux, George, 259n33

Cailloux, Hortense, 48

Cailloux, Jean Louis, 34–37, 53, 82, 155, 258

Cailloux, Josephine (mother of André Cailloux), 15–17, 22–26, 45, 45n8

Cailloux, Odile, 48

Cailloux family genealogy, 38

Cailloux Leagues, 225, 233

Camaire, Marie Justin, 53

Canal Street, Battle of (1877), 261

Canby, Edward R. S., 220

Cantiques (religious folk songs), 49–50

"Captain André Cailloux and His Companions in Arms," 153–54

"Captaine Caillou," 159–60

Capuchins, 18, 19, 21, 24, 235, 238

Carmelites, 18

Carriere, Augustin, 230–31

Carroll, Bishop John, 19

Case, George, 86

Catholic Church: conflicts between Maistre and Odin, 1–2, 6, 106–07, 132–36, 155–56, 190, 235–37, 239, 260; and free people of color and freedpeople, 6–7, 11–12, 23, 37,

48–53, 84, 103, 136, 165, 196–97, 241–47, 250–52; baptism of slaves by, 11–12, 13, 20, 21n17, 23, 24, 31, 31n30, 33, 166; and slaves, 11–13, 20–24, 50–53, 165; and African animism, 13; as slaveholder, 18, 22, 100, 108; weaknesses of institutional church, 18–20; white Catholics' laissez-faire attitude toward, 18, 19–20, 51; *marguilliers* (lay wardens) of, 19, 64, 64n32, 101–02; women's role in, 19, 20–21, 50, 51, 165; Lenten observance and Easter duty in, 20, 49; sacraments of, 20–23, 49, 51, 114, 244, 246–47; and slave marriages, 21, 21n17, 22–23, 23n18; and *cantiques* (religious folk songs), 49–50; popular devotionalism in, 50, 51; and voodoo, 50; racial discrimination by, 51–52, 94, 112–14, 199–200, 236, 249–50, 262–63; and education of blacks, 53–56, 243, 244, 254–55, 262, 262n36; in France, 57; and Freemasonry, 63–65; and black troops, 94, 112–14; liberal Catholic thinkers, 97, 246; and abolitionism, 100–101, 109, 242, 243–44; in Texas, 104, 105, 108; and Confederacy, 107, 107n14, 191–94, 192n8, 199–200; moral teaching on slavery, 108–12; and occupied New Orleans, 191–93; and peace initiatives during Civil War, 191–93, 192n8; and black demands for separate black churches, 196–99, 199n16, 241, 246; criticisms of, by Afro-Creole leaders, 199–200; negotiations for end of impasse between Maistre and Odin, 234–40, 252, 261; black priests in, 241, 241n11, 242, 262; segregation of churches, 243, 244, 262–63; Maistre's submission to and termination of schism with, 254–56, 261. *See also* Maistre, Claude Paschal; Odin, Jean-Marie; St. Louis Cathe-

Fort St. Leon, 126, 210
Fort St. Philip, 74, 121
Fort Wagner, 5, 205–06
Fourteenth Amendment, 249, 254
Foy, Octave, 74–75, 76
France, 11, 18, 21, 41, 56–57, 61, 64, 69, 86, 95, 97, 100, 111–12, 246
Francisca (mother of the senior André), 9–10, 11
Frank Leslie's Illustrated Weekly, 119
Free people of color: at Cailloux's funeral, 2–5, 62, 155–56; mutual aid societies for, 2, 3, 44–45, 61–63, 65, 65*n*33, 71, 103, 114, 190, 198, 234; relationship between Afro-Creole and Anglophonic free black communities, 5, 7, 86, 155, 163, 186–87, 250–51; Catholicism of, 6–7, 11–12, 23, 37, 48–53, 84, 103, 136, 165, 196–97, 241–47, 250–52; population of, 9, 12, 33, 34, 41–42, 60–61, 90–91; and Spanish slave code, 21; female *marchandes* (peddlers) among, 28, 35; female domestics among, 35; real estate holdings of, 35, 42, 45–47, 57, 61–62, 73, 79, 81, 252, 256, 257–58; and manumission of slaves, 36, 44; prenuptial pregnancy among, 36, 37, 39; baptism of, in Catholic Church, 37, 45, 48, 80, 136; education and literacy of, 37, 40, 53–57, 60; marriage of, 37, 39; legal and social position of, 40–41, 60, 61, 66, 186; as slaveholders, 40, 41, 43–45; wealth of, 40–41, 59, 61, 81; in colonial Louisiana, 41; employment of, 41, 42, 43, 57–58, 61, 84; whites' fears of and repressive measures against, 60–61; in Confederate army during Civil War, 68–75; in Union army during Civil War, 74–94; relationship between slaves/freedpeople and, 87–89, 186–87; tributes to Cailloux after death, 152–55; suffrage for, 185–90, 223–25, 232–33, 234, 240, 249,

254, 255; and Union Association, 185–86, 188; and abolitionism, 186–87; criticisms of Catholic Church by, 199–200, 241, 246; economic difficulties of, 216–17, 257–58. *See also* Black troops in Civil War
Freedmen's Aid Association, 87, 187
Freedmen's Bureau, 248
Freedmen's Savings and Trust Company, 258
Freedpeople: relations between free people of color and, 186–87; suffrage for, 186–87, 223–25, 232–33, 234, 240, 249, 254, 255; contract labor system for, 187; Banks's policies on, 191; prisoner-of-war status of, 203–05; Black Codes on, 240; and Catholic Church, 241–44
Freeman's Journal, 107*n*14, 192
Freemasonry, 63–65, 65*n*33, 185, 189, 195, 215, 225, 245, 247, 260
French immigrants, 27, 102
Freret, James P., 73
Friends of Order, 2, 3, 62–63, 65, 71, 78, 79
Friends of Universal Suffrage, 195, 233, 234
Frisbie, Henry N., 219–23

Garcia, Céline Fremaux, 205
Gardner, Franklin Kitchell, 139, 148
Gardner, Samuel S., 84, 226–27, 228, 230, 231
Garland, J. P., 129
Garnet, Henry Highland, 224
Garrison, William Lloyd, 149, 255
Gaudin, Juliette, 51, 52
Gens de couleur libre. See Free people of color
George, Louis, 214
German immigrants, 25, 102
Glaudin, Achille, 241
Glaudin, Clemence, 45
Glaudin, Henry, 43
Glaudin, J. B., 27, 36, 43, 48
Glaudin, Meurice, 45, 258

Glaudin, P. F., 241
Golard, Jules, 214
Gonzalez, Armand, 195
Gould, Lois Virginia Meacham, 188
Grand Ecore, 212
Grand Isle, 30
Grant, Ulysses S., 139, 261, 263
Great Britain, 86
Gregory XVI, Pope, 109
Gros, Joseph, 80
Gueno, Madeleine, 102–03

Hahn, Michael, 189, 190
Haiti (St. Domingue), 41, 42–43n4, 50, 61, 112
Halleck, Henry W., 77, 150
"Halleck's Guards," 77, 78n12. *See also* Louisiana Native Guards (Union)
Hamelton, Warren D., 216
Hamilton, Thomas, 51
Hardee, William J., 203, 204
Hawkins, John P., 228
Hayes, Rutherford B., 263–64
Healy, J. W., 253
Healy brothers, 241n11
Hennesey, James, 192n8
Henry, Julia, 23n18
Henry, Patrick, 23n18, 128, 128n20
Holy Family Sisters. *See* Sisters of the Holy Family
Holy Name of Jesus Church, 193–94, 198–99, 246, 250–52, 256, 257
Honoré, Charles W., 195
Hooker, James, 214
Hospice of the Holy Family, 53
Houzeau, Jean Charles, 255
Hughes, Archbishop John, 191, 192

Immigrants, 25, 27, 48–49
Indians. *See* Native Americans
Ingraham, James H., 6, 207, 223–25
Institute Catholique, 53–56, 63, 68, 72, 74, 77, 79, 81, 88–89, 114, 187, 214
Institution des Orphelins Indigents, 244–45

Irish immigrants, 25, 48, 64, 107n14, 241n11
Irwin, Richard B., 125

Jackson, Andrew, 56, 69
Jackson, Stonewall, 137
Jeannetti, C., 195
Jesuits, 18, 22, 241n11
Jim Crow. *See* Segregation
John (slave), 27–29
Johnson, Andrew, 239–40
Jolibois, Charles, 63
Jones, Michael, 26
Josaphat, Father. *See* Kleiber, Father Josaphat
Joseph, Alcide, 217
Joseph, Edmond, 195, 218
Jouan, Father Pierre-Marie, 113
Joubert, Blanc F., 89

Kellogg, William Pitt, 261
Kennedy, John A., 144
Kenrick, Archbishop Francis Patrick, 108–09, 242, 243
Killborn, Captain C. W., 134, 197
Kinney, Isidore, 206–07
Kleiber, Father Josaphat, 235, 237, 238
Know-Nothing Party, 49, 104, 105

Labatut, Félix, 70
Lachant, G., 195
Lacordaire, Jean Baptiste Henri, 97
Lacroix, François, 53
Lafon, Thomy, 47, 245n16, 265
Lamanière, L., 88
Lambert, Lucian, 56
Lamennais, Félicité Robert de, 97
Lanusse, Armand, 54–55, 74
LaPorte, Father Pierre, 263
Laprade, Louise, 9, 11, 14
Larrieu, Louis, 145
Lartet, Aimée., 15, 17, 24–29
Lartet, Firmin, 27
Lartet, Marie, 27
Lartet, Mathieu, 26–29, 35–36, 36–37n38

Stanton, Edwin M., 75, 83, 204, 216, 225
Stevens, Thaddeus, 259–60
Straight University, 252–55
Streetcars, segregation of, 92
Strong, George L., 93
Strunke, Elias D., 148–49
Suffrage for blacks, 185–90, 223–25, 232–33, 234, 240, 249, 254, 255, 264
Sumner, Charles, 189
Swails, Stephen A., 208

Taylor, Richard, 152, 155
"Ten Percent Plan," 188, 190
Texas, 104, 105, 108, 193
Therese (sister of the senior André), 11, 14, 15, 16
Thibaut, Louis H., 145, 202, 207
Thomas, Colonel, 116, 117
Thomas Aquinas, St., 108
Tignon (kerchief), 168
Timon, John, 108
Tinchant, Joseph, 89
Tocqueville, Alexis de, 62
Trepagnier, F. B., 83
Trepagnier, J. Frank, 83, 143
Trévigne, Hortense, 244–45, 247
Trévigne, Paul, 89, 244, 265
True Friends Mutual Benevolent Association, 65n33
Tureaud, A. P., 6, 6n5
Turner, Walter Stephens, 147–48

Ulgere, Athanase, 144
Ullman, Daniel, 148–51, 216
Union. See L'Union
Union Association, 185–86, 188
U.S. Colored Infantry: 73rd Regiment,
183, 212–23, 225–33; 83rd Regiment, 221; 92nd Regiment, 221. *See also* Louisiana Native Guards (Union)
U.S. Colored Troops, 85th, 213
Urquhart, Victor, 80
Ursulines, 11–12, 18, 21, 23, 39, 248

Van de Velde, Bishop James Oliver, 96, 97, 98–99, 133
Vaughan, Archbishop Herbert, 262
Venereal disease, 124
Vermont 2nd Battery, 203
Vermont 8th volunteers, 116, 117
Verot, Bishop Augustin, 109–10
Vicksburg, 137, 152, 242
Vincentians, 18, 20, 104, 108, 193
Vinet, Emile L., 199n16
Violence against blacks, 204–05, 226, 240
Voodoo, 13, 50
Voting rights. *See* Suffrage for blacks

Walsh, Rev. Patrick, 19
War of 1812, 68, 69–70, 189
Warmouth, Henry C., 250–51, 255
Weekly Anglo-African, 149, 156, 164n37
Weitzel, Godfrey, 116–17, 121, 139–41
White League, 259, 261, 262, 263
Wickliffe, Charles Anderson, 118
Williams, George Washington, 6
Wilson, Joseph T., 6
Wisconsin 11th Regiment, 231

Yellow fever, 48, 49, 103

Zardais, Joseph Martin, 61, 62
Zenon, Hillaire, 85
Zumpt, James E., 122